PRINCIPLES OF ETHICAL ECONOMY

Issues in Business Ethics

VOLUME 17

The titles published in this series are listed at the end of this volume.

Principles of Ethical Economy

by

PETER KOSLOWSKI
Forschungsinstitut für Philosophie Hannover,
Hannover, Germany

KLUWER ACADEMIC PUBLISHERS
DORDRECHT / BOSTON / LONDON

A C.I.P. Catalogue record for this book is available from the Library of Congress.

ISBN 0-7923-6713-8

Published by Kluwer Academic Publishers,
P.O. Box 17, 3300 AA Dordrecht, The Netherlands.

Sold and distributed in North, Central and South America
by Kluwer Academic Publishers,
101 Philip Drive, Norwell, MA 02061, U.S.A.

In all other countries, sold and distributed
by Kluwer Academic Publishers,
P.O. Box 322, 3300 AH Dordrecht, The Netherlands.

The translation of this book was supported by a grant from the DaimlerChrysler Fund.

English translation of Peter Koslowski, Prinzipien der Ethischen Ökonomie, Grundlegung der Wirtschaftsethik und der auf die Ökonomie bezogenen Ethik, J.C.B. Mohr (Paul Siebeck), Tübingen, 1988. Translated by David W. Lutz.

World wide English rights obtained from J.C.B. Mohr (Paul Siebeck)

Printed on acid-free paper

Printed in the Netherlands.

FOREWORD

John Maynard Keynes wrote to his grandchildren more than fifty years ago about their economic possibilities, and thus about our own: "I see us free, therefore, to return to some of the most sure and certain principles of religion and traditional virtue – that avarice is a vice, that the exaction of usury is a misdemeanour.... We shall once more value ends above means and prefer the good to the useful" ("Economic Possibilities for Our Grandchildren," pp. 371-72). In the year 1930 Keynes regarded these prospects as realizable only after a time span of one hundred years, of which we have now achieved more than half. The present book does not share Keynes's view that the possibility of an integration of ethics and economics is dependent exclusively on the state of economic development, though this integration is certainly made easier by an advantageous total economic situation. The conditions of an economy that is becoming post-industrial and post-modern are favorable for the unification of ethics, cultural theory, and economics. Economic development makes a new establishment of economic ethics and a theory of ethical economy necessary.

Herdecke and Hanover, October 1987 P.K.

TABLE OF CONTENTS

Foreword v

Introduction 1

0.1. Ethical Economy and Political Economy 1
  0.1.1. Ethical Economy as Theory of the Ethical Presuppositions of the Economy and Economic Ethics 3
  0.1.2. Ethical Economy as Economic Theory of the Ethical or Ethics Oriented toward Economics 3
  0.1.3. Ethical Economy as Substantive Theory of Goods and Cultural Economics 4
0.2. Why the Interest in Economic Ethics Today? 5
  0.2.1. Increasing Side Effects of Economic Activity 6
  0.2.2. Rediscovery of the Human Person 8
  0.2.3. Normative Penetration of the Economy as Complement of its Differentiation 9
0.3. Overview of the Structure of the Book 12
0.4. Missing Mediation of Economics and Ethics in Modernity – Ethical Economy as Post-Modern Economics 13

1. Economics, Ethics, and Religion: Positive Theory of the Coordination of Self-Interested Actions 17

1.1. Internalization of Side Effects and Inclusion of Persons Affected as Criteria of Social Coordination 17
1.2. Private Vices - Public Benefits: The Good as Side Effect 18
1.3. Economic Failure 20
1.4. Ethics as Corrective for Economic Failure 26
1.5. Religion as Corrective for Ethical Failure 31
1.6. Self-Interest, Corporate Ethics, and Employee Motivation 34

2. Economics and Ethics I: Formal Ethics 38

2.1. Ethics and Economics: Global and Local Maximization 39
2.2. Unifying Universalization and Exception: Ethics and Religion 46
2.3. Economic, Ethical, and Religious Rationality: Extending the Limits of the Self 48

2.3.1. Love of Self – Love of God – Love of Neighbor: Augustine's Understanding of the Transformations and Coordinations of Self-Interest ... 49
2.3.2. Economization of Ethics and Religion? ... 51
2.4. Rationality and Coordination ... 54
2.4.1. The A Priori Nature of the Principle of Rationality ... 54
2.4.2. Formal Rationality and Non-Formal, Substantive Rationality ... 57
2.5. Ethics as Form of Social Coordination ... 59
2.5.1. Convergence of Ethical Universalization and Market Coordination in the Formal Nature of their Laws ... 60
2.5.2. Kantian Ethics as the Solution to the Prisoner's Dilemma ... 64
2.5.3. Formal Ethics as Internal Pre-Coordination of the Economic Coordination of the Price System ... 67
2.5.4. Deepening Social Coordination by Ethics ... 69
2.5.5. Ethics as the Reduction of Uncertainty about the Decision Behavior of Other Persons and its Composition into Patterns of Social Interaction ... 70
2.6. Ethics and Religion as Ways of Increasing Economic Rationality and Coordination ... 72
2.6.1. Ethics as the Ability to Endure the Consequences of One's Own Actions ... 75
2.6.2. Ethics and Economics in the View of Interpretive Sociology ... 77
2.7. Formality and Materiality ... 78

3. Economics and Ethics II: Substantive Ethics ... 81

3.1. Ethical and Economic Theories of Goods ... 82
3.1.1. The Theory of the Highest Good ... 83
3.1.2. Scheler's Substantive Ethics of Values ... 85
3.2. Experiencing Values and Understanding Cultural Meaning ... 87
3.3. Side Effects between Experiences and Value Convictions, "Is" and "Ought" ... 89
3.4. Substantive Value-Qualities and Degrees of the Publicness of Goods ... 91
3.5. Ethics as Theory of Virtues ... 96
3.5.1. The Interchangeability of Means and Ends and the Economics of Sublimation ... 98
3.5.2. Proper Conduct, or Appropriateness to the Nature of the Matter, and Justice as Virtue ... 101
3.6. The Unity of Ethics as the Theory of Duty, of Virtue, and of the Good ... 104
3.7. Everything Worth Doing Is Worth Doing Well, or The Good as Perfection ... 108

4. Economics and Culture 112

4.1. Cultural Economics and the Cultural Philosophy of the Economy 112
4.2. The Culture of Production 114
4.3. The Culture of Consumption 115
4.4. Technological Progress and Transformations in the Meaning of Work in Society 117
4.5. Art and the Economy 121

5. Economics, Ethics, and Decision Theory: The Problem of Controlling Side Effects 123

5.1. The Law of Intended Side Effects in the Firm 125
5.2. Side Effects as Decision Problem 128
5.2.1. Uncertainty about the Consequences of Actions in Ethics, Economics, and Decision Theory 129
5.2.2. Probabilism 131
5.2.3. Criticisms of Probabilistic Decision Calculi 134
5.2.4. The Principle of Double Effect 137

6. Economics and Ontology 142

6.1. Intentional or Natural-Scientific Ontology of the Economy? 143
6.2. The Inconceivability of an Objective General Equilibrium and Universal Mechanism 149
6.3. The Market Economy as Teleological Mechanism 151
6.4. General Equilibrium as Transcendental Ideal 153
6.5. Poietic Imagination of New Possibilities in the Market Process 157
6.6. The Market as Social Discourse and Process of Entelechial Coordination 159
6.7. Not Value Subjectivism, but Subjective Value-Realization 160
6.8. Ethical Economy or Subjective Economics as General Theory of Human Action? 164

7. Economic Ethics in the Market Economy 169

7.1. Does the "Mechanism of Competition" Make Ethics Superfluous? 169
7.2. Morality and Advantage: The Costs of Economic Ethics 174
7.3. Morality at the Margin 178
7.4. Proper Conduct and Appropriateness to the Nature of the Subject Matter in Question 181

8. Commutative Justice 184

8.1. Commutative Justice as Appropriateness to the Nature of the Matter of Exchange: The Equivalence Principle 184
8.2. How Do We Determine What Each Person is Entitled to in Exchange? ... 185
8.2.1. Joining the Prevailing Price by the Actual Contract Price 186
8.2.2. Appropriateness to the Nature of the Item Exchanged: No Exchange of Sham Goods 193
8.2.3. Mutually-Advantageous Exchange: Neither Party Suffers a Loss of Net Wealth 195
8.2.4. Commutative Justice as Virtue 197
8.2.5. The Unavoidability of the Question of Justice 202
8.3. What Is the Basis of the Obligation to Give Each Person What Is His or Hers in Exchange? 205

9. Just Price Theory 211

9.1. Preliminary Historical Remark: The Significance of Early-Modern, Probabilistic Just Price Theory 212
9.2. Natural Law and Forces of Nature in the Legitimation of the Price System 215
9.3. What Distinguishes the Price System from Other Forms of Price Determination? 218
9.4. Formal and Non-Formal or Substantive Conditions of Price Justice 219
9.4.1. Unification of Procedural and Structural Justice 223
9.4.2. Allocation and Distribution 225
9.5. International Price Justice 227
9.6. Justice as Satisfying a Criterion or as a Synopsis of Several Criteria? 229
9.6.1. Rawls' Criterion of a Veil of Ignorance 230
9.6.2. The Utilitarian Criterion of Total-Utility Maximization 231
9.6.3. Justice and Games: Hayek 235
9.6.4. Nozick's Criterion of the Justified Claim 237
9.6.5. Unification of Procedural and End-State Criteria 238
9.7. Justice in Interaction with Nature 241

Conclusion: Morality and Efficiency 244

Bibliography 247

Index of Persons 266

Index of Subjects 271

INTRODUCTION

The ordering of the economy and society must make use of both the strongest and the best of human motives. Economics, since its beginnings as an independent science, has assumed as its starting point the strongest of human motives: self-interest. Philosophical ethics has traditionally aimed at what is considered the best of human motives: striving for the good, performance of duty, the attainment of virtue. If economic theory analyzes and designs social institutions and rules of action on the basis of self-interest, and if ethical theory provides arguments for institutions and norms that are to provide opportunities for the best of human motives to develop and to be fully realized, then both disciplines are concerned with the same subject matter: the acting human person and the coordination of rational actions.

Since economics and ethics are concerned with the same subject matter, they are not independent of one another. The necessity of unifying the economic and ethical views of human action and its coordination arises, therefore, from the very nature of human action itself and from the requirement that the social order permit both economic and ethical theories of action to become effective. As Alfred Marshall's *Principles of Economics* has already postulated, a comprehensive theory of the economy need not base its analysis on narrow self-interest alone. At the same time, a realistic theory of ethics cannot close its eyes to the economic circumstances of ethical actions. Ethics and economics must instead accept one another's insights and unite themselves in a comprehensive theory of rational action.

0.1. Ethical Economy and Political Economy

Economic ethics or ethical economy is a theory of the economy and of ethics, which seeks to meet this challenge. As ethical economy, it unites ethical and economic judgments and constitutes the complement of political economy. It examines, on the level of ethics, the ethical presuppositions and structural conditions of economic actions, just as political economy examines the political and legal presuppositions of economic actions and institutions. Both ethical economy and political economy are based upon the same formal economic theory of rational action, as it is developed in microeconomics. The analytic instrument of the pure theory of rational action according to the economic principle or principle of rationality is no less compatible with different political structural conditions and institutional arrangements than with different traditions of moral philosophy, with Kantian ethics and utilitarianism. The theory of rational action serves both ethical and political economy by shedding light on the rationality of norms and institutions and on their appropriateness for previously-determined ethical or political purposes.

Pure economic theory is a powerful instrument for the analysis of rational action and the efficient coordination of rational actions. If the rational and efficient pursuit of objectives is the distinctive characteristic of human persons, and if both ethics and politics seek to promote the rational and efficient pursuit of objectives by individuals and communities, then it is reasonable to conclude that both refer to the economic principle and economic theory. Political economy, the union of political philosophy and economics, is an economic theory of the political, the economics of political institutions and the political presuppositions of the cultural sphere of the economy (i.e. the political presuppositions of market coordination and economic control through the price system). Since Adam Smith's theory of "the wealth of nations," political economy has had a fundamental influence on the societal form that makes possible the free pursuit of objectives and responsible business management by its members, and is closely related to the history of political liberty and the liberal coordination of the economy.

Economic ethics or ethical economy is, accordingly, on one hand, an economic theory of the ethical and of the economics of ethical institutions and rules and, on the other hand, the ethics of the economy. Like political economy, it has a double meaning. It is a theory of ethics that uses economic instruments of analysis, a theory of ethics oriented toward economics, just as political economy is a political theory that uses economic instruments of analysis. But ethical economy or economic ethics is also a theory of the ethical presuppositions of the cultural system of the economy, a theory of the ethical rules and attitudes that presuppose market coordination and the price system in order to function. This component of ethical economy, which is more strongly oriented toward application, is called here "economic ethics" (*Wirtschaftsethik*), although the terms "ethical economy" and "economic ethics" merge and the present work also attempts to deal with fundamental and applied questions of ethical economy and economic ethics.[1] The term "ethical economy" (*Ethische Ökonomie*) goes beyond the research objectives of economic ethics, understood as the eth-

---

[1] Since 1959, only one longer monograph with the term "economic ethics" ("*Wirtschaftsethik*") in its title has been published in the German-language literature: Arthur Rich, *Wirtschaftsethik* (Gütersloh, 1984). Its title is less than completely accurate, however, since it is the first of two volumes and is concerned almost exclusively with general questions of the foundation of social ethics from a theological perspective, while the promised second volume, which is to deal specifically with *economic* ethics, has not yet appeared. [Translator's note: The second volume was published in 1990.]

ics of the economy, to achieve an integration of ethical theory and economic theory. Ethical economy must be more than simply "economics & ethics."

0.1.1. ETHICAL ECONOMY AS THEORY OF THE ETHICAL PRESUPPOSITIONS OF THE ECONOMY AND ECONOMIC ETHICS

Political economy and ethical economy – the latter introduced here as a new term – constitute the political and ethical presuppositions of the pure economics of markets and the price system. Market coordination and control by the price system can work only when certain institutional structural conditions are met. The New Institutional Economics has recently reminded us forcefully of this fact once again. Among these institutional presuppositions of market coordination are those that political economy examines (i.e. the political structural conditions of rights of ownership, contract rights, the administration of justice, etc.) and those that ethical economy investigates (i.e. the ethical structural conditions that the principle of *pacta sunt servanda* is universally valid and trust in the fulfillment of contracts is justified, that quasi-rents neither come into existence nor are exploited in labor relationships by a possibly-existing quasi-monopoly of employees or employers, etc.).

0.1.2. ETHICAL ECONOMY AS ECONOMIC THEORY OF THE ETHICAL OR ETHICS ORIENTED TOWARD ECONOMICS

The other subject of economic ethics or ethical economy is the clarification of ethical problems that include components from economic theory. The economic theory of ethics expands the analytic power of ethics by applying economic theory, for example, the theory of economies of scale, to the problem of universalization and the efficiency of different degrees of inclusiveness of universalization,[2] or by integrating maximization calculations into ethical decisions. The economic theory of ethics also examines the question of the relationship between morality and advantage, or self-interest and universal interest, which is essential for ethical motivation.

---

[2] Cf. Allan Gibbard's important book *Utilitarianisms and Coordination* (Cambridge, Mass., 1971).

0.1.3. ETHICAL ECONOMY AS SUBSTANTIVE[3] THEORY OF GOODS AND CULTURAL ECONOMICS

Finally, in addition to the theory of the ethical presuppositions of the economy and the economic theory of ethics, there is a third sphere of ethical economy or economic ethics, which examines the mutual penetration of economics and ethics in the theory of goods. Things become goods for individuals by certain value-qualities and by the perception of these value-qualities. The economic effectiveness of these value-qualities is not independent of their perception by the human subject, the consumer. In the penetration of economic and aesthetic-ethical theories of goods, ethical economy or economic ethics proves to be at the same time a theory of corporate culture, of cultural economics, and of the cultural philosophy of the economy.

The three areas of ethical economy – the theory of the ethical presuppositions of economics, the economic theory of ethics, and the ethical-economic theory of goods and cultural value-qualities – show that ethics and economics unite to form a comprehensive theory of human action and human praxis,[4] in which the cultural understanding of human institutions and rules of conduct must be included. The theory of human manners and customs, the theory of the virtues of conduct, also belongs to this comprehensive theory of human action.

Ethical economy or economic ethics returns to the older philosophical tradition of Aristotelian practical philosophy, the union of ethics, economics, and politics. This unity of practical philosophy has been dissolved since the establishment of economics as a self-sufficient science by Adam Smith and the emigration of pragmatic and social ethics from moral philosophy with Kant.[5] The triad of ethics, economics, and politics has been replaced by three independent disciplines. Ethical economy and political economy show that this segmentation of the components of practical philosophy is not irrevocable, but rather that individual and social actions have political, economic, and ethical presuppositions and that analyzing and understanding human action requires an economic theory of ethics, an ethical theory of the economy, an economic theory of politics, and a political theory of the economy.

---

[3] [Translator's note: German: *material*. If the German adjectives *material* and *materiell* were both translated into English as "material," the distinction between them would be lost. In the present work, *material* means "material" as distinguished from "formal," and *materiell* means "material" as distinguished from "immaterial." In order to preserve this distinction, *material* and *materiell* are translated here in most cases as "substantive" and "material," respectively.]

[4] It is appropriate here to point out Ludwig von Mises' important work *Human Action* (New Haven, 1949), which outlines economics as a general theory of human action, but incorporates ethics into economics insufficiently.

[5] On the relationship between economics and ethics in Kant and Adam Smith, see Koslowski, *Gesellschaft und Staat* (Stuttgart, 1982), pp. 185-237.

Ethical economy and economic ethics constitute the attempt to integrate ethical aspects of action in the economic action model of the economic disciplines. Ethical economy attempts to close the gap between the totality of the ethical relationships of economic action and the necessary abstractions of *homo oeconomicus* (economic man). Because the world of the lived ethos or the totality of our ethical-social relationships is the world in which we live and work, an adequate theory of economic action must do justice to this totality.

Philosophical ethics also gains analytic and normative power from the reunification of ethics and economics, because it seeks to impart ethical reflection and judgment to economic praxis, as to every other praxis. The mission of ethics as *practical* philosophy, as the theory of right action, cannot be merely the establishment, nor even the *ultimate* establishment, of norms, but must also be the impartation of well-founded norms to concrete life and the world of action. Ethics cannot be merely metaethics or the theory of the ultimate foundations of morality. It must also be oriented toward action in the various spheres of human action; it must be a moral reflection *immanent* for them. A theory of economic ethics and ethical economy immanent to economics in this sense must be developed, because of all systems of action and cultural spheres of society, the economy is the most important and determines the lives of most persons during the largest segments of their lifetimes. The role of philosophical ethics is likewise the communication and the foundation of ethics, imparting ethics to the concrete circumstances of human life. Without this communication, the fate of philosophical ethics is practical ineffectiveness. It remains in the precociousness of the "ought," facing the so-called "real-world" arguments of practitioners and experts.

Ethics focuses on inciting human praxis: "Its end is action, not knowledge."[6] This is especially true of economic ethics or ethical economy. Economic ethics must also be the practical ethics of the cultural sphere and system of action of the economy. It must impart itself as business ethics and the ethics of work to the concrete life situations of human persons and must ethically clarify and form their motives and actions.

0.2. Why the Interest in Economic Ethics Today?

Interest in economic ethics and business ethics and publication in the field of business ethics have increased rapidly in recent years, especially in the United

[6] Aristotle, *Nicomachean Ethics*, trans. Terence Irwin (Indianapolis, 1985), I, 3, 1095 a 6.

States, but also in Europe.[7] Three reasons can be identified for this newly-awakened interest in the old discipline of economic ethics, and thus in an integral component of practical philosophy.

The new discipline of economic ethics consists of 1) a consciousness of the increasing cultural and ecological side effects of our economic actions and the need for their ethical accountability, 2) the rediscovery of the human element in technical economic science and the growing expectation of the accountability of leaders of the economy, and 3) the need to counteract a wider separation of the spheres of culture and especially the alienation of the economic world and the intellectual and material culture.

0.2.1. INCREASING SIDE EFFECTS OF ECONOMIC ACTIVITY

Interest in economic ethics has increased, because the unintended side effects (externalities) of our actions in the economy and technology are increasing with the growing power of human action. Increasing side effects point out the need for an integrated assessment of the consequences of actions (i.e. for an integrated ethic of the spheres of the culture), which contains, not merely in the narrower sense, economic and natural-scientific viewpoints. Side effects are not only a *problem* of, but also a *reason* for economic ethics. They not only present to economic ethics the task of analyzing and evaluating side effects, but are at the same time a reason that economic ethics comes into existence as a normative science and a social investigation of values within the intersection of economics and general ethics.

How are side effects to be understood? They are effects that are accepted in addition to the primary effect, which is identified as the objective by the acting person before the action takes place. Side effects present two challenges: first, the challenge of the ethical-economic analysis of their causes by the acting person and their imputation to the acting person and, second, the ethical and economic challenge for the person making the decision of predicting and evaluating side effects.[8]

Our power over nature and our room for social action are increasing. With the ability to act, the number of possible side effects also increases. Increasing

---

[7] Cf. Donald G. Jones and Helen Troy, eds., *A Bibliography of Business Ethics, 1976-1980* (Charlottesville, 1982); Tom Regan, ed., *Just Business* (Philadelphia, 1983); and Richard T. De George, *Business Ethics* (New York, 1982).

[8] Cf. Robert Spaemann, "Nebenwirkungen als moralisches Problem," in Spaemann, *Kritik der politischen Utopie* (Stuttgart, 1977), pp. 167-82; and Koslowski, "Nebenwirkungen," in Joachim Ritter and Karlfried Gründer, eds., *Historisches Wörterbuch der Philosophie*, Vol. VI, Basel, 1984, pp. 659-62. For the economic literature on externalities, see E. J. Mishan, "The Postwar Literature on Externalities," *Journal of Economic Literature*, 9 (1971), pp. 1-29; and Koslowski, "Markt- und Demokratieversagen?" *Politische Vierteljahresschrift*, 24 (1983), pp. 166-87.

power calls not only for more analytic knowledge, but also for a growing sensibility to its effects and side effects. It calls for practical-ethical action-knowledge that takes into account the side effects of one's own actions as the decision is being made.

The awakened ecological consciousness and the debate concerning the use of energy are expressions and manifestations of the increase in side effects. As Nicholas Georgescu-Roegen has shown,[9] the second law of thermodynamics is the physical cause of the problem of economic and ecological scarcity. This law of nature means for economics, first of all, that energy flows on its own only from warm bodies to cold ones, thus exactly in the direction we do not wish it to go. Secondly, it means that energy cannot be converted into work or raw materials without side effects for the environment. These side effects of energy conversion, like all negative side effects of economic activity, must be taken into account and minimized as much as possible. At the same time, any possible positive side effects, synergies, and symbioses must be maximized.

In order to observe the repercussions of the environment on actions, adaptability of thought, attentiveness, ability of perception, and ethical reflection – in Pascal's terms, not only *esprit de géometrie*, the spirit of the exact, geometrical sciences, but also *esprit de finesse*, the spirit of fine, practical discretion – are required. Economic ethics should also promote these qualities.

An example from environmental economics can serve to illustrate this point. In certain regions of Bavaria, farmland was reallocated from small pieces of land into larger units by an integration of tracts, in order to bring about an increased agricultural yield. After the reallocation, it was observed that all natural biotopes had disappeared and that there was no longer room for natural species. These biotopes must now be recreated artificially, by breaking up the larger tracts into smaller pieces of land, leaving room at the edges for natural biotopes. And this must be done by a "re-disintegration of farmland." The farmers are now being paid to reverse the reallocation of land and to create artificial biotopes.

According to biologist Jakob von Uexküll, the environment of a living being consists of the possibilities of action that are opened up for it.[10] The social and natural environment of human beings, the possibilities of action opened up for us, have become greater and greater in this sense. And as our environment has grown, so has our responsibility for it. But we can cope with the growth of our power only if the increase in our ability to bring about changes by our actions is accompanied by an increase in our ability to endure. Consideration of the side effects of our actions contains an element of the ability to endure the conse-

---

[9] Cf. Nicholas Georgescu-Roegen, *Energy and Economic Myths* (New York, 1976).

[10] Cited by Carl Friedrich von Weizsäcker, "Die Einheit von Wahrnehmen und Bewegen," in von Weizsäcker, *Der Garten des Menschlichen* (Frankfurt, 1980), pp. 164.

quences of our own actions, the ability to tolerate the repercussions that our actions cause. The necessity to consider the side effects of economic activity on human persons themselves and on nature is the first reason that there is a greater need today for economic ethics.

0.2.2. REDISCOVERY OF THE HUMAN PERSON

The second reason that economic ethics is needed is the phenomenon of the "rediscovery of the human person" in the social sciences. Ethics asserts the "primacy of practical reason" (Kant) in the sciences, as distinguished from the autonomy of scientific and technological research. Ethics reminds us that science is a praxis, and that as scientific praxis it must pose to itself the question of the scholarship and adequacy of its paradigm for the self-understanding of the human person. For economics, the move from scientific paradigms of the inanimate world, of physicalism, to a science that considers the subject of the science, the human person, in the scientific praxis itself, is especially significant, because it is a practical science, a science of conscious activity. Economics, as a theory of the conscious action of the intellectual nature of human persons, is more a humanity than a natural science.

The process of the "re-anthropomorphization" or "re-humanization" of our scientific understanding and greater consideration of the human subject in science is strengthened by socio-economic developments in the transformation of the industrial society into the service society. Anthropomorphism expresses itself in the economy.[11] The post-industrial economy calls for a stronger consideration of the human factor, an anthropological or anthropomorphic point of view. The relationship of human persons to themselves, their ability to engage in taking ethical distance, and therefore their need for justification and grounding, must be more strongly observed in an economy that increasingly shifts from the quantity of the material production of goods to the quality of a service economy. The expectation of accountability in leaders and institutions increases with the higher qualification of workers and the higher demands for labor-productivity in the micro-electronic age. The transition from the energy-processing machine to the information-processing machine replaces energy and matter with knowledge. Information is substituted for energy. This development also has repercussions for the increasingly spiritual character of work. "Bringing mind back in"[12] was a demand of organization theory in the previous decade. Since then, this process has advanced. Economic ethics is the way to bring mind back

---

[11] Johann Wolfgang von Goethe, *The Maxims and Reflections of Goethe*, trans. Bailey Saunders (New York, 1893), Aphorism 165, p. 94: "A man never understands how anthropomorphic he is."

[12] Louis R. Pondy and David M. Boje, "Bringing Mind Back In," in *Paradigm Development as a Frontier Problem in Organization Theory* (Urbana, 1976).

into our picture of the economy and once again to base economics to a greater degree on the concept of the conscious action.

If the expectation that managers must be accountable increases, the danger of tribunalization is great. The tribunalization of the economy is a form of the "re-moralization" of the economy, which is no longer economic ethics, but moral aggression, aggression clothed in morality against those who have decision-making power. Promoting an ethic of the cultural spheres[13] and an economic ethic of the economy as a cultural sphere is not the same as rash moralizing. Moralizing spheres of activity always runs the risk of deteriorating into resentment, the resentment that clothes its envy in the formula that the action of the competent person is insignificant, because it is not in accordance with morally dressed-up mediocrity. Since the conscious life must struggle for and attain its self-consciousness anew daily, it must overcome its inclination to resentment once again every day. In the same way, the economic-ethicist will also have to struggle for an adequate form of economic life and to seek a middle way between ivory tower moralism and uncritical apology, between abstract moral postulates and unreflective acceptance of the status quo.

0.2.3. NORMATIVE PENETRATION OF THE ECONOMY AS COMPLEMENT OF ITS DIFFERENTIATION

The third reason that interest in economic ethics has increased is found in the growing differentiation of modern society and the danger arising from it that modern culture will lose its unifying meaning. Economic ethics attempts anew to answer the question of how the interpretation and the objective meaning of the economy relate to the totality of social life in its political, cultural, religious, and aesthetic dimensions. What is the place of the economy within the totality of the purposes and cultural spheres of a society? The differentiation of the economic system from the entire system of society leads to a conflict between the economic functional conditions of the market – competition and the formation of market prices – and the sociological requirements of social cohesion and integration (i.e. of the common features of the symbolic world view and the conformity of behavior). Considered in economic terms, the market and the price system can better perform their controlling and coordinating function the larger and less personal the market and the competition between buyers and sellers and, thus, the more anonymous and objective the social relationships among the participants.[14] Whether and at what price we obtain meat, as Adam Smith wrote,

---

[13] See also Oswald von Nell-Breuning, "Wirtschaftsethik," in *Staatslexikon*, 6th Ed. (Freiburg, 1963), Vol. XIII, pp. 773-80.

[14] Cf. James M. Buchanan, "Ethical Rules, Expected Values, and Large Numbers," *Ethics*, 76 (1965), pp. 1-13.

should not depend on the benevolence of the butcher, but on his self-interest and on the supply of and demand for meat in the market.

In the transition from the hierarchical society to the market society – in Ferdinand Tönnies' terms, from *Gemeinschaft* to *Gesellschaft* – from substantive to instrumental rationality, from integration by shared culture and life-world (*Lebenswelt*) to integration by economic exchange, a loss of accepted norms and values relevant to conduct and related to small-group environments takes place. One characteristic of the development of subjectivity and the market society is an ambiguity that can be called the dilemma of giving more room to subjectivity and at the same time reification. Economic rationality and liberty promote a large market with purely economic expectations of behavior and the coordination of subjective demand, measured only in terms of the readiness and ability to pay. The larger the market, the greater the economic rationality and division of labor, but the lower the sense and experience of community. This dilemma is brought about by the differentiation of society as a whole and the autonomization of the economy. The differentiation and autonomization of subsystems creates social costs and cannot be considered good in itself. It reaches internal limits, where the community of individual persons' expectations of meaning and the functional conditions of the subsystems are too widely separated. It is, consequently, no longer possible for an all-embracing sense of community to be experienced in the role-expectations of individuals.

The goal of ethics is to penetrate all spheres of action with value orientations. The social function of ethics is to formulate the common values and norms that serve the action orientations of the members of a society. Ethics aims at *penetrating* society and the economy with common values and norms. This ethical penetration must counteract the tendency in modern society toward the differentiation and separation of the spheres of life. The life-world and the "secondary systems," the unity of everyday life and the instrumentally-rational systems of the economy, have separated and grown apart from one another so widely that they threaten to become completely unconnected. The separation of a common social sense of meaning and common value convictions into partial rationalities will become apparent in the following discussion.

In nations with market economies, a cultural tension emerges between the culture of the sphere of production and that of the sphere of consumption. In the sphere of consumption, the functional principle of the economy is based on hedonistic calculation and constantly expanding consumer demand. In the sphere of production, it is based on a strict work ethic, discipline, and the renunciation of immediate satisfaction of needs. Because the cultural context of Western society is formed almost entirely by the sphere of consumption, the culture and the economy develop in different directions. The norms of the economy operate outside those of the consumer culture. The other spheres of the culture – science, art, and religion – now have little to do with the sphere of work, and the values and forms of expression of the extra-economic culture are no longer connected to the world of work. Daniel Bell has portrayed this development as a phenomenon of American society and of capitalism.[15] The tense relationship between producer culture and consumer culture is, however, not restricted to capitalism, but exists in all economic systems, because each human person is at the same time a disciplined producer and a hedonistic consumer.[16]

The drifting apart of the cultures of the world of work and economic activity and the world of consumption and leisure, and the separation of culture from the everyday world into a specialized cultural professionalism can be seen in all Western societies. The separation of the economy and the culture, of renunciation in production and hedonism in consumption was, however, accelerated considerably by the Keynesian version of the market economy. The ethos of "inner-worldly asceticism," of saving and investing, becomes obsolete when the quantitative aspect of the fiscal and psychological expansion of demand stands at the center, even though the rest of a work ethos in production is still as necessary as always. The virtues of thrifty, frugal economizing are anachronistic and foreign under conditions of fiscal expansion policies. But because of the unity of the life-world and of our sense of action, the development toward the differentiation of the cultural spheres cannot continue without restriction. At the present time, consequently, a tendency can be noted away from differentiation and toward a growing reintegration of the cultural spheres of science, the economy, and art, toward a cultural interpenetration of the cultural spheres of society.[17] The value-orientations of the economy and the other cultural spheres, of the worlds of work and leisure, cannot be constantly separated from one another without the emergence of the phenomena of crisis. Economic ethics and the cultural philosophy of the economy are the attempt to create, in opposition to this development toward cultural segmentation, a new unity between the economy and culture, the work-world and the life-world.

The interest in an expansion of political economy by ethical economy and a cultural philosophy of the economy corresponds to the transformations of modern technology and economy. The expansion of room for freedom of action and the increased prosperity of the individual mean that the social question of the nineteenth century, the question of the worker and property in the means of production, as the theme of nineteenth-century political economy, must take second place today to the challenges of the ethical and cultural formation of highly-developed societies. Political-economic analysis – the theory of ownership and production relationships and the political-legal frameworks of the market econ-

---

[15] Daniel Bell, *The Cultural Contradictions of Capitalism* (New York, 1976).

[16] Cf. Eduard Spranger, "Die Wirtschaft unter kulturphilosophischem Aspekt," in Spranger, *Kulturphilosophie und Kulturkritik*, ed. Hans Wenke (Tübingen, 1969).

[17] Cf. Koslowski, *Die postmoderne Kultur* (Munich, 1987), pp. 89-98 and 133-47.

omy – must be expanded by ethical-economic analysis, by the question of the ethical presuppositions of an advanced, post-industrial, and individualistic economy, in which the "intelligent" technology of microelectronics is dominant. The ethical-economic analysis of individual actions and their coordination, ethical economy, is performed alongside the political-economic analysis of the frameworks of the economy and state action, political economy.

0.3. Overview of the Structure of the Book

The present work takes up the three questions of ethical economy identified above. It examines the ethical presuppositions of the economy, especially those of the market-economic order and the coordination by the price system, and develops an economic theory of ethics and of the economic conditions of ethical rationality (Chapter 2: Economics and Formal Ethics). It poses the question of the relationship of ethical and economic theories of the good, of ethical and economic experiencing of value and understanding of meaning (Chapter 3: Economics and Substantive Ethics), and determines their relationship to the culture of a society within a cultural philosophy of the economy (Chapter 4). Side effects are consequences of our actions that unintentionally extend into other areas of conduct and spheres of culture and, by definition, exceed the limits of their spheres and disciplines. Controlling them, therefore, presents a problem for ethics, economics, and decision theory (Chapter 5).

One prerequisite of a theory of ethical economy and economic ethics, and one condition of achieving the integration of ethics and economics in a comprehensive theory of the coordination of self-interested action, is an expansion of ethics to include metaphysics, which remains, nevertheless, within the bounds of a general theory of rationality (Chapter 1: Economics, Ethics, and Religion: A Positive Theory of the Coordination of Self-Interested Action). The principles of ethical economy presented in this book begin with the conviction that, without metaphysics, economics and ethics are possible, but not very effective. The reference to metaphysics or religion as a theory of totality is valid for both ethics and for economics.

An economic theory that seeks to be more than a variation calculus within given parameters and more than a consideration of variability within *ceteris paribus* conditions already forms in itself an ontological theory of the maximization of existence and the realization of values in a world of scarce resources. Economic ontology, as the ontology of every sphere of existence presented by the economy, examines the basic concepts and assumptions of economic theory, such as general equilibrium, etc. (Chapter 6: Economics and Ontology). The fact that the ontology of mechanics is only applicable to economics to a limited degree and has led to an underestimation of the ethical factor in the market economy is evident not only from ontological reflections, but also from practical, economic-ethical reflections on the opportunities for ethical action and the relationship between morality and advantage in the competitive market (Chapter 7: Economic Ethics in the Market Economy).

The theory of the ethical presuppositions of the market economy, the economic and ethical theories of the good, and ethics oriented toward economics are unified in dealing with the problem of justice. Substantive and formal ethics must come together in the theory of justice, because the problem of justice has both a formal side of deontological justice and a material or substantive side of appropriateness to the nature of the particular subject matter at hand. The "theory of just processes of price formation" proves itself in the process to be a central theoretical element of a "neo-Aristotelian synthesis" of natural law and classical liberalism, and to be necessary for the market economy. Moreover, it is capable of acting as a link between pure process justice and pure end-state justice (Chapters 8 and 9: Commutative Justice and Just Price Theory).

0.4. Missing Mediation of Economics and Ethics in Modernity – Ethical Economy as Post-Modern Economics

Since the divorce of economics from moral philosophy with Adam Smith's theory, a tense relationship has existed between the disciplines of economics and ethics. One cause of this tense relationship is found in the orientation of the mainstream of economics toward the natural sciences – an orientation that from the outset put ethics in the position of being insufficiently scientific and precise.

The separation of ethics and economics is a consequence of the triumphant progress of the modern, mechanistic conception of the world and its application to the economy since the works of Thomas Hobbes and Bernard Mandeville. Economics followed the mechanization of the world view that is characteristic of the modern age.[18] The mechanization of economic theory is true of classical and neo-classical, as well as of Marxist economics.[19] Economic subjects are viewed as acting persons driven by insatiable desires, whose productive activities must be mediated mechanically and technically by either market equilibrium or central control. Ontologically, the discipline of economics is classified as a natural science and – as with Kant, for instance – practical reason is restricted to the interior of morality, to the pure will. This ontology of the economy as a technical or natural sphere is just as characteristic of the pre-Marxist political

[18] Cf. Anneliese Maier, *Die Mechanisierung des Weltbildes im 17. Jahrhundert*. 2nd Ed. (Rome, 1968).

[19] The sole exception is the Austrian school of political economy, above all, Mises' *Human Action*, with his a priori argument for the economic principle. This school is, consequently, of considerable significance for the establishment of a theory of ethical economy.

tinue to exist in a relationship of mutual exclusion and irreconcilable opposition to one another, because they refer to the same subject matter, the activities of conscious, rational human persons. Ethics and economics must merge and become a theory of ethical economy and of ethics oriented toward economics. Their distinctiveness and the fact that they belong together are clear in all action orientations that aim at the integration of economic and ethical action perspectives and purposes, in economic ethics. Economic ethics is not an oxymoron of two mutually exclusive theory-components, but the recognition of the distinctiveness and affinity of the strongest and the best of human motives and the outline of rules and institutions that make use of *both* of these motives.

CHAPTER 1

ECONOMICS, ETHICS, AND RELIGION

Positive Theory of the Coordination of Self-Interested Actions

Economics is concerned with two main questions:

1. The question of how the use of scarce means for given ends can be economized, the economic problem in the narrower sense; and

2. The question of the optimal coordination of individual actions that result from the self-interest of acting persons in alternative economic systems and decision processes.

Both questions have an ethical dimension and refer to the interdependence of ethics and economics, of the ethical and the economic orientation and coordination of actions.

It is not the normative viewpoint of economic ethics, but the metaethical analysis of the relation of economic and ethical rules in the coordination of actions that should be treated first. Is social coordination possible without ethics, or is the introduction and the obligation of ethical codes of conduct necessary in social coordination, so that the economy can realize its full potential? Are ethics and economics in fact complementary? And if so, does their complementarity apply to the decentralized coordination of market societies?

1.1. Internalization of Side Effects and Inclusion of Persons Affected as Criteria of Social Coordination

For every system of coordination the question is posed: Which groups and individuals should be taken into account in the coordination and to what extent and to what depth of differentiation should the effects and side effects of the process of interaction arising from the coordination be taken into account? The best system of coordination is one that achieves the most comprehensive inclusion of persons affected and the most extensive internalization of effects and side effects. An ideal system of coordination includes everyone affected and internalizes all side effects.

To what extent can side effects become a problem of the theory of social coordination? Societies can control production and distribution by one of three systems of decision and coordination: by the market, by voting, or by central control. The theory of social coordination must investigate which of these social systems of decision and coordination is best able to realize the objectives of society and of individual persons (i.e. the needs of the members of a society) in an efficient manner.

The ideal of a free-market society is that of contractual agreement between individuals. If two parties close a business contract, all side effects of a good, all secondary gains and losses, are known by the parties to the contract and are included in their utility calculations. No side effects can arise for a third party: all effects are internalized and everyone affected by the contract is included or, in the case of a third party, unaffected.[1] If one extends these criteria of mutually-advantageous exchange to entire social systems of decision, the *internalization* of all effects and side effects of actions and the *inclusion* of everyone affected become the criteria of social systems of decision.[2] All effects and side effects and everyone affected by a decision should be taken into account in the process of coordination and decision. This means that for the process of decision and coordination of democratic elections, the conditions of equal voting rights, and for that of the market and price system, the condition of unlimited market access, must be met. These conditions form the meaning of liberty and equality in a democracy and an economy: no one may be excluded from the formal rights of political co-determination and market access, and no negative (side-)effects may be passed on to other persons without a legal reason or their own agreement.

1.2. Private Vices – Public Benefits: The Good as Side Effect

The central premise of market theory is that the market, under conditions of perfect competition, not only ensures the inclusion of the persons affected and the internalization of negative side effects, but also produces efficiency as a positive side effect (externality) in a process that is intent on something completely different from the common good. Economic subjects pursue their own interests in the market. They seek their own profit and are led by the invisible hand of competition to produce efficiently and to sell at the equilibrium price.[3] A motive that is either not extremely ethical or ethically-neutral, such as profit maximization, leads by market forces to a social good, efficiency.

---

[1] Cf. James M. Buchanan, "Social Choice, Democracy, and Free Markets" and "Individual Choice in Voting and the Market," *Journal of Political Economy*, 62 (1954), pp. 114-23 and 334-43.

[2] See also Koslowski, "Markt- und Demokratieversagen?" *Politische Vierteljahresschrift*, 24 (1983), pp. 166-87 and "Market and Democracy as Discourses," in Koslowski, ed., *Individual Liberty and Democratic Decision-Making* (Tübingen, 1987), pp. 58-92.

[3] Cf. James M. Buchanan, "Rent Seeking and Profit Seeking," in Buchanan, Robert D. Tollison, and Gordon Tullock, eds., *Toward a Theory of the Rent-Seeking Society* (College Station, 1980), pp. 3-15.

Bernard Mandeville reduced this ability of the market to produce efficiency as an externality, a *side effect*, in a process that actually aims at something else to the well-known paradox: "private vices – public benefits." Not only an ethically neutral motivation, such as striving for profit, but even immoral motives, vices, are transformed by the invisible hand of the market into positive side effects, into goods. Non-ethical behavior is transformed behind the backs of the contestants into socially advantageous conduct.

One can place Mandeville's paradox near the center of a series of other paradoxes of this kind, such as Adam Smith's invisible hand and Hegel's cunning of reason in history, which achieve their goals behind people's backs. His paradox, however, goes beyond these authors, because it explicitly considers not merely ethically-neutral actions, but also unethical actions, to promote the common good. Mandeville's principle resembles that of Mephistopheles in Goethe's *Faust*: "I am a part of the power that always wills evil and always does good." The good is the side effect of someone who does not at all desire the good. It is not necessary to desire the good, because it comes into being anyway, as the side effect of egoistic motives.

In Mandeville's theory, ethics is eliminated from the market economy. It no longer has a function. His theory is consistent: the direct intention of the good is not economically desirable, because the consequence of the good always also has bad side effects. On the other hand, the consequence of the bad always also has *good* side effects. There is, therefore, no reason to prefer the good to the bad. Every action has good side effects for someone and bad side effects for someone else. For example, according to Mandeville, the Fire of London provided employment for many firemen, and for construction workers during the rebuilding of the city, while the frugal consumption of the prosperous classes promoted unemployment in the lower classes.[4] Mandeville's thesis is that in the market society a consistent ethos, an ethical theory free of contradiction, is no longer possible. Good brings about bad and bad brings about good. This is opposed to the proposition of Thomas Aquinas, "*bonum est diffusivum sui.*" [5] The good brings about good and, therefore, should always be strived for as the purpose and the effect of actions. It does not come into being, as with Mandeville, only as an unintended side effect of actions.

---

[4] Cf. Bernard Mandeville, *The Fable of the Bees*, ed. F. B. Kaye (Oxford, 1924), Vol I, p. 367: "It is in Morality as it is in Nature, there is nothing so perfectly Good in Creatures that it cannot be hurtful to anyone of the society, nor any thing so entirely Evil, but it may prove beneficial to some part or other of the Creation." – On Mandeville, see also Koslowski, *Gesellschaft und Staat* (Stuttgart, 1982), pp. 174-85; and Alois Riklin, *Wissenschaft und Ethik* (St. Gallen, 1982).

[5] Thomas Aquinas, *Summa contra Gentiles*, Book III: *Providence*, trans. Vernon J. Bourke (Notre Dame, Ind., 1975), Chap. 24, Para 8, p. 96: "The better a thing is, the more does it diffuse its goodness to remote beings."

The influence of Mandeville's paradox was and is extraordinary. Adam Smith was concerned with Mandeville's *Fable of the Bees* as early as his *Theory of the Moral Sentiments*, and was brought not least by these lectures to found economics as an independent discipline in his subsequent *Wealth of Nations*.[6] For the Cambridge tradition of ethics and economics, with G. E. Moore and John Maynard Keynes,[7] Mandeville's paradox became a crucial stimulus.

The question posed by Mandeville's paradox is: How can we defend the promotion of acting well when we cannot at all see which positive or negative side effects our actions will cause in the infinity of the interdependence of reality? If truth is the correspondence of the understanding to the subject, if justice is the correspondence of the will and of action to the good, and if the *oeconomia*, the true economy, is the appropriateness of the action to the situation, how can we always be sure that we have acted rightly? In the network of causalities, the basic norms cannot be completely specified for concrete actions and all of their consequences. The truth is not the individual action, but the entirety of the effects of actions. No appropriateness of an action to reality can be perfect in the immeasurable eventfulness of the world. Therefore, every specific truth that we express and every particular deed that we perform is blemished by the error that remains with even the careful decision and without which we could hardly live.

1.3. Economic Failure

Ethics, however, does not become superfluous as a consequence of this phenomenon. The model of the invisible hand, of a market free of ethics in Adam Smith's philanthropic version and Mandeville's cynical formulation, is valid only under three very restrictive conditions. The invisible hand leads from completely egoistic motives to the optimum when the number of suppliers and demanders is extremely high, when all adaptations can be made with neither cost nor loss of time, and when the contractual agreements can be kept or enforced without cost (i.e. without transaction costs). Only if these conditions are satisfied are egoistic efforts transformed by the invisible hand of the market into socially-advantageous market results. Only under these conditions are ethics and

---

[6] On Smith's contradiction of Mandeville, see his critique of Mandeville's principle in *The Theory of Moral Sentiments*, ed. E. G. West (Indianapolis, 1976), p. 499: "Virtue is the great support, and vice the great disturber of human society," but also his agreement: "But how destructive soever this system may appear . . . , in some respects [it] bordered upon the truth (*Ibid*, p. 495).

[7] G. E. Moore, *Principia Ethica* (Cambridge, 1903), pp. 150-55 and John Maynard Keynes, *A Treatise on Probability* (London, 1973), pp. 309 ff. According to Moore, all actions aimed at the long term require the fundamental presumption that short-term charitable results also translate themselves into charitable consequences in the long term.

ethical conduct superfluous in the market, because social coordination and the common good are brought about without the onerous imposition of ethics.

The conditions of perfect competition and costless enforcement of contracts are, however, ideal conditions that are not met in the reality of the market economy. The market is not the ideal mechanism that the neo-classical theory of general equilibrium assumes, but is instead a context of the interaction of acting and communicating individuals. In this context of exchange, ethics remains necessary for economic activity. Contrary to Mandeville's conviction, ethics, understood as desiring and doing the good, also promotes the economic good in the market. One cannot discharge one's duty of responsible decision-making by referring to the automatic mechanism of the market, even if the side effects of our actions are not completely foreseeable in their ultimate ramifications. The economic significance of ethics in the market can be seen in the consequences that mutual trust and the reliability of business partners have for reducing the cost of closing deals, and in the room of action for free decisions that managers have in the market to set prices and to fulfill their contractual obligations from a sales or labor contract – above all with asymmetric knowledge between seller and buyer and with the uniqueness of the position of the seller or buyer. This room for action exceeds mere acceptance of the market price, as is assumed of the behavior of a price taker, who can vary only the amount sold, and not the price of the good, in the theory of perfect competition.[8]

The reliability of business partners and their trust in one another bring about a decrease in the costs of economic exchange. All economic exchange activities, all transactions between producers and suppliers, employers and employees, contain an element of uncertainty about the performance of contracts. This undefined and uncontrollable element is created as a side effect of a contractual transaction, one that cannot be completely internalized by economic or legal means – not even with high costs of monitoring the contract or obtaining private economic insurance. The element of uncertainty is greater in a free economic order or a market system than in centrally-controlled economies, because the former leaves room for free contractual agreement, while the latter chooses from the start control and supervision, which indeed reduce uncertainty, but create in its place even greater problems of coercion, motivation to work, and the control of contribution to the production of collectivized firms.

---

[8] John von Neumann and Oskar Morgenstern, *Theory of Games and Economic Behavior*, 3rd Ed. (Princeton, 1953), pp. 9-15; and Morgenstern, "Thirteen Critical Points in Contemporary Economic Theory," in *Selected Economic Writings*, ed. Andrew Schotter (New York, 1976), pp. 271 ff. and 283 ff., show that the picture of the market as a flexible equilibrium of unlimitedly adaptable individuals is accurate only for market openings and the beginning of market transactions. Once the individuals have determined their preferences and have entered into their exchange-relationships, the free market is transformed into a market with established and rigid relationships and commitments, and, therefore, also with expectations of ethical behavior.

The pursuit of *mere* self-interest by everyone engaged in commerce does not lead to optimal efficiency, because trust in the performance of contracts and in the sincerity of the parties to the contract is not established and, therefore, does not exist on the basis of mere self-interest. A lack of trust in the other party to comply with the rules and a lack of willingness on both sides to keep to the rules when short-term advantage can be attained by breaking one of them create costs that are economically wasteful from the perspective of production – costs of monitoring and enforcing the fulfillment of contracts by legal means.

In addition to the problem of the costs of enforcement, there are also instances of the violation of contracts in which the expansion of economic control according to self-interest and of contractual agreement by legal regulations is impossible, because the evidence of a breach of contract cannot be adduced, or can be adduced only with great difficulty. Two examples of such economic failure follow:

Asymmetric Knowledge:
If one of the parties to a contract possesses superior knowledge about the object of exchange, the other party must trust that the knowledgeable party will use his or her knowledge conscientiously and will not cheat the party with less knowledge. The physician may not misuse her superior knowledge of medicine to advise her patient to undergo an operation that she knows to be unnecessary; the geologist exploring natural resources must pass on the results of his research to the client according to their contract; etc. The transmission and application of knowledge, including economically-relevant knowledge, is an ethical problem, because an external observer or court cannot determine and prove beyond doubt whether a person acted without possessing the knowledge or consciously applied it incorrectly or harmfully.[9] It can be determined that knowledge is applied knowledgeably only by a self-relationship of the knower with himself, only by responsibility and conscientiousness, not by a relationship with someone else and external control. External control or monitoring of the conscientious application of knowledge can detect and punish only gross negligence. It cannot establish the efficient use of knowledge in everyday economic life. The transmission of knowledge is always an ethical phenomenon.

Monopoly in Employing the Resources of one's own Actions:
All persons have a monopoly regarding knowledge of their own ability to perform and, above all, their willingness to perform – a monopoly concerning their own goodwill. Whether they use the resources of their actions, abilities, and will optimally and according to contract cannot be determined economically and le-

[9] Cf. R. C. O. Matthews, "Morality, Competition, and Efficiency," *The Manchester School of Economic and Social Studies*, 49 (1981), p. 294.

gally in detail by other persons. This monopoly in the use of one's own person is especially visible in long-term contracts or contracts that are closed with the implicit intention to repeat their terms. The repetition of commercial relationships, repeat business, is more common than the one-time commercial relationship and is more efficient for the economy as a whole than the process of conducting every transaction in the market and price competition anew. Repetition of commercial relationships leads to economies of scale in avoiding transaction costs. Transaction costs sink in proportion to the repetition of the contractually-agreed performances. The implicit contract of repeated commercial relationships has one difficulty, however. It increases the opportunity for the parties to the contract to derive advantages from their quasi-monopolistic positions as established businesspersons and to set excessive prices on the basis of their special positions relative to the other parties.

Taking advantage of a relative, short-term, monopolistic position in long-term contracts, without considering criteria of fairness, makes the economically-efficient establishment of enduring business relationships more difficult and, as far as the entire economy is concerned, leads to a suboptimal allocation of resources, because the transaction costs of searching for markets and forming contracts with unnecessary frequency occur with every transaction. A party to a contract who draws every short-term advantage from a long-term business relationship and his growing monopolistic position calls the long-term advantage of the repetition of business relationships into question.

The monopolistic position of the parties to a contract relative to one another in the case of repeated business relationships also exists with enduring work relationships between employers and employees. Both sides have a monopolistic position, since they cannot be replaced in the labor market by other employers or employees in the short term and without costs. The existence of larger firms with salaried employees is only possible when the labor contract is based upon an ethical relationship of trust between employers and employees. Otherwise, it would be necessary to reemploy workers in the labor market for each transaction of the firm. The "internal labor market"[10] of the firm would have to be completely replaced by the external market. The economies of scale resulting from the repetition of transactions without repetition of the contract for each particular transaction would be impossible. The gain in efficiency resulting from it would be lost. Without the social validity and expectation of a relationship of trust between employers and employees, the only possibility of concluding long-term labor contracts without costly contract negotiations for each transaction is that of contracts between family members. Nepotism is a rational option – if also an inefficient one for the economy as a whole – when people

---

[10] Cf. Oliver E. Williamson, "Firms and Markets," in Sidney Weintraub, ed., *Modern Economic Thought* (Philadelphia, 1977), pp. 185-202.

believe that the only workers they can trust are their own relatives. That is why Alfred Marshall believed that the modern business corporation with salaried workers became possible only after improvement in "commercial morality."[11]

Uncertainty in contractual agreements can either be accepted by trust or be somewhat reduced at high cost by legal control and sanctions. Trust reduces transaction costs, because the parties to a contract reach an agreement more quickly and require less control.[12] Following rules voluntarily and ethically, when doing so is not observable or is observable only at high cost, reduces the costs of economic transactions and, consequently, the costs for the entire economy, without reducing the economic returns of the parties to the contract. An economic ethic living with the members of an economy and an expressed ethos of economic reliability increase the welfare of an economy.

The opposing position is maintained by Robert Axelrod:

> The individuals do not have to be rational: the evolutionary process allows the successful strategies to thrive, even if the players do not know why or how. Nor do the players have to exchange messages or commitments: they do not need words, because their deeds speak for them. Likewise, there is no need to assume trust between the players: the use of reciprocity can be enough to make defection unproductive. Altruism is not needed: successful strategies can elicit cooperation even from an egoist. Finally, no central authority is needed: cooperation based on reciprocity can be self-policing.[13]

It should be said concerning such a "mechanistic" theory of cooperation that the acceptance of a situation of interaction is already intentionally and linguistically mediated: the other person does not have a mechanical effect upon oneself, but influences oneself as a perceived person in a relationship of mutual perception. Axelrod is correct in saying that a minimal form of cooperation may develop with mutual adoption of the "tit-for-tat" strategy ("I'll do to you what you do to me"). This situation, however, is not the optimum, but merely the social minimum of cooperation. And there is no reason to be satisfied with a minimalism of social cooperation.

Even Axelrod is forced to admit that cooperation increases with certain modifications, such as 1) readiness to cooperate at the beginning of interaction, 2) leniency or readiness to forgive after responding to a provocation by the other person[14] and 3) anticipation of the continuation of interaction and of repeat business in the future (i.e. extension of the time horizon and a lower preference

---

[11] Alfred Marshall, *Principles of Economics*, 8th Ed. (London, 1961), pp. 252-53.

[12] Cf. Horst Albach, "Vertrauen in der ökonomischen Theorie," *Zeitschrift für die gesamte Staatswissenschaft*, 136 (1980), pp. 2-11.

[13] Robert Axelrod, *The Evolution of Cooperation* (New York, 1984), pp. 173-74.

[14] *Ibid.*, p. 20.

for present utility – a lower discount rate).[15] These modifications of mere retaliation are, however, already *ethical* transformations of the tit-for-tat strategy, going beyond a mechanical reaction and assuming that the acting person anticipates the anticipations of the other party.[16] Furthermore, trust is not, as Axelrod presumes, an altruistic disposition. Trust does not seek primarily the utility of the other person, but rather common benefit, the mutually-advantageous increase of cooperation.

Axelrod's work is handicapped by an incorrect, complete disjunction of egoism and altruism, of strategic and moral action, in which the acting person either is completely egoistic or immediately takes on the character of altruistic sacrifice. The dichotomy that he makes between strategic and ethical action excludes the ability to conceive of developing forms of social cooperation. He also overlooks the possibility of a synthesis of self-interested and other-interested action (i.e. economic-ethical cooperation). Strategic game theory and ethics can be unified in a theory of ethical economy.

Trust, reliability, fidelity, and faith presuppose ethical attitudes of managers that go beyond the model of mere utility maximization. Since these ethical attitudes decrease transaction costs, they increase the capability of the market to perform, reduce the probability of market failure, and reduce the incentive to disregard governmental coordination of obligations. Ethics is a corrective for economic or market failure, because it decreases the costs of sanctions and controls.[17] Since governmental control by the organs of the executive and judiciary branches is also costly, ethics reduces the costs of state action and the probability of "governmental failure" in the public sector.

There is, therefore, an unequivocal argument for ethical conduct. But the macroeconomic argument is not compelling at the level of individual, personal economics. It is not persuasive for those who follow only their own interests, for utility-maximizing economic man. It has persuasive power only for those who make the universal interest, total utility, or simply morality, their own interest. Decentralized, uncontrolled coordination attains it optimum only where not only the special, but also the universal interest is adopted in the maxims of acting persons, where the universal becomes the motive of the individual (economic) acting person. If this does not occur, the consequence is either a loss of welfare due to the high transaction costs of control and implementation, or prohibitively-high transaction costs, market failure, and, therefore, the compulsory direction of the economy by the state.

---

15 *Ibid.*, p. 128.

16 A decrease in the discount rate for present utility by anticipating and discounting the future into the present is, as is pointed out on p. 43 below, a proto-ethical phenomenon.

17 On ethics as a corrective for market failure, see Kenneth J. Arrow, "Political and Economic Evaluation of Social Effects and Externalities," in Michael D. Intriligator, ed., *Frontiers of Quantitative Economics* (New York, 1975), pp. 3-25.

1.4. Ethics as Corrective for Economic Failure

In response to this insight into the relationship between ethics and economics, between ethical conduct – such as rule-compliance, trust, reliability, fidelity, and faith – on one hand, and the reduction of transaction costs, on the other, the individual has three options:[18]

Case 1: The person can simply act morally. He then makes the insight into the economic total utility of ethical conduct also the *motive* of his *own* action. He makes the universal interest his own interest. He acts morally, independently of the conduct of the other person. For example, an employee of a firm strives, independently of what his co-workers produce, to achieve his full output. Or, a manager seeks to be fair, despite widespread, unfair competition.

Case 2: The person can act partially morally. He is ready to obey ethical rules, if others, or at least most of the others, do so as well. He breaks the rules himself, however, whenever he feels that he is being "duped." For example, a worker performs his job well, as long as everyone else also does so.

Case 3: The person may understand that a better condition will be attained for all if everyone obeys the rules, but considers the best situation to exist when everyone except himself obeys the rules. For example, a worker knows that everyone must produce his full performance for the survival of the firm, but decides that he would rather be an exception.

The immoral individual of Case 3 interprets the situation, in terms of game theory, as the "prisoner's dilemma," as the dilemma of a utility-maximizing prisoner among other prisoners. If everyone follows the ethical rules, the best condition for everyone will be realized.[19] Each individual can, however, improve his or her own position even more by not following the rules, while everyone else does. But the dilemma of this prisoner is that he cannot be certain that, if he violates the rules, the others will not respond by breaking them as well, with the consequence that he himself and everyone else will be worse off than if everyone followed the rules. In the small, observable group, this problem of the prisoner's dilemma is not so significant, because each group member can monitor the conduct of the others and can insist on the observance of mutuality. In larger groups, in which this transparency does not exist, implementing universal rule-compliance encounters greater problems. The individual can no longer adapt his behavior immediately to that of all others and, therefore, runs

---

[18] On the following, see also Koslowski, "Religion, Ökonomie, Ethik," in Koslowski, ed., *Die religiöse Dimension der Gesellschaft* (Tübingen, 1984), pp. 76-96.

[19] The prisoner's dilemma is usually presented in terms of the number of years of confinement two prisoners will receive as a consequence of confessing or not confessing to a crime, without the possibility of communicating with one another. It is applied here to the problem of rule-compliance under uncertainty about the rule-compliant behavior of other persons.

the risk that he alone will obey the rules, while the others break them "at his expense."

In the modern commercial society, there arises the moral problem of the free rider: Some persons wish to claim the advantages of a moral situation for themselves, without participating in the costs of restraining unethical desires by converting their own desires into ethically-universalizable and rule-conforming desires.[20] This free rider problem increases with the number of members in a group and with the reduction of the transparency of the conduct. A "dilemma of large numbers" (James Buchanan) emerges. With the expansion of the market, the scope of transactions, and the number of groups to which the individual is related, face-to-face monitoring and informal pressure to follow the rules in small groups, which compelled social conformity in societal forms before the commercial society, become impossible.

One way to oppose this development of the commercial society would be to redivide the reference groups into smaller, more observable units – as regionalism, for example, attempts to do. This solution, however, contradicts the other, highly useful consequence of the growth of the market and of the dilemma of large numbers. In the large market, the individual is compelled by the competition of the large number of suppliers to become a price taker and economically-efficient acting person, thereby increasing the efficiency of the market. A dilemma of economic ethics and of the relationship between ethics and economics arises here: in the economy, impersonality and large numbers of persons are beneficial; but in ethics, they are a hindrance. The larger and less personal the society, the greater is the opportunity for the individual, at the cost of others and in the anonymity of large numbers, to break the rules without being caught. The greater also, therefore, is the effectiveness of market competition and price control, and thus the efficiency of the economy.

Those who make the universal – the universalizable moral rule or the imperative of morality – the rule only of the moral conduct of others, but not their own rule and the motive of their own actions and who, consequently, exploit the morality of others to their own advantage by the opaqueness of the situation and the ability to conceal their actions, act economically, not morally. It should be noted, however, that this economic conduct does not lead to a stable situation in terms of game theory. Case 3 above is a typical dilemma situation, within which one cannot remain. The prisoner's dilemma describes a situation in which everyone improves his condition if *everyone* follows the rules, but in which every individual has an interest in being the only person who breaks the rules. The rule will thus collapse, if complying with it is neither compelled from outside by monitoring and sanctions nor compelled by the individuals themselves for ethi-

[20] James M. Buchanan, "Ethical Rules, Expected Values, and Large Numbers," *Ethics*, 76 (1965), p. 8.

cal reasons. Case 3 must be converted into the ethical option of cases 1 or 2, or into an external system of coercion.

Consider Case 2. This is a typical intermediate situation, which possesses high plausibility for depicting the conduct of most persons. They act morally when others do so as well. They cease acting morally when they feel that everyone else has done so. Ethics is a means of converting the situation of the prisoner's dilemma, which presents a case of economic failure, into the situation of trust or assurance. The universal observance of ethical rules in a society would thus turn what Sen calls the "isolation paradox"[21] of Case 2 into a situation of relative certainty. The isolation paradox says that in isolation and under uncertainty about the behavior of others, the individual will not follow ethical rules, because he fears being cheated, although he is fundamentally prepared to apply universal principles to himself.

The three cases can also be described formally as follows: In Case 3, where the individual is economically motivated, the individual prefers situation A_1E_0 to A_1E_1. A_1 means that the others *(alter)* obey the rules; E_1 means that oneself *(ego)* obeys them. A_0 and E_0 are the negations of A_1 and E_1, respectively.[22] According to Buchanan, the individual will not act ethically if he experiences no external, informal monitoring in small groups; he prefers A_1E_0 to A_1E_1 when he can avoid being caught. Thus he does not really act ethically. He never acts as one who makes the universalizability of ethical rules his own free will, or, in Kantian terms, as one who makes the moral law his own law.

When seen from the ethical point of view, the problem appears differently. If the individual takes the universal as one of his preferences, his preference is transformed in such a way that he prefers alternative A_1E_1 to A_1E_0 (Cases 1 and 2). When moral motivation is universalized, there is no longer a prisoner's dilemma. The individuals are no longer taking advantage of the rules. They prefer the situation of universal rule-compliance to the situation of their own exception from the rule. Ethics is thus a solution to the prisoner's dilemma. If direct monitoring is no longer possible, but keeping the rules is not always in accordance with the immediate preferences of the individuals, the individual must revise the maxims of his will, his preferences themselves, in such a way that he prefers the universalizability of a maxim to the particularity of excepting himself. The individual prefers a world in which no one, including himself, lies to a world in which everyone except himself tells the truth. The moral, as opposed to the economic assessment of the situations of rule-compliance are characterized by the preference of A_1E_1 to A_1E_0.

---

[21] Amartya Sen, "Isolation, Assurance, and the Social Rate of Discount," *Quarterly Journal of Economics*, 81 (1967), p. 112.

[22] Sen provides the formal notation in *On Economic Inequality* (Oxford, 1997), pp. 96-99.

The individual is, however, never certain whether this moral preference for the universality of rules is also shared and followed by the others. Only if the ethical preferences in a society are manifested and universalized (i.e. if everyone, or at least nearly everyone, likewise prefers A_1E_1 to A_1E_0), can the individual act under conditions of uncertainty regarding the strategies of others. If the moral preferences are not universal, however, the individual can find himself in the situation of one who produces a moral prior concession and precommitment that is not reciprocated by others. A situation in which no one except himself obeys the rules, A_0E_1, is certainly not desirable.

This means that Case 2 is also unstable, because the assurance that everyone else, or at least the majority, will obey the rule is always given only partially and with reservations. Indeed, Sen assumes that universally recognized moral values convert Case 3 of the prisoner's dilemma into Case 2 of the "assurance game," because if these values are valid, the individual no longer acts with uncertainty about the morality of the preferences of others.[23] This assumption is, however, a *petitio principii*, that no longer helps the individual. It says only that if ethical conduct is universal (i.e. if "values" are recognized), individuals have additional incentives to act ethically. Whether the values are universally recognized and whether the individual perceives social reality in such a way is, however, precisely what is in question in Case 2, the isolation paradox. How can the universal recognition of moral "values," the situation in which others act ethically and the individual likewise makes the rule his own motive, be achieved? The element of uncertainty is not eliminated here, the assurance is always only partial. Therefore, Case 2 is indeed more stable than Case 3, because in Case 2 the individuals are at least partially moral. But Case 2 cannot produce assurance of the moral conduct of others, and therefore cannot establish such assurance as the basis of the acting person's own conduct.

Two questions arise, consequently, for Case 2, the isolation paradox. First, how long will the person be willing to obey the moral rules, when most other people break them or when the actual conduct of the others is not completely known? Second, how can uncertainty about the behavior of other persons be reduced? These questions cannot be answered by ethics alone. Attempts to answer them within ethical theory lead again and again to the *petitio principii* that ethics will be accepted and find universal recognition, if it is already universally recognized. It claims fallaciously to have proof that the isolation paradox of the acceptance of ethics can be overcome, if ethics already has universal validity.

Case 2 shows that the prisoner's dilemma and the isolation paradox can be overcome by ethics, only if individuals recognize the moral rules and make them their own motive freely and without considering the behavior of others. Since uncertainty about the behavior of others cannot be eliminated, the ethical

---

[23] Sen, *On Economic Inequality*, pp. 98-99.

rule can find acknowledgement only when it is acknowledged independently of the behavior of others. This is precisely the demand of Kant's categorical imperative: the ethical maxim must be seized out of mere respect for the law, without consideration of empirical utility. As soon as the maxim of conduct that is supposed to be capable of universal validity is chosen on the basis of considering the consequences of one's own action and the conditions of the action of others, it is no longer morally "pure," and also – more significantly in the present context – no longer chosen with certainty. One must then worry about what others will do, which effects one's action will have under such and such conditions, etc. Ultimately, one will no longer be able to decide anything at all, or to be persuaded by the obligation of the moral maxim.

For our Kantian Case 1, pure morality without consideration of the behavior of others, however, there arises the problem of the empirical realization of transcendental morality under the conditions of human finitude. How long will the individual be ready to follow the categorical imperative and to obey the moral rules, when others break them? How long will the moral individual be willing to maintain situation A_0E_1, instead of A_0E_0? According to the morality of Kant's ethic, the behavior of others is of no importance to the choice of an action-guiding maxim. The moral subject acts according to the rule of the categorical imperative, even when the consequences are unpleasant and when others do not obey it, but instead pursue their own selfish goals. The isolation paradox does not exist for the Kantian. In the reality of social life, however, this transcendental moralism can hardly be action-guiding, because it is unable to serve as a link between the empirical and the a priori, as Hegel[24] objected to Kant, or because its extremely high demands create the danger of an idealistic over-valuation of the self, as Herder[25] criticized Kant.

If we summarize the results of discussing these three ethical cases, it appears that Case 3, the prisoner's dilemma, and Case 2, the isolation paradox, are not stable. Case 1, pure morality without consideration of the behavior of others, however, is extremely improbable and requires moral heroism. An ethically-immanent grounding of morality "out of pure respect for the law" is indeed possible. But the incentives for the individual to adopt a "pure" ethic for himself are similarly low. In analogy to market failure, it is highly probable that the consequence here will be "ethical failure."

---

[24] Georg W. F. Hegel, *The Philosophy of Right*, trans. S. W. Dyde (Amherst, N. Y., 1996), §§ 135 ff.

[25] Johann Gottfried Herder, *Vernunft und Sprache*, in *Sämtliche Werke*, ed., B. Suphan (Hildesheim, 1967), Vol. XXI, p. 289.

1.5. Religion as Corrective for Ethical Failure

Kant saw the problem of ethical failure completely. If the moral individual follows the categorical imperative, but everyone else follows the rule of his or her own happiness, the individual's harmony of morality and happiness will be disturbed considerably. Kant saw the solution to this problem in the theory of the postulates. The postulates of practical reason – God, freedom, and the immortality of the soul – once again produce trust in the significance of ethical action, in the harmony of happiness and morality. The presupposition that the individual will be prepared to realize the situation of universal rule-compliance, A_1E_1, even when the preferences of others concerning their alternatives A_1E_1 and A_1E_0 are not known, finds its foundation in religious faith in the transcendental reconciliation of morality and happiness for the immortal soul. With the postulates that make this reconciliation persuasive, it is meaningful for the individual to prefer situation A_0E_1, in which only he acts morally, to situation A_0E_0, in which no one acts morally.

Religious faith transforms ethical failure into trust in the significance of ethics, the empirical uncertainty of the isolation paradox into the faith-convictions of the significance of morality. First of all, religion can bring about what Sen already attributed to ethics: transforming the situations of the prisoner's dilemma and the isolation paradox into those of an "assurance situation" or "assurance game." Assurance and trust in the significance of moral action are not to be attained from ethics alone, but instead from the religious establishment of morality. Religion – for example, in the form of postulates with Kant, as the idea of the good and the myth of the judgment of souls after death with Plato – assures the subject that morality and happiness converge in the long run. It makes action under certainty possible in ethics, even when the individual, because of uncertainty about the behavior of others, stands in an isolation paradox or prisoner's dilemma.

The objection could be raised against this argument that it regards religion only as a clever means of social control and the accomplishment of conformity, because expectations of social behavior are simply internalized, and thereby become even more oppressive. It must be made clear, in response, that ethical rules must be able to stand the test of truth, that the religious assurance of the significance of ethics must have validity for everyone, and that this religious faith, when it is universal, actually improves the position of everyone.[26]

But more important than the fact that the individual is moved by religious faith to prefer situation A_0E_1 to A_0E_0 (which could also apply to a masochistic

---

[26] Religion, in this sense, is not bound to any organized, confessional religion. Even an atheist can have religion in this sense, if he is prepared to bring his life under a holistic point of view and to justify it as a whole.

disposition or lead to the exploitation of the individual by others) is the following: Trust that others are moral and obey ethical rules, trust that A_1E_1 will appear more frequently, even when this trust is occasionally disappointed, is strengthened by religion. Thus the readiness of the individual to prefer situation A_0E_1 to A_0E_0, and not to favor situation A_0E_0 out of fear of A_0E_1, is increased. For the fear of delivering without reciprocity leads ultimately to the realization of situation A_0E_0, because everyone believes this. The danger that from this fear of realizing A_0E_1 ultimately no one will obey ethical rules and the worst alternative, A_0E_0, will be realized can be counteracted by the postulates of practical reason. Because individuals are more willing to accept A_0E_1, trust that A_1E_1 will be realized is strengthened and with it also the probability that A_1E_1 will actually appear. The religious validation of the proposition that it is better to endure injustice than to act unjustly, the preference of A_0E_1 to A_1E_0, leads, as Plato already saw, to an increase of trust in the behavior of others, and thus to a greater probability that the situation of universal rule-compliance, situation A_1E_1, will be realized. This avoids a self-fulfilling prophecy, in which mistrust of others and fear of A_0E_1 leads to the realization of situation A_0E_0.[27]

By increasing the willingness to produce moral precommitment, religion reduces the costs of complaining about and adapting to the behavior of others. Because it reduces fear of A_0E_1, it increases the probability that A_1E_1 will be realized. That means that religion not only increases the readiness to produce moral precommitment, but also that it increases the probability that moral action will not have the character of prior concession, but instead that of universal conduct. The steps of our argument – economic or market failure, ethics as corrective to economic failure, religion as corrective to ethical or ethics failure – show the close ties between economic, individual-ethical, and religious orientations of action. They show that economics transcends itself to the level of ethics, and ethics transcends itself to the level of religion.

The small transcendence of the economic contract that exists in passing over from the interaction of one party to a contract with the other, and in passing over from the separateness of persons in economic exchange, points in the direction of the intermediate transcendence of ethics, in which the separateness of persons is transcended even further to the commonality of the ethical rules and values and anticipation of the common interest or common good. The intermediate transcendence of ethics transcends self-interest and the simple balancing of interests in the mutually-advantageous exchange of the commercial contract, the consideration of the universal in the particular interest. The intermediate transcendence of ethics refers once again to the greater transcendence of religion, and is unified within it into a meaningful life option, in which ethical be-

[27] On this danger of the self-fulfilling prophecy in collective actions, see Mancur Olson, *The Logic of Collective Action* (Cambridge, Mass., 1965), pp. 105-10.

havior is thought of as advantageous in the long run and for the most part. The greater transcendence of religion is the condition of the individual meaningfulness of ethical conduct. It is the prerequisite for fulfilling the meaning of the intermediate transcendence of ethics, and for uniting morality and reason or self-interest.[28]

Economics, ethics, and religion constitute a system of transcendences, of going on to something different, and an iteration of compensations, or, in Hegel's words, "sublations" *(Aufhebungen)*. Ethics is the corrective to and compensation for market failure; religion the corrective to and compensation for ethical failure. When economics fails, ethics enters the scene; when ethics fails, religion enters. The transcendences of self-interest take the place of one another; the higher levels compensate for the deficiencies and fill the gaps of the lower levels. The danger is, of course, that ethical failure will be repeated in religious failure, that religion will also be unable assure the person of the significance of ethical action, because there is no ultimate assurance of the truth of religion. Religious failure cannot be compensated by any additional iteration. Religion is the *assurance* of religious-transcendental "payment" for the commitment to ethical behavior, and for the precommitment of trust, for the commitment that concern for the universal interest and the ethical rule is better than disregarding ethics, because of one's own mistrust that others will not act ethically. This assurance of religion is, however, the expression of basic ontological trust and remains in itself the consequence of this trust.

The model of the triad of economics, ethics, and religion presented here is, like Kant's philosophical ethics and practical metaphysics, a very rational argument for the validity of a monotheistic religion and theory of metaphysics. Philosophical ethics is capable of rationally grounding traditional metaphysics, with its specialized metaphysics of rational theology (the concept of God) and ration-

---

[28] The concept of small, intermediate, and great transcendences originates with Thomas Luckmann. See his "Über die Funktion der Religion," in Koslowski, ed., *Die religiöse Dimension der Gesellschaft* (Tübingen, 1985), pp. 28-29: "The distinction of I-related and I-surpassing experiences is encountered by everyone without great consideration; it is the basis of knowledge about the transcendence of the world. This distinction is based on the universal structure of experience. Each (at the time) present experience has an imaginary core and a horizon of present non-experiencing: The experience-core refers automatically to not yet and no longer experiencing. From this circumstance derives an elementary 'co-experience' of transcendence. The distinction of I-relating and I-surpassing in experience and this 'co-experience' of transcendence for the experience-matter, out of which for everyone the consciousness of the borders of the everyday life-word form themselves. We can already formulate here a typology of 'transcendence' based on the general structure of human experience: 1) If the non-experience shown in present experience is fundamentally just as capable of being experienced as the present experience, we wish to speak of 'small' transcendences. 2) If the present is fundamentally experienced only indirectly, and never directly, but therefore as a component of the same everyday reality, we wish to speak of 'intermediate' transcendences. 3) If something is only grasped at all as *reference* to another, non-everyday reality, as such not capable of being experienced, we speak of 'great' transcendences."

al psychology (the freedom and immortality of the soul). But it cannot cause or compel by argument the validity of and belief in these metaphysical theories. The same is true of ethics, which also remains dependent upon being freely recognized by human persons. Ethical discourse is ontologically closer than religious discourse to economic discourse; it requires only a moderate transcendence of experiencable reality, not a large one. On the other hand, to speak in economic terms, the profits of ethics are lower than those of religion, which means that the risk of ethics is smaller than that of religion, but so is the return. Religion is thus closer in economic terms, considered from the perspective of the individual's advantage, to economics than ethics is. The fact that economic ethics – like ethics in general – is linked to metaphysics and religion and is given substance by them is shown not the least by the economic-ethical systems of the world religions and the extraordinary significance of the world religions for the development of economic forms of ethos, of convictions concerning economic ethics.[29]

1.6. Self-Interest, Corporate Ethics, and Employee Motivation

If one disregards the religious solution to the isolation paradox and the coordination problem, only ethics can convert Sen's isolation paradox into a situation of assurance of universal rule-compliance for the individual. The function of ethics consists essentially in assuring the individual, by the universal validity of a code of ethics, that others will also obey the rules. The function of a specific theory of economic ethics is to give the individual the assurance that universal rule-compliance is also valid for action in the economy, both within the firm and in the market, and thereby to strengthen his will and his incentives to follow the rules that promote the common good in economic life. Through general and economic ethics, the moderately moral person of Case 2, who acts morally if and only if others do so as well, is assured that most of the others will also behave ethically.

Business firms are, consequently, also concerned with the development of a code of ethics that provides mutual assurance of ethical conduct. IBM, for example, has developed an explicitly formulated system of values for its workers

---

[29] Cf. Max Weber, "The Social Psychology of the World Religions," in *From Max Weber: Essays in Sociology*, trans. and ed. H. H. Gerth and C. Wright Mills (New York, 1946), p. 268: "The religious determination of life-conduct, however, is also one – note this – only one, of the determinants of the economic ethic." See also Werner Sombart, *The Quintessence of Capitalism*, trans. Mortimer Epstein (New York, 1967), pp. 228 ff.; Sombart, *Der moderne Kapitalismus*, 2nd. Ed. (Leipzig, 1916), Vol. II, Part 1, pp. 36 ff; and Heinrich Pesch, *Ethik und Volkswirtschaftslehre* (Freiburg, 1918), pp. 84 ff.

that includes basic beliefs, policies, and business practices.[30] It is noteworthy that the development of the system of values, or better, of the practical philosophy and world-view of this firm, follows the system of transcendence from economics to ethics, and from ethics to metaphysics. The sequence of rules in this firm, from the rules of the particular and operative level of business practices, through the more universal levels of strategy, up to universal convictions about the totality of the firm and its environment, become progressively more universal and universalized. This example shows that even business ethics assumes basic beliefs about the total reality of the human person and the world that assure people of the significance of ethics.

The process of developing a theory of business ethics must, however, note that ethics cannot be introduced merely functionally, in order to attain something completely different, namely profit maximization, and that ethics must be universally valid in its core, not specific to a single firm. There can, of course, be firm-specific forms of ethos, habits, customs, etc. But the universal rules of a theory of business ethics cannot be firm-specific in the sense of being valid only for a single firm, because they are good only for that firm. Attempts to introduce firm-specific codes of business ethics, useful functionally only for the financial goals of the firm in question, are subject to the same objections as are functionalistic establishments of ethics in general.

Ethical theories introduced in order to serve functionally a purpose that is outside ethics itself are always in danger of failing to serve their purpose, because people see through their purpose, with the consequence that the ethics is not recognized. Functional establishments have the weakness that they argue, and must argue, with functional equivalents. Something is good for the performance of a function. But something else can perform the function just as well, which means that the something *else* can always take the place of that which performs the function. If ethics is introduced only in order to attain something totally different, namely higher profit, when it is not also recognized as valid in itself and desirable by all members of a firm, including its managers and owners, it achieves no power of persuasion with the workers, because its ethos and ethic are used as means to something completely different and are not recognized as a representation of an absolute and as a challenge of the workers' free moral decision.

Functionalistic foundations are insufficient for the development and expansion of a theory of economic ethics. In ethics, it must be recognized at the same time that human freedom is an absolute and end in itself. Ethics must portray the fact that, in Kant's words, one must never regard oneself or others only as a

---

[30] Cf. Walter Trux and Werner Kirsch, "Strategisches Management oder die Möglichkeit einer 'wissenschaftlichen' Unternehmensführung," *Die Betriebswirtschaft*, 39 (1979), p. 232, n. 23.

means, but instead always at the same time as ends in themselves. That does not mean that one may *never* consider other persons and ethics as a means to something completely different. Such a hyper-moralism would make the idea of economic cooperation and division of labor impossible. Kant's claim means instead that one may never use a person and ethics *only* as a means. When applied to economic ethics, this means that business ethics can and should be beneficial to economic purposes, but that it may never be founded only for these purposes and may never be completely instrumentalized for acquisitive purposes.

Economic ethics is a theory of the norms and motives of economic action and exchange in the external market of the economy and in the internal market of the business firm.[31] It is, like general ethics, a theory of duties, virtues, and goods. The connection of these parts of ethics will be further established below. Economic ethics is the reflection, illumination, and foundation of the norms, the deontology that the businessperson should follow, and at the same time a theory of the correct (economic) life, of the virtues and goods of management. As a virtue theory of the manager, economic and business ethics not only portrays the virtues of just business management, but also attempts to strengthen the motives to correct action and ethos in the market and the firm. Economic and business ethics aims not only at an "ethical minimum" of ensuring efficiency and economic survival, but also at ethical and meaningful management. The theory of the virtues of the manager, with the theory of the duties of the manager and the theory of goods, belongs to economic and business ethics, though virtues, unlike norms, cannot be made obligatory and, by their very nature, allow room for creativity in the perfection of action.

The deontological ethics of the manager, the ethics of following rules and of the "*pacta sunt servanda*," reduces the negative side effects of business contracts that become visible as transaction costs resulting from uncertainty about observing the fulfillment of contracts in the market and the firm. They create positive side effects (externalities), such as trust, goodwill, etc. The theory of duties, the deontology of the economy, increases the firm's and the economy's performance and ability to grow. The theory of the virtues of the economy, surpassing the theory of duties, establishes a kind of economic lifestyle that aims not only at survival, but also at the good or perfect life. It thus seeks to promote, in the cultural sphere of the economy, a perfection of economic style and corporate culture.

Economic ethics is a necessary component of a general theory of social ethics, because not all ethically-relevant side effects of actions in the market are avoided and internalized. Side effects are a problem of the social ethics of the economy, because the principle "private vices – public benefits" is not valid in

---

[31] On the firm as an internal market, see Williamson, "Firms and Markets," and "The Modern Corporation," *Journal of Economic Literature*, 19 (1981), pp. 1537-68.

the sense that it produces the good as a side effect and makes ethics superfluous in the competitive market. The "ethical minimum" of following economic rules and the principle *pacta sunt servanda* require, where external control is not possible, that the individual makes the universal interest his own interest. The validity and individual appropriation of an ethical code by the manager reduces the side effects of the business contract that appear as transaction costs. Economic ethics thus brings about an increase, not only of morality, but also of welfare.

The universality of the validity of a theory of economic ethics as a corrective for failure of control by mere self-interest in the market is, however, not ensured. Market failure can repeat itself in ethical failure. Ethical failure refers to the necessity of metaphysics and religion as theories of total reality. The context of economics, ethics, and basic assumptions about reality also assert themselves at the level of the firm, with the way in which worker motivation, business ethics, and basic convictions about reality mutually refer to one another. The side effects of economic activity that are not internalized in the market and the interrelatedness of economic, ethical, and metaphysical orientations of action show that the economy and the market are not ethically-neutral zones.

CHAPTER 2

ECONOMICS AND ETHICS I

Formal Ethics

The preceding chapter has shown that the market can perform its coordination function fully only when there exists a minimum of mutual, justified trust that the other market participants will comply with ethical rules, because otherwise the transaction costs of the market become too high and the repetition of business relationships is reduced to a smaller and, in terms of allocation theory, inefficient size. Market coordination does not function so ideally that the pursuit of self-interest by market participants leads to the efficiency of the entire economy without consideration of the ethical norms of contract compliance and without transaction costs resulting from the absence of trust. Ethics is, therefore, by no means superfluous in the competitive market. The ethical rules, for their part, are not appropriated to such a universal extent that ethical failure is excluded and the religious assurance of ethics is superfluous. Only if ethics is universally acknowledged and the assurance problem is solved will ethical failure be avoided and will it be unnecessary to compensate for ethical failure by religious assurance and to validate ethics religiously.

A society that knows neither market failure nor ethical failure is a society without the introspection of those who perceive and desire, without the self-relation of acting persons to what they do, and thus without persons able to accept differences of actions. In such a society, human persons do mechanically what contracts and ethical rules demand of them. But there is no society and no market economy in which persons do not have a self-relationship of freedom to their own actions, and thus also the opportunity to refuse to obey the rules of the market and of ethics. There is, therefore, no economic and social order without economic and ethical failure. As compensation for ethical failure, only two correctives and two social solutions are conceivable. Ethical failure is either compensated by religion or eliminated by complete, external control in a social and economic order that replaces ethics with social control and the abolition of free decision-making.

The transcendence and the displacement of economics by ethics and of ethics by religion are not unequivocal causal relationships. Economics, ethics, and religion instead form a living network of conditions of different stages of rationality and levels of coordination in the life of a society. Ethics and religion represent in a way something related. They form a "super-rationality" of economic rationality, a transcendence of immediate self-interest in human persons that is not given, but is given up, and is thus often missed and leads to ethical and religious failure, because the forms of rationality corresponding to ethics and religion are less robust than that of immediate self-interest. An example of a nation without ethical failure is the nation of animals. It includes the economics of nature, bio-economics, which is an economics without peaceful and conscious exchange. Peaceful and (self-)conscious exchange is, according to Adam Smith, not only an exclusive feature of the human economy, but also the very characteristic that distinguishes human persons from animals. Without ethics and religion, the bio-economics of nature is a closed system. Only with ethics and religion does human economics become a unified and meaningful whole.

2.1. Ethics and Economics: Global and Local Maximization

The approach developed here is not merely a voluntary, theoretical, religious extension of economics. The model of *homo oeconomicus* in the narrow sense does not form the action-theoretical and rationality-theoretical background of the theory of the relationships among economics, ethics, and religion. The conception of *homo oeconomicus* is too narrow for a game theory and theory of rationality that seeks to integrate economics, ethics, and ontology in a comprehensive theory of rational action, taking into account the rational action of others. It goes beyond the classical theory of *homo eoconomicus* to a "*homo strategus*." With game theory, as the following discussion will demonstrate, the traditional boundaries of economics and ethics are no longer valid and their fields of study are no longer well defined. The game theory of rational, strategic action makes the development of an economic theory related to ethics and an ethical theory that does not exclude considerations of economic efficiency possible. The boundary between economic theory and ethical theory cannot be well-defined, because the unity of action must also connect them theoretically.

Given the presupposition that human persons act rationally, one can recognize a complete context that is determined by the described relationship of economics, ethics, and religion and that constitutes a structure of ethical, religious, and economic self-interest for a rationally acting person. This theory is, admittedly, of little use for persons who do not act fully rationally, in the sense of an extensive rationality. But for the person who acts with comprehensive rationality, the structure of economics, ethics, and religion has an internal coherence. Within the boundaries of advanced societies, which have gone through rationalization and have taken the step from objective, substantive rationality to subjective, instrumental rationality, the orientation of action toward rationality has more than marginal significance. For this orientation is what is required above all in the sphere of the economy, a conduct orientation from which the acting person *cannot* withdraw. Expectations of rationality are taken over from the social form of organization to the individual person.

The relationships of the coordination of economics, ethics, and religion – of economic self-interest, ethics' assurance of universal rule-compliance, and religion's assurance of the universality of ethics – transcends the coordination model of perfect competition, as it is depicted in microeconomics. If the model of perfect competition agreed completely with social reality, economic ethics, understood as the formal ethics of rule-compliance and coordination, would be superfluous. If high transaction costs did not lead to market failure, a formal ethic of the *pacta sunt servanda* would be unnecessary. Since transaction costs do not play a role in the coordination of the market system in the microeconomic theory of perfect competition, economic ethics is not relevant to it. In fact, if no problems of externalities, no transaction costs, and therefore no necessity of trust and the repetition of commercial relationships arose in the social reality of rational, self-interested action, but instead all free agreements among persons, all free contracts, were kept, as they were decided by the parties to the contracts, the existence of ethics, a legal system, and a religion would be superfluous in human society. But since the reality of market coordination cannot be perfectly and exclusively described by the theory of perfect competition's pure ideal of economic coordination, ethics, religion, and a legal system are indispensable for the social-economic order.

The action-theoretical background of the theory of the coordination of rational action, of the context of reference of economics, ethics, and religion presented here, is not the theory of economic man in the narrower sense, but rather a theory of rational action in which ethics and metaphysics or religion are seen as also belonging to the *environment* of the acting person and as dependent upon him or her. The model of economic man, in contrast, begins with an assumption of action under conditions of certainty in a stable environment. Economic man maximizes his utility under conditions of certainty and boundary conditions of his action. He behaves in an environment that is viewed as established and parametric. The actions of others and changes in the environment are seen by the acting person as parameters that cannot be influenced. Only in the theory of monopolistic and oligopolistic competition, in which the action of the monopolist or oligopolist is assumed to be limitedly strategic, is the assumption of the parametricity of the environment replaced by the assumption that the acting person has some ability to influence the environment.

Game theory transcends economic theory's model of rationality, to achieve a comprehensive theory of strategic, rational action in which the actions of other persons and changes in the environment become variables that one's own actions can influence. Strategic action means regarding changes in the environment as anticipatable and influenceable, and anticipating the decisions of others and taking them into consideration when making one's own decisions. The "assurance game" of ethics is an adaptation of one's own action to the actions of others, with the assurance of universal rule-compliance.

According to Jon Elster's theory of rationality, the coordination of economic and ethical motivations of action in the acting person means that the ethical person, in the sense of the assurance game and of universalization, is a "global maximizer," as distinguished from a local maximizer. The ethical person is in a position to wait. She is capable of rejecting a strategy that is advantageous in the short-term. She does not take advantage of available opportunities to break ethical-economic rules without sanction. She refrains from taking advantage of these opportunities, in order not to endanger the greater advantages of universal rule conformance, so that she can benefit later from these advantages. The ethical person is capable of following indirect strategies. She chooses a strategy that is less advantageous immediately, in order to benefit from a more advantageous strategy later. She prefers the rule-compliance of everyone, including herself, (A_1E_1), to the alternative of making herself an exception, (A_1E_0). In other words, she follows an indirect strategy. Indirect strategies are, like the ability to wait, a consequence of human intentionality and distinguish human persons, who are able to realize comprehensive maxima, from animals, who are able to achieve only local maxima.[1] In the case of the assurance game, the ethical person chooses *not* to take advantage of the rules, the option that is not advantageous in the short term, in order to secure the subsequent option of universal rule-compliance, which is more advantageous in the long run. But the ethical person cannot be certain that this indirect strategy will be advantageous ultimately, because the universality of rule-compliance can collapse if too many other persons are rule-breakers.

The ethical and religious person will, therefore, repeat the wait for the even more advantageous option and the indirect strategy of the renunciation of the strategy most advantageous in the short term in favor of the strategy most advantageous in the long term, as the assurance game of ethics requires, once again in the "super-assurance game" of religion. This "game" iterates the indirect strategy of ethics to the doubly-indirect strategy of religion and to the religious "assurance" of ethical action. The religious person transcends the situation of the ethical person, for whom the environment of the other person's actions is still parametric. For the ethical person, the environment remains parametric and heteronomous, in as much as he is enduring in relation to the universality of the ethical conduct of other persons. The conditions of the actions of other persons are imposed on him. The ethical and religious person, going beyond the ethical view of his situation, attains a view of total reality, in which the universality of ethical conduct becomes insignificant for him. He makes complete reality something dependent upon himself. Complete reality becomes what

[1] Cf. Jon Elster, *Ulysses and the Sirens*, 2nd Ed. (Cambridge, 1984), pp. 9-10.

the person is willing to see in it, according to his moral decisions. Johann Fichte's saying – "The kind of person one is determines the kind of philosophy one advocates" – or Leibniz's – "Not to see the world as the best of all possible worlds is a lack of love for God" – prove to be globally-maximizing strategies at the level of a theory of rational action: one must see the world in such a way that ethical action is meaningful in it. And if one sees the world in this way, ethical action is meaningful in it. How one sees the world depends on what kind of person one is; what kind of person one is depends on how one sees the world.

The indirect strategy of the ethical renunciation of short-term advantage is advantageous in the long term under two conditions. Ethical conduct is advantageous, if it has universal validity in the environment of the acting person. It is also advantageous, if the person does not care which strategies other persons choose, either because ethical action as such has value for him or because he sees it in an environment and totality in which ethical action, going beyond death, is always also the indirect strategy that is advantageous in the long term, because of the transcendental compensation of divine justice. In the latter case, the choice of a view or theory of complete reality becomes itself the rational choice of an indirect strategy. It becomes a variable of the ability to wait and of the ability to renounce strategies that are advantageous in the short term in order to adopt strategies that are advantageous in the long term. Kant's theory of the postulated existence of God and the postulated immortality of the soul can be viewed as a globally-maximizing strategy of the individual. The maximizing character of this strategy is guaranteed, because the time horizon of its maximization extends even beyond the death of the individual. The deficiency of the Kantian theory of religion does not lie in its practical character (i.e. in that the choice of a theory of complete reality is linked back to practical reason or rationality), but in the fact that it *remains* postulated and only practical, and that the *theory* of complete reality, of theoretical philosophy capable of truth, is external to it.

The super-rationality of economics, ethics, and religion (i.e. of ethics as the assurance of individual rule-compliance and religion as the assurance of ethics and collective rule-compliance) resolves the parametricity, the determination of the environment, into a strategic situation in which complete reality and seeing it as complete become the object of a rational decision and globally-maximizing strategy. Through ethics and religion, the acting person's decision-relevant environment is transformed into something that depends completely on his or her moral decision and does not influence his or her decision as a compulsive and heteronomous parameter. The model of the "super-assurance game" of religion as the assurance of the assurance of ethics makes action possible under conditions of *certainty* about the environment and the effects of one's own actions. The "super-assurance game" returns in certain respects to the simple utility-maximizing decision situation of action under certainty, as it appears to economic man. For economic man, the environment is completely parametric. For the ethical-religious person, it is completely *un*parametric and dependent upon his or her decision alone for a theory of complete reality, one that is simultaneously a consequence and a condition of his of her moral choice of a globally-maximizing strategy.

Both decision models and representations of reality agree in making action under conditions of certainty possible. The utility maximization of economic man is action under certainty, because his control of the environment is limited and his decision situation is well structured. The super-assurance game of the religious theory of complete reality is action under certainty, because the view of reality itself has become a completely unparametric, ethical variable. The theory of complete reality is dependent on the ethical attitude of the acting person. The most poorly-structured decision situation of strategic action with uncertainty about the behavior of other persons and about the composition of the individual strategies of others toward the environment of each acting person is converted into a well-structured decision situation of action under certainty, because the actions of other persons have become irrelevant for the religious strategy of the super-assurance game, which is completely indirect in comparison to the economic and ethical strategies, because of the religious assurance of one's own action.

The theory of rational action, understood as the union of economics and ethics, presents a continuum of increasing inclusion of the persons affected and increasing internalization of side effects in the meaningful construction of the various steps of the rationalities and strategies. Economic action according to the model of utility maximization under the condition of keeping the environment parametric or beyond the acting person's influence, does not take into account the actions of other persons and does not orient its strategies according to the anticipation of the anticipations of others. The subjectivity of the utility-maximizer does not expand into intersubjectivity. The game-theoretical model of rational action transforms economizing into strategic action, in which it anticipates and takes into account the reactions of other persons to one's own actions. Strategic action transcends subjectivity to the level of intersubjectivity, or better, trans-subjectivity. Two forms of trans-subjectivity are possible with game theory: strategic trans-subjectivity and ethical trans-subjectivity. Strategic trans-subjectivity takes the actions and reactions of the other person or persons into account only as a means or handicap for the purposes of the ego. Ethical trans-subjectivity anticipates the other person and his actions as a cooperating partner and as a factor to include in one's own utility function.

Oswald Schwemmer[2] has reformulated the categorical imperative as the proposition "Transcend your subjectivity." The continuum of game theory cases

2 Oswald Schwemmer, *Philosophie der Praxis* (Frankfurt, 1971), p. 114.

extends from the parametric behavior of economic man to the strategic action of the non-cooperative game, which nevertheless anticipates the strategies of others, and to those of cooperative games, all the way to the super-assurance game of ethical-religious action. This continuum is, to use Schwemmer's terms, one of increasing transcendence of one's own subjectivity and the immediacy of self-interest. It can be presented in Sen's symbolism as follows: Economic man prefers the situation in which everyone except himself obeys the rules to the situation in which everyone including himself obeys the rules. He prefers A_1E_0 to A_1E_1. The qualified-ethical person of the assurance game prefers A_1E_1 to A_1E_0. And the religious person of the super-assurance game is indifferent between A_1E_0 and A_1E_1. The local maximization of immediate self-interest becomes, through inclusion and internalization, an ever more comprehensive and inclusive maximization.

The continuum of the transcendence of immediacy and subjectivity extends from saving money as the transcendence of immediate desire and present consumption to religious ethics as the transcendence of the principle of universalization. Adam Smith correctly recognized the beginning of the ethical in the ability to wait.[3] Therefore, one must also see saving as an ethical phenomenon and classify it as belonging to both economics and ethics. In saving, as in all ethical action, the immediacy of subjective desire is transcended in order to attain a wider time-horizon and a chronologically-indirect strategy. Saving is the transcendence of the immediate present; investment is an act of generosity or munificence.[4] Capital formation contains an ethical element of the transcendence of immediacy. The inclination and the will to follow ethical maxims assumes a low discount rate; it is difficult to reconcile a high discount rate, a high preference for present utility, with ethical conduct.[5] A high preference for present utility, a high discount rate, is an expression of the inability to wait, of the inability to transcend the immediacy of desires for the sake of the long-term

---

[3] Adam Smith, *The Theory of Moral Sentiments*, ed. E. G. West (Indianapolis, 1976), p. 312: "The pleasure which we are to enjoy ten years hence interests us so little in comparison with that which we may enjoy to-day; the passion which the first excites is naturally so weak in comparison with that violent emotion which the second is apt to give occasion to, that the one could never be any balance to the other, unless it was supported by the sense of propriety, by the consciousness that we merited the esteem and approbation of every body."

[4] Pius XI, Encyclical *Quadragesimo Anno – On Reconstruction of the Social Order* (Rome, 1931): "Expending larger incomes so that opportunity for gainful work may be abundant, provided, however, that this work is applied to producing really useful goods, ought to be considered. as We deduce from the principles of the Angelic Doctor (Thomas Aquinas, *Summa theologica*, II-II, Q. 134) an outstanding exemplification of the virtue of munificence and one particularly suited to the needs of the times."

[5] Cf. Richard B. McKenzie, "The Economic Dimension of Ethical Behavior," *Ethics*, 87 (1977), p. 219: "Needless to say, persons with high discount rates on future income . . . would be less inclined to behave ethically."

future of strategies. Since ethics also promotes the transcendence of immediate desires, the ability to wait and a low discount rate are preliminary stages of the ethical.[6] Not only is ethics a phenomenon of capital formation and ethical conduct a capital or public good, as Buchanan writes,[7] but capital formation is also a proto-ethical phenomenon and an instance of ethical conduct, transcending immediate self-interest. Capital formation, like ethical conduct, is an indirect strategy of the ability to wait and the renunciation of the immediately-advantageous strategy in favor of a strategy that is advantageous in the long term.

A strengthening of the transcendence of subjectivity leads from the temporal transcendence of one's own subjectivity from present to future utility to the intersubjectivity of universalization. The person who makes the universalization argument and universalizable maxims her own transcends her subjectivity to attain the intersubjective ability to coordinate individual efforts. She prefers a situation of universalization to a situation in which she makes an exception of herself. The preference for universalization is ultimately capable of transcending once again to become a preference for totality and perfection.

The case of ethically preferring A_1E_1 to A_1E_0, the situation of universal rule-compliance to the situation in which the individual can except herself without adverse consequences, must be subdivided once again. The readiness to transcend subjectivity, which leads both to universal rule-compliance and to following the rules oneself, can arise from either of two motives. It can arise from the belief that with the universality of rule-compliance the assurance of the totality that universal rule-compliance is the case will grow and that one's *own* utility will thereby also be maximized, because self-utility is greater in the long term with the validity of the universalization argument. The readiness to universalize maxims can, however, also arise from an attitude and interest that does not see the significance of ethical conduct in the universalization itself and the utility for the individual flowing from it, but rather recognizes universalization only as an expression of an ethical totality, in which not the universalization, but the greater perfection flowing from the universalization is the real purpose and meaning. Kant's assertion that only actions that are motivated not by the utility of universalization, but by pure respect for the law are moral describes this difference between strategic universalization as a presupposition of utility maximi-

---

[6] The condition of a low time-preference or discount rate for the present as a preliminary stage of the ethical is also in agreement with the observation of Robert Axelrod, *The Evolution of Cooperation* (New York, 1984), pp. 124-28, that a decrease in the preference for present utility and a reduction of uncertainty about the future increase the readiness for cooperation in interactions and reduce the tendency toward non-cooperatively taking advantage of other persons. The anticipation of repeat business in the present increases the readiness to cooperate, as well as both the inclination toward and the probability of repeat business.

[7] James M. Buchanan, "Ethical Rules, Expected Values, and Large Numbers," *Ethics*. 76 (1965), pp. 10-11.

zation and moral universalization as the representation of a totality and the state of everyone making this totality his or her own. Kant himself obscured this distinction by relating morality too closely to the law, with the consequence that a respect for and pleasure in the law that transcends legality to achieve the affirmation of a moral and ontological totality is decreased too much in importance, relative to obedience to the law.

2.2. Unifying Universalization and Exception: Ethics and Religion

The fact that the law of universalizability cannot be the highest level of ethics follows from the problem of the exception. Economically, it is to be maintained that the *perfect* universalization of a way of conduct as law is suboptimal or inefficient in many cases. When walking on the grass is forbidden in a public park, in order to protect the grass, the intent of the law may still be attained if a few persons who enjoy walking on grass very much do so. Total utility is higher with 90% rule-compliance than with 100%.[8] The optimum is achieved with the coexistence of universalization and exception. Thus, Kierkegaard placed the category of exception, understood as a religious category and as the specific attribute of religious existence, above aesthetic existence, and even above ethical existence.[9]

The category of exception must be considered along with the category of universalization and the category of efficiency, or the economic principle. It proves, in turn, that ontology, ethics, and economics belong to one another. The principle of efficiency, which is based upon immediate self-interest, does not achieve an efficient solution if the universality of the maxims must be ethically anticipated and must be desired in the transcendence of immediate self-interest, as in the example above of walking on the grass, but also in other variations of the prisoner's dilemma. Strict universalization of the categorical imperative, for its part, is, on the contrary, suboptimal in many situations, because it is "super-ethical" and represents, in economic terms, an over-investment in restrictions of behavior. The ethical and the religious, in the sense of a global maximization, a perfection of the totality, require at the same time the exception from the rule and the universalization of the rule.

---

[8] James M. Buchanan and Gordon Tullock, "Economic Analogues for the Generalization Argument," *Ethics*, 74 (1964), pp. 300-301.

[9] Søren Kierkegaard, *Either/Or*, Part II, trans. Howard V. Hong and Edna H. Hong (Princeton, 1987), p. 270: "The childish rigorism with which I at that time distinguished between rule and exception, in life as well as in grammar, has certainly been mitigated, but I still have the distinction with me. I know how to call it up, especially when I see you and your kind, who seem to advance the doctrine that the exception is the more important – indeed, that the rule exists only so that the exception can show up to advantage."

The superiority of the religious-ethical super-assurance game to the assurance game of ethical universalization consists in the fact that the one who sees the rule as a means to the optimization of the totality and not only as a means of assuring the meaning of his *own* ethical action is also in a position to recognize exceptions from the rule and the simultaneous validity of the rule as an improvement of the overall situation. That does not mean that he makes himself an exception rashly, but that he is ready to permit others to be exceptions and to recognize that an increase of value-realization for the totality follows from the validity of the rule and the simultaneous granting of exceptions. The exception, however, may be neither economically nor ethically intended. The individual instead strives ethically for the rule as the rule, if he receives the maximum of value-realization of the totality as a universal, ontological-ethical purpose in his subjective will.

Taking the actions of others and the effects of one's own actions on others into account leads to a transcendence of subjectivity and immediate self-interest that can be either strategic or moral. The *strategic* transcendence of subjectivity implies, according to game theory, that cooperative or non-cooperative interaction and intersubjectivity occur. *Moral* transcendence of subjectivity leads to an ethical assurance of universal rule-compliance. *Religious* transcendence of subjectivity brings about the intention to optimize the totality, with the help of the ethical, universal rule and, at the same time, the readiness to permit exceptions and to acknowledge that they can increase the value-realization of the totality.

Elster's conception of the animal organism as a "locally maximizing machine" and human intentionality as a "globally maximizing machine" is helpful here – if one deletes "machine." The economic calculation of economic man is a "locally-maximizing calculation" with respect to the inclusion of other individuals – even when the acting person makes decisions of great consequence. The calculation is *locally*-maximizing, because only his or her own goal variables enter into economic man's process of maximization. The calculation of game theory is indeed strategic calculation, but still only a *locally*-maximizing calculation, even if it is more comprehensive than economic calculation, because while it does include others in its calculations, it does so only strategically. Finally, the ethical calculation of the assurance game is a *regionally*-maximizing calculation, one that includes intersubjectivity, because it includes the universality of the rule, its validity, and the repercussions of one's own action on its validity in the maximization calculations, but does not represent within itself the totality outside the rule and the category of the exception. Only religious-ethical "calculus" can be considered a *globally*-maximizing calculation, one that includes trans-subjectivity. It is, of course, not a maximizing calculation in the categorical sense, but only in the trans-categorical sense of a regulative comprehension of a gestalt or idea.[10] For a finite consciousness, contrary to Elster's position, global maxima are not possible in the categorical and discursive sense, but only in the analogous sense of an intention toward totality in the transition through rational and discursive cognition and decision analysis, according to economic *and* ethical rules. The direct intention of a global optimum or maximum, global maximization in the sense of the choice of the best of all possible worlds, is conceivable only for an infinite consciousness.[11]

2.3. Economic, Ethical, and Religious Rationality: Extending the Limits of the Self

The relationships among economics, ethics, and religion can be understood as a continuum of an increasing expansion and inclusiveness of what is meant by the term "self" in the expression "self-interest." Economic self-interest refers to a narrow self, defined by the ego. At most, the family is included in addition to the ego among those whose interests the economic motivation and goal-pursuit seek to maximize. The self, however, in agreement with Carl Jung, goes beyond the domain of the ego. Self-interest expands when the ego expands to a broader inclusion of other persons and a broader internalization of the consequences of one's actions. Such an extension of self-interest occurs in the case of ethical assurance. The expansion of the self in the ethical can extend as far as the elimination of limits and the inclusion of the totality of the self.

In the tradition of philosophy, this sequence of expanding the limits of the ego and the sequence of economics, ethics, and religion are comprehended conceptually by the triad of self-love, love of neighbor, and love of God. Love of God means – if God is equated in the present context with the totality of being and is understood as the unity of existence and meaning – the intention to make totality and the globally-maximizing decision one's own. God is, agreeing with Wittgenstein, how everything is related. Love of God is the belief and the intention that everything, the totality of being, is well, that the world's realization of value is maximized. Extending the limits of the self is the goal of ethics. Maximal expansion of the self is the goal of religious ethics and the theory of complete reality.

---

[10] Cf. Koslowski, "Economy Principle, Maximizing, and the Co-Ordination of Individuals in Economics and Philosophy," in Koslowski, ed., *Economics and Philosophy* (Tübingen, 1985), pp. 39-67, for a discussion of the range of maximization concepts.

[11] Thus in Leibniz's metaphysical theory of the choice of the best of all possible worlds.

2.3.1. LOVE OF SELF – LOVE OF GOD – LOVE OF NEIGHBOR: AUGUSTINE'S UNDERSTANDING OF THE TRANSFORMATIONS AND COORDINATIONS OF SELF-INTEREST

Augustine described the transformations of self-interest into an extended self, one interested in the totality of being, as transformations from self-love to love of God and from love of God to love of neighbor. For Augustine, the individual attains self-realization in the totality, in the love of God. The human self does not lose itself in the Deity to something different, external to itself, but realizes its own true purpose and its own self in this love.[12] The love of God and striving for love of the totality are, therefore, nothing other than the individual's properly-understood pursuit of the realization of happiness and himself or herself:

> For our goal (or, as the philosophers in their endless disputes have termed it, our end or good) is nothing else than union with Him . . . . For, in order that a man might learn how to love himself, a standard was set to regulate all his actions on which his happiness depends. For, to love one's own self is nothing but to wish to be happy, and the standard is union with God.[13]

Striving for God, an interest in the totality, and pursuing happiness or self-interest are identical, according to Augustine. Self-love, properly understood, and the pursuit of happiness urge the human person toward consideration of the whole, toward the love of God, which the enlightened, human self-interest must regard as its own goal, because happiness is in God. The perfection command of the observance of totality and the law of universalization (i.e. the law of the love of God) are individualistic demands on the individual and establish a personal interest of the individual in the totality. The human person realizes himself or herself in the individual love of God.

According to Ernst Troeltsch, the absolute individualism and the radical affirmation of the human self in Christianity by the conviction of being personally created in the image of God and of being loved by God is rationally defensible:

> It is clear that an individualism of this kind is entirely radical, and that it transcends all natural barriers and differences, through the ideal of the religious value of the soul. It is also clear that such an individualism is only possible at all upon this religious basis. It is only fellowship with God which gives value to the individual.[14]

---

[12] Augustine, *The City of God*, trans. Gerald G. Walsh and Grace Monahan (Washington. 1952), Book X, Chap. 3, pp. 121-22.

[13] *Ibid.*, p. 121. On the philosophy of Augustine, see also Koslowski, *Gesellschaft und Staat* (Stuttgart, 1982), pp. 58-90.

[14] Ernst Troeltsch, *The Social Teaching of the Christian Churches*, trans. Olive Wyon (Chicago, 1981), Vol. I, p. 55.

Love of God and love of neighbor are, according to Augustine, identical commandments, because the love of God is realized in love of neighbor. Those who love themselves in the right way love God. Those who follow their self-interest are led to an interest in the whole. But those who have love of God and love of the totality also love their neighbor, incorporate the universal interest of ethics into their self-interest, and expand their self-interest into an interest in universality and the ability of their own actions to coexist with those of other persons. Self-love, correctly understood, leads to love of God, which in turn includes love of neighbor. But if the self-loving human creature should love his neighbor as himself, and if his self-love leads him to love God, then he must will that others will what he wills, namely, love of God. Self-love and love of neighbor have the same goal, the love of God, in which the interest of the self encounters interest in others and the interests of others. Self-love and love of neighbor coincide in interest in the totality.

The love of God, which follows from properly understood and enlightened self-love, requires the sublation of the difference between the individual and the neighbor or other persons. The interest in the perfection of the totality excludes a complete separation of self-interest and interest in the being of others, a disjunction of economics and ethics. In the love of God, love of neighbor becomes self-love and self-love becomes love of neighbor, because the limits of the self are extended. One's own self and the selves of other persons become united in the intention to totality, in love of God: "When, therefore, a person who knows how to love himself is bidden to love his neighbor as himself, is he not, in effect, commanded to persuade others, as far as he can, to love God?"[15] The will to ethical universality and to the integration of the universal interest in one's self-interest involves the desire and the ethical demand to help the other person to understand the transformation of his or her self-interest into an interest in the totality and universality as worth striving for, and to persuade him or her to undergo this transformation. In the bilateral, successful intention on the universal, in the union of the self-interests of *ego* and *alter* in the love of God, the difference between one's own striving and that of others for God and happiness, between the universal interest of the self in the other and the particular interest in oneself, is sublated.

Love of self and love of neighbor are united in the love of God. It converts individualism into a comprehensive universalism of the common good and the love of neighbor. The antinomy of economic interest and ethical universality, of individual nature and social nature, the splitting[16] of the selves of human persons, is sublated in the love of God. In the comprehensive order of love *(ordo amoris)* there is no longer an unbridgeable chasm between self-interest and the

---

[15] Augustine, *The City of God*, Book X, Chap. 3, p. 122.

[16] On Hegel's concept of splitting, see Koslowski, *Gesellschaft und Staat*, pp. 6 ff.

interest of others, because the efforts and interests of individual persons are united in the love of God. According to Troeltsch, this religious individualism

> also contains within itself a strong idea of fellowship; this idea is based just as clearly upon the specifically religious fundamental idea. This cannot be explained simply by pointing out that the altruistic commandments are bound up with the commands to consecrate the self to God .... In the last resort the idea of fellowship springs from the fact that those who are being purified for the sake of God meet in Him ... ; so from this same fundamental idea this absolute individualism leads to just as absolute a fellowship of love among those who are united in God.[17]

Augustine's doctrine of the love of God is in accordance with the theory of the "super-assurance game" of religious ethics, which is described here in terms of game theory. For Augustine, the path of the transformation of self-interest leads from love of self through love of God to love of neighbor, from economics to religion and from religion to ethics. The locally-maximizing strategy is first converted into the globally-maximizing strategy of religion, and then, with the help of religion, into the regionally-maximizing strategy of ethics, whose comprehensiveness stands between the local-maximization of economics and the global-maximization of religion. Economic self-interest is led by the conviction of the truth of religion to ethics and the universalization of the maxims of actions, and then is also caused by religion to *will* the universalizability of the maxims.

Augustine's eudaemonism and egoism in the founding of ethics and religion have been criticized. For him, ethics is based only on self-interested calculation, which seeks to realize self-love and the individual pursuit of happiness simultaneously by love of God. Love of God and neighbor is desired, for Augustine, only out of self-interest. Religion – in the language of game theory, the "super-assurance game of religion" – is adopted only out of economic motivation. And the assurance game of ethics is adopted only out of economic *and* religious necessity.

2.3.2. ECONOMIZATION OF ETHICS AND RELIGION?

The question is posed, therefore, whether in the Augustinian model and the model of economics, ethics, and religion presented here in terms of game theory, ethics is not in the end adopted for non-moral and non-ethical reasons, so that the characteristic feature of the ethical is not at all obtained with this model. The answer is to be found in two phenomena, which simultaneously refute the suspicion of sheer eudaemonism against the present argument and refute the Augustinian model.

---

[17] Troeltsch, *The Social Teaching of the Christian Churches*, p. 56.

First, the existential acceptance of religion and the requirement to adopt the comprehensive ontological perspective and "globally-maximizing strategy," instead of the locally-maximizing strategy, presuppose themselves a moral element, transcending the immediacy of self-interest. *Neither* the ethical *nor* the religious perspective imposes itself; both require instead the "will to believe" (William James), which is itself an ethical phenomenon. Ethics and religion are, therefore, always directly related and must be affirmed together by the individual. Ethics does not compel religion, nor does religion quasi-physically compel ethics. Ethical failure does not call deterministically for the corrective of religion, nor does faith in the truth of religion call "from itself" for ethical conduct. Both stand instead in a mutual relationship; each requires free recognition of its truth.

Second, the ethical is itself already religious, as has been shown above, if it accepts the characteristic form of the absolute (i.e. if it is not adopted because of the greater advantages for oneself that follow from universal rule-compliance, but instead out of observance of the law and for the sake of greater value-development), which is made possible by the fulfillment of the law in the world. Because the absolutely ethical and the religious coincide in this sense, for Augustine love of neighbor and love of God, ethics and religion, also agree with one another in having the same intention of the good.

The disagreement about whether religion and the love of God can be founded on self-interest, *amour de soi*, or on the absolute, disinterested, pure love of God, *amour pur*, without looking at the (eudaemonistic) consequences of religion, gained importance in intellectual history as early as the famous argument between Jacques Bossuet, Bishop of Meaux, and François Fénelon, Archbishop of Cambrai, at the end of the seventeenth century. This argument anticipated, more than a half-century before the discussion that brought economics into existence, the latter's question whether self-interest depicts the dominant motive of all human action. In this argument, Fénelon defended the mystical position that human love of God, the love of human persons toward God, must become like God's love, the love with which God loves human persons. It is the duty of human persons to love God in a way similar to the way in which God loves them. Just as God does not love the world and human persons out of any need or to increase his own happiness, so human persons may not love God for the sake of their own advantage and happiness. They must instead love God (and the totality of being) according to the image and likeness of God, *ad imaginem ac similitudinem*, disinterestedly, without compensation *(gratis)*, and without the motive of increasing their own happiness.[18] Echoes of the fundamental idea of Christ-

[18] François Fénelon, *Dissertatio de amore puro*, in *Oeuvres complètes* (Paris, 1851), Vol. III, p. 424: *"Deus . . . creaturam suam amat, non ex motivo suae beatitudinis, quae ex hoc nullatenus pendet; sed gratis amat, non ut ex eo quod amat, aliquid proveniat sibi, et suae beatitudini perficiendae conducat. Eâ purè gratuitâ voluntate mundum extra se condidit; voluntate aequè*

ian gnosis that the resemblance to God is the mission of man become perceptible here with Fénelon.

Bossuet maintained, on the contrary, the essential distinction between God's way of existence and love and the way of human existence and love. Only God's love, the love of God toward human persons, can be disinterested and free of striving for the increase of one's own happiness. The love of God, the love of human persons toward God, is always at the same time self-interested and exists out of neediness. Human persons are capable of loving – and that, according to Bossuet, is the (ontological) difference between God and man – only out of need and with an interest in increasing their own happiness through their own love.[19] In this conflict, Fénelon's position of the pure love of God and the resemblance of the human person to God was dogmatically inferior to Bossuet's orthodox defense of the self-interested, rational basis of the love of God.[20]

The question that the conflict about self-love and love of God still poses today, above and beyond its historical importance, is whether a fully disinterested love and the idea, originating in Gnosticism, that human love can become equal to divine love are at all possible. At the same time, this conflict raises the question whether there is not even in the love with which God loves himself, an element of self-interest or a response of love within the Trinitarian divine "self." A love without an interest in a self that remains in the love would be the love of a completely undefined self, one no longer existing. The self cannot be extended so far that reflexivity and self-regard are no longer possible, because the self would then undergo a lack of self-regard. Even perfect love includes self-regard and self-interest, because otherwise the subject of the love would disintegrate. A completely disinterested, pure love would lead to the annihilation and disintegration of the self in the other, which would no longer be the self, but instead an unbounded and indefinite substance.

Both in God's love, God's love of Himself and the world, and in the love of God, love of humans toward God and intention on the totality, therefore, reference to self, the self-reference of the divine self and of human subjects, must be preserved. In trinitarian theology, the absolute or God, understood as the opposite person of love, is also in himself self-referential, a relational and personal

---

gratuitâ homines lapsos in Christo redemit. Haec est ea magna voluntas; hic est ille perfectus amor, nostri amoris pro modulo forma et exemplar. Ad illius imaginem ac similitudinem facti, debemus velle et amare, quemadmodum ipse vult et amat, id est gratis et absque beatitudinis comparandae motivo."

19 Jacques Bénigne Bossuet, *Cinquième écrit ou mémoire de M. l'Évêque de Meaux à M. l'Archevêque de Cambrai*, in *Oeuvres Complètes* (Paris, 1846), Vol. IX, p. 368: *"Il n'appartient qu'à Dieu seul d'aimer sans besoin; notre besoin essential nous attache et nous assujettit à lui comme à celui qui nous rend heureux en se donnant lui-même."*

20 Twenty-three of Fénelon's propositions were condemned by Pope Innocent XII in 1699. On Fénelon, see Robert Spaemann, *Reflexion und Spontaneität* (Stuttgart, 2nd Ed., 1990), especially pp. 34-57.

self, not a mere substance in which the human self could disintegrate without limits. The unity of human self-interest and universal interest is not a perishing of the self without distinctions in the universal and in pure identity, but a union in the difference, identity of identity and non-identity of self-interest and universal interest.

2.4. Rationality and Coordination

Ethical universalization and the religious orientation toward the totality have been portrayed as rational strategies following from the extension of self-interest in the direction of a greater inclusion of persons affected and a more comprehensive internalization of side effects, from the extension of utility maximization from the locally-maximizing to the globally-maximizing strategy. But to what extent are the ethical principle of universalization and the religious principle of totality forms of rationality?

2.4.1. THE A PRIORI NATURE OF THE PRINCIPLE OF RATIONALITY

The principle of rationality, or the economic principle, says that, for the attainment of a given end, the minimum of means should be used. Or alternatively, with given means or resources, the maximum degree of goal-attainment should be achieved.

As a formal principle, the economic principle or principle of rationality is not concerned with the content of the end, with the matter or material of the will. Every goal, regardless of its content or the manner in which it is defined, can and should be pursued rationally. The principle of rationality is, therefore, indifferent to its application (i.e. the ends that are drawn from it). It is a formal and a priori principle,[21] which determines the logic of human preference. Just as the laws of the logical syllogism prescribe the rules of drawing theoretical conclusions, the economic principle determines the rules of the practical syllogism. If the premises of the end and the available means are formulated, the economic principle demands that the solution of maximal goal-achievement with the given means or the solution with the least use of means with the given ends is drawn from these premises as the conclusion.

But there are obviously types of rationality in which the economic principle attains a distinctive character and individualization. Thus Max Weber distinguished "formal" or "instrumental" rationality (*Zweckrationalität*) from "non-formal" or "substantive" rationality (*Wertrationalität*) as follows:

---

[21] Ludwig von Mises, "Soziologie und Geschichte," *Archiv für Sozialwissenschaften und Sozialpolitik*, 61 (1929), p. 485. Cf. below, Section 6.1, pp. 143-49.

> The term "formal rationality of economic action" will be used to designate the extent of quantitative calculation or accounting which is technically possible and which is actually applied. The "substantive rationality," on the other hand, is the degree to which the provisioning of given groups of persons (no matter how delimited) with goods is shaped by economically oriented social action under some criterion (past, present, or potential) of ultimate values (*wertende Postulate*), regardless of the nature of these ends. . . . Calculation in terms of money, and not its actual use, is thus the specific means of rational, economic provision.[22]

In another passage he writes, somewhat differently, that formal or instrumental rationality orients itself toward the market situation and that persons who act according to instrumental rationality assess their actions rationally with the help of financial calculations concerning ends, means, and side effects.[23]

In Weber's account of the distinction between formal or instrumental rationality and non-formal or substantive rationality, it is not clear whether the attribute distinguishing the former from the latter is the possibility of formal calculation or the orientation of the use of means and ends to the market situation. Thus Ludwig von Mises objected that the Weberian distinction, if it takes account of the possibility of calculation of action, is incorrect, since substantive values[24] can also be pursued with strong calculation in a traditional society. The pursuit of substantive values, such as duty, dignity, and beauty, also involves goals, and one easily recognizes that "for this reason, conduct directed toward their realization must likewise be classified as formal rationality."[25]

Mises is correct in emphasizing the fact that substantive values can be pursued or realized just as rationally or irrationally as the goals of formal rationality that orient themselves toward economic values and market opportunities. The distinction between substantive and formal rationality is indifferent to, or at least incommensurable with, the principle of rationality. There is, to be sure, a greater proximity of market-oriented economic action to monetary calculation and to formal rationality than is the case with economic action oriented toward substantive goals, because market price formation and the availability of a market price make an unambiguous monetary calculability and actual calculation easier. But even economic behavior oriented toward market conditions can be "incalculable" and proceed according to intuitions, and nevertheless be rational and successful, just as the substantive orientation can proceed strictly according to economic calculations and rationally, in the sense of a formal monetary cal-

---

22 Max Weber, *Economy and Society*, ed. Guenther Roth and Claus Wittich (New York, 1968), Vol. I, pp. 85-86.

23 *Ibid.*, pp. 24-26.

24 [Translator's note: *Materiale Werte* is translated here as "substantive values," rather than "material values," because the latter expression has the connotation of mundane or crass, but *materiale Werte* does not. See also p. 4, note 3.]

25 Mises, "Soziologie und Geschichte," p. 479.

culation, to traditional values or values predetermined in other ways, for instance, by an authoritative planning department – if one ignores for the moment the question whether there can be genuine scarcity prices with this kind of calculation.

The economic principle, understood as the a priori principle of rational action, is superior to and comprehends Weber's distinction between formal and substantive rationality. Just as all thought-acts obey the logical law of non-contradiction, all conscious choices must follow the economic principle. Both principles have an a priori character – the economic principle for human decision, the law of non-contradiction for human thought. The two principles, however, are not realized optimally in all human decisions or thought-acts. Neither complete or maximal rationality nor strict logical thought is realized in all human life-expressions. Mises correctly emphasized the intellectual and a priori nature of the economic principle, but erred when he equated human action to rational action.[26] The full measure of possible rationality is not realized in each action, although there is no action that does not follow the economic principle at least partially. One must assume that Mises saw the necessity of equating action and rational action in the necessity of anticipating the obvious objection that the economic principle cannot be a priori if it is not applied universally and is not true for all actions.

From the fact that the principle of rationality is not always obeyed and is not observed as a maximum or minimum principle in every decision, it does not follow that it lacks universal and a priori validity. Karl Popper raised the objection against the a priori character of the economic principle that the principle of rationality is not an empirically or psychologically verifiable proposition, because it always refers to the situation and the purpose as a rational agent perceives it. We cannot perceive externally how a person has perceived *his* decision situation, however, because we are not completely able to penetrate his view of things. The principle of rationality is also not an a priori principle, according to Popper, because it is not always applicable: human persons do not always behave rationally. From that, Popper concludes that an a priori principle that is not always true is either false or not a priori. Therefore, according to Popper, the principle of rationality is indeed an indispensable principle, but one of little content. It involves a minimum principle: we conform our actions to the situations as we perceive these situations.[27]

Two decisive objections can be made against Popper's critique of the a priori nature of the principle of rationality. First, if one follows Popper, the principle

---

[26] Mises, *Human Action* (New Haven, 1949), p. 18: "Human action is necessarily always rational. The term 'rational action' is therefore pleonastic and must be rejected as such."

[27] Karl Popper, "La rationalité et le statut du principe de rationalité," in Jacques Rueff and Emil M. Claassen, eds., *Les fondements philosophiques des systèmes économiques* (Paris, 1967), pp. 142-50.

of rationality cannot be refuted by an external observer. Thus, since the principle of rationality is not falsifiable, it also cannot be decided externally whether an actor has acted rationally. Second, a priori principles are not always followed. Popper's definition of the a priori as strict necessity is incorrect. Not all a priori principles are always obeyed. Even the laws of logic, though valid, are not always followed, and do not thereby lose their a priori character: "What makes logic a priori is the impossibility of illogical thought."[28] From this proposition of Wittgenstein it does not follow that everything *is* always thought logically. Nothing can be thought *without* logic, but not everything is thought logically. There can be no action without rationality, but not all actions are rational.

Logicalness and rationality are not discrete, but continuous characteristics. The a priori character of the logic of thought and the logic of action are, however, not refuted by the fact that there are degrees of logicalness and rationality. From the fact that human persons do not always behave rationally, it does not follow that the economic principle is not valid a priori for conscious decisions and actions, since an external observer cannot recognize how the decision situation was perceived by the acting person ex ante, how his or her decision calculation conformed to the perceived situation, and how the means-end relation was anticipated. Just as there are degrees of logicalness, there are also degrees of rationality. A lack of logicalness in the thought of an individual is not a valid objection to the validity of logic: "Indeed people even surmised that there must be a 'law of least action' before they knew exactly how it went. (Here, as always, what is certain a priori proves to be something purely logical.)"[29] Just as with logical thought the laws of logic do not guarantee correct conclusions, so also in the conscious decision the a priori nature of the principle of rationality does not ensure the rationality of the decision and action. The laws of logic, like the principle of rationality, "show how little is achieved when these problems are solved."[30] The formality of logic and of the economic principle ensure that when the formal problems have been solved, the real problems begin.

2.4.2. FORMAL RATIONALITY AND NON-FORMAL, SUBSTANTIVE RATIONALITY

If the principle of rationality is an a priori principle, valid for all human acts of choice, and if it implies that the choice of means for an established end in the situation, as it is perceived, is appropriate, it is impossible that the distinguishing feature of formal and substantive rationality consists in the viability of

---

[28] Ludwig Wittgenstein, *Tractatus Logico-Philosophicus*, trans. D. F. Pears and B. F. McGuinness (London, 1961), Proposition 5.4731, p. 47.

[29] *Ibid.*, Proposition 6.3211, p. 67.

[30] *Ibid.*, Preface, p. 4.

formal calculation. Both with the orientation of setting and pursuing goals according to the market situation and monetary parameters, and with the pursuit of substantive values, formal calculation or the process of calculation can be rational or irrational, appropriate or inappropriate, depending upon whether the end and the means permit a process of calculation to appear "rationally" and whether the cost of the calculation is justified economically.

The Weberian distinction between formal and substantive rationality is nevertheless illuminating, if it is not interpreted as a distinction between ways of economizing and forms of the rationality of the choices of means and ends, but as a distinction between two ways of coordinating rational persons. Formal and substantive rationality do not describe different ways of optimizing the means-ends relationship or of employing means toward ends economically. Ends are pursued rationally with both formal and substantive rationality. The distinction refers instead to different socio-economic forms of integration and coordination.

Formal rationality is realized in a type of social coordination that does not commit persons to "substantive" ends and values that are defined in terms of their content, and does not achieve the coordination of individual actions by the advancement of these substantive ends in communities. Formal rationality instead leaves the setting of goals open and attempts to coordinate their pursuit by formal rules in such a way that the maximal attainment of subjective ends is possible. The market society sets the individual pursuit of ends free and permits its members to determine their ends autonomously and individually. It pursues a form of coordination and rationality that does not establish socially compulsory, substantive ends or values, such as the attainment of a definite quantitative production goal (e.g., "the primacy of heavy industry") or the realization of substantive values (e.g., national autarky) and seeks to realize this with the minimum total cost to society. It realizes, instead, a formal kind of coordination that seeks to arrange subjective ends, whose content is left open, rationally or efficiently, according to formal, universal rules, which are the same for all persons. Formal coordination establishes rules of the coexistence of diverse plans and actions, which allow any particular ends – which must be within definite boundaries, but are not socially and culturally established – to be realized at the lowest cost. The costs are not measured in substantive terms, but in formal terms, according to the smallest opportunity costs, expressed in monetary terms. The costs consist in the restriction that the attainment of the goals of one individual imposes upon the realization of the goals of other persons.

The market and democracy, as social decision systems, do not decide and act with substantive rationality (i.e. concerning substantive value-claims and value-realizations, to integrate with the lowest expenditure and by substantive values into a symbolic and valuable unity), but with formal rationality, according to universal rules of the ability to exist with one another, according to the maximum ability to coordinate all individual goals of the actors in the market and ballot box. The expressions of the will of individuals, their ends (preferences) and their urgency of ends (intensity of preferences), are coordinated with those of everyone else in the coordination system of the market according to readiness to pay, and thus through price signals. Political preferences are coordinated in the voting process of the majority electoral system, according to the principle "one man – one vote."

It should be noted that social and economic mediation by substantive rationality can be uncoerced, if the substantive values are accepted universally. The criteria of substantive rationality, however, are not derived from subjective goals and individual goal-setting, but from predetermined goals. Since the sphere of consumption in the economies of prosperous societies, in which basic subsistence needs are met, can almost be defined by the fact that the subjectivity of the self is effective in them and is acknowledged in the endless duplication of needs, a complete control and arrangement of the economy and the price system according to substantive values would not meet the principle of the market economy, to meet subsistence needs *and* subjective consumer needs. Coordination according to substantive rationality in the sphere of market coordination would not assume the character of coordination, but that of subordination. Substantive rationality, however, remains rationality in the sense of the economic principle. Its bearer or subject is not the composition and coordination of individual "rationalities" into the formal rationality of the price system, but rather the central decision-maker, who "economizes" the social resources for the substantive goals predetermined by himself. Substantive rationality also remains necessary in the democratic market society beside formal rationality in the integration by shared values and in governmental action. But it cannot become the determining principle of the economy.

2.5. Ethics as Form of Social Coordination

The coordination of formal rationality, the arrangement of the subjective, rational pursuit of goals, takes place in the market through the rules of the price system. These rules of exchange and rights of ownership are universal, formal principles, which are not oriented toward substantive values and do not observe the substantive features and individuality of the acting person at the level of the rules. The principles of formal arrangement and coordination according to individual instrumental rationality correspond to the principles of the ethics of universalization, and above all its development by Kant to such a degree that universalization as the internalization of coordination ideals, as it also serves as the foundation of market coordination, can be seen in the ethical decision process of the individual.

2.5.1. CONVERGENCE OF ETHICAL UNIVERSALIZATION AND MARKET COORDINATION IN THE FORMAL NATURE OF THEIR LAWS

The formal rationality of the market aims at the ability of individual demands and expectations regarding the national product to coexist and at the coordination of actions in market exchange. The problem of economic individualism and its formal rationality is: What must I do in order to realize efficiently my goal with the existing economic and social boundary conditions and under the condition that others also pursue their goals? How must the coordination system of the price system be designed, in order to realize these individual goals economically? The problem of the formal ethic of universalization and formalism in ethics is: Of which maxim of my action can I will that it become a principle of universal legislation or a universal rule of action?

Unlike the formal rationality of market coordination, which aims at the ability to coordinate actions, as well as plans and preferences that are already determined, formal ethics aims at the formation and coordination of preferences and maxims in the inner being of the acting person. One should choose that maxim of action of which one can will that it become a universal principle.

Like market coordination, the ethical coordination of formal ethics does not select and designate any goals ahead of others. The two forms of coordination determine – in Kant's words – not the material, but the form of the will (i.e. they ask about the ability of individuals' inner preferences *and* the decision-actions flowing from them to coexist). Market coordination brings about a conformity of plans and revealed preferences in the market, up to the point of their ability to coexist. The ethical coordination of universalization aims at a transformation of preferences that are not yet shaped into rational (i.e. universalizable) preferences. In both forms of coordination, the ideal of coordination itself, and not one of the coordination of an external, substantive criterion, should become the standard of the coordination process. The means of social coordination is at the same time its own ideal.

The external coordination of formal rationality in the market should be anticipated conceptually by anticipation of coordination in the inner coordination of the autonomy of the will, according to the criterion of the universalizability of the maxim of action. The correspondence of formal rationality and external coordination in the market and the formal internal coordination of maxims to the universalizability principle consists in the fact that a substantive goal or principle of the will of the acting person should not coerce or influence from outside, but instead that the will should be determined only formally by the necessity to be compatible with the equal freedom of will of other persons. The autonomy of the will and of action should be limited in ethical and economic coordination only by the freedom of others to be able to act similarly and, therefore, by the principle of coordination, but not by other substantive principles or goals. Consequently, according to Kant, there is only one categorical imperative and principle of ethics, not several competing principles: "There is, therefore, only one categorical imperative. It is: Act only according to that maxim by which you can at the same time will that it should become a universal law."[31]

The will should not be determined ethically, nor conduct economically, by the material of the will (i.e. by some conditional principle or predetermined goal). The will should instead be determined ethically only by the possibility of the universality of the maxim (or preference) of the acting person and the actions following from the preferences. And it should be determined economically only by its compatibility with the expectations and plans of other persons. Both ethics and economics should be determined exclusively by the ideal of coordination itself. The content of the formal ethic of universalization and the formal rationality of the market is the idea of coordination itself.

The Kantian ethic of universalization and its ideal of coordination is, however, not *completely* formal, because it contains at least two value judgments that are subjective (i.e. not derived from the mere universalization of the coordination rule). First, the ideal of coordination in ethics assumes as a value that there should be maximal coordination, and thus that it should be and is willed by the acting person. Second, it assumes as a value that forms of action, not mere events or atomistic components of behavior, are coordinated. The value judgment that there should be coordination by formal coordination, and not subordination by substantive coordination, is shared by the economic theory of the market with the formal ethic of universalization. The value judgment of preferring forms of action to atomistic behavioral events is, however, shared with ethics only by a market theory that recognizes in the market a context of conscious interaction, not a context of external optimization. The question of what the unity of actions and the maximandum of maximizing actions in the economy should achieve, of what is to be maximized, is unanswered in positive economics.

The standard of the notional, anticipated coordination of ethics is the universalizability of the maxim. In Kant's words, "So act that the maxim of your will could always hold at the same time as a principle establishing universal law."[32] For Kant, the principle of universalization contains two conditions. First, the *maxim* of the action – not the action itself[33] – must be universalizable and must permit itself to be universalized. The maxim must be of such a kind that the ac-

[31] Immanuel Kant, *Foundations of the Metaphysics of Morals*, trans. Lewis White Beck (New York, 1959), p. 39.

[32] Kant, *Critique of Practical Reason*, trans. Beck (New York, 1985), p. 30.

[33] R. C. O. Matthews, in "Morality, Competition, and Efficiency," *The Manchester School of Economic and Social Studies*, 49 (1981), p. 295, overlooks this distinction between the universalization of actions and the universalization of maxims. He raises against Kant the objection that the individual would no longer be able to do anything at all, if he had to examine the universalizability of *all* of his actions.

tion following from it can coexist with the actions of others who also follow this maxim. Second, it must be possible for a decision-maker to *will* that his or her maxim be universalized.

Kant's formulation of the categorical imperative avoids the deficit that exists in the similar principle of the Golden Rule. The Golden Rule – that one should not do to others what one would not want to be done to oneself – leaves open the possibility that an evil doer could respond that he is quite willing to have precisely the same thing done to himself. He can reply that he, like a gambler, would run the risk of having to endure the universalization of his action. The murderer can reply to the prosecutor that he is prepared to risk being murdered himself, in order to be able to commit murder. According to the categorical imperative, the acting person must not only ask himself whether the maxim is universalizable, but also whether he can *will* that it be universalized and become a universal law of nature: "Act as though the maxim of your action were by your will to become a universal law of nature."[34] In the law of nature formulation of the categorical imperative, the proximity of ethics to ontology, as it is understood by Kant, becomes apparent. The pure formalism of universalization transcends itself to the level of the preservation-idea of the ontology of the natural. The maxim must not only be universalizable, and its universalization must not only be capable of being willed, but the situation of the whole that follows from its universal validity (i.e. the model of the coordinated actions) must also be capable of becoming nature (i.e. be capable of preservation).

Kant's formulation of the categorical imperative also avoids another deficit that exists in the simple principle of universalization. It is not a principle of the universalization of actions, but one of the universalization of maxims – the universalization of the subjective, practical principle of the acting person. The maxim is, for Kant, a subjective, practical principle that is valid for the person and to which more specialized rules are subordinated. The maxim becomes an objective, practical principle or law when it is recognized as valid for the will of every rational being.[35] Actions are individual and, therefore, like all individual entities, cannot be formulated and universalized. Only that within the individual action which is already directed toward universality, the subjective principle, is universalizable. Kant's concept of the maxim responds, therefore, to the objection that each acting person could reply to the requirement that his *actions* be universalized by saying that his particular situation is not at all universalizable, or that his action is thoroughly universalizable if the singular situation and indi-

---

[34] Kant, *Foundations of the Metaphysics of Morals*, p. 39. Kant's solution to the problem of understanding the relationship between the individual case and the natural law, and his definition of natural law for the concept of nature in ethics and "human nature" leaves questions open, of course, because the particular receives too little space in his ethical theory. Cf. below, Section 3.5, p. 104.

[35] Kant, *Critique of Practical Reason*, p. 17.

vidualization of the action are taken into account. He could will absolutely that every acting person in the same situation in which he himself is found would act in the same way. His action could be its own genus or its own class and set, which has been thus far only a one-member set, but could in the future become an *n*-member class or set and, therefore, be universalizable. He could will that everyone who comes into precisely the same situation in the future would perform the same action.

The maxim as a subjective principle, not the action itself, is the object of universalization. The description of the individual action according to its maxim ensures that the action is already considered from the point of view of its species. The universalizability is related to the nature or kind of action and not to the universalizability of the individuation of the kind of action in time and space and in the action of an individual. Universalizability is only possible in a thought that already moves in the medium of the universal and in universals. Universalization presupposes that there are already universals of actions, types of acting.

Kant's formal ethics of universalization presupposes the existence of substantive forms of action, not merely formal combinations of events into actions. An action is not a combination of events that takes place ex post and could have received a different name. Kant's ethics contains no complete formalism, because it presupposes that an action has a nature. A lie, for example, is not for Kant a formal action consisting in a statement that is false and takes place under certain circumstances. A lie is, instead, a type of action of the intentional, false statement, in a situation that requires a truthful statement, and to a person who is justified in assuming that the statement is true. Kant's formulation of the categorical imperative, as the demand to be able to will that a principle of action becomes natural, is connected to the law of nature. Kant's formulation of the universalizable maxim as a law of nature confirms the insight of Heinrich Rickert: "Empirical reality becomes nature when we view it with respect to its universal characteristics; it becomes history when we view it as particular and individual."[36] If there were not also an element of the universal and the natural in the action, there would be no formal ethics and no possibility of universalization.

---

[36] Heinrich Rickert, *Science and History*, trans. George Reisman (Princeton, 1962), p. 57. Rickert introduces this principle thus: "With the object of making clear and explicit *two purely logical, and hence purely formal, concepts of nature and history* – by which I mean not two different *domains* of reality, but the same reality seen from two *different points of view* – I myself have attempted to formulate the fundamental logical problem of classifying the sciences according to their methods in the following way..." (p. 56). See also Rickert, *The Limits of Concept Formation in Natural Science*, trans. Guy Oakes (Cambridge, 1986).

2.5.2. KANTIAN ETHICS AS THE SOLUTION TO THE PRISONER'S DILEMMA

According to R. C. O. Matthews, all defects of market control and all cases of market failure belong to the universal set of situations that can be described by the prisoner's dilemma.[37] Prisoner's dilemma situations exist when the pursuit of self-interest does not lead to an efficient coordination of actions. In cases of high transaction costs, non-rivalry of consumption, non-exclusion of non-paying customers, etc. in the price system of the market, the pursuit of self-interest does not bring about an efficient solution. In such cases, the coordination of prices must be replaced by other forms of control, such as voting or central control. The coordination problem is especially difficult to solve when central control and enforcement eliminate universality for systematic reasons, when, as in the case of asymmetric knowledge or a "natural" monopoly, governmental monitoring and control are impossible or are possible only with great difficulty. In such cases, if both central control and decentralized coordination by the price system are impossible, the dilemma situation is characterized by the interest that every individual has in universal rule-compliance and the realization of the common good of the group. But each individual is also subject to the incentive to make an exception of himself, at the expense of the group. In such a situation the only solution is the ethical solution (i.e. the anticipation of the universal in the will of the individual and the ethical will toward this anticipation and following of the universal).

The task that the prisoner's dilemma presents for a group in which each individual exploits the universal rule for his or her own benefit as a "free rider" and wishes to make an exception of himself or herself is the following: How can the group, whose coordination cannot be ensured by central control, arrive at a situation in which each individual makes the universal law and welfare also the maxim of his or her individual actions? The task is an eminently ethical one: The universal should become the motive of individual action; the universal interest should also become the self-interest of all. Kantian ethics establishes a demand for the individual, which is, at the individual level, an exact mirror image of the demand that the prisoner's dilemma situation establishes at the collective level as a universal demand for the group affected by the dilemma as a whole. The demand of the categorical imperative for the individual and the response of Kantian ethics to the question "What should I do?" is: "Act in such a way that you can make your maxim a universal law." This answer corresponds to the question that the prisoner's dilemma poses for the group: "How can we make the universality of the rule also the maxim of individual action?"

---

[37] Matthews, "Morality, Competition, and Efficiency," p. 295.

The group in which a prisoner's dilemma arises is confronted by three problems: the problem of motivation, the problem of universalization, and the problem of the excuse or exception. It must create a motive for rule-compliance. It must formulate the universalization of the rule. And it must ensure that the universal principle of the group is reshaped into the correct individual maxims (i.e. that the correct individual maxim is universalized or the individual maxim is correctly universalized), so that with the application of the universal rule to the individual maxim of action, no mistakes are made and the problem of the excuse or exception does not become dominant.

The problem of motivation consists for the group in creating an individual motive for an action that is not in one's immediate self-interest, for a regionally- or globally-maximizing strategy, for members who otherwise pursue their short-term self-interest and locally-maximizing strategies. The transformation of the strategies of immediate self-interest into regionally- and globally-maximizing strategies takes place, as has been shown above, through ethics and religion. For ethics, the problem of its application and specification consists in the fact that the universalization of the individual maxim or rule of action as the solution to the prisoner's dilemma must find a mean between the extremes of rules that are too general and those that are too specific. The rule *pacta sunt servanda* is only the major premise of the solution to the problem of the transaction costs of contracts. It must be expounded in more specific maxims of economic activity and specific solutions to the prisoner's dilemma.

At the same time, in addition to the motivation of universalization, it must also be ensured that the persons in the prisoner's dilemma do not describe their action-situations in such a way that they do not fall under the rule, and that the rule is not formulated in such a way that their actions are not subsumed under it. They must be prevented from adopting either of two classic strategies of the excuse. Finally, the ethical solution to the prisoner's dilemma must prevent persons from choosing and adopting the universalization of the rule that is precisely not the solution of the dilemma. The "prisoner" of the dilemma situation can represent the universal rule and demand that every person make an exception of the rule for himself, and thereby make it impossible to solve the dilemma.

Kantian ethics replies to this problematic situation of the prisoner's dilemma. The attempt is made to preserve the motivation toward universalization, with Kant, according to the schema of the "assurance game" of ethics and the "super-assurance game" of religion, by the categorical imperative and postulational religion. He establishes the motivation to ethical action with the specific dignity of the moral in human persons as end in themselves, with the "fact of reason" in human persons, and with the postulates of practical reason – God, freedom, and the immortality of the soul – which have been reconstructed above in terms of game theory.

The possibility of the excuse and self-exception from the rule by the construction of individual exception situations is reduced by the concept of the maxim. The universalization of the maxim, not of the individual action, ensures the internal universalization of the action into the action-type. The action-type is then examined in a second step, to determine whether it is universalizable. The prisoner of the prisoner's dilemma cannot universalize his or her concrete action situation – that would lead to the problems already noted of the non-universalizability of the singular. He or she must instead first formulate the maxims of his or her alternative actions, in order then to universalize the maxims.

The criterion of universalizability requires that the universalization is of such a kind that it can also be willed by the acting person and not just be accepted by him or her indifferently as a theoretical possibility. Furthermore, it requires that the universalization of the maxim also ensures the long-term preservation of the individuals and the group as a whole. In other words, it must be capable of becoming a valid law of nature. Both components of the requirement of universalization – the ability to be willed and the ability to become a law of nature – prohibit the prisoner in the prisoner's dilemma from turning the exception into the rule and declaring the exception of himself or herself from the universal law to be the universal rule of the group. Kantian ethics makes it impossible for individuals to elevate the exception to the rule to the level of a universal law, which could be followed by all acting persons in dilemma situations, all prisoners. The Kantian solution to the prisoner's dilemma is more satisfactory than the governmental solution of central control, because the ethical solution creates no costs of control and monitoring. This analysis confirms that *the state is only an imperfect substitute for ethics*[38] and that the ethical solution to the dilemma is more efficient than the governmental solution.

Kant's emphasis on individual, moral motivation and the universalization of ethics' sphere of application to encompass all situations to be assessed and all groups to be included in the universalization makes his ethical theory suitable not only for avoiding situations of the prisoner's dilemma in small groups, but also for avoiding dilemma situations in large groups. The group whose dilemma situation must be solved is, for Kantian universalism, humanity as a whole. Universalization is demanded in Kantian ethics for all prisoner's dilemma situations and for *all* affected persons. As an ethical theory for large groups, Kantian universalism represents the ethics of the market society, with high mobility and fluctuation in the formation of groups, which make it impossible to tie ethics and ethos down to particular groups. Given the mobility between groups in modern society, it is a rational strategy for individuals, according to Richard McKenzie, to develop a type of ethics that contains universalistic ethical rules,

---

[38] Cf. McKenzie, "The Economic Dimension of Ethical Behavior," p. 221.

so that members in new groups are accepted quickly when they must change their groups and local memberships.[39] Kantian universalism meets this demand.

A mobile society of changing group memberships and changing situations of the prisoner's dilemma requires an ethical theory with high universality of validity and comprehensive inclusion of individuals and groups affected. The Kantian ethic of the coordination of maxims toward universalizability is an ethical theory that defines the groups of the prisoner's dilemma so widely that *all* changing groups that can fall into a prisoner's dilemma situation are included by it, because the addressee of the Kantian ethic of universalization is the individual as a representative of humanity. In the modern commercial society, the market's need for coordination and the number of cases of the prisoner's dilemma can become quite large. The ethical theory corresponding to it must, therefore, demonstrate a high capability for coordination and inclusion. It is necessary that ethics, under the conditions of a mobile market society, expands the groups that should make the universality of the rule and the universal interest also the motive of individual action to include all members of the affected society, and claim validity for everyone. The ethical theory must not be of a kind such that it has validity only for small or specific groups and that it is limited in its range, because the interactions and side effects of the members of the commercial society are not restricted to small groups.

2.5.3. FORMAL ETHICS AS INTERNAL PRE-COORDINATION OF THE ECONOMIC COORDINATION OF THE PRICE SYSTEM

The inclusion of the persons affected and the internalization of consequences comprise the criteria of social coordination. The economic theory of the market and of the price system puts forward the claim concerning the market's ability to coordinate that the market, with the exception of situations of *economic* market failure, produces inclusion and internalization. General equilibrium theory adds that the market, under conditions of perfect competition, guarantees not only inclusion and internalization, but also the attainment of the social optimum or economic efficiency. The process theory of the market in the Austrian school and Buchanan's contractualist school sees, on the contrary, the market as a process of interaction that guarantees inclusion and internalization, without the possibility of saying that optimality is thereby attained, since optimality cannot be defined independently of the market process (i.e. not as an extra-procedural criterion). According to the interactionist-contractualist approach, the *coordinating function of the market* is the decisive argument for a market-economic constitution of the economy, while the question of the total economic optimum is undecidable, because of the lack of knowledge about the parameters of the

[39] *Ibid.*, p. 214.

economic situation, uncertainty about the future, and the acting person's subjective assessments of goods, which are not conclusively recognizable from the outside.[40]

Our model of interaction, understood in terms of game theory, between economics, religion, and ethics has shown that the market's ability to coordinate and its efficiency are increased by the validity of a formal theory of the ethics of universalization and rule-compliance. Ethics increases social coordination, and thus also economic coordination itself, when the coordination efficiency of the market is given with perfect competition, in the sense of general equilibrium theory. The ethical coordination of actions takes place by the anticipation of universality (i.e. the anticipated consideration of the composition of one's own actions with the expected actions of other persons in self-interested economic decisions). The coordination of actions *in foro interno* according to the rule of assumed universalization performs a pre-coordination of one's action with those of everyone else in the interior of the action and before the action is performed. The individual fulfillment of a contract and the keeping of contractually agreed performances of the self and others are not first coordinated *ex post* after the action by control and sanctions, and the coordination of the previous time periods are not first corrected afterwards. The coordination, instead, already takes place by reflection on and anticipation of the universalizability of one's own action before the action.

The individual's ethical reflection and decision anticipate market coordination and at the same time create motives to produce social coordination individually by universalization, because the principle of universalization has the character not only of a means, but also of a demand. The universalization principle of ethical reflection is at the same time an instrument of coordination and a motive to perform ethical pre-coordination according to universalizability. The universalizability of the maxim of action is the conceptual anticipation of actual coordination: "So act that the maxim of your will could always hold at the same time as a principle establishing universal law."[41] In other words, "Act in such a way that your individual maxim can coexist with the same maxim of other persons and that the actions of everyone flowing from it can be coordinated."

The fact that ethics represents the internal, intra-subjective pre-coordination of the economic, coordinating interaction of the market can be seen in Sen's "assurance game." If the validity of a code of ethics in a group guarantees that the majority will obey a particular ethical rule, the acting person anticipates the universalizability of this rule and the ability to coordinate the actions flowing from it before she herself acts and chooses a particular form of action. She is at the same time prepared to aim her own action at the principle of universaliza-

---

[40] On the theory of general equilibrium, see Chapter 6 below.

[41] Kant, *Critique of Practical Reason*, trans. Beck (New York, 1985), p. 30.

tion. The ability to coordinate an action with the actions of others, abiding by the terms of a contract for instance, must not be first guaranteed by sanctions *ex post* and *externally*, with the consequence that the coordination is carried out at a high cost. The coordination is instead anticipated *ex ante* and carried out *internally*.

Ethics is the pre-coordination of action-guiding interests and maxims. The fact that, in this function, it reduces the actual, external coordination needs at the economic level can be seen in the fact that ethics promotes trust, which in turn alleviates interpersonal coordination. The validity and moral obligation of ethical rules increases both trust in the promises of others and the predictability of their actions universally, not merely economic-specifically. Since the contract is a promise and constitutes the dominant principle of the market economy, the promotion of trust by ethics has a specifically economic effect. The importance of trust in a society built upon voluntary contracts shows why both the state and the economy must be particularly interested in whether business-persons trust one another, and whether that trust is justified.

2.5.4. DEEPENING SOCIAL COORDINATION BY ETHICS

Ethics and religion reduce uncertainty regarding which options the other person will select from the range of available, alternative actions. Ethics is the self-obligation of the acting person to reduce the field of alternative actions to those that are ethically justifiable. By ethical pre-coordination, which takes place before market coordination, the ethical person obligates himself to choose among alternative actions only universalizable options in ethically questionable cases (i.e. options that satisfy the requirement of the universalizability of the maxim and confirm the "assurance game" of the validity of universal ethical rules), while assuring other persons that the ethical norms are universally valid in the society.

The self-obligation of the acting person to ethical norms and to the principle of the universalizability of the maxim in cases in which no explicit norms exist is a "precommitment" (Elster) to obey ethical norms and to restrict the range of alternative actions voluntarily. This self-restriction in the choice of alternative actions reduces the uncertainty of others about the conduct of the acting person and decreases the need to coordinate the interactions. At the same time, the individual is also able to act with the universal validity of ethics under lower uncertainty about the emerging composition of his action with the actions of others and about the composition of the actions of the others among one another, when he can assume that ethical rules show universal validity. Ethical rules reduce, as a pre-coordination in the interiority of the acting person, the need for coordination in the market and in politics, because they reduce the spectrum of alternative actions and the variance of the interaction patterns that emerge from the composition of individual actions.

The reduction of uncertainty by the universal validity of an ethical code of conduct has not only the compensatory function of correcting market failure and governmental failure, but also the positive and even economically advantageous function of additional coordination. Ethical coordination facilitates *all* social interactions. Ethics is to be understood both as a means to the compensation of governmental and market failure and, at the same time, in a positive sense as an end in itself, as strengthening social coordination in *all* action situations. It is a strengthening and deepening of social coordination, which has at the same time the character of an end in itself. The universality of ethics and of an ethos in a society intensifies and facilitates social coordination, because it reduces uncertainty about alternative actions and about the composition of individual actions into patterns of social interaction.

2.5.5. ETHICS AS THE REDUCTION OF UNCERTAINTY ABOUT THE DECISION BEHAVIOR OF OTHER PERSONS AND ITS COMPOSITION INTO PATTERNS OF SOCIAL INTERACTION

The anticipation of the patterns of social interaction that arise from individual strategies of action and, therefore, both the anticipating pre-coordination of ethics and the actual coordination of the market and voting (democracy), as social decision systems, are aggravated by the so-called problem of composition. The composition of individual decisions into a pattern of coordination resulting from them and the side effects of the individual decisions on one another and on the developing pattern, as they emerge in the process of composition, can be known in advance neither by the individual nor by any central decision and observation authority. The repercussions on the original goals of the individual that arise from the composition of individual actions in a market in the course of market coordination and *ex post* when markets close cannot be known *ex ante* by the actors pursuing their individual goals and strategies in the market. They can only be imagined in anticipation. This anticipation is all the more difficult, the less the actions of individuals correspond to rules or typical patterns and the more they are subjective or random.

In the external, individualistic, social coordination of the market, therefore, a problem of summation often arises. Many individually insignificant side effects of the interaction of the many individual actions that are not recognizable at the point in time of the action and that were not grasped under universalizable points of view can, in the external coordination of the market, add up to a difficult, socially undesired total pattern. If each individual attempts to protect himself or herself from inflation by refuge in tangible assets, galloping inflation can arise, precisely *because* each individual seeks to avoid the effects of inflation on himself or herself. Another example is the over-development of especially beautiful scenery: Each individual builds a house in order to enjoy it. But from the composition of these individual strategies, too many houses are built, thwarting the individuals' original goal.

The problem of the composition of individual actions,[42] which is inherent in the external, individualistic-discursive coordination of the market and in democracy, is reduced by internal ethical coordination, the anticipation of external, social-economic coordination. To say that the problem of the composition of individual actions is defused in its urgency by ethics assumes that the individuals wish to *and* are able to anticipate ethically the composition of their actions with those of other persons. The problem of composition includes both an ethical and a pragmatic dimension. Its ethical dimension consists in the fact that individuals often do not *desire* to consider the effects of their actions on others, and do not *wish* to act under conditions of universalization or in anticipation of an overall result, even though the anticipation of the composition of actions is cognitively possible, internal ethical coordination according to the principle of universalization could be willed, and the universal observance of the ethical rules would also reduce uncertainty about the results of coordination. The pragmatic problem of coordination consists in the fact that individuals are in many cases *unable* to see clearly or to anticipate the interaction between their actions and those of other persons at all and, therefore, *cannot* plan harmonious coordination, even if the ethical will to universalization and to the anticipation of the overall result of the composition of individual strategies in the individual decision exists.

The ethical and pragmatic sides that the problem of the anticipation of composition and coordination reveals show that without the validity of rules neither ethical pre-coordination nor economic-legal, external coordination is possible, because the interaction patterns that arise from disorderly action are completely singular and therefore unrecognizable. Social (i.e. economic, legal, and ethical) rules reduce the possible number of the patterns that the composition of individual actions can assume. They make patterns of the composition of social interaction recognizable and anticipatable.

In situations of asymmetric and externally-unobservable knowledge and the absence of markets (i.e. in situations in which legal and price control are impossible) economic coordination by the price system indispensably requires ethical coordination. In all other cases of economic interaction, the economic coordination of the price system is facilitated and intensified by ethical pre-coordination, because the validity of ethics reduces the transaction costs of commercial relationships. The cooperation of the acting person, which constitutes the nature of

---

42 On the problem of market failure and democratic failure as failure of discourse, see Koslowski, "Markt- und Demokratieversagen?" *Politische Vierteljahresschrift*, 24 (1983), pp. 166-87, and "Market and Democracy as Discourses," in Koslowski, ed., *Individual Liberty and Democratic Decision-Making* (Tübingen, 1987), pp. 58-92.

the exchange economy, is increased and in some cases first made possible when the economic actors and the group members of an economic project of cooperation orient their actions toward ethical rules and universalizability.

Economic theory must, therefore, take ethics into consideration as a discipline and ethical norms as action-guiding (or at least action-influencing) motives and as factors in the formation of preferences, and must integrate them into a comprehensive theory of economic action and its coordination.[43] A causal or functional explanation of economic action is only possible on the basis of the decisions of human persons. In these decisions, ethical precommitments and self-obligations play a role that can no more be ignored in the analysis of individual economic action than in the analysis of the coordination of these actions in the market or in other social decision systems.

When seen in terms of game theory, ethics is an intensification of economic coordination and cooperation, and religion is an intensification of ethical coordination. Ethics and religion lead to an enhancement of a society's ability to coordinate and cooperate. Seen *ex post*, they are correctives for a lack or failure of coordination in the economic sphere of the market. Seen *ex ante*, they are instead pre-coordination within decision-makers and within their structures of preferences, which lie outside the actual coordination of actions in the market. As pre-coordination of the economy, ethics and religion bring about an increase in the ability of individual persons to coexist in the economy and society.

2.6. Ethics and Religion as Ways of Increasing Economic Rationality and Coordination

Expansions of self-interest into an interest in a more comprehensive inclusion of the external world within the self that pursues its "self-interest" are expansions of formal rationality and coordination, but not of substantive rationality and coordination, which orient themselves toward predetermined, substantive goals. Market coordination mediates between the subjective strategies of the market participants, who are not questioned and coordinated from substantive points of view, but from their compatibility with the preferences and strategies of everyone else. The ethical coordination of the principle of universalization seeks to coordinate one's own preferences within the medium of universality and to choose those preferences and actions that can coexist when universalized and adopted as maxims by everyone else. Finally, religious coordination aspires to proceed from the mere coordination of actions to the coordination of the maximum of value-realization of the totality, and seeks to choose globally-maximizing strategies.

---

[43] Johannes Messner, *Sozialökonomik und Sozialethik*, 2nd Ed. (Paderborn, 1929), pp. 50 ff.

At all three of these levels of coordination – in the market economy, the ethics of universalization, and the religious ethics of the maximal realization of values – there is a priority of the formal to the substantive, if the three levels cannot in fact be seen as completely formal. The formalism of the law, as it determines price control and market processes in the economy, is repeated in the formalism of the universalizability of the maxim, in the Kantian "moral law," and in the qualified formalism of a maximization of value-realization of the totality. This agreement in the type of economics and ethics is not accidental. The formalism of economics and ethics is, instead, closely related to the principle of liberty and the subjectivity of modernity. Uncoerced coordination is possible at the level of external, social systems of decision and coordination, only if they have the character of formal coordination and instrumental rationality. Formal, instrumentally rational coordination receives the individual expressions of will as they are, and does not seek to shape and form them according to a substantive value point of view. The form of the coordination at the external, social level has priority to the content of the coordination, and the form of the maxim in ethics has priority to the content of the maxim – which is not to say that formalism in ethics covers the entire field of ethics.

Formal ethics and its pre-coordination according to universalizability constitute the correspondence to formalism and to the subjectivity of the market at the level of interiority. Formal ethics, like market coordination, does not question the determining factors of the will concerning their content, but according to their universalizability. The maxim of the autonomous will should not correspond to substantive criteria of the moral, but should instead be subjected to their form, according to the moral law (i.e. should be able to take on the form of a universal law).

The relationship of the progressive levels of rationality and coordination from economics to ethics to religion is likewise formally determinable. Their difference lies in the different degrees of inclusion, in the increasing inclusion of persons affected in the formally-rational decision. Rationality has been used in the present analysis as a generic term naming both the economic principle itself and the type of rationality level. The subjective conception of rationality, as adaptation to the situation as we see it, and the conception of rationality as an a priori economic principle are not only compatible, but also connected. The a priori nature of the principle of rationality consists in maximum and minimum calculations, realizing the maximal degree of goal attainment with given means, or attaining a given end with the least necessary expenditure of means. This principle is applied in *every conscious* decision, whatever the *content* of the person's action may be. The content of individual goals is not predetermined by the concept of rationality. The content of the rationality follows from the perspectives of individuals, which can be economic, ethical, and religious.

In the case of the formal ethics of moral freedom, the form of the economically-rational action becomes itself the content of the higher rationality levels of ethics. The formal principle of economic rationality and coordination, to coordinate self-interested, economically-rational actions, becomes the content of ethical coordination in the interior of the acting person. The ethically-rational decision-maker makes the formal principle of the capacity for economic coordination the content and material of his own will when he himself wills the realization of the categorical imperative, and thus the maximal capacity for the coordination of actions, his own goal – and not only as an external principle of social coordination – and acknowledges the increase of coordination made possible by ethics as his self-legislated goal. The form of the universalization of the maxim becomes the "content" of his own, ethically-rational decision.

Since it is not committed to an objective concept of utility or rationality, the subjective concept of rationality permits planning the expansion of the economic rationality of ethical and religious rationality. In the subjective concept of rationality, ethical and religious rationality form expansions of the individual setting of goals, whose ethical and religious goals are "economized" and rationally pursued with the help of the a priori economic principle. The expansion of the maximandum in the individual ethical-religious maximization strategy deepens and facilitates the internal and external coordination of society and increases the inclusion of persons affected and the internalization of side effects in the subjective, rational calculation.

According to Plato, the highest form of knowledge is that which includes all other forms of knowledge within itself and is able to represent them. The superiority of the more inclusive to the less inclusive levels is also true of levels of rationality. The superior form of rationality is an expansion of the subordinate levels of rationality, and contains them within itself. The expansion of the maximandum in ethical rationality into the regionally- and globally-maximizing strategy, the extension of the inclusion and internalization of the totality, as it can be seen in the strengthening of the coordination of economics to the precoordination of ethics, makes it possible to see an increasing level of economic rationality in ethical rationality.

This assessment of the forms of rationality is in accordance with a conclusion that Gary Becker draws from his economic analysis of human behavior; namely, that an altruist can actually be better off than an egoist, even from the perspective of economics. The positive side effects of the utility that others have for her own utility can outweigh the direct disadvantages for herself that result from her altruism.[44] In the framework of an enlarged rationality-calculus and a regionally-maximizing strategy, an altruist is better off than an egoist who maximizes his self-interest locally (i.e. in a petty way). A higher level of inclusion

---

44 Cf. Gary S. Becker, *The Economic Approach to Human Behavior* (Chicago, 1976), p. 287.

of other persons in one's own rational pursuit of goals also means a higher level of *positive* interaction between the self and other persons and increased sources of individual utility arising from the intersubjectivity and interdependence of the utility function.

2.6.1. ETHICS AS THE ABILITY TO ENDURE THE CONSEQUENCES OF ONE'S OWN ACTIONS

With the question of the interdependence of the utility function of the moral agent and those of other persons, however, it is necessary to distinguish between the interdependence of the utility functions in acting and in enduring. In the interdependence of his actions with those of other persons, the moral agent does not endure primarily the existence and suffering of others, but the effects of his *own* actions on others. If he experienced the actions and the suffering of other persons as his own, he could no longer act with mere sympathy. Enduring the existence and actions of others is not identical to enduring the effects of one's own actions on the existence and actions of others. If the two forms of enduring were identical, the inclusion of other persons in one's own actions would lead to an interdependence in enduring that could hardly be overcome. If one understands the ethical inclusion that is greater in ethically-oriented behavior than in economically-oriented behavior as the identity of the suffering of others and one's own suffering, then all negative and positive effects that affect other persons work out their repercussions symmetrically on the self – even if perhaps in a somewhat narrower scope.

Such a situation of the approaching identity of experience between persons is possible only in the family, and even there only with an asymmetry between sorrow and joy. The positive effects that other persons experience are accepted differently with the interdependence of utility functions in the family than are the negative effects. Sharing in happiness is not symmetrical to sharing in unhappiness. Positive empathy is not identical to negative empathy or sympathy. Sharing in the sorrows and sharing in the joys of others are included in one's own experience in different ways. Complete co-suffering with others would make a person incapable of action, which is true only to a lesser degree of co-rejoicing.

The case of the interdependence or partial identity of utility functions in personal relationships and the family is not to be confused with the case of ethical action in the general social context of large groups. The case of sympathy, the interdependence of utility functions, is not the case of ethics and of ethical action according to a regionally- or globally-maximizing strategy. The situation of a partial identity of the utility functions of individuals is not ethically relevant, because it represents a situation of mere endurance, not one of consciously and freely grasping trans-subjectivity. An action situation in which the utility functions of the ego and of other persons are identical is incommensurable with ethical criteria, because it is passive and involuntary.

Ethics does not include the endurance of the suffering of other persons, but instead the endurance of the effects of one's *own* actions on others, and requires the anticipation and endurance of the effects of one's own actions on others. In the case of the negative repercussions of our own actions on other persons, ethics requires that we experience the endurance of these effects in such a way that we refrain from actions with negative side effects. The ethical is not primarily the endurance of the sorrows of other persons, but the consideration and avoidance of the side effects that our own actions have on others. The moral agent is in the position to endure the effects of her actions on other persons, to experience the suffering that has become, through others, her own suffering. In contrast, the unethical action does not consider the side effects of its own actions.[45] It is the distinctive characteristic of an evil will that it cannot endure its own effects.

From the insight that the character of the ethical is enduring the effects and side effects of one's own actions on other persons, the necessarily moral character of politics follows. Since the effects of political actions on the lives of other persons have the greatest impact of all possible effects of actions, the ability to endure the effects that one's own actions have on others, and the ability to anticipate these effects (i.e. their ethical consideration in the action) are most comprehensive and intense in the political decision.

The subjective concept of rationality permits thinking about levels of rationality that are distinguished by the degree of inclusion and internalization produced by economic, ethical, and religious rationality. The subjective concept of rationality understands rationality as the adaptation of actions to the situation, as we perceive it, according to the economic principle. The theory of subjective rationality is superior to the objective concept of rationality of economic man and utilitarianism, above all the variant of utilitarianism that takes essentially measurable and intersubjectively comparable utility as its starting point, because subjective rationality does not attempt to fill the formal, even metaphorical, concept of utility with a supposedly objective and substantive content. Subjective rationality instead takes into consideration the fact that the concept of utility can accept a great diversity of content in a maximization calculus or in other possible rationality calculi, such as "satisficing" (Herbert Simon). According to the theory of subjective rationality, "utility" can also exist in the "formal" content of ethical universalization or the content of the maximal coordination of being, as it does in religion. Both contents are, for those who make them their own, both "utile" and rational to follow.

---

[45] Cf. Robert Spaemann, "Nebenwirkungen als moralisches Problem," in Spaemann, *Kritik der politischen Utopie* (Stuttgart, 1977), pp. 167-82.

2.6.2. ETHICS AND ECONOMICS IN THE VIEW OF INTERPRETIVE SOCIOLOGY

Ludwig von Mises and Alfred Schütz have called economics the most highly-developed branch of interpretive sociology.[46] The principle of interpretive sociology is to understand action by fitting a subjective context of meaning into an objective context of meaning.[47] One of the central objective contexts of meaning in society is that of the economy. The definition of the social context of meaning and the definition of behavioral situations and expectations are clearer in the economy than in other cultural spheres. The ascertainment of success is also easier in the economy than in other cultural spheres, due to the calculability and monetary calculation of the price system. On the basis of the mostly-correct presumption that economic, locally-maximizing rationality characterizes the pursuit of goals by individuals, economic action is clearer and easier to "interpret" than other social action. The statement that economics is the most highly-developed branch of interpretive sociology is supported by the fact that the interpretive social science of the most quantifiable and calculable cultural sphere or partial system of society, the economy, must also be the most calculable and clearest part of social science. We understand rational, economically self-interested behavior and its coordination with other self-interested behavior better than all other behavior – better than, for example, action that is more diffuse in its rationality, its means-ends relationships, and is not oriented toward instrumental rationality and monetary calculation according to market success, but seeks instead to realize non-formal, substantive goals.

Nevertheless, an "interpretive" access from interpretative sociology to ethics is also possible. Ethics appears to interpretive sociology and, if we consider economics to be one of its sub-disciplines, also to "interpretive economics" as one kind of rational action, one that interprets the subjective and objective contexts of meaning more comprehensively and grasps the action-situation and self-interest of the individual more widely than economic rationality. It extends the subjective context of meaning by expanding the limits of the self to global maximization and inserts this subjective, ethical context of meaning into the objective context of meaning of the maximum of compossible value-realization, as it is based on ontology. Interpretive economics, which comprises the non-normative part of ethical economy, and interpretive sociology are able to grasp ethical rationality as the rationality of an expanded self that maximizes a more comprehensive goal function. From the perspective of interpretive sociology, ethical rationality is the fitting and subsuming of a subjective context of meaning into

---

[46] Mises, "Soziologie und Geschichte," p. 467, and Schütz, *The Phenomenology of the Social World*, trans. George Walsh and Frederick Lehnert (Evanston, 1967), § 49, pp. 243-48.

[47] Schütz, *The Phenomenology of the Social World*, § 49, p. 241.

an objective context of meaning, whereby both the subjective and the objective meaning contexts are more comprehensive in the case of ethical rationality than in the case of economic rationality.

There is, of course, one place in which economics transcends interpretive sociology, namely, where the economic goes beyond the social world and extends to natural economics and the discussion of human persons and of economic cooperation with nature. Economics, when understood as the economics of nature, touches ontology and transcends the social and cultural sciences, the interpretive sciences of the "meaningful construction of the social world" (Schütz), because it, like ontology, must see complete reality as a unity of nature and culture. An ontologically comprehending theory of economics comprehends the world as a limited whole and a unity, in which limited means must be employed economically for human *and* natural goals. Bio-economics[48] and ecology point out the ontological dimension of the economy, which goes beyond social economics. In a world of finite resources, in which many species – not only the human species – compete for the resources of the earth, economics and ethics have not only a social function, but also a bio-economic-ecological function. They must ensure the maximization of value-realization in the *total economy* of the earth, not just in social economics. The expansion of human economics into bio-economics makes the environmental ethics of the businessperson a necessary addition to a theory of economic ethics that is directed first of all and above all toward human economics.

2.7. Formality and Materiality

Making economic coordination possible is the central function of the price system. The knowledge and the analysis of economic systems of coordination, and especially of the price system, are the main subjects of economic theory and social economics. Increasing economic-social coordination and unification is one of the functions of ethics. Formal ethics is the coordination of free, market coordination. The "super-assurance game" of religion is the coordination of ethical coordination. The iterations of coordinations in ethical economy, which understands the relationships among economics, ethics, and religion as the coordination of coordination, raises the question whether economics and ethics can be completely described as ways of coordination and whether the arguments of economic and ethical rationality can be based on the formal concepts of coordination alone. Even if the central roles of the universalization principle in ethics and the price system in economics are granted, the question still remains wheth-

[48] On the problem of bio-economy – socio-biology, see Koslowski, *Evolution und Gesellschaft* (Tübingen, 1984).

er coordination, the central concept of market economics, and the coordination of coordination (i.e. universalization), the determining principle of the ethical will, are sufficient.

Is the human will described sufficiently and comprehended fully in ethics, if its ethical side, its existence as practical reason, is defined only as obedience to the law and the agreement of maxims with the categorical imperative, thus with its content as an ethical will always remaining formal? Is it an appropriate theory of ethics, if all other substantive reasons of the determination of the will are, as with Kant, classified as belonging to the non-ethical domain of bondage and heteronomy of the will? Or must not substantive reasons of the determination of the will and the substantive value-qualities of the goods strived for also be acknowledged in their significance for ethical formation and the cultivation of desiring and striving?

Is it instead acceptable in economics to leave all human value viewpoints and all substantive value-qualities of economic goods (i.e. the substantive and value-based determinants of subjective demand) solely to the arbitrariness of preferences and their ethical-economic non-questionableness and to insert them into the black box of revealed preferences, as is the case with revealed preference theory?

Formal ethics and the classical liberal theory of markets and prices agree concerning the ideal of coordination. Just as Kantian ethics' pure ideal of coordination acknowledges only the formality of the principle of universalization as a basis of the determination of the moral will and as the principle of ethics, and refers all substantive determinants of the will to the extra-ethical field of sensibility, economics excludes all viewpoints of substantive values and goods and the problem of the formation of individual preferences from economic theory and assigns the formation of preferences to the extra-economic field of mere subjectivity. For the theory of a pure market economy or catallactic, only revealed preferences, the subjective acts of choice that actually become effective in demand, are of significance. For formal ethics, only the universality of the maxim is significant. Both market theory and formal ethics banish substantive considerations of the formation of preferences from economics and ethics.

From the perspective of ethical economy, *three objections* can be raised against the formalism that demands exclusiveness and the sole validity of the coordination principle in economics and ethics:

First, in the economy, as in all other spheres of action and culture, a non-formal, substantive ethic, a theory of the good and of virtue, is indispensable.

Second, the start-up conditions, the conditions of maintaining, and the end-state conditions of the formal coordination of economics and ethics must be considered in economic ethics and their efficiency, justifiability, *and* justice must be examined, because the problem of justice is imperative and cannot be completely converted into a formal problem of coordination.

Third, although the mere formal coordination of coordination, understood as the ultimate purpose of the social order and of the individual will, requiring affirmation by the individual person, is not a vicious circle, it is nevertheless underdetermined and inadequate. The ethical content of the social order and the economy cannot be merely coordination and the ethical goal of the individual cannot be merely the formality of universalizability. The question of the finality of formal ethics and the meaning of social coordination cannot be answered by maximal coordination. The purpose of social coordination is directed not merely toward coordination. *The purpose of economic-social coordination is to ensure that the non-formal, substantive value-qualities and higher-order goods of human culture are developed* and that the growth of the inner person is made possible.[49]

A theory of non-formal, substantive ethics and an ethical-economic theory of the good are indispensable to ethical economy and the sphere of the economy, because we will not only the universality of the law or the ability of maxims and actions to be coordinated, but also at the same time specific goods and substantive qualities of values and goods. Economic ethics or ethical economy can restrict itself to the universalizable form of the rule and universal following of the rule no more than general ethics can. Ethics and ethical economy must instead also investigate the question of the content of the will, and lead and form the striving of the human person and the individual's rational and emotional perception of values. Ethical economy or economic ethics is also substantive ethics. As a theory of the goods and the virtues of economic behavior, it completes formal, deontological ethics and its ideal of universalization and coordination with a theory of goods and value-qualities.

---

[49] The first objection will be presented in Chapter 3, the second in Chapters 8 and 9, and the third in Chapters 4 and 6.

CHAPTER 3

ECONOMICS AND ETHICS II

Substantive Ethics

The rationality of formal ethics and economics follows two principles: the individual maximization of the attainment of subjectively-defined goals and the coordination of maximization. Coordination takes place as ethical coordination within the decision-maker by means of universalization, and as economic coordination externally by the decision-maker and the price system. The formation of preferences is directed toward universalization; the economic coordination of preferences is directed toward the ability of persons to live together. In the formal ethics of rules, as in the economic coordination of the price system, the content of the *ethical* will is formed by rules. Can the *ethical* side of the determination of the will, which should be achieved by ethics, consist only in the formal principle of universalization? If ethics is determined only by the categorical imperative, is it not underdetermined, because it should not merely clarify the question of how I can best achieve what I already intend here and now – as economics does – and because it should not merely answer the question of what I should do – as Kantian ethics does? Ethics must instead also provide an answer to the question of what I should or can *desire*, if I have become conscious of my will by taking distance and expanding the perspective of my self and the situation in which I stand. Ethics must seek to explain what a successful life is on the whole, not merely which actions are universalizable. Ethics serves to answer the question of what I actually do and can desire. It is not only a theory of duty, following rules, but also just as much a theory of the formation of the will, and a development, therefore, not only of an order of obligations, but also of an order of desires and aspirations.

Kant's formal ethics is deontological. The form of the will should be examined for its agreement with an absolute obligation, the categorical imperative, and should be brought into agreement with it. The mainstream of ethics, however, since its founding as in independent discipline by Aristotle, has been teleological. The aspiration of the human person, in whom elements of will, habit, conduct, and inclination unite, the *orexis* of Aristotle, should be joined to the good, and to the good life.

The idea that ethics is related not only to the will and the rules of obligation, but also just as much to the aspiration and the content of the good aspired to and desired, must go beside the idea of the coordination of formal, deontological ethics and market economics. The desires and aspirations of the human person have ethically as their object not merely the ability to coordinate and universalize any subjectively maxims. The acting person must instead be in a position to evaluate comprehensively (i.e. ethically, aesthetically, and economically), not merely ethically *or* economically. The question "What should and can I will?" is prior to the question "What should and may I do?" and is not to be replaced by the latter. In order to be able to pose to the will the deontological question whether its maxim can be a principle of universal legislation, I must first know what I actually will, to which goals and goods I aspire. Only if I have become conscious of the content of my aspirations can I examine the maxim of the action that is directed toward the realization of these goods for its ability to be coordinated with other aspirations.

3.1. Ethical and Economic Theories of Goods

From the perspective of a complete theory of ethics, one that encompasses *both* the formal ethics of rules *and* the substantive ethics of goods and values, the content of willing is of ethical significance. The desires and aspirations must be capable of choosing between goods and value-qualities, not only economically, but also ethically and aesthetically. The economic concept of the good is, first of all, no less formal than the rules of economic coordination. According to Richard Strigl, a good is defined by opening alternative opportunities for utility.[1] An alternative opportunity for utility becomes a good or a value for a person who has been determined in some particular way and who discovers and recognizes it for himself. If alternative opportunities for utility are made into goods or values by the subject alone, that which makes something an economic good depends upon the subject's assessment. For economics, the question of the good stops at this point. What it is within the subject that makes a utility opportunity into such a thing is, for economics, a black box, which is not to be questioned further, but is instead to be taken for granted. According to revealed preference theory economics, whose function is only to coordinate preferences, does not need to be interested in the interiority of preference formation.

For ethics, however, the formation of preferences and the development of the perception of value-qualities and opportunities to increase utility is precisely the true function. The good of economics may consist in opening alternative opportunities for utility. But if this good enters into ethics, which seeks to illuminate the process of preference formation and to expand the ability to perceive opportunities for utility in order to pre-coordinate the social coordination of the preferences of economics, it cannot be defined again by alternative opportunities for utility, without leading to an infinite regress. Economics coordinates the use of

[1] Cited by Hans Albert, *Marktsoziologie und Entscheidungslogik* (Neuwied, 1967), p. 42.

goods whose utility opportunities are seen as arbitrary and subjective, whose character as goods follows from subjective preferences. Ethics, as the illumination and coordination of these preferences, cannot, with the determination of the good and preferences for the good, give again as the answer to the question of what the good should be and for what the alternative utility-possibilities should be good: "for alternative utility opportunities." At some point the definition of good as "good for something else" must arrive at the place where the good itself is reached.

3.1.1. THE THEORY OF THE HIGHEST GOOD

In the tradition of ethics one can distinguish two types of theories that go beyond the closed circle of the concept of economic goods as alternative opportunities for utility to achieve a substantial concept of the goods or good in itself. The first type is described by the theory of the highest good, in which the good in itself, which is not merely good for something else, is grasped as the highest good. The other type of theory of the good is represented by substantive value ethics, which attempts to develop ultimate kinds of goods and values, or good- and value-qualities, which cannot be traced back further to other means of assessment and utility.

According to the tradition of the ethics of the highest good, all individual goods are related to a final and highest good. The individual goods receive their character of the good from their relation to and their beneficence for the highest good. In this tradition, goods are not defined by alternative opportunities for utility, which are once again good for other utility opportunities, but instead by their contribution to the attainment of the highest good. This highest good can be determined, as with eudaemonism, as individual happiness (*eudaimonia*) or, as in Platonism, as the idea (or form) of the good.

With eudaemonistic ethics, all goods become means to the attainment of the highest good. Its weakness is that it must instrumentalize all goods and value-qualities other than happiness itself, and that it is not able to accomplish the concrete mediation between the final cause of the highest good and the subordinate goods – the answer to the question of how one must utilize all interim goods for the highest good. Eudaemonistic ethics contradicts the feeling of the self-value character of goods and actions and the desire for the concretization of action strategies for the highest good. In addition, eudaemonism has difficulty accomplishing the social-ethical mediation between the individual's pursuit of happiness and everyone else's pursuit of happiness. The coordination of everyone's individual pursuit of happiness is not solved satisfactorily in eudaemonistic ethics. It is solipsistic. The modern problem of unifying the pursuit of happiness of independent beings, the ability to coordinate the pursuit of happiness of all human persons, remains substantively underdetermined.

The Platonic theory of the highest good as the idea of the good is the second approach of a theory of the highest good, and avoids the danger of eudaemonistic solipsism. Platonic ethics defines the good as that which allots the character of goodness to and is the cause of all individual goods. The idea of the good is the cause of all goods and the cause of their recognizability as goods. The individual good is, for Plato, the realization of the idea of the individual good or thing. Because the realization of the idea of a being is its purpose and is the good for it and good in itself, but its idea in the idea of the ideas, the idea of the good, shares and receives its idea and goodness from it, the realization of the idea of the individual is both the purpose in itself and a partner in the highest good. The good is participation in the realization of the ideas according to the order of the idea of the good. In the Platonic theory of the good, relatedness to the highest good and the value of the individual good are united in a unique way. In contrast to the eudaemonistic theory of the highest good, neither is the individual good merely instrumentalized for the highest good nor do the individual goods fall apart without relationship to one another. The idea of a being as the individual good represents, instead, both the highest good and itself. The individual good is the idea of itself and shares in the highest good, the idea of the good. The Platonic ethical theory is the most highly developed theory of the ethics of the good and of the highest good, because it is equally capable of conceiving the orientation of goods toward the highest good and of conceiving the independent value and self-worth of the individual being as the realization of its idea that participates in the good.

The Aristotelian, eudaemonistic theory of the highest good has the advantage, relative to the ethics of universalization, of subsuming goods under an ultimate good and final cause. The Platonic theory of the highest good as the idea of the good has the additional advantage, relative to eudaemonism, that it is able to bring the individual good into an order of the good and is able to determine it relationally by its relation to the highest good, the idea of the good, and by sharing in it. The substantive quality of the good itself, that which makes the individual good the good for me, however, also threatens to become lost in the relation to others with the theory of the highest good, as with the economic concept of value. The substantiality of the good and the qualities of goods are in danger of being lost beside the relational determination of the means for and the sharing in the highest good. The qualitative, material objective of the will and the quality of that which becomes the object of the will is, of course, philosophically problematic in ethics, as with all recognitions of qualities, since only relationships appear to provide universality, unambiguous nameability, and therefore mental certainty, whereas the knowledge of qualities in themselves is considered to be fluctuating and subjective. Max Scheler's substantive ethics of values attempts to accomplish precisely this difficult thinking of the qualities of the good and the recognition of the substantive nature of value-qualities.

3.1.2. SCHELER'S SUBSTANTIVE ETHICS OF VALUES

Max Scheler's substantive ethics of values (*materiale Wertethik*) is an approach to ethics that seeks to go beyond both the relationality of the ethical theory of the highest good and the economic theory of goods and values of the good as alternative opportunities for utility, to those goods that are not goods for the highest good and to those value-qualities that are not only of value for other uses, thus value in exchange or value in use for alternative utility opportunities. The substantive ethics of values stops the external relatedness and iteration of the economic category of values, in which a value is always valuable only for something else, and seeks to define values as qualities in themselves, as a priori value-qualities or value-modalities. Scheler's approach helps us to recognize that something other than the mere aspiration for utility opportunities is expressed in the aspiration for goods. In the striving for genuine goods, the aspiration to experience goods as such and the will to realize good-qualities in and for themselves is shown. No one maximizes utility for the sake of utility, because no one wants to have utility. One wants to have something definite, which can be understood as utility, in common with everything else one wants, only in an extremely remote abstraction. To call the pursuit of all of the good-qualities that someone wants the "maximization of utility" is a metaphorical way of speaking. Utility stands for everything that the acting person actually wants.

The substantive ethics of values seeks to identify that which is strived for as itself in its substantive quality and not in its formal abstraction as utility or the universality of a maxim. According to Scheler, the value-qualities of goods can be distinguished according to the fundamental value modalities of the pleasant, the useful, the noble, and the holy, where this sequence represents a ranking of values from the lowest value of pleasure to the highest of holiness.[2] The value-qualities define what is aspired to in the goods and what constitutes the good of the goods. They do not represent alternative utility- or utilization-viewpoints, but instead the a priori qualities of the good itself, which form the ultimate goals of willing and aspiring and between which (rather than between alternative opportunities for utility) choice acts of preference take place. To classify a good as more valuable than others is to assess the others as lower and to weigh their realization or their existence as less important. The other goods and values are determined to be less valuable than the chosen value and are placed below it. To emphasize the value of the noble and to make the noble the goal of one's own actions and the standard of one's evaluation of a good is to place the pleasant and the useful below the noble.

[2] Cf. Max Scheler, *Der Formalismus in der Ethik und die materiale Wertethik*, 6th Ed. (Bern. 1980), pp. 122-26, 493-94, 111.

According to Scheler, however, the higher value does not attain its higher rank from the preference actions of the human person, from the "preference" for the "noble" opportunity for utility, but instead from the intrinsic characteristic of the value itself. The value is not created by the subjectivity of the human person; the value-quality exists and is preferred and actualized by the subjectivity of the person. The higher value reveals its greater degree of value, according to Scheler, by not using itself up, like substantive values, by not wearing out, like sensory values, and by not miscalculating, like useful values. If, going beyond Scheler, one uses the conceptualization of the economic theory of public goods, the phenomenon of the higher degree of value can also be expressed thus: The higher value reveals its higher rank and superiority in being a public good in a greater measure and showing a higher degree of publicness. The higher value carries the stigma of freedom, and all the more, the higher its value rank. Value-characteristics and virtues, such as friendship, kindness, unselfishness, justice, courage, love, and faith, cannot be compelled or brought about by rules. Similarly, the highest intellectual values and goods, such as those of art, science, and religion, cannot be produced and reproduced in the strict sense. They are, instead, the work of free devotion and "being affected," which are motivated by the higher value rank. It follows from their higher value-quality relative to mere material goods that all goods bearing higher value-qualities are perceived as enduring and lead to deeper fulfillment of meaning and satisfaction and to a lesser degree of exclusion of others than the material goods of the useful and the pleasant. They are "more open" and more inclusive in character than goods of lower value-quality.

The ability to perceive and experience higher value-qualities requires, however, a corresponding *experience* of the forms of the freedom of human potential, which is at its core an ethical experience and acquisition and not merely a decision of the will for a universalizable maxim. The ability to experience the higher value does not arise on its own, but instead requires practice or exercise of a kind that imparts itself in the higher value, requires "asceticism" (i.e. in the original meaning of the word "exercise"). When this exercise is required in the ability to experience the higher value, it develops its own action-guiding gravitational force: "Some things allure us by their own force, and attract us by their own worth."[3] By the power of its nature, the higher value wins us; by its dignity, it pulls us into its spell. It is the higher value, according to Scheler,[4] that assigns to the lower the position appropriate to it, thereby in this sense giving

---

[3] Marcus Tullius Cicero, *De Invent. Rhet.* II, 52, as cited by Thomas Aquinas, *Summa Theologiae*, II-II, q. 145, a. 1.

[4] Scheler, *Der Formalismus in der Ethik und die materiale Wertethik*, pp. 114-16.

foundation to it and in the process determining the order of preference and priority in the concrete situation.[5]

3.2. Experiencing Values and Understanding Cultural Meaning

Scheler's *rank*-ordering of the values shows that his theory is an ethical theory. It is not merely a theory of understanding value-qualities, but also one of arranging them in order of preference. The need to develop the ability to perceive and understand and the need for the acting person to express his or her opinion concerning goods and value-qualities point out the close relationship between ethics, aesthetics, and cultural philosophy. The experience of value-qualities is related to the development of the ability to experience, to express oneself, and to understand. Eduard Spranger's theory of understanding is helpful here. Wilhelm Dilthey defines understanding as circulation of the experience of the artist, of the expression of his experience in art, and the reexperience of the experience of the artist by the observer.[6] This circulation of the understanding demonstrates the proximity of substantive ethics and culture, of understanding values and expressions of culture and art. Stating one's opinion is, according to Spranger, the catchword of the intellectual world: the ability to accept and to reject.[7] Expressing one's opinion is also a key concept in the substantive ethics of values: It is impossible to perceive the value-qualities of the higher vital and intellectual values without expressing one's opinion.

The economy, along with science and art, is one of the three main provinces of culture. These provinces of culture are distinguished by the different intentions, peculiar to each of them, of the actions that build them up. In the three cultural spheres – the economy, science, and art – the acts or actions of persons are directed in specific intentions toward particular goods and value-qualities. They are directed toward the economic, theoretical, or aesthetic value that corresponds in the sphere of the things to the consumption, knowledge, and artistic goods. To be able to state one's opinion about the content of the economy, science, and art meaningfully is an essential achievement in carrying out the intel-

---

[5] Cf. Wilhelm Korff, "Ethische Entscheidungskonflikte," in *Handbuch der christlichen Ethik* (Freiburg and Gütersloh, 1982), Vol. III, p. 79.

[6] Wilhelm Dilthey, *Der Aufbau der geschichtlichen Welt in den Geisteswissenschaften* (Frankfurt, 1981), pp. 235 ff. See also Eduard Spranger, "Wilhelm Dilthey," in Spranger, *Vom pädagogischen Genius* (Heidelberg, 1965), pp. 209-10.

[7] Eduard Spranger, "Vom Wesen des Geistigen," in *Gesammelte Schriften*, ed. Hans Walter Bähr (Tübingen, 1980), Vol. VI, p. 307. Earlier, Heinrich Rickert, *Science and History*, trans. George Reisman (Princeton, 1962), p. 65: "The science of psychology aspires to *explain* the nature of psychical existence by seeking to discover its general laws or any other general concepts. But the 'psychological' knowledge of mental life that we seek to acquire in the study of history consists in *re-experiencing* it in its individual course."

lectual life.[8] Teaching others how to attain this ability is the function of training and education. Training takes place in the presentation of meaning to inner learning. Education takes place in the formation of one's own nature, which takes place in meaning-understanding, value-experiencing, self-reflecting, and self-deciding.

The theory of the meaning-understanding of the intellectual and cultural sciences is closely related to the theory of the substantive ethics of values, understood as the theory of the preference of value-qualities. Together, they show that the understanding and preference of goods and training for the perception of value-qualities that goods possess are prior to the process of external and internal coordination. The substantive ethics of values and the theory of meaning-understanding are prior to both economics, which is oriented toward the coordination of preferences, and formal ethics, which seeks to achieve the internal formation of preferences according to the law of their ability to be coordinated with other preferences. First, when value-qualities are perceived and experienced, preferences can be formed. Then, in a second step, these preferences can be coordinated by the principle of universalization. The substantive ethics of values, as a theory of teleological ethics, intersects with the economic theory of the goods of the useful in the same way as with the aesthetic theory of the goods of the beautiful. In the theory of the good, or substantive ethics, the interpretation of economic, ethical, and aesthetic meaning-understanding, value-experiencing, and decision-making prevails. The alternative utility opportunities of the economic good are not already here in themselves by the physical existence of the good. Their superiority to the utility opportunities of the lower values of the pleasant and the useful must first be experienced, understood, and realized by the opinion-expressing subject.

In understanding the meaning and experiencing the value of the substantive value-qualities of a good, mutual effects between experiences and value-convictions exist, between the actual existence of a good and its evaluation. These mutual effects sublate the familiar distinction of "is" and "ought." Experiences of things have an effect on the value experience; the ability to judge and experience value-qualities reacts on the experience of things or economic goods. The alternative utility opportunities of a good are not given, but instead depend on the ability of the user to utilize them, on his or her ability to perceive and experience, on the formation of his or her receptivity for substantive value-qualities.

The economic value of a good is not independent of its aesthetic, ethical, and cultural value. Understanding an economic good and using it efficiently require (if it is more than a trivial, consumer good) that the user has at his or her disposal the ability to experience and assess, in order to understand the higher, substantive value-qualities and to use them ethically, aesthetically, and economi-

[8] Cf. Spranger, "Vom Wesen des Geistigen," p. 311.

cally. The qualities of the good must be experienced, expressed, and imparted to the addressee, the consumer. Economic activity has in common with artistic activity the circulation of the experience and its expression by the producer and the reexperience and understanding by the recipient. Above and beyond the demands that confront the artist, the economic producer must also ensure that the circulation of understanding between the producer's experience and expression of the experience and the consumer/recipient's after-effect and understanding of the expression also actually ensures, by appropriate forms of marketing, that the consumer/recipient "understands" the producer. In his or her experience and expressions of the qualities of a good, the economic producer must consider the recipient in the production process to a greater degree than the artistic and the scientific producer.

3.3. Side Effects between Experiences and Value-Convictions, "Is" and "Ought"

The substantive ethics of values shows that there exists no complete separation between experiences and value-convictions in the area of the higher, intellectual and vital values and goods and, therefore, that also no strict separation between formal and substantive principles of ethics is possible. The content of the maxim that should become the universal principle is already characterized by substantive value-qualities in its being experienced and understood. The ability to experience determines the experiences and actions, as the experiences and the experience of the effects of one's own actions on others and the environment likewise react on the acting person's ethical and aesthetic ability to experience and his or her value-convictions. A complete separation of "is" and "ought," of economics, on one hand, and ethics and aesthetics, on the other, is impossible.

The physical side effects of our actions can change our value-convictions. We change our value-convictions and normative statements on the basis of statements of fact about the side effects of our actions and about the effects of those value-convictions that we previously had when the experience of the consequences of our values elicits serious value-arguments *and* fact-arguments for a change of our value-convictions. The side effects of our actions and our lifestyles on ourselves and the reality about us change our previous value-convictions, as an insistence on one's own value-convictions is likewise ethically required, if the reality of our value-convictions, and not our ethical stance of reality must be adapted.

The acting person acts into an external world, one whose factors are subject to self-legislation. It is true of our goal-directed actions that what is actually attained never completely agrees with our previous conceptions of our success. The discrepancy between willing and accomplishing is no mere psychological phenomenon, but a phenomenon at the boundary between the way of the world and the process of perceiving the way of the world. The gap between will and accomplishment is a realization and statement about events with the clash between the subject and the objective course of the world, between imaginations, establishments of goals, and assessments of the way of the world and its actual course.[9]

All unintended side effects have in common the fact that they subsequently react in a correcting manner on the will, its emotional, evaluative, and objective elements, and on the consciousness of the intending and acting subject. What Max Weber held to be impossible, that the value-attitude is reconstructed by recognition of that in the intellectual world which follows from the action in accordance with the predetermined value-attitude, takes place with the side effects of actions and the discrepancy between will and accomplishment.[10] It is impossible that value-convictions change only as a result of changes within the sphere of values, because the sphere of values is directed toward the sphere of facts. It must be possible for side effects to change value convictions, because otherwise the consequence would be a complete solipsism, a window-less monadism of the individual sphere of value. The most important case of a correction of one's own goal-setting and value-acting as a result of the experience of the success of one's own actions is that of a change of convictions and of the standards of value elicited by enduring the effects of one's own actions. The genuine revolutions of the inner person are those that are provoked by the reaction of one's own action on the complete attitude of the person.[11] The phenomenon of the transformation of the ego and its values by facts and experiences sublates the supposedly clear separation of "is" and "ought" statements. Arguments about facts and values, about economic and ethical points of view, are not completely separable, but are instead interdependent and have side effects on one another. Merely understanding existing facts and contexts of culture and social institutions, without guiding and tacit values, is already impossible. Therefore, economic considerations can also influence changes of attitude, and changes in attitude can change economic arguments. The two strands of reflection do not run independently of one another, but beside one another in parallel. For example, on the basis of cost considerations (i.e. economic side effects), in public health service, certain procedures can be excluded from general use and the value of "equal treatment" can be restricted for *economic* reasons, when the efficiency of measures is low and the social total return does not increase in proportion to increasing universalization of the procedures. On the other hand, in questions of

---

[9] Cf. Wilhelm Wundt, *System der Philosophie* (Leipzig, 1889), Vol. I, p. 337.

[10] Cf. Spranger, *Das Gesetz der ungewollten Nebenwirkungen in der Erziehung*, 6th Ed. (Heidelberg, 1960), p. 101. See also Otto Bollnow, *Existenzphilosophie und Pädagogik*, 5th Ed. (Stuttgart, 1977), pp. 105 ff.

[11] Cf. Spranger, *Ibid.*, pp. 94-95.

fundamental life interests and health, cost viewpoints in medical care must be set aside by value-convictions as irrelevant and unethical.

Ethics, understood in the comprehensive sense, cannot accept an opposition of conviction (morality) and success orientation (economics), the world of facts and the world of values. Success and side effects are just as much to be observed and accepted in the mind as the consequences become through evaluation what they are: not mere events, but effects of actions. The decision-maker must design and assess the value of his or her strategies, the possible environmental events, and the consequences of his or her actions *ex ante* from preference rules or perspectives, from value points of view. Values are not objective constructions, but perspectives, perceptions of preferences.

A person's value perspectives form the foundation for describing the influence that expectations and imaginations of the future have on her present choice acts. Social values describe how a social group wants the future to influence a person's choice acts. Ethical values are values that can be universalized and agreed with, that the individual makes her own as evaluating the future in her choice act, and about which rational discourse is possible. The acting person selects her strategies from the "possible worlds" that her actions will bring about, according to preferential points of view. Acts of choice are not choices between actual states of the world or events, but between ideas of states of the world. The acting person does not choose between acts, but between imaginations and ideas of acts.[12] Since acts of choice take place in the sphere of representation and the imagination, just as they do in the world of actual events, reality and the representation of reality, "is" and "ought" statements, presuppose one another. That the acting person chooses between possible worlds is true of all choice acts of greater range, for economic, ethical, and political choice acts. The choosing person imagines *ex ante* possible worlds, whose realizations are evaluated *ex post* by herself and others according to success *and* action-guiding motives and values.

3.4. Substantive Value-Qualities and Degrees of the Publicness of Goods

The rationality of formal ethics and economics follows the logic of maximization and the coordination of maximization. The content of the maximandum that the individual establishes for his rational actions is, for formal ethics and economics, not relevant. Only the form of the maximization's ability to exist with other maximizations is of ethical and economic significance. For formal ethics and economics, it is also not significant whether the content and the substantive value-quality of the goods have ethical and social-economic side effects on the

---

[12] Cf. G. L. S. Shackle, *Imagination and the Nature of Choice* (Edinburgh, 1979), pp. 2 ff.

form of coordination and the social unification of individuals beyond market exchange. Economic theory recognizes only one case in which the substantive content of goods is significant for socio-economic coordination, the case of the public good. The public good brings about, by its substantive characteristics, a failure of market coordination. Its "publicness" is its specific substantive value-quality. According to the economic theory of public goods, the substantive characteristics of a good, not the utility opportunities subjectively related to it, determine whether a good is private or public (i.e. whether exclusion or rivalry of consumption prevails when it is consumed) and, therefore, whether it permits market coordination or makes it impossible, or at least more difficult. The non-applicability of the exclusion principle implies that non-paying consumers cannot be excluded from consumption of the good. The non-competition of consumption implies that the consumption of one good does not compete with the consumption of the other, that the consumption of one does not reduce that of the other. An example of a public good, in this sense, is the good of national defence, from which non-payers cannot be excluded and with which, therefore, market coordination is impossible.[13]

In the theory of market failure, a dichotomy between private and public goods is generally observed, which does not do justice to the actual continuum from completely private to completely public goods. The theory of merit goods is not a counter-example, because it sees merit goods as private goods that are produced publicly.[14]

The problem of public goods points to the economic relevance of substantive theories of goods and values, because the substantive characteristics of goods, their "publicness," changes the way in which they are economically coordinated. The substantive theory of goods exerts a direct effect here on economic theory, the goods-quality on the manner of the coordination of goods. It can be seen at this point not only that the substantive theory of goods is economically and ethically relevant in the dichotomy of "public" and "private" goods, but also that wide-ranging conclusions for the relationship of the substantive ethics of goods and values and economic coordination can be drawn from this phenomenon. Substantive goods-qualities and, therefore, the substantive ethics of values exert an influence not only indirectly as ethics on economic coordination in the way that substantive ethics – like the formal, deontological ethics as pre-coordination of preferences – influences economic coordination, but in the way that goods-qualities *directly* change economic ways of coordination. Value-qualities exert a direct influence on the form of economic coordination, because the high-

[13] On the theory of "public goods," see Richard A. Musgrave and Peggy B. Musgrave, *Public Finance in Theory and Practice*, 2nd Ed. (Englewood Cliffs, N. J, 1976), pp. 49 ff.

[14] An example of a merit good is free, public education, which is produced publicly, but whose goods are appropriated privately.

er rank of value-modalities that are attached to a good not only elicits a perception of higher value-qualities with the user of the good they are attached to, but also changes the manner of use and the scarcity relationship for goods on the whole. The higher value is less competitive and exclusive in consumption than the lower value. It proves its higher rank by not being competitive in consumption. The higher value reveals its higher rank in the fact that, in contrast to substantive values, it is not used up (in economic terms, does not demonstrate non-competitiveness of consumption), that in contrast to moral values, it does not wear out (is not subjected to diminishing marginal utility), and in contrast to the useful values, cannot miscalculate (does not permits clear exclusion). The higher value requires a different experience of use and coordination than does the lower value, because it is not used up, is not worn out, and does not miscalculate. Its economic characteristics of non-competition, constant marginal utility, and the impossibility of exclusion make a way of production determined purely by immediate self-interest and a purely private-economic way of coordination inefficient. The manner of market coordination must be appropriate to the nature of the higher value-qualities. Mere self-interest would lead to an underproduction of the higher value or public good, because of the inability to exclude non-paying consumers with non-modified price control.

It is of great importance, however, that just as the value-qualities range from the lowest to the highest value, the goods corresponding to them also range from private through intermediate to public goods. The highest value of the holy is the most public value, not in its ability to be perceived, but in its effect on the environment. With the higher value modalities, as the value level increases, their effects take on a growing public and collective character. Their ability to be communicated or to be perceived, on the contrary, decreases with increasing value level. With the higher values, the individual's perception of utility and actual public utility can diverge, if the formation and ability to experience are not so widely learned and spread among other people that they are able to perceive the public character of the highest values. Certain personal value-qualities or virtues, such as courage, kindness, justice, etc., and certain intellectual values and goods, such as art, science, and religion, are difficult to miscalculate, demonstrate less slowly diminishing marginal utility or lower wearing out than moral goods, and use themselves up, because their "consumption" competes with the consumption of others within a smaller range than those of material goods.

Intellectual goods, such as art and science, and personal virtues, such as kindness and courage, are neither completely public nor completely private, but instead demonstrate degrees of "publicness." They must be acquired privately by effort and education. Their benefit, however, goes beyond their private acquisition. They cause public side effects or spillovers, because they do not lose anything and are not worn out when they are used. A great work of art loses none of its value when millions of people look at it. The virtue of justice is not used up when it is called into action. The utility derived from reading a truly great book increases all the more, the more often it is read.

The virtues and intellectual goods are goods with a public character, or of a semi-public, semi-private nature. They are of significance economically in two different respects, and in increasing measure in the post-industrial and post-modern economy. With growing distribution, on one hand, semi-public goods change the relationship of resource-consuming to resource-conserving goods in economic output. On the other hand, they facilitate social coordination and cohesion, because they help to produce the public good or capital of the validity of the ethical rules and trust in their validity.

Intellectual goods, which are produced privately and acquired publicly, demonstrate the characteristics of higher values noted above: not using themselves up, not wearing out, and non-competitive consumption. At the same time, fewer natural, non-renewable resources are required for their production and consumption. Therefore, in a world of exhaustible resources, their production can be ensured for a longer time than those of material goods, because intellectual and cultural goods require smaller quantities of exhaustible resources. Their consumption, however, also involves lower costs, both lower consumption-induced additional costs of material goods, in order to facilitate consumption generally, and reduced quantities of the concerned consumption good, because the consumption of one does not drive out consumption of others. Cultural goods are not used up when they are consumed, although, of course, even with them, as with other public goods, a problem similar to that of the competition of consumption can arise: the problem of congestion.

Congestion in the use of a public good can lead to the necessity of exclusion mechanisms and rationing, which shift the public good's character in the direction of a semi-private and semi-competing good. Nevertheless, the shifting of preferences from competitive private goods to less-competitive public goods remains a crucial development-potential of the post-modern society in the transition from the commercial to the cultural society. In the transition (sketched more thoroughly below) from the commercial and consumer society to the cultural society, the theory of semi-public goods and substantive value-qualities receives its resource-economic foundation. The consumption of culture – in contrast to the consumption of material goods – demonstrates environmental-economic side effects. Culture is more conservative of resources than are material consumption or the leisure-consumption habits of certain sports, such as automobile racing, skiing, etc.

One can see in the fact that higher value-qualities and goods are not used up by being perceived and experienced not only that the "economic" characteristic of these goods is one of non-competitiveness, but also their potential for bringing about social cohesion. Higher value-qualities and the consumption of intellectual goods demonstrate not only the characteristic that their consumption does not lead to competition (i.e. that no side effect analogous to a quasi-externality of consumption arises), that their consumption by one person does not reduce the amount available for others. Higher value-qualities also demonstrate, going beyond non-competition of consumption, that use by one person and use by others could be regarded as indifferent, the *positive* side effect that as they are consumed, they do not bring about division, but cohesion of the "consumer." While the consumption of substantive, private goods and the realization of their value-qualities brings about social division, the perception and realization of higher value-qualities by the individual leads to cohesion with others who also perceive these value-qualities.

The semi-public goods of art and religion promote what the philosophy of German idealism called the "unification" (*Vereinigung*) of individuals. It promotes social cohesion and non-coerced unity.[15] The unification of persons in a society cannot happen merely by exchange and the price system, on one hand, and governmental central control, on the other. It must also – for cultural *and* economic reasons – arise from shared value-judgments and value-perceptions. Only the cultural commonality of value-judgments lets language and a common ethos be possible. And they are, in turn, presuppositions of the intensive economic exchange and market interaction of individuals. With the cultural unification of individuals, the economic unification and coordination and, with growing non-competition of consumption, the range of the quantity of goods available for the entire society also increases. Social coordination is not only economic coordination, but also just as much cultural and ethical coordination. Economic coordination is coordination not only of quantities and prices, but also of coordination goods-qualities and value-qualities. Growing unification through a growing share of semi-public goods and higher value-qualities in the quantity of goods and degree of value-realization for the entire economy increases the welfare and cultural level of the economy. It expands the limits of the economically-realizable maximum of value-realization.

---

[15] The phenomenon of cohesion and separation through the pursuit of different goods has already been seen by means of the example of Augustine. The genus of private (earthly) goods excludes others, according to him, since with the genus of the goods of this world is necessarily tied to "competition of consumption." Therefore, there will always be envy and strife in the state. It is otherwise, according to Augustine, with the good of the *civitas Dei*, of the love of God. Possession of it does not create strife, but community and unity: "Unlike material possessions, goodness is not diminished when it is shared, either momentarily or permanently, with others, but expands and, in fact, the more heartily each of the lovers of goodness enjoys the possession the more does goodness grow . . ., it is [a possession] that increases the more its possessor loves to share it" (*The City of God*, trans. G. G. Walsh and G. Monahan (Washington, 1952), Book XV, Chap. 5, p. 421). The *amor sui* creates strife and division, but the *amor Dei* creates community and unity, because no one can have possession of the love of God "who is unwilling to share it" *(Ibid.)*. The *amor Dei* has eminently political significance as the principle of reconciliation and political cohesion.

3.5. Ethics as Theory of Virtues

The unifying potential of the higher value-qualities and "more public" goods represents a public good and capital that flows from these goods and value-qualities, if they are realized by the human person. Unification is a characteristic of substantive value-qualities and goods, and the substantive ethics of value is the way to promote the perception of the value-qualities and the realization of their unifying potential. At the same time, an additional side effect with ethical and economic significance for the problem of assurance arises from the unifying potential of the substantive ethics of values and of the culture. The substantive ethics of values creates the motivations that are necessary for the rules of formal or deontological ethics to be followed and for economic failure, in the form of coordination failure, to be avoided. The virtues that flow from the substantive ethics of values and the higher value-qualities help to produce the public good and capital of rule-compliance and the assurance of the universality of ethical action. They strengthen the readiness to collaborate in the production of capital and the public good "universality of following ethical rules."

The substantive ethics of values and ethical-cultural formation increase the accessibility of value-qualities and the ability to perceive them. The habituation and development of the ability to evaluate higher value-qualities lead to attitudes, habit-formations, and dispositions for the perception of values. Together with the conscious affirmation of this formation of habits and the deliberate control of the intention and disposition toward the habituation of correct value judgments, there arises what has been called in philosophical tradition since Aristotle "virtue." Virtue is not a characteristic of the individual action, but of the attitude and state of character on which the action is based. It is the cause and result of virtuous action, a psychological state *(hexis)* acquired and strengthened by practice. Virtue arises from the mutual effects between attitude, action, and experience or endurance of the consequence of actions, which has been described above. The psychological state brings about a specific action; actions and experience react on the state. The two elements influence and shape one another. Virtue is the disposition to good action; good actions creates the disposition to virtue and correct state of character.[16]

Virtue, understood as a state of character and development of habits toward good actions and the perception of the higher value-qualities, creates the disposition for the performance of duty, compliance with the rules of formal ethics, and the realization of ever higher values. Virtue, motivation for action consistent with duty and for the higher value, is at the same time motivation for the

---

[16] Aristotle, *Nicomachean Ethics*, trans. Terence Irwin (Indianapolis, 1985), III, 8, 1114 b 27: "Certain actions produce [the virtues], and they cause us to do these same actions, expressing the virtues themselves."

nature of the particular subject matter in question and, therefore, is not to be separated from the economic-technical assessment of a good. Virtue creates the disposition for the objectivity of the life of the higher levels. It helps to realize the higher value-qualities of the person and the subject matter.

The development of dispositions toward the good is, in economic terms, the formation of the motivation to participate in the production of public goods. At the same time, the virtues, understood as habitual dispositions, are themselves already goods that are not purely private. The virtues of kindness and justice are value-qualities that are not used up when they are realized. When they become the property of other persons, they remain with those who possess them. They are useful both to the person who possesses them and to those around him. The person who exercises a virtue produces a semi-private, semi-public good, which benefits himself and others, but whose costs, in the form of the reduction of his own action and the proximity of the desires, accrue to him. Virtue, understood as a disposition, as distinguished from duty, understood as urging and strict rule, demonstrates by the ethical law of the preference that actions from virtue, as distinguished from actions performed merely out of duty, contain the element of inclination to the good and not merely of the duty to rule-compliance.

The costs of restricting immediate self-interest by virtue are reduced, relative to the costs of action in accordance with duty, by gradual habituation and the formation of dispositions to the good. Virtue leads out from the dichotomy between the public good of rule-compliance and the private good of being able to do whatever one pleases. The virtues bring about a shaping of the will and of actions into habits, states of character, and motives that are "tuned" to the realization of the good or dutiful, as is required by deontological ethics. A consequence of the restriction of natural aspiration and disposition by the virtues is that the restriction of the will by duty to action conforming to rules in the concrete, individual case fails less drastically than in the case of a clash of the merely dutiful with the merely natural desires. The virtuous habit has already made, by inclination, part of the journey that duty demands of the acting person. The development of the virtues thus reduces the private, individual costs of dutiful ethical action, or at least stretches these costs over a longer period of time of adjusting to the demands of the dutiful or the virtuous. The investment in ethical conduct is spread out over a longer period of time, so that the demand of ethical renunciation is less painful in individual cases. By seeking to accomplish the reconciliation of duty and inclination, universal interest and self-interest, virtue stands between the completely public good of obeying the ethical rule out of duty (i.e. from mere observance of the law, as required by the categorical imperative) and the completely private good of the satisfaction of inclinations.

3.5.1. THE INTERCHANGEABILITY OF MEANS AND ENDS AND THE ECONOMICS OF SUBLIMATION

The development of the virtues takes advantage of a positive externality or side effect that exists between the formation and the realization of preferences, between setting and pursuing goals. The virtuous person attempts to desire to do what she should do. She aspires to a situation in which she does what duty requires, not only out of duty, but also out of inclination. One way to make herself inclined to do her duty is to make the fulfillment of duty a side effect of something else that she does out of inclination. An example of a positive externality between something done out of duty and something done out of inclination is the conversion of the goal in accordance with duty into the side effect of an action that is performed out of inclination. Phenomena of forming virtue and sublimation apply the logic of ends, means, and side effects to the field of the obligatory and the forbidden. They redirect the inclinations and dispositions from their original goal in such a way that the inclinations become means to other goals, by the pursuit of which the attainment of the original goal of the inclination is taken care of as a side effect of the fact that it is no longer used as a means. Duty and inclination lose their mutually-restrictive relationship when the inclination becomes through the virtue the means and the disposition for the dutiful.

The relationship between duty and inclination, or deontological ethics and virtue ethics, is economically relevant, because virtue ethics is an attempt to arrive at a transformation and refinement in the natural relationship of means and ends: the means should also become ends, the obligatory should also become the desired. The opposition of the natural economics of desires and the dutiful economics of goals and renunciations should be transformed into a refined economics of the virtues, in which the renunciations of the virtues serve as means for sublimated satisfactions or as these themselves. The sublimated economics of the virtues, or virtue economics of sublimation, is superior to the opposition between the immediately self-interested economics of means and ends and the formal, deontological ethics of universalization.

Economics is the calculation of means, circumstances, and side effects, given particular ends. Marcus Aurelius, in his *Meditations*, uses "economics" (*oikonomía*) in the sense of doing things with a certain reference to circumstances and side effects.[17] Ethics is reflection on the goals that we should set for ourselves, and on the agreement of these goals with their universalizability. Both ways of reflection, the ethical and the "economic" in Marcus Aurelius's sense, can be integrated into the comprehensive ethics of the simultaneous consideration of means and ends in their interdependence. Means and ends are not inde-

---

[17] Marcus Aurelius, *Meditations*, trans. George Long (London, 1862), XI, 18.

pendent of one another, but are instead interdependent and capable of taking one another's place. Because means and ends are interdependent, economics and ethics cannot be separated from one another. An end can become a means, and vice versa. One person sees gardening as a means and as work, the another as an end and as pleasure.

"The wisest mind so acts, as far as it is possible, that the means are also in a sense ends."[18] According to this definition of the wise person, wisdom is the economic ability of the human person. Wisdom attains its goals without use of resources, because it makes what *must* happen also its own goal and enjoyment. Wisdom, in the Leibnizian sense, transforms the necessary into the desired by the attitudes toward what must happen. It transforms investment into consumption, use into profit. Interchanging means and ends, letting means and ends be identical, brings about a savings effect, because use becomes at the same time the increase of utility, the means of investment becomes at the same time the means of enjoyment. If consumption is the goal of every economic action, all economic activity that is an end in itself is, according to this model, consumption. Consequently, each investment activity that is at the same time an end in itself for the acting person changes itself into a consuming and satisfaction-bringing activity. If the means are turned into ends, the genuine goal of the activity is already attained along the way. The strategy that refines the means of earning a living, labor, and the business enterprise (i.e. makes them at the same time ends and bearers of meaning and culture), is therefore the most economically efficient way of attaining goals and the satisfaction of needs.[19] The wise person knows, according to Leibniz, the law of the interchangeability of means and ends in actions. He or she can make the means into its end with the consequence that what was at first an end for him or her is co-attained as a "side effect" of the now-purposeful means.

The person who converts means into ends gains a quasi-rent: she does with pleasure what she must do anyway. The utility from what is done with pleasure is additional utility or economic rent, going beyond the utility or return from the use of labor as the means to another goal, which was necessary anyway. That which must be done anyway, becomes the intended side effect of something that is done with pleasure. This is a reconstruction, in terms of the theory of externalities, of the processes of refinement and sublimation. As Hegel says, culture makes itself noticeably stronger in the refinement of means than in the refinement of ends. We already have refined ends in general, but we do not desire most of the means to them, because they are arduous. Because the means to

---

[18] Gottfried Wilhelm Leibniz, *Theodicy*, trans. E. M. Huggard, 1952, § 208, p. 257.

[19] See also Serge-Christophe Kolm, "Must One Be Buddhist to Grow?" in Koslowski, ed., *Economics and Philosophy* (Tübingen, 1985), pp. 225-28, on the relationship between the principle of "the end in the means" in Buddhist ethics and Japanese economic growth.

noble ends are laborious, there is an inadequate provision of superior ends with adequate means.

To develop virtues is to make the means to the dutiful and obligatory the ends of the self. The virtuous person makes the means of duty, the dispositions and good habits, his own ends. In the pursuit of his new ends, the exercise of virtue becomes the means to the fulfillment of the dutiful; the dispositions for the good are co-realized. Sublimations are reversals of the direction of the original ends toward (un)intended side effects that are accepted with the pursuit of new, different ends and as a side effect of the employment of means. In sublimation, the logic of means, ends, and side effects is applied to the field of the obligatory and the forbidden. Sublimations direct the libidinous energies toward other permissible ends, by whose pursuit the attainment of the original ends of the desires are reached as side effects of the pursuit of the new ends by just the original libidinous energies. Virtue is, in this sense, a transformation of libidinous energies into dispositions, brought about by the substantive ethics of values, which makes these energies suitable for every end that requires deontological ethics as obligatory for the individual. Virtue creates the disposition not only for itself and for dutiful actions, but also for the sublimation, the redirection of the drive-energies toward refined and economically-maximizing actions. It is maximizing insofar as it avoids, or at least reduces, the conflict and the loss of energy that originate from the opposition of duty and inclination.

Virtue ethics is superior to deontological ethics in all ethically-relevant situations that are, by their nature, unattainable by universal rules. Among such situations are singular, non-repeatable decision situations, for which universalization of the maxim yields nothing, and which do not permit the formation of a subjective rule. Also included are cases of completely self-related obligation, which present a special case of the singularity of a decision situation. Duties to oneself cannot be established by deontological ethics, because the subject and the object of the rule are identical. The object of the rule of duty to myself – myself – cannot be examined by universalization. I myself cannot be for myself the object of universal legislation, and the maxim of conduct to myself cannot become the principle of a universal legislation, since no one can give universal laws that are valid only for oneself.

In the relationship of the human person to himself or herself, as in other singular situations that are not attainable by a rule, ethics can only be virtue theory, not deontological ethics. Kant saw this difficulty and introduced the term "virtue-duty to oneself." This expression, however, joins mutually-contradictory terms, because, according to Kant, that which is duty is not virtue, and that which is done from duty cannot also be done from virtue, because morality, for Kant, is only that which can be done *only* out of duty. Schleiermacher elaborated this contradiction in Kant's term "virtue-duty." Kant required a merger of duty and virtue in this term, although he otherwise decisively advocated the separation of virtue ethics and the ethics of duty.[20]

With the relationship of the human person to himself or herself, it can be seen that the ethical cannot be merely the subject of rules and duty, but must also be just as much virtue as a state of character and conviction toward the good. In the singular situations of the relationship to oneself and to other persons, it is necessary for the theory of virtue to complete the theory of duty.

An example from economic ethics of this necessity of completing deontological ethics with virtue ethics is consumer ethics. The question of the justifiability of one's own consumption cannot be answered by universalization alone. The question is not about the justifiability of a universal pattern of consumption, but about my own, singular, consumption. Another example is the singularity of contractual situations in which the contract cannot use the prevailing market price, but the degrees of freedom of setting the contractual price are higher and, therefore, a higher degree of ethical decision-making about the just and the fair remains, which can be achieved only by the question of the virtuous action.[21]

Duties arise from rules, virtues from the motive and the conviction toward the good. "Virtue-duties" are conceivable only in an analogous sense, when the concept of duty is unable to formulate a rule, but an "obligation" to the good is based without a rule on the nature of the matter at hand. An essential "virtue-duty" of this kind is the duty and virtue to correspond to the nature of the particular subject matter in question and to be just, to act "appropriately to the matter."

3.5.2. PROPER CONDUCT, OR APPROPRIATENESS TO THE NATURE OF THE MATTER, AND JUSTICE AS VIRTUE

The concept of justice shows in an exemplary way that deontological ethics and virtue ethics belong together. An action is "just" (*gerecht*) if it corresponds to the rules of justice (*Gerechtigkeit*) and of "correct" (*richtig*) law. An action is "proper" or "appropriate" (*sachgerecht*) if it not only corresponds to the rules of action in the subject or field (*Sachgebiet*) in question, but is also "just" to the particularity and uniqueness of the subject matter (*Sache*) in question here and now. Justice describes both the state of corresponding to the rules and the virtue of justice, which consists in the firm resolve to see that justice is done to every person and that every subject matter receives that which is proper or appropriate

---

[20] Friedrich Schleiermacher, *Grundlinien einer Kritik der bisherigen Sittenlehre* (Berlin, 1803), pp. 176-77: "So Kant has both duties that are virtue-duties and duties that are not virtue-duties, but are nevertheless ethical duties; then also various duties whose performance is virtuous, but not virtue-dutiful. And one minute he writes that one can say that we are obligated to virtue, then the next minute he writes that one cannot say that it is obligatory to possess the virtues."

[21] Cf. below, Section 8.2.4., pp. 197-202.

to it, above and beyond the universality of the rule. Justice is a principle of the critique of positive law, an ethical rule, and a virtue. As a principle of the critique of positive law, justice describes the quality and the condition of a legal system. If the laws of a legal system correspond to the requirements of ethics, with the categorical imperative for instance, so that each person receives his right and the laws can be thought of as those to which every person agrees, the legal system in question may be called just.

A legal system is just if it gives every person what is due him or her according to laws that correspond to the standard of the preceding paragraph. An action is just in the sense of deontological ethics, if it follows the rule to give each person what is due him or her according to the law and to justice. Justice as a virtue, in the sense of virtue theory, is the state of character that aspires to treat every person justly. An action and a state of character are appropriate, if they give not only what is due in social relationships according to justice, but also see that justice is done to each individual thing or person, independently of the rules. In the tradition of ethics, the deontological concept of justice and the related social virtue of justice compete with the comprehensive virtue of justice as a generic term for the unity of ethics as a whole.

The deontological ethics of justice requires obedience to just laws. The specific virtue of justice, which corresponds to the deontological ethics of justice, requires and promotes the state of character and steadfast disposition to give and to take justly in the exchange of goods between citizens in civil law (*iustitia commutativa*), to give and to receive justly in the allocation of goods by the state to its citizens (*iustitia distributiva*), and to realize justice as the obedience of citizens to the laws of the state, including tax and contributive obligations (*iustitia legalis*).[22]

The content of the just law is embodied in the specific virtue of justice in the steadfast state of character, aspired to by the will and guided by reason, to give to each his or her due, and to realize this in every situation. According to Aristotle, "Justice is the state that makes us doers of just actions, that makes us do justice and wish what is just."[23]

The comprehensive concept of justice is, in contrast, not bound to a rule or the just law. Within the Platonic tradition, justice is not a virtue among others, and does not correspond to the virtue of special justice, the rules of exchange, of allotment and contribution obligations,[24] but is instead the totality and the orderer of the specific virtues. Justice is, for Plato, the order and harmony among the

---

[22] Cf. Josef Pieper, "Justice," trans. Lawrence E. Lynch, in *The Four Cardinal Virtues* (Notre Dame, Ind., 1966), pp. 70-75.

[23] Aristotle, *Nicomachean Ethics*, V, 1, 1129 a 8-9.

[24] For an investigation of the specific justice of exchange and distribution, and the general justice as virtue simply, see Aristotle, *Ibid.*, V, 2, 1129 b 25 ff.

virtues of wisdom, fortitude, and temperance.[25] The comprehensive virtue of justice follows an ontological concept of justice and relates to the entirety of the cosmos, which is joined together and set in order by justice, is just and appropriate because of the comprehensive virtue of justice. Socrates says that justice is that which penetrates everything.[26] He articulates here the Greek, ontological concept of justice. In the Greek tradition of thought,[27] justice expands into a cosmological-ontological principle for penetrating everything that brings about the orderliness and structure of the whole. Justice is the characteristic of being ordered and the harmony of the parts. Thus Solon of Athens could say that the sea is most just when it is calm, and that it is lashed and unjust during a storm.[28] Justice is that which penetrates everything, and the virtue of justice, in the complete sense, is the state of character that seeks to make the justice that penetrates everything for its part "just."

Justice gains here the dimension of the comprehensive penetration and providence of the world. The virtue of justice is the state of character to realize in one's own will and actions that which brings things into a correct fit and joins them together.[29] For Plato, therefore, the comprehensive virtue of justice consists in doing justice to everyone and everything, and realizing the just, which penetrates and puts together the world, in one's own action and production.

The comprehensive concept of justice aims at the moral or the ethical as such, at the *intentio recta* to correspond to the nature of the subject matter and not merely to a rule. According to this theory of justice, when no rule exists, there is still justice, namely proper conduct, appropriateness to the nature of the matter in question. And when a rule of exchange and distribution does exist, that does not necessarily mean that justice is realized by applying it blindly. To correspond to the nature of the person and the subject matter means, likewise, to do justice to that universal nature of the thing that the rule is in a position to seize as the specific characteristic feature of the nature of *this* thing, its singularity, which the rule is not able to reach. The complete virtue of justice comprehends the universality of the rule of justice and the particularity of the individu-

---

[25] Plato, *Republic*, trans. Paul Shorey, in *The Collected Dialogues*, ed. Edith Hamilton and Huntington Cairns (New York, 1961), IV, 441 c ff.

[26] Plato, *Cratylus*, trans. Benjamin Jowett, in *The Collected Dialogues*, 412 e.

[27] The Greeks, in the words of Werner Jaeger, *Paideia*, trans. Gilbert Highet (New York. 1939), Vol I., p. 158, saw "creation to be a cosmos 'writ large' – namely a community of things under law."

[28] Cf. Heraclitus: "The sun will not overstep his bounds; if he does, the Erinnyes, allies of justice, will find him out," Fragment 29, in Milton C. Nahm, ed., *Selections from Early Greek Philosophy*, 3rd Ed. (New York, 1947), p. 90.

[29] According to J. and W. Grimm, *Deutsches Worterbuch* (Munich, 1984), the meaning of the German adjective *passend* (fitting, appropriate, suitable) is central to the meaning of the German adjective *gerecht* (just).

al case and individual thing. Because justice is that which penetrates everything, the virtue of justice must also penetrate the universality and the particularity of its object, above and beyond that of universal nature. Justice is not merely compliance with the rule, though without the rule there is no justice. Justice is not merely that which complies with the rule, because the rule is not able to penetrate the individual person without doing injustice to him in his particularity.

The just law is one that allows room for the particular, just as the natural law of the organic world gives the particular organism room for action for its individuality. The organic law of nature penetrates the organism without destroying its particularity. The abstract rule compels the individual from outside into the universality of regularity. The relationship of the individual to the whole is not merely negative here. Schleiermacher criticizes Kant's deontological ethics for adopting a false, inorganic concept of the law of nature:

> Kant himself indeed claims that he has always chosen the equations of a natural law as the model of his equations; but he is unable to convey this belief to anyone else. For a natural law is conceivable only when it contains the seed of the division of the identical in its opposite, and with the universal simultaneously creates space for the particular, because only in this way does an organic conjunction originate, for which there can be only a natural law.[30]

The just action is one that is appropriate to the subject matter at hand. The action that is just by nature is determined by the organic law of nature, which penetrates everything individual, without destroying its particularity. The virtue of justice is the state of character to do justice to this penetration and to realize it in actions. At the same time, justice is the representation of the moral as complete and the intention to the whole of the moral. *One* of the forms of justice is, therefore, to do justice to the various value-qualities of a thing or person (i.e. to realize the various levels of values). The Platonic concept of justice, the unification of all virtues, refers to the unity of the virtues, which can indeed be distinguished from one another in the individual cardinal virtues of prudence, temperance, fortitude, and "special justice," but which constitute a whole as a moral state of character, conviction, and motivation. Virtue presents the ethical as a state of character and motive. In all individual virtues, virtue finds expression as a unified whole, and as a moral state of character and disposition.

3.6. The Unity of Ethics as the Theory of Duty, of Virtue, and of the Good

Morality understood as virtue, cannot oppose morality understood as duty, and morality understood as the good, because duty does not require anything that contravenes virtue, virtue does not require anything that contravenes the order

[30] Schleiermacher, *Grundlinien einer Kritik der bisherigen Sittenlehre*, p. 87.

of goods, and the order of goods does not require anything that contravenes duty. The great insight of Schleiermacher's critique of Kant is that Kant's ripping apart of duty and virtue destroys the unity of moral action. The separation of the theories of duty, virtue, and the good does not do justice to the unity of ethics. Theories of duty, virtue, and the good can neither require contradiction nor displace one another. According to Schleiermacher, each action is determined by the reason of obligation, by the motive, and by the content of the good aspired to. The theory of duties provides the reason of obligation and the rule of moral action; virtue theory provides the motive of the action; and the theory of the good provides the content of the good aspired to. Morality is realized as duty, as a state of character, and as the good; each of the three aspects of morality represents in itself the entirety and the unity of morality. Every theory of ethics is at the same time a theory of duties, a theory of virtues, and a theory of goods.

It is this unity of morality that Plato portrayed with the concept of justice as the totality of virtue. Platonic justice is the realization of the idea of the good and is directed toward unifying law and state of character, duty and virtuous motive, as aspects of the good. Justice is the idea of the good, from the point of view of the law and of the state of character to realize the good. Penetrating justice must be understood as the manifestation of the idea of the good in the law and in the penetration of being. Just as the *idea* of the good is the good under the perspective of the cognoscibility of being and forms the source and ordering of the ideas of total reality, justice is the side of the idea of the good that presents itself as the habit to act, as action and deed. Justice reflects the act and the habit from the three viewpoints of the good: law, virtue, and good. As the habit of justice, it is the idea of the good under the aspect of the ordering that penetrates everything. The human virtue of justice seeks to follow the justice that penetrates everything by the world-forming state of character and act, and to do justice to the nature of each thing. The law of justice is the side of the idea of the good that is the establishment of order. Human justice seeks to correspond to this side of the idea of the good by just rules and laws.

Duties, virtues, and goods are the realizations of the good and the moral. The law is the side of the idea of the good that is the establishment of order. Human morality seeks to fulfill it under the concept of duty. Virtue is the side of the singular that is the penetration of being. Human morality seeks to correspond to it as state of character and virtue. Finally, the goods represent the side of the idea of the good that is abundance and cognoscibility. The abundance and cognoscibility of goods seek to do justice to human insight by the recognition of the value-qualities and the conditions of their realization. Morality follows the order of the goods in the recognition of their value rank and order of realization. Duty according to the law, state of character according to virtue, and knowledge of the goods in their orientation toward to the highest good are the manifestations of the idea of the good in ethical action and knowledge.

The course of our investigation has followed this structure. The deontological ethics of the categorical imperative, as it is presented in the Kantian tradition, proves to be suitable for developing the rules to which the ethical pre-coordination of economic coordination must correspond, so that it is possible for free human persons to coexist. Deontological ethics needs, however, the motive- and action-foundation of virtue theory, most of all for the relationship of the human person to himself or herself and for behavior in singular decision-situations. Both the theory of duties and the theory of virtues must, in turn, be completed by a theory of goods and substantive ethics of values, because the perception of value-qualities within what corresponds to the obligatory and the virtuous is neither a question of duty alone nor a moral state of character alone, but is just as much the ability to perceive and to experience.

Schleiermacher's idea of unifying deontological theory, virtue theory, and the theory of goods is superior to Scheler's substantive ethics of values, because Scheler takes as his theme exclusively the aspect of virtue theory and the theory of goods in ethics and his critique of Kant leads him to a denial of deontological ethics and an underestimation of the formal ethics of rules. In contrast to Schleiermacher's critique of Kant, Scheler's critique overlooks the significance of deontological theory and rules for the core sphere of ethics. Deontological theory formulates the universalizable rules that form the load-bearing framework of the house of ethics. Without the concept of duty and rules of the ethical, the theories of the virtues and of goods threaten to cause the substantive ethics of values to lose firmness and stability and to become subjective and aesthetic. Above all, in value conflicts the theory of duties must unambiguously provide duties as reasons of obligation, so that value-qualities are not played off against necessary, universal rules. On the other hand, the formal ethics of rules and its ethical coordination must rely on the theories of goods and virtues for the motivation and perception of goods, in order to be able to realize proper conduct in particular cases. Deontological ethics' ideal of duty and coordination does not do justice to the obligation to proper conduct and individual justice, because it understands all beings and things in the medium of the universal and of the rule as understood in terms of natural law. The ideal of universalization stands in a tense relationship to proper conduct, which understands the just as penetration of the individual and singular decision situation.

The theory of goods of the substantive ethics of values must be united with the theory of duties to form a theory of the highest good that goes beyond the disconnectedness of value-qualities and their mere value rank ordering to a principle of unity of the plural value-qualities. The Platonic theory of the idea of the good, and of the goods as the realization of the individual idea, make it possible to achieve such a viewpoint of unity in the theory of goods. The good is the realization of the idea, the state of character motivating to the realization of the good is the virtue, and the obligation and that which guides the coordination of the actions to the realization of the idea is the obligatory action out of observance of the law that follows the universalizable maxim and the categorical imperative. The purest concept of ethics is found in Plato's theory, to which the later insights of philosophical ethics, the element of the substantive value-qualities from Scheler's theory and the element of universalizable duty from Kant's ethics must be added. Plato's ethical theory introduced the concept of the idea of the good into philosophical discussion, Scheler introduced the idea of substantive value-qualities, and Kant introduced the idea of duty. Without the ideas and the highest of the good, which unifies them and puts them in order, however, the concept of duty remains empty and formal. Without the idea of the good and the concept of duty, the substantive ethics of values and its value-qualities remain without a context, without the order and force of the "ought."

Schleiermacher wrote correctly that Plato's ethics is the origin and the foundation of ethics:

> For he considered the human person's similarity to God to be the highest good, in such a way that all being is a portrayal and representation of the divine nature. So also the human person, first inwardly himself, but then also outwardly, should shape that part of the world that is given over to his power according to the ideas and should represent the moral everywhere in this way. Thus the distinctive feature of the concept becomes clearly evident here and the identity of the concept with itself distinguishes itself both from the act and from the mental attitude.[31]

The act and the will alone, even if they obey the universal of the categorical imperative, do not realize the highest good, because the highest good is not only act, but also active word and creative idea. The act that only fulfills the form of the law remains empty, because the content of the highest good is not law, but idea. The conviction without the content of the concept or the idea remains impotent, because it does not find the concretion of the conviction in the active realization of the idea. The idea of the good is the union of action, feeling, and understanding. Morality, understood as participation toward the realization of the idea of the good, is the union of duty, state of character, and ability to perceive. The moral agent realizes the idea by his or her act, state of character, and understanding.

The idea of the good requires the realization of the maximum of value-realization, the maximum of compossible realizations of goods and value-qualities. This idea is also the actual coordination and maximization ideal of economics, which is required by economic ethics. The maximization of existence,[32] the greatest value-realization of persons, goods, and value-qualities in the world, is not identical to the maximization of material output. The maximization of value-realization requires a realization of values, to which not only material goods,

[31] Schleiermacher, *Grundlinien einer Kritik der bisherigen Sittenlehre*, p. 247.

[32] Cf. Koslowski, "Maximierung von Existenz," *Studia Leibnitiana*, 19 (1987), pp. 54-67.

but also to a special degree the higher-ranking value-qualities of the intellectual and vital values and goods belong. These maximize existence to a higher degree than material goods do, since they are goods whose degree of publicness is higher and that therefore are used up, wear out, and miscalculate less quickly. A comprehensive economics, a universal economics, is not possible in the sense of a maximization of material output. It must be thought of as the maximization of compossible realizations of values, as the maximization of existence. If it is understood as such an economics of the maximization of compossible realizations of values, it is universal economics and at the same time ethical economy and the ethics of a universal theory of values and goods, which includes the various value-qualities.

3.7. Everything Worth Doing Is Worth Doing Well, or The Good as Perfection

The side effects between the ethical pre-coordination of formal ethics and the economic coordinations of the price system, which have been described in the previous chapter, "Economics and Ethics I," and the side effects between the substantive ethics of values and the economic theory of goods, which are examined in this chapter, "Ethics and Economics II," show that an unambiguous separation of economics and ethics is not feasible. We must judge each significant decision economically *and* ethically at the same time in a theory of ethical economy and ethics related to economics. The idea of a theory of ethical economy takes this fact into account. The idea of ethical economy connects to the Aristotelian tradition of practical philosophy, to the fact that economics, ethics, and politics belong together, and at the same time completes political economy with a theory of the ethical presuppositions of economic action and the economic presuppositions of ethics.

The comprehensive concept of ethics says: Everything worth doing is worth doing well. All actions, primarily life-world social, primarily economic, and primarily political actions, are directed toward the acting person's unique perfection, toward doing good and becoming good. One cannot say that only what is ethically valuable is worth doing well, but what is economically valuable is only worth doing efficiently. Aristotle says that everything we do at all should be done well.[33] James Buchanan has put forward the opposite thesis: For the econ-

[33] Aristotle, *Nicomachean Ethics*, I, 7, 1098 a 10: "Now we take the human function to be a certain kind of life, and take this life to be the soul's activity and actions that express reason. The excellent man's function is to do this finely and well. Each function is completed well when its completion expresses the proper virtue. Therefore, the human good turns out to be the soul's activity that expresses virtue. And if there are more virtues than one, the good will express the best and most complete virtue. Moreover, it will be in a complete life."

omist, *not* everything worth doing is worth doing well.[34] According to this claim, the essence of economics consists precisely in showing that it would be economically good to do some things not so well.

Is there an actual contradiction here between ethics and economics? G. E. Moore maintained that the word "good" (like the names of other simple qualities) cannot be defined.[35] The problem with defining the ethical and the good only as duty, only as virtue, or only as the good to which one aspires confirms that the determination of the content of the word "good" is difficult, even if not impossible. A contradiction between "ethically good" and "economically good" is, however, logically and ontologically impossible and social-philosophically and social-economically improper, because it leads to the dualism of the good and the useful, which tears apart the unity of a person's life. One must find a definition of the good that sublates the dualism and overcomes the contradiction of ethical goodness and economic goodness. In free recourse to Aristotelian ethics, "good" is defined as follows: to attain the excellence *(areté)* or perfection peculiar to a thing or action. The ethical concept of the good extends to the meaning of morally and economically good. If one distinguishes, as is customary in economics and ethics today, between economically good, in the sense of profitable or efficient, and ethically good, in the sense of absolutely good, it follows that it can also be economically good not to do something so well. It is thus economically good to make mass products not so well, in order to reduce the price.

The contradiction that many people believe they can see here is not a true contradiction. The ethicist also says that mass production is good, if it leads to an expansion of opportunities for consumers, even if the products are "not so good." It would be even better, though, if the mass products were good, not only from the perspective of good as in cheap, but also from the perspective of good in itself (i.e. qualitatively good). If the completely good mass product is not possible, because of the cost situation, the circumstances, and the side effects of production on other economic goals, the mass production of cheap and moderately good products attains the degree of excellence possible in those circumstances. It is, then, also ethically good – which does not rule out the possibility that it could and should be even better in the future.

The example of mass production shows that the ethical view of the good is not a viewpoint in addition to the economic viewpoint of the economically good (i.e. the useful) and the aesthetic viewpoint of the aesthetically good (i.e. the beautiful). The ethical point of view is, instead, the viewpoint of looking at all

---

[34] Cf. James M. Buchanan, "Economics and Its Scientific Neighbors," in Buchanan, *What Should Economists Do?* Indianapolis: Liberty Press, 1979, p. 118. With Buchanan, to be sure, this position has the features of a thought experiment.

[35] G. E. Moore, *Principia Ethica* (Cambridge, 1903), p. 6.

aspects of the good, of the moral, the useful, and the beautiful, together and integrating them. In the individual decision, the ethical is not an aspect besides others, but a way to take notice of the perspectives and arguments of the sciences, to order and evaluate them, and to let them become action guiding. This definition of ethics is true of both individual ethics and social ethics. The question of the ethical justifiability of an economic order, capitalism for instance, cannot read, "Is capitalism moral?" but must instead be, "Is capitalism – under the conditions of human nature and the scarcity of resources, according to the integration of the analyses of the sciences of the human person and of nature, and taking the assessment viewpoints of ethics, economics, and aesthetics into account – a humane and good economic order?"[36]

The absolute, the dignity of the human person, and the value of life are the goods that cannot be adequately measured in the *unity* of economics and ethics as a weighing of goods. They are conditions of the personality of the human person and, therefore, are presuppositions of all evaluation. They stand outside the weighing of goods, because they are goods for a conscious self and make the weighing of goods by persons possible. Their acknowledgment by each person as independent of weighings of goods is, therefore, a duty. The human person, according to Kant, has no price and no value, but instead dignity.[37] He or she is the condition of epitome of value and price and, therefore, cannot be assessed like a commercial value, with other non-absolute things as something non-absolute. The human person has dignity, not a price of an equivalent that can be assessed relative to other equivalents.

The definition of ethics related to economics and ethical economy as a theory of the realization of the comprehensively understood good must be expanded even further with regard to the concept of *the dignity of the human person* and be defined as follows: The ethical viewpoint is the viewpoint and the virtuous state of character that integrates assessment perspectives into a whole and performs a comprehensive weighing of goods under the obligatory constraint, under the side condition, that the dignity of the human person represents the limit of the weighing of goods. A human action is good, according to this definition of ethics, if it corresponds in every respect (i.e. according to the goal or intention of the acting person, according to the result, the means, the circumstances, and the side effects of actions) to the nature of the state of affairs or action. It is bad if it exhibits a deficit in any of these respects. The observance of the negative constraints is moral duty, the state of character and the motive to realize the perfection of action is moral virtue, and the content of the action is the realization of the idea of the thing. In the fifth century Pseudo-Dionysius Areopagita

---

[36] Cf. Koslowski, *Ethik des Kapitalismus*, 6th Ed. (Tübingen, 1998).

[37] Immanuel Kant, *Foundations of the Metaphysics of Morals*, trans. Lewis White Beck (New York, 1959), p. 53.

reduced this principle to the succinct formula: "*Bonum ex integra causa, malum ex quocumque defectu.*"[38] The good consists in the perfection of the thing, the bad in showing a deficit in some respect.

Ethics takes as its theme the unity of the life-world in actions relative to the identification of action-guiding goals and assessments of action in aesthetic, economic, and moral values and principles. Ethics must bring to evidence and realize the good in the intention on the obligatory, in the moral attitude, and with the aspiration to realize the idea of the thing, according to the three most important value-qualities. It realizes the good according to the value-qualities of the useful *(utile)*, the beautiful *(pulchrum)*, and the moral or noble *(honestum)*. As the science and wisdom of integration, ethics balks at dividing up the unity of our action into economic, ethical, and aesthetic aspects. It is, instead, directed toward achieving a comprehensive action orientation for the acting and deciding person, an aid to decision-making for the self-design and self-realization of the human person.

The successful business firm must also achieve the integration of utility or efficiency, ethics, and aesthetics. The concept of corporate culture or identity shows that the need for a refinement of the internal life of the firm above and beyond the purely utilitarian and economic aspects of achieving profits is perceived. The significance of culture for the economy and of cultural philosophy for the theory of the economy make an expansion of economic theory to a cultural economy and theory of the economy as a cultural sphere necessary. Since the transition between cultural and ethical action orientations is fluid, since ethical norms are culturally mediated and cultural interpretations of existence and orderings of life are ethically based, cultural economy forms a part of non-formal, substantive ethical economy.

---

[38] Thomas Aquinas, *Summa theologiae*, I-II, q. 18, a. 4, ad. 3, with reference to Pseudo-Dionysius, *De divinis nominibus*, c. 4: "Evil results from any single defect, but good from the complete cause." Cf. Peter Lombard, *Libri Quatuor Sententiarum*, 1158, II, d. 36. See also [Cursus] Collegii Salmanticensis, *Cursus Theologicus*, tract. XI, disp. IV, dub. 1 (*Comm. in S. Thomae s. th.* I-II, q. 18, a. 3): Because each substance becomes perfect in the physical order by those accidentals, so also each moral act becomes perfect in its order by whatever circumstances and receives from them the completion of its morality, whether goodness or evilness." Leibniz also defines the good as the possible perfection of a thing or action. Kant (*Foundations of the Metaphysics of Morals*, pp. 61-62), objects, incorrectly, that the concept of perfection is empty. Even if there is no universally and categorically applicable rule of perfection, it does not follow that the concept of perfection is empty. It is a concept at the limit, whose function is orientation.

CHAPTER 4

ECONOMICS AND CULTURE

The insight into the need to unite economics, ethics, and aesthetics and their respective primary values of efficiency, morality, and beauty in our way of life and in our economies, as it is evident in new theories of business ethics and corporate culture, points to the fact that the economy is one of the main spheres of culture, and economic ethics, understood as ethical economy, is not only a theory of economic rationality and coordination, but equally a theory of the culture of the economy and of the economy as a cultural sphere.

4.1. Cultural Economics and the Cultural Philosophy of the Economy

The economy, as it is understood in cultural and moral philosophy, is a cultural sphere – in the terminology of systems theory, a social subsystem. It is, on one hand, an object of the theory of society that seeks to determine the fundamental law-governed regularities of all social action and all formation of social institutions. On the other hand, the economy appears to be the most autonomous and self-governed of all spheres of culture, with its logic given by economic rationality and its norms by profit and loss calculations according to double-entry accounting. The economy is, therefore, the object of its own science, economics, which fluctuates in its self-understanding between the natural sciences and the social sciences or humanities. Since the economy is a part of culture and is determined by cultural and ethical norms and values, economics must also be cultural science and cultural economics.

Economics, as the science of the economy, is, as has been shown above, both the most developed branch of interpretive sociology and a theory of action involved with technology and the natural sciences. It is the best understood part of interpretive sociology, because we understand rational, self-interested action better than all other types of action. At the same time, it is a science containing natural-scientific elements of a mechanics of the movement of goods and factors, because it has to do with quantitative and measurable prices.

The economic-technical paradigm tends toward underestimating and disregarding the degree to which human praxis is determined by cultural meaning. As a result, countless economically-relevant actions are culturally determined and shaped. Our consumption and investment decision are thus always also culturally and religiously formed and defined, for instance, in the symbolic meaning of goods and the religious foundation of renouncing consumption and saving for the future. Habits of energy use and attitudes toward conservation of the natural environment are also culturally shaped. The substantive ethics of values and the theory of cultural meaning-understanding show that, as consumers, we must understand, comprehend, and express our opinions on goods and their value-qualities and that, as producers, we must express and communicate our experience of goods and value-qualities in our products in such a way that they are understood by consumers.

Economics, like its object of study, the economic safeguarding of the means of subsistence, ranges from inanimate matter, raw materials, to symbolic and aesthetic content, from the natural to the spiritual. Economics is neither entirely a natural science nor entirely one of the humanities. It is a cultural, natural, and technical science. It ranges from bio-economics and technical economics to ethical and cultural economics. The genuine achievement of the entrepreneur or manager consists in the integration of technological, economic, and cultural-aesthetic knowledge and ability. This integration achievement of technology and culture, of industrial economics and cultural economics, is continually becoming more significant for the fields of management and marketing.

The post-industrial economy must pay greater attention to the factor of culture. Aesthetic and cultural dimensions of the worker's daily routine in production, leisure, and consumption must be observed increasingly in an economy that makes the transition from the quantity of material goods produced to the quality of a service economy. The cultural expectations of firms increase with the higher qualification of the worker and the higher production demands of the work in the micro-electronic age. The transition from energy-processing to information-processing machines replaces energy and matter by knowledge. This also has repercussions on the increasingly more intellectual character of work, which is defined by symbols and cultural meaning.[1]

Cultural economics, or the cultural science of the economy, takes into account the "refinement" and aesthetization of needs that increase in an economy with growing prosperity. Cultural philosophy takes as its theme the meaningful construction of the social world and the unity of the life-world in actions and institutions. It attempts to preserve the aspect of the unity of human existence relative to the differentiating out of action orientations in economic, aesthetic, and ethical action- and judgment-guiding values and principles. As an integrative science, it balks against the division of the unity of the acting subject into economic, ethical, and aesthetic roles. Cultural philosophy is directed toward comprehensive action orientations, toward an action orientation to which the successful firm must also aspire. It must achieve the integration of economic efficiency, economic ethics, and aesthetics. The term "corporate identity" shows

---

[1] The ideas in this chapter have already been partially published in Koslowski, *Die postmoderne Kultur* (Munich, 1987), Chap. IV.2.

that the need for a refinement of life within the firm going beyond the pure function of production is perceived. The goal of the firm in the cultural society must be not only to be a site of production, but also a place of corporate culture and human relationships. The goal is the "refined firm." It is of great significance for the vivacity of the culture that the economy and culture, the firm and art, do not become opposites, but are instead "reconciled."[2]

4.2. The Culture of Production

When seen from the supply and production side of the economy, business culture requires that the patterns of action and forms of organization of production be determined and refined as social and meaningful action. Transformations in the culture of production of the economy follow the transition from the industrially-oriented economy to the service-oriented economy. A shift in emphasis from the production of material goods to the production of immaterial goods takes place. The shift of emphasis from the production of material goods to the production of immaterial, intellectual goods and services corresponds to the increasingly more "intellectual," immaterial character of post-modernity and its technology. The industries with the highest rate of growth at the present time are the "cultural industries," such as films and television, consulting firms, etc.

The production culture of industry is characterized by the ability to predict, full control, and an orientation toward the end product. Output is crucial. It can be described as a function-oriented and quantity-oriented, modern, "masculine" culture of production. The production culture of the service society, in contrast, is process-oriented, does not have complete control of the manufacturing of goods, and is directed not only toward the end product, but also toward the manner of production. It bears strong characteristics of the ideal type of a communicative and contextual, post-modern, "feminine" culture of production. The

---

[2] Joseph Beuys, in Beuys, *et al.*, *Ein Gespräch: Una discussione*, ed., Jacqueline Burckhardt (Zürich, 1986), p. 126: "The situation in which we find ourselves shows that the guiding force is the economy . . . . If one wishes to change this and to make art or culture the guiding force, then one must develop methods that influence the heart of society, in order to transform the economic concept into a cultural one." – On the cultural philosophy of the economy, see Eduard Spranger, "Die Wirtschaft unter kulturphilosophischem Aspekt," in Spranger, *Kulturphilosophie und Kulturkritik*, ed. Hans Wenke (Tübingen, 1969); and Kenneth E. Boulding, "Toward the Development of a Cultural Economics," *Social Science Quarterly*, 53 (1972), pp. 267-84. On the economics of culture, the arts, and the "cultural industry," see William J. Baumol and William G. Bowen, *Performing Arts* (New York, 1966); Mark Blaug, ed., *The Economics of the Arts* (London, 1976); Dick Netzer, *The Subsidized Muse* (Cambridge, 1978); William S. Hendon, "An Observation on Arts and Economics," in Hendon, James L. Shanahan, Alice J. MacDonald, eds., *Economic Policy for the Arts* (Cambridge, Mass., 1980); Hendon and Shanahan, eds., *Economics of Cultural Decisions* (Akron, 1983); Hendon, *et al.*, eds., *The Economics of Cultural Industries* (Akron, 1984); and Edward C. Banfield, *The Democratic Muse* (New York, 1984).

"products" of the service economy are also more strongly culturally and symbolically shaped than those of industry.

The change from the modern production culture of industry to the post-modern culture of the service society is typically linked to the change from the hierarchical to the cooperative organization structure. If patterns of the service economy mix with those of the industrial economy, they must change old industrial hierarchies and the industrial culture of production.[3] Some of the new social movements formulate a protest against the "masculine" form of industrial culture of production, which stresses hierarchy, requires discipline, and is characterized by the end product. The actually realizable production culture of post-modernity will bear neither purely "masculine" nor purely "feminine" characteristics, in the ideal-typical sense used here, because the "masculine" industry remains necessary. It will, however, show, relative to the "industrial culture," stronger characteristics of an immaterial production culture and will form a mixture of industrially-oriented and service-oriented production cultures.

4.3. The Culture of Consumption

On the demand and consumption side of the post-modern economy, changes in the social and cultural patterns of consumption are taking place. The consumer culture of the present time is making the transition from mass consumption to aesthetic and culturally-discriminating consumption. Cultural points of view are playing greater roles in the assessment of merchandise. Prestige is shifting from the material qualities of goods (e.g. the horsepower of a car) to its symbolic-cultural qualities (e.g. the design of the car, the "snob effect" of scarcity, etc.). To the extent that recreation, entertainment, and culture are blending today and cultural and entertainment activities are no longer seen as completely separated, merchandise and cultural consumption are also blending. Leisure time is being spent in "joint consumption" as culture-consumption-entertainment time. The demand for culturally "enriched," aesthetically refined goods is increasing. The universalization of former cultural-aesthetic consumer behavior, restricted to prosperous (educated-)classes, is becoming effective in broad demand. Some examples are the trend toward traveling for experience, the widening of the social basis of buying and reading books, the increase of festivals, and the increase of visiting and tours to museums.

Culture is becoming an economic factor in marketing, in the advertising and design of products, in consumer goods marketing and the marketing of industrial sites. With the increasing purchasing power of the entire population, the sig-

[3] Cf. Kjell Eide, "Cultural/Economic Relationships," in Douglas V. Shaw, *et al.*, eds., *Artists and Cultural Consumers* (Akron, 1987), Vol. III, pp. 202-6.

nificance of price competition is decreasing, but the significance of non-price, cultural product- and promotion-competition is increasing. Product marketing and *promotion* marketing work with cultural and symbolic elements, with the cultural additional use or "cultural value in use" that is added to the value in use and the value in exchange of merchandise. The architect and designer Matteo Thun-Hohenstein writes concerning these development as follows:

> The new situation of consumption is characterized by the search for social identity. Consumption means building a new emotional relationship between person and object, between person and habitat. The consumption of recent decades means above all the consumption of graphic impressions. That means constant renovation of the sign language. The idea that consumption is in a process of continuing acceleration, the idea of stylistic mobility and exchangeability, requires a new readiness on the part of industry. This radical change is taking place at the same time as the beginning of post-industrial culture.
>
> Post-industrial culture – a culture that is no longer able to achieve a monolithic production policy, but is instead dealing with various decentralized, sectoral products. An industry that renews itself on the basis of that culture, that has co-produced itself. Standard products for the large market (i.e. products not aimed at any particular market sector) are no longer in demand today, since the large market has itself been replaced by various specialized markets that have organized themselves into cultural groups involving various traditions of speaking and ways of behavior. Advertising – no longer the target, but the psychological cluster. In other words, one asks about products whose sales motivation does not correspond to the general satisfaction of needs, but instead appeals to a specific cultural class. Thus *products with unambiguous cultural appeal.* That means a re-definition of the functional, an inclusion of imaginary elements and an *enrichment of metaphors at an intensified level of speaking.* A new equation comes into being: DESIGN = COMMUNICATION = SIGN. Is the equation correct? The "Silver Prince of the *Bauhaus*" is still among us. The dilemma "technical design" vs. "new design" has begun.[4]

Cultural marketing plays an important role in competition for industrial locations, because what a city is able to offer culturally determines its leisure value and the attractiveness of its leisure value to workers. The cultural promotion of cities and communities serves not least the goal of "site marketing." On the international scale, foreign cultural policy can be seen, in addition to its diplomatic-political role, as "cultural marketing" for the exports of a nation and as advertisement for the cultural surplus to the value in use of its merchandise. Cultural value in use plays a significant role with imported goods ("Italian design," "French chic," "German workmanship"). The marketing of a nation's

---

[4] Matteo Thun-Hohenstein, *Ein neues Affektverhältnis zwischen Mensch und Objekt*, unpublished manuscript, Vienna School of Applied Arts, October, 1984 and Letter of 28 August 1986.

economy, through a prudent "cultural marketing" of foreign cultural policy, provides meaningful assistance, especially when the foreign cultural policy is discriminating (i.e. does not permit its content to be produced for instrumental promotion of the economy, but instead for "high culture").

The immaterial activities of the economy grow more quickly today than the material activities; the cultural side of the (service-)economy more quickly than the material production of the industrial economy. The symbolic and immaterial value component in the assessment of commodities increases, relative to the material value of the commodities, as the material saturation of the economy increases. Smaller nations, such as Norway, have already adapted their export policies to this development and have shifted the emphasis from the quantitative-material side of exports to the qualitative-cultural side. The motto of their export promotion is, "Sell the culture!" The emphasis in export marketing is on the interplay of the cultural and economic characteristics of export goods.[5] Exports have a cultural component. The cultural character of the export good of a nation ensures that it is not substitutable for the same good of another exporting nation. Giovanni Agnelli of Fiat sees the cultural competitive advantage of the European nations as the only opportunity to be able to keep up with the United States and Japan in competition. With mass production and technological development, the latter nations have had such quantitative advantages in research and such economies of scale in production that smaller nations have not been able to keep up, even with great efforts in research and production.

Cultural goods have smaller economies of scale than material goods. The relative reduction per piece by production of large quantities is much less than in industry. This is not, however, entirely a disadvantage, because the cultural economy is also able to employ more workers and to decrease unemployment.

4.4. Technological Progress and Transformations in the Meaning of Work in Society

The appearance of the possibility of saturation is a historically unique phenomenon in the nations of the "First World."[6] Instances of saturation make a new cultural orientation of society possible. The problem of saturation, however, does not completely change the "logic of the labor society." The thesis that the logic of "work creates prosperity" or "economic growth secures jobs" is obsolete is incorrect. Our present level of consumption saturation, rationalization of production, and national welfare can be preserved only by great intellectual effort, especially if one wishes to reduce the environmental pollution caused by this

[5] Cf. Eide, "Cultural/Economic Relationships."

[6] Cf. Josef Falkinger, *Sättigung* (Tübingen, 1986).

level of prosperity. Maintaining a high level of technology, science, art, philosophy, and economic organization is almost as difficult as achieving it in the first place and creating it anew. The abilities of a society must be learned and earned anew in each generation, because the condition of having learned something is not inherited genetically. For this reason, it would be a mistake to declare the work ethos to be obsolete. The same is true of rationalized and automated production. Rationalization does not free us from work, only from prolonged, monotonous, and difficult physical work. The demands of work for concentration, precision, and dependability increase with rationalized production, even though its duration and physical strenuousness decrease.

A high level of unemployment is seen by some social scientists not primarily as a scandal, as a political and social problem, but as an opportunity for a new form of human existence. According to the advocates of this thesis, work is not the medium of meaning and self-realization of the human person, as modern philosophy has maintained since Descartes and Locke, through Hegel and Marx, up to Max Scheler. Work is instead a means of alienation of the human person from his or her nature, while the liberation of the person from work is an opportunity for meaning, leisure, and self-realization. But is this thesis correct?

The release of the human person from coercion to constant physical work by the rationalization of production and organization is a new opportunity for human self-realization. This opportunity consists, however, less in liberation *from* work than in liberation to meaningful work, from the drudgery of monotonous, manual work to the liberty of creative work. One can see a complete liberation from work (i.e. from serious, planning, realizing, responsible engagement with nature and other persons) as a dreadful vision. It demands too much of the person, because it lets him or her have a meaningless and non-committal "everything is possible," with which one cannot cope. For one thing, it is based on a false concept of freedom, understood merely as freedom of choice and arbitrariness of action. Freedom, understood as the freedom to choose, without work makes the development of the personality into the environment and community, which form "the other" of the freedom, impossible and reduces self-actualization to the arbitrary ability to choose among meaningless activities or hobbies. Moreover, the utopia of "unemployment" ignores the fact that the human person is the animal that becomes bored (Werner Sombart). For the human person, a world without work is insufficiently significant. We cannot live like lower animals, because only a world with symbols and cultural meaning has sufficient significance for our reason (Claude Lévi-Strauss). Without this cultural meaning, the world and our lives are insignificant for us. But the significance of the world is created only by work or serious effort. Even if the utopia of liberation from work were possible economically, the problem of meaningfulness would still arise. Because meaning is possible only with work, one must reject the thesis that the liberation of the human person from work offers the opportunity for meaning and leisure time and, therefore, for self-fulfillment.

Normal work creates five experiences:

1. The division of time or structuring of the course of the day.
2. The experience of the necessity of division of labor and cooperation.
3. The enrichment of social experience by interaction in the workplace: the human horizon expands.
4. The status and identity of the human person in our society are defined above all by work.
5. Work means regular activity, work with and in reality.[7]

According to Freud, the strongest bond of the human person is in the reality of work. Mere free time, without meaningful activity, is the opposite of self-fulfillment. It is noteworthy that the nature of the human person has been defined since Aristotle as *energeia*, active realization of the rational nature in human praxis. One can argue about whether praxis can be equated with work. But one certainly cannot *separate* praxis completely from work and consider leisure-time activity or hobbies to be arbitrary. The link between occupation and vocation must also be preserved in a society in which the struggle against nature has lost its intensity. Perhaps such a society first offered the possibility to open a link between occupation and vocation for more persons.

The human person does not tolerate being inactive. In the Middle Ages inactivity, *acedia*, was seen as a vice and sickness, especially one of monks and philosophers. Later the definition of sadness and melancholy accompanied that of inactivity. This ambiguity of *acedia*, as both inactivity and sadness, throws light on the present problem. A world without work can become extremely sad, because it is a world without a future perspective. For the life of the human person, the direction of the changing of his or her life perspective is of particular importance. Someone who is spiritually and economically wealthy in younger years and then constantly becomes poorer finds himself or herself in a worse situation than someone who is poor at the beginning of life and then continuously become wealthier – even if the total quantity of wealth for both of their entire lives is the same. What is true of individuals is also true of nations: The genuine pleasure is not being rich, but becoming rich. When seen in this way, the economic phenomenon of the saturation of an economy can become more of a problem than an opportunity.

Maintaining a high level of prosperity, conserving the environment and eliminating the damage to the natural environment of recent decades, as well as the problem of evening out economic differences among the different regions of the world, will require so much of us that life without work will not become a reali-

---

[7] Marie Jahoda, "Arbeitslose haben alles Recht der Welt, über ihre Lage unglücklich zu sein," in Psychologie-heute-Redaktion, ed., *Geschafft* (Weinheim, 1985), pp. 16-23.

ty. Therefore, the opportunities of the contemporary economic situation are dominant. Unemployment will require a redistribution of labor to more persons *and* in favor of more leisure time. Consequently, not only the duration of work, but above all the density of work, should be reduced. Not only the duration of work, but also the intensity of work is of significance for the ability to participate in the culture and for the dominance of working for a living in society. Preindustrial societies work more than modern societies, but are less defined by work, because cultural and communal activities take place *during* the work time. Reducing work time by half is not synonymous with reducing work by half. Culture, in the sense of "cultural entrepreneurship" and "cultivation" or refinement of the economy, should be carried on in the world of work, not away from the work world in cultural leisure-time ghettos. Reducing the density of working for a living[8] would mean furnishing longer breaks during the workday for rest and education, but also opportunities for educational vacations and sabbatical years.

The reduction of the density of working for a living by the cultural enrichment of work reduces the tempo of work and thereby perhaps also competition pressure among individuals. Work will be able to assume a stronger character of play. If work becomes play or joy, the life of the human person becomes longer, because he or she gains in addition full time instead of empty time. The "refinement of work" is the best strategy for lengthening life that a society can adopt. It is more appropriate than the present experience of pursuing at life's end – after a very demanding and intensive work life, and with medical high technology made possible by health insurance premiums that are just barely still affordable – artificial extension of life by high-technology medicine. A dietetics of life and work and a reduction of the mad rush of economic life would produce greater success than an updating of work intensity and of curative medicine to compensate for it.

With the increase in leisure time and education sabbaticals, art, play, science, and spirituality, the riches of culture, will take on a more important position in contemporary life. This is a special opportunity for philosophy and religion. Such a development can mean the end of modernity, understood as a society determined primarily by the economy, and lead into a *returning progress* to a society characterized by religion, spirituality, and art. Such a cultural society will not be able to live without work and an economy. But work will have a spiritual and playful form within it. Culture, philosophy, and religion achieve the meaning orientation of the human person, so that she does not lose herself in mere consumption. If the pressure of the production problem eases, the liberty of the culture increases. The hour of culture, philosophy, and religion is thus still to

---

[8] Cf. Jürgen P. Rinderspacher, "Der Feierabend, der keiner ist," in *Geschafft*, pp. 38-41: and David Riesman, *Abundance for What?* (New York, 1964).

come. The tradition of the *vita contemplativa* will perhaps dispose of its esoteric character in this historical epoch and become a general form of life. But even if the contemplative life does not become general, it can still transform the existence of *homo oeconomicus* (economic man) or *homo faber* (industrial man) in a socially effective merger of active-economic and contemplative-cultural life. It is in this sense that the contemporary economic situation is an opportunity for human self-development – not as liberation from work, but as liberation to genuine human activity.

4.5. Art and the Economy

The development from the industrial economy to the service economy leads to a shift from emphasis on the material aspects to emphasis on the immaterial aspects of management. The economies of scale of mass production lose significance in the economy. Cultural aspects of work and production conditions gain significance on the supply side; cultural aspects of goods, marketing, and the image and corporate identity of the producer on the demand side. New opportunities for collaboration between the economy, art, and cultural sciences also arise here. The promotion of art by private firms, corporate sponsorship, can be seen in the framework of a global corporate strategy as a component of firm- and product-marketing. The promotion of art by promoting artists and works of art is, within a unified corporate strategy, a marketing and advertising measure.

The development of the part of the culture that demanded until now to be as autonomous as possible from the culture as a whole, the development of the self-legislating industrial economy into a culture of the economy and a cultural economy, shows that culture runs through and characterizes all activities of the human person. The development into the cultural economy is a part of the post-modern development into cultural contextuality and penetration of the cultural sphere. The cultural economy makes it clear that culture and the economy must be seen as belonging together, and that cultural and economic policies must be pursued together. The merger of cultural and economic policy into *one* policy is the contemporary task of cultural policy. At the same time, cultural-economic policy must not restrict itself to giving support of the fashion industry and consumer culture, though these cultural economic factors also belong to cultural *and* economic policy.

Cultural economy and cultural economic policy are directed toward the cultural side of economic goods and the economic side of cultural and artistic goods. The fact that material goods exhibit cultural elements and cultural goods exhibit economic elements shows that the economy and art border one another and constitute together a part of a society's culture. Technology plays a central role in the production of *both* the economy *and* art. In both, it serves production, *poiesis*, and makes possible the appearance of the idea that was previously created as an image in the imagination. Corporate sponsorship that establishes for itself the function of direct promotion and exchange between the artist and the firm is able, on the basis of the shared trait of commercial and artistic production in *poiesis*, to lead to fruitful, mutual cooperation and to synergy between the economy and art, to an exchange from which both sides profit. The mutual stimulation between economic and artistic production includes aesthetic learning, researching materials, testing new techniques, and learning skilled trades. In the interaction between art and industry, it is often art that introduces new materials and techniques, and industry that follows the artistic avant-garde.

The increasing penetration of the cultural sphere of the economy by art is an example of the penetration of the cultural sphere in post-modernity. It satisfies a demand of art and of industry, if industrial production becomes more artistic and art finds increased entry into the daily routine, and is not pushed aside in the sterility of *l'art pour l'art*.

CHAPTER 5

ECONOMICS, ETHICS, AND DECISION THEORY

The Problem of Controlling Side Effects

Ethics and economics have the same object of knowledge, if the maximum of value-realization, according to the rank ordering of value-qualities, is understood as the final cause of a theory of universal economics or ethical economy. In addition to the commonality of their final cause and highest good, evidence of the convergence of economics and ethics is also found in the numerous side effects between ethical and economic goods and, therefore, also between ethical and economic assessments of actions. These side effects can be seen, first of all, in the mutual influence of experiences and value-convictions, economic cost-utility calculations and ethical value judgments, as they have been depicted above.[1] Economic and ethical assessments of goods do not take place independently of one another, but instead exist in positive and negative side effects, in strengthening or conflicting mutual effects on one another. Secondly, the interchangeability of means and ends and the sublimation phenomenon of the attainment of original goals by reducing them to side effects, which are co-attained in the pursuit of something completely different, prove the ubiquity of the phenomenon of side effects. They show how important the ability to control side effects or externalities is for general ethics, ethical economy, and general economics.

Action is subject to the necessity of the finite to realize itself in a structure of effects that is not under its complete power of disposal. Actions and their goals are determined by the definitions that we give to goods, values, and goals. Consequently, the difference between the intended effect and realization of an objective and value defined in one way or another and its unintended side effect becomes somewhat blurred. The action produces side effects that it is not completely able to predict, that it often does not intend, and whose subsequent assessment does not agree with the anticipated assessment. The positive or negative side effects that the economic action and every action of great depth of effect produces are, neither in ethics nor in economics, a trivial matter. Negative side effects can cause unintended damage and thwart the actual intention of an action. Positive side effects can create utility and profit not seen in advance and reveal new possibilities of action to the conscious life.

[1] Cf. above, Section 3.3, pp. 89-91.

Positive side effects arise from the social spillovers, the overlapping and unifying effects that the higher value-qualities of public and semi-public goods produce. The unifying power of these goods or value-qualities brings about positive side effects between the substantive ethics of values and economics. Great works of art create non-competitive individual utilities. Negative side effects between economics and ethics exist, however, in the case of the prisoner's dilemma, when instead of expanding the assurance game, the pursuit of immediate self-interest brings about an erosion of ethical rule-compliance that aggravates the dilemma situation, leading to a reduction of assurance of universal rule-compliance and to broader erosion of rules.[2] For the theory of economic ethics, therefore, the side effects and mutual effects between ethics and economics, ethical and economic action orientations, are of particular significance.

The individual-ethical and individual-economic decision is also quite interested in recognizing and controlling side effects. The ethical and economic interest in side effects is concerned not only with controlling negative instances, but also with controlling positive side effects and spillovers. Positive side effects are a crucial source of increases in the ability to act and to realize values, especially in managerial action. Since side effects are in themselves external to the structure of actions and effects, they exhibit the peculiarity of being unattainable, or barely attainable, by rule-guided thought and action. An effect that appears regularly is, general speaking, not an (accidental) *side* effect. It is extremely difficult to get a handle on side effects in terms of deontological ethics or economic law-governed regularities. They require, as has already been pointed out, *esprit de finesse*, thought in intuitions, not *esprit de géometrie*, thought in rules.

Deontological universalization and the laws of the economy achieve only primary effects. Secondary or side effects, which cannot be universalized, are conceptually difficult for them to comprehend. The maximum of compossible realizations of values, as the final goal of totality, however, requires that precisely the positive externalities of actions and systems of action are used and promoted together. Overlappings of systems of rules can exercise both negative and positive side effects on goals of action. To recognize and to promote them is a globally-maximizing strategy of value-realization, not merely one related locally to *one* system of rules and actions.

The following observations on the calculability of side effects relate, first of all, to the phenomenon of the maximization of positive side effects in the firm as the specific achievement of the manager. They formulate the "law of intended side effects in the firm," which makes it possible to grasp anew the peculiarity of the managerial function. The discussion is concerned, secondly, with the

---

[2] The phenomenon of sinking marginal morality follows from this attenuation of assurance. Cf. below, Section 7.3, pp. 178-81.

problem of the individual decision and the controllability of side effects in individual action. Since the problem of the inclusion of the persons affected and the internalization of side effects at the socio-economic level and as a problem of social coordination and social decision systems has been treated in the first two chapters, the following chapters will discuss the problem of how the individual decision-maker can analyze and control the side effects of his or her actions. Besides probabilistic decision theory, this will take place above all with reference to the principle of double-effect (side effects), as earlier moral theology has developed it.

5.1. The Law of Intended Side Effects in the Firm

Eduard Spranger formulated "the law of unintended side effects in education."[3] It says that every theory of education and pedagogy that is directed only toward the primary effect of the practice of educational action and toward the goal at the end of the educational process of having taught the student *one* and only one well-defined skill, misses the point of the genuine process of education. It consists not only in the primary effect, but also in considering the side effects of the process of education on the other person. It is necessary to observe what the student does with the education, and how he or she creatively uses it and changes it for himself or herself.

From the law of the interchangeability of means and ends and from the law of unintended side effects and the heterogony of objectives and effects, a third law, which is important for economic ethics, can be derived: "the law of intended side effects in the firm." A theory of managerial action can, at the same time, be developed from it. First, the term "intended side effects" appears to be self-contradictory, because side effects as such are understood in action theory to be effects of actions that are not intended as goals or as means to ends. Side effects must be sincerely unintended (i.e. not consciously taken into account for the attainment of a goal). A side effect that is consciously taken into account is, in legal terms, an "indirect intention" (*indirekter Vorsatz*).[4] Side effects must really be accidental, secondary, and thus not essentially connected to the primary

[3] Eduard Spranger, "Vom Wesen des Geistigen," in *Gesammelte Schriften*, ed. Hans Walter Bähr (Tübingen, 1980), Vol. VI, pp. 305-12. See also Robert Spaemann, "Die Herausforderung," in *Mut zur Erziehung* (Stuttgart, 1978). Spaemann – going beyond Spranger – sees the task of education as the explicit observance of personality-forming side effects on the persons being educated. With Spranger, however, the question should be asked whether education can achieve this at all, or whether the side effects of education will not always remain as such.

[4] Cf. Adolf Schönke and Horst Schröder, *Strafgesetzbuch: Kommentar*, 22nd Ed. (Munich, 1982), pp. 199-204; and Gustav Radbruch, *Der Handlungsbegriff in seiner Bedeutung für das Strafrechtssystem* (Darmstadt, 1967).

effect of the means. According to this definition, one cannot directly intend side effects, because they would no longer be side effects, but objectives.

One can, however, intend effects that unintentionally produce side effects. I can intend side effects of the actions of another person, if I cause someone to do something without coercion and intentionally, and thereby unintentionally to create externalities of his or her action that are side effects in the sense of unintentional results of an action for him or her, but effects and intentional utility for me. Someone who enjoys working in the quiet of the night also protects the house in which he works with the light by which he works. For him, the night watchman effect is an unintended side affect. But for those who rent the room to him, it is an intentional effect. The "law of intentional side effects" says that an individual can will that another person produces unintentional externalities, and thus side effects. This phenomenon is distinguished from co-production by the fact that the externality is unintended.

The law of making full use of externalities has been known until now from the sociobiology of the symbiosis of various animal species. Various species use the side effects or externalities of the life-process of another species to promote their own life process. Ants, which milk aphids for their own nourishment, are a well-known example. One species produces externalities as output, which serve the other species as input for its own production. The problem of externalities and symbiosis is also the explanation of the practice of raising various species together within a single biotope. Breeders and herdsmen are in a position to increase the natural yield from natural capital by "rational selection."[5] They can transfer biological mutual or side effects – externalities – between species in exchanges that are mutually advantageous for themselves and these species. The output of one species becomes the precommitment and input of the other. The beekeeper is of use to himself, the bees, and the plants that are pollinated. The human person is able to use possible positive externalities that the species in the exchange produce together and the side effects between the natural species and his own production for himself. Plato saw in the prudent use of these externalities the art of the herdsman. The good herdsman pursues his own interest and the interest of his animals simultaneously.

Applied to the theory of the firm, this means that each business enterprise achieves by prudent management the highest yield for its members, which exhibits the highest density of the exchange of positive externalities, positive side effects, to its members. The firm, as an internal market and an economic organism, uses the unconscious and unintended side effects of the actions of its members toward one another for the goals of the firms. The successful and creative

[5] Cf. Gordon Tullock, "An Application of Economics in Biology," in *Toward Liberty* (Menlo Park, 1971), Vol. II, p. 391; and Koslowski, *Evolution und Gesellschaft* (Tübingen, 1984), pp. 49ff.

firm must promote the unintentional, positive side effects of the actions of its members on one another and on the overall goal of the firm and take them into consideration in remuneration. It must compensate overall performance, with all positive mutual effects, justly according to performance. It is crucial that the principle of intentional, positive side effects in the firm allocates to the manager the function of imagination, of envisioning and realizing such positive side effects. This function cannot be performed by conceptual, analytic thought alone. It requires powers of creative imagination that put oneself in the position of the interests of other persons and combine their actions and goals into a new symbiotic whole of side effects.[6]

The theory of the entrepreneur as someone who imagines and realizes the positive side effects of actions is more appropriate to the interdependence of the participants in an organization than is the neo-classical, microeconomic theory of the firm, which sees the entrepreneur or manager only as someone who assembles already prepared and fixed factors of production into technologically and economically optimal combinations, in order to make some predetermined product. Neither quantitatively nor in terms of price are the factors of production predetermined and constant. The assumption of a fixed and determined factor of labor in the theory of production and of the firm is especially unrealistic. The factor of labor becomes what it can be only in the interactions of the firm. The neo-classical theory of production presupposes that the causal relationships among the factors of production and between the factors and the product are invariable and well known. According to this point of view, the creative achievement of the manager consists merely in calculating and implementing the best recombination of factors.

The assumptions of this neo-classical model of the entrepreneur or manager that the relationships of production and the entrepreneur's information about them are fixed and predetermined are unrealistic. The decision-maker, on one hand, knows less about the environment and the process of corporate performance planning and, on the other hand, is able to imagine creatively the new and the hitherto not yet existent to a greater degree than the microeconomic theory of the firm assumes. The theory of symbiosis, in contrast to this static model of fixed factor relationships, takes as its starting point the conscious corporate use of unintended side effects or externalities, whose combination is imagined by the firm's managers as they promote the positive side effects of the organization's members on one another. The model of imagination and symbiosis is more adequate for the exchange process of corporate life than the microeconomic model, because it is more robust concerning presuppositions about information and considers the side effects of the life process.

---

[6] On the role of imagination in managerial action, see also G. L. S. Shackle, *Imagination and the Nature of Choice* (Edinburgh, 1979); and pp. 157-58 below.

The entrepreneur or manager is someone who attempts to maximize the positive side effects and symbiotic phenomena among the members of the firm for the entire firm, including the workers, and not only for herself or her own profit. The expression "maximization of positive side effects" is, of course, used here in an analogous sense. In the literal sense of a calculating maximization according to a formal calculus, the "maximization" of positive side effects is impossible, since the manager neither knows nor can know the maximanda and the equation of the maximization.

5.2. Side Effects as Decision Problem

To demand precision where calculation and formal systems of equations are impossible by the very nature of the subject matter is a dubious action. Unjustified declarations of precision are a decision-theoretical, economic, and ethical problem. They are a problem in decision theory, because they challenge the imagination of decision theorists. They are an economic problem, because the misallocation of efforts to be precise in places where they are, by the nature of the subject matter, doomed to failure creates considerable and avoidable costs. Finally, they are ethically problematic, because unjustified claims to precision, where it *necessarily* cannot be attained, are immoral according to the ethical responsibility of the scholar, and also create doubts in the theory of economic ethics for the person who offers misplaced precision and claims to be able to attain it in the wrong place.

The degree of precision that can or may be claimed for the analysis of complex phenomena presents in itself a decision-theoretical and ethical problem. In cases of complex phenomena, decision theory and ethics must apply their theoretical tools to themselves and ask themselves what degree of precision of decision calculus is rationally responsible with decisions under uncertainty and what claim to precision is ethically responsible in the advocacy of a recommendation to other persons.

The problem of precision presents itself in a special way for side effects that exceed the boundaries of rule systems, and with which the actions of a finite being necessarily extend into the sphere of the accidental. When the distinction between accidental side effects and necessary consequences of actions is somewhat vague and flexible, powers of cognition, ethical judgment, and powers of imagination are challenged. The various disciplines of the practical decision – ethics, economics, decision theory, and operations research – strive to reduce the vagueness of the effects of actions and the uncertainty about them. With the decision to consult a particular discipline for the clarification of a decision problem, Jean-Paul Sartre's statement that to choose an adviser is already to choose his advice[7] is often valid.

Relative to the "precise" decision disciplines, such as decision theory and operations research, ethics is left at the back of the pack, because of its alleged imprecision. The supposed imprecision of ethics has also damaged the assessment of economic ethics. A more accurate analysis of decisions, however, with more profound effectiveness and with uncertainty about the future and the non-controllability of the environment – conditions that apply to all sorts of constitutive decisions – demonstrates that the assessment of ethics as imprecise is incorrect. Decision theory's claims to precision must be rejected whenever it is asserted that it can achieve precise control of the events of subjective assessment, estimations of probability, and uncertainty about the future (i.e. of phenomena that, by their very nature, are not mathematically or "scientifically" controllable). Economic ethics, as a decision theory, not least of all, makes the boundaries of the controllability of decisions and the necessity of personal decision visible once again. It immunizes against the experiments of decision-theoretical and practical scientism and makes it possible for the individual to obtain the degree of decision certainty that is available to the finite and time-bound creature.

5.2.1. UNCERTAINTY ABOUT THE CONSEQUENCES OF ACTIONS IN ETHICS, ECONOMICS, AND DECISION THEORY

Every scientistic and consequentialist approach to ethics and decision theory that makes the empirical results of actions its ultimate criterion, such as teleological ethics and operations research, is confronted by the problem that empirically-oriented theories, in cases of decisions that are of a constitutive kind and exhibit great depth of effect, can make no decisions under certainty possible, only statements of probability about the consequences of decisions. An ethical theory or decision theory that affirms as its standard or guiding principle of action that a greater part of the empirical world *maximizes* an empirical variable in the strict sense, cannot provide the acting person with a universal and valid decision criterion. Neither the boundary conditions of action nor other persons' strategies of action are completely under the control of the individual. A truly maximizing action would require complete information about all antecedent conditions *and* about the actions and reactions of other persons.

Even in the improbable case that complete knowledge of the past and present were available, the fact would remain that knowledge of the future cannot be

---

[7] Jean-Paul Sartre, *Existentialism and Humanism*, trans. Philip Mairet (London, 1948), p. 37.

acquired.[8] With respect to the long-term future consequences of an action and changes in its environment, the decision-maker always finds herself in a situation of uncertainty. She acts under uncertainty about the results of her particular kind of action and under even greater uncertainty about the causal results of her actions that can be anticipated only on the basis of conclusions drawn from the assumption that certain consequences of her actions have been realized that caused other consequences from these actions and their coincidences with other events. According to Scheler, these causal results, which arise from the action's success and are established by conclusions, do not belong to the morally relevant unity of the action.[9] Every ethical theory that seeks to arrive at genuine decisions and ethical judgments must follow him at this point.

Consequentialist ethics and maximizing decision theory, however, also make the categorial causal results of an action's success, which cannot be completely determined according to the causal principle, the criterion of the correctness of an action. Both ways of clarifying decisions, consequentialism and maximization calculus, fall thereby into the boundlessness of the categorial determination of the causal results of the consequences or success of an action, because they no longer determine the decision and the success of its action as a form and according to a "nature of action," but instead see it as an event that brings about (infinitely many) other events. Uncertainty about the causal results of actions makes it impossible to use utility maximization as a principle of ethics and decision theory. The requirement of act utilitarianism, for instance, that the decision-maker must choose from all possible actions the one that will bring about the greatest possible quantity of utility for everyone, cannot be met, because our knowledge of the future is never sufficient to identify the *one maximizing* action or combination of actions out of the multitude of possible actions and the series of events caused by them.

Armen Alchian has criticized the economic concept of utility maximization as a rule for managerial action in an analogous way, which is also valid for the rule of act utilitarianism that the moral agent must select the action with the greatest total utility. Action under uncertainty, according to Alchian, does not permit the identification or anticipation of an action resulting in optimal, profit or utility maximization, but only the anticipation of a judgment of the probability of possible results. Therefore, only the maxim "positive profit or utility" can be a maxim of action, not profit or utility maximization, since the individual acts under uncertainty: "Uncertainty arises from at least two sources: imperfect

[8] G. L. S. Shackle, *Imagination and the Nature of Choice*, pp. 18 ff.; and *Epistemics and Economics* (Cambridge, 1972), p. 47: "If we are candid, knowledge of the future is a contradiction in terms."

[9] Cf. Max Scheler, *Der Formalismus in der Ethik und die materiale Wertethik*, 6th Ed. (Bern, 1980), pp. 137.

foresight and human inability to solve complex problems containing a host of variables even when an optimum is definable."[10]

The fact that it is impossible for an acting person to gain certain knowledge about other persons' types and strategies of action is central to the difficulty of estimating action results as causal results of actions, and is a limit for each optimizing action. Act utilitarianism, if it really wished to determine the maximizing action alternatives, would have to include the actions of others to an unlimited extent in the utilitarian estimation of the results of actions. An action *a* of individual *A* can only be utility-maximizing if *A* includes all boundary conditions and results of *a* in his calculus. These boundary conditions also include the actions of other persons. Assume that *a* is optimal, if *B* chooses action *b*, *C* chooses *c*, etc., to *N* chooses *n*. Under these conditions, action *a* becomes immediately suboptimal, if *B* or *C* chooses a maxim or action other than the one anticipated by *A*. *A* could be compelled to select action $a\_$, in order to maximize the total utility under the condition "*B* chooses $b\_$." Such a solution $a\_$, which would be second-best when seen from the moral point of view, could guarantee more utility in the overall context than keeping to *a*, the action that would actually be ethical for *A*.[11]

Since a truly maximizing, utilitarian solution cannot be achieved without taking *all* boundary conditions or constraints into account, it proves to be an optimization problem under constraints, whose borders with the environment can be marked out only arbitrarily. In all approaches to maximization, the individual must solve *n* equations with *n* unknowns under the constraints of, again, *n* equations with *n* unknowns, without knowing the content of all of these equations. The arbitrary restriction of included constraints and misjudgments of secondary results lead, however, to suboptimal solutions. A discursive-analytic, purely consequentialist ethical and decision theory is, therefore, in view of the information and ascription problem, confronted by insoluble problems.[12]

5.2.2. PROBABILISM

The optimal, deterministic solution of the decision problem, as it is calculable with action under certainty, is impossible with all actions that exert a continuing

[10] Armen A. Alchian, *Economic Forces at Work* (Indianapolis, 1977), p. 17.

[11] The problem corresponds to the theory of the "second best" for conditions of *imperfect* competition, developed by Richard G. Lipsey and Kelvin Lancaster, "The General Theory of the Second Best," *Review of Economic Studies*, 24 (1956), pp. 11-32. If the optimality conditions in a sector of the economy are not met, it can be more efficient to make adjustments in the other sectors that yield solutions that are, when judged by the ideal conditions of perfect competition. "second best." See also Charles K. Rowley and Alan T. Peacock, *Welfare Economics* (London. 1975), Chap. 2.

[12] Cf. Koslowski, *Gesellschaft und Staat*, pp. 230 ff.

influence on the course of events. Decision theory attempts, therefore, to create precise calculations for action under uncertainty with the help of probabilistic approaches. The self-contradictory concept of an exact probabilistic calculus for action under uncertainty already reveals the problem with this attempt.

A distinction can be made in ethics between traditions that place more emphasis on the calculation of the effects of actions, described above, and the advice of external advisors, and traditions that see the prerequisite of the ethical decision in the inner advice of the ego to itself and in the validity of strict rules. Both forms of ethics ultimately agree, however, that neither the internal advice and assessment of decisions within the decision-maker nor the external calculation of possible effects can be completely disregarded. The will to achieve a responsible estimation of results and to state correctly the external probabilities of occurrence and the internal assessment of the expected results of actions cannot be separated in ethics.

In order to analyze the decision situation, it is advisable first to distinguish the ex ante assessment of the expected results and side effects of actions from the estimation of the probability of their occurrence. The analytic, heuristic distinction between determining the probability of the occurrence of the effects of actions and establishing their assessment has been refined by probabilistic decision theory into an instrument of decision analysis. Probabilistic decision theory, however, asserts additionally and incorrectly that a clear *separation* can be made between the ethical assessment and the decision-theoretical analysis of probable environmental events, between possible action strategies and probable effects of actions. Since this separation is supposed to be possible, decision theory has become a discipline independent of ethics. It is considered not to be ethics, in the sense of analysis and assessment, but instead to be an entirely positive analysis of alternative actions and their consequences.[13]

With this assumption that decision analysis and moral decision or ethical commitment are separable from one another, decision theory is close, despite many differences, to a tradition of ethics that sees the role of ethics above all – even if not exclusively, as with decision theory – in the analysis of the probability of the ethical justification of a decision, the tradition of probabilism in ethics. Probabilistic ethics analyses the probability with which it can be assumed in an ethical dilemma that an external authority approves, or at least does not prohibit, a decision that must be made. Probabilistic decision theory[14] shows close parallels to probabilism in early-modern ethics. According to ethical probabilism, the correct action among alternatives is determined by recourse to the

---

[13] Wolfgang Stegmüller, *Probleme und Resultate der Wissenschaftstheorie und Analytischen Philosophie*, Vol. I: *Personelle Wahrscheinlichkeit und rationale Entscheidung* (Berlin, 1973), p. 325.

[14] On the metaphysics of decision theory, see also Patrick Suppes, *Probabilistic Metaphysics* (Uppsala, 1974).

probabilitas externa, to the probability of the approval of a decision problem by an external authority.[15] The individual's own ethical assessment is secondary to the *probabilitas externa* of the agreement of an external authority.

If probabilism traces the question of the action to be chosen and the burden of the decision back to the choice of the authority whose opinion, among other possible authoritative opinions, has the greatest probability of being correct (i.e. to the choice of the advisor), so decision theory attempts to hand the decision over to a decision calculus and to replace the question of ethical assessment by one of decision-analytic calculation. Decision theory reduces the decision to selecting the alternative that the probabilistic decision calculus calculates as the one with the highest utility value – in the Bayesian decision calculus, to the adoption of the alternative with the highest expected value. That the decision arises "automatically" from the external calculus, is the objective of decision theory.

The Bayesian decision calculus has the following basic structure: The expected value is the expected utility E of a decision that is measured according to subjective assessments of the consequences of decisions and of the probabilities of the occurrences of environmental events. Assume that someone must decide, under conditions of uncertainty about the weather, whether to risk become wet. The choice from the given decision alternatives d_1, d_2 (d_1 = "take an umbrella," d_2 = "don't take an umbrella") is a function of the expected conditions of the external world, which the decision-maker cannot influence, s_1, s_2 (s_1 = "it will rain," s_2 = "it won't rain"), whose subjective probabilities of occurrence p_1, p_2 are assigned, and a function of the assessment of the consequences of the decision c_1, c_2, c_3 (c_1 = "get wet," c_2 = "stay dry, but have to carry umbrella," c_3 = "stay dry without taking an umbrella"). The consequences of the action are functions of the decisions of the individual (d_i) and of the conditions of the external world (s_j). Let c = f ($d(s)$), thus:

$$d_1(s_1) = c_2, \quad d_1(s_2) = c_2, \quad d_2(s_1) = c_1, \quad d_2(s_2) = c_3,$$

where:

$$d_1(s_1) = d_1(s_2) = c_2.$$

The individual assesses the consequences (i.e. assigns them numerical utility values u and assigns the conditions of the external world the probabilities of occurrence p). In this example:

$$u(c_1) = -10, \quad u(c_2) = 5, \quad u(c_3) = 7 \text{ and}$$

$$p(s_1) = 0.8, \quad p(s_2) = 0.2$$

---

[15] On probabilism in ethics, see Charles Sainte-Foi, "Du Probabilisme," *Le Correspondant*. 2 (1843), pp. 145-59; Ignaz von Döllinger and Fr. H. Reusch, *Geschichte der Moralstreitigkeiten in der römisch-katholischen Kirche* (Nördlingen, 1889); and Heinrich Klomps, *Tradition und Fortschritt in der Moraltheologie* (Bonn, 1963).

The rule of the maximization of the decision's expected utility requires selecting the alternative that has the highest expected value, according to its possible consequences. The expected value is defined as the sum of the products of the utility of the possible consequences and the probability of the occurrence of each possible environmental event. $E(d_1)$ is the expected value of decision d_1, $E(d_2)$ corresponds to that of decision d_2.

$$\text{Let } E(d_i) = \sum_{i,j=1}^{n} u(c_i) \cdot p(s_j)$$

In the example:

$$E(d_1) = u(c_2) \cdot p(s_1) + u(c_2) \cdot p(s_2)$$

$$E(d_2) = u(c_1) \cdot p(s_1) + u(c_3) \cdot p(s_2)$$

$$E(d_1) = 5 \cdot 0.8 + 5 \cdot 0.2 = 5$$

$$E(d_2) = (-10) \cdot 0.8 + 7 \cdot 0.2 = -6.6$$

According to the rule that the decision alternative with the highest expected value is to be selected, alternative d_1 must be chosen, which means that the umbrella must be taken.[16]

5.2.3. CRITICISMS OF PROBABILISTIC DECISION CALCULI

Several objections can be made to a determination of decisions by the Bayesian decision rule, or by any other calculation of utility and probability external to the decision-maker. The essence of these objections is that the *probabilitas interna*, the conscientious assessment of expected "outcomes" and their probabilities of occurrence, and the *probabilitas externa*, the external calculation of "objective" probabilities, should not and cannot be separated in the responsible decision.

The assessment of the utility of the effects and side affects of actions and the estimation of the probability of their occurrence are not independent of one another. They are separable, at most, only heuristically. A person interested in a particular outcome will consider something else to be probable than someone not interested in the outcome. According to John Henry Newman, a moral person has different beliefs about what is probable than an immoral person.[17]

In the great discussion between Jansenistic and probabilistic ethics, the Jansenist critics of the *Port Royal* were proved correct in arguing that the external

---

[16] On the theory of expected value maximization, see also R. Duncan Luce and Howard Raiffa, *Games and Decisions* (New York, 1957); and Patrick Suppes, "Decision Theory," in Paul Edwards, ed., *Encyclopedia of Philosophy* (New York, 1967), Vol. II, p. 311.

[17] John Henry Newman, *An Essay in Aid of a Grammar of Assent* (London, 1870).

probability can never replace the inner discussion of the choice of actions. Blaise Pascal pointed out the significance of sincerity in the determination of intended primary effects and unintended secondary effects: "... when the person is not of such a wretched disposition as this, we try to put in practice our method of *directing the intention (diriger l'intention)*, which simply consists in his proposing to himself, as the end of his actions, some allowable object."[18] This re-labeling of the genuine intention as the side effect that is only taken into account is to be assessed critically when the intention is directed toward an intrinsically bad action.

The danger of this "directing the intention" also exists with the way in which a Bayesian decision calculus is constructed: The interest of the decision-maker is not irrelevant to the determination of the expected utility and the probability of the occurrence of the events. His interest will "direct" his intentions to their favor in such a way that the (subjective) probabilities of the occurrence of desired outcomes are somewhat higher than those of undesired side effects. This direction of the intentions by interests can also be seen in the assessment of experts' reports that are based upon probability estimations.

John Maynard Keynes summarized additional objections to the probabilistic formation of expected values: 1. The expected value ignores the weights of the arguments, the degree of evidence, on which each probability is based. 2. It ignores the element of risk: a situation of equal probabilities of heaven and hell is, according to this approach, exactly as desirable as certain mediocrity.[19]

The following objections from D'Alembert can also be added: 1. The methods of measuring probability are not persuasive. 2. The expected value is not linearly proportional to the probability. There exist economies of scale with the expected value: the expectation grows over-proportionally with increasing probability. 3. The probabilities and utility expectations cannot simply be added, especially not negative and positive expected values.

Keynes' probabilistic decision theory and his and D'Alembert's critique of the Bayesian rule reach the same conclusion as Aristotelian ethics: the action decision must be based on the assessment of the form of the action and on the intuitive estimation of its causal results, not on the components of the particular estimation of the results. The inevitability of the internal, comprehensive estimation of the results and the overall ethical assessment of the action, from which the decision cannot be removed by external authorities, is implied in the "paradox of choice."[20] If an act of the will is effective, we cannot know what

[18] Blaise Pascal, "The Provincial Letters," trans. Thomas M'Crie, in Mortimer J. Adler, ed., *Great Books of the Western World*, 2nd Ed. (Chicago, 1990), Vol. XXX, p. 45.

[19] John Maynard Keynes, *A Treatise on Probability* (London, 1973), Chap. 26: "The Application of Probability to Conduct."

[20] On the "paradox of choice," see Shackle, *Imagination and the Nature of Choice*, p. 19.

effect the decision following from it will have ultimately. Because the decision is supposed to change the course of the world, we cannot project forward or extrapolate the course of the world. If, on the other hand, we already know the future course of the world exactly, including the effects of our action, before the action is taken, it is beyond our influence and our free-will decision is without significance. We then have no genuine choice.

The boundaries of decision calculi, the paradox of choice, and the necessity that the deciding self takes a position internal to the decisions that he or she must make, show that the intuitive judgment of a decision situation and the decision itself must be based on an inner probability, a *probabilitas interna*, on every kind of provisional certitude or *certitudo moralis*[21] that is accessible to finite creatures alone. Decision-theoretical knowledge is much weaker than uncertainty about the future.[22] Uncertainty about the future constantly overcomes decision knowledge. Decision knowledge is always less than the sphere that should be known. What is rescued from the unknown of the future in the decision analysis remains uncompleted, because our decisions create new reality and new possible worlds in the process of the recognition and decision of reality.

The problem and paradox of probabilistic certitude presented itself at the beginning of the modern era in the ethical tradition of probabilism, just as it can be seen today in the approaches of probabilistic decision theory. From the critique of ethical probabilism of the first generation, which was overly committed to the externality of probable authoritative opinions, John of Saint Thomas, Bartholomew Medina, and the authors of the School of Salamanca[23] – above all, Domingo de Santa Teresa – developed a qualified and critical probabilism that attempted to mediate between the ethical inner freedom of the decision, the *probabilitas interna*, and the necessity of the analysis and assessment of expected external consequences and consultation with other, experienced persons, the *probabilitas externa*.

---

[21] Cf. Henry G. Van Leeuwen, "Certainty in Seventeenth-Century Thought" and Shirley Robin Letwin, "Certainty Since the Seventeenth Century," in Philip P. Wiener, ed., *Dictionary of the History of Ideas* (New York, 1968), Vol. I, pp. 304-11 and 312-25; and Helmut Thielicke, *Theologische Ethik* (Tübingen, 1965), p. 88.

[22] Aeschylus, *Prometheus Bound*, trans. James Scully and C. John Herington (Oxford, 1975), p. 53, verse 514: "Art is far feebler than Necessity."

[23] On the School of Salamanca, from an ethical perspective, see Friedrich Stegmüller, "Zur Literaturgeschichte der Salmanticenser Theologen," *Theologische Revue*, 29 (1930), pp. 55-59; and "Die spanischen Handschriften der Salmanticenser Theologen," *Theologische Revue*, 30 (1931), pp. 361-65; J. T. Mangan, "A Historical Analysis of the Principle of Double Effect," *Theological Studies*, 10 (1949), pp. 41-61; and Jozef Ghoos, "L'acte à double effet," *Ephemerides Theologicae Lovanenses*, 27 (1951), pp. 30-52. For an economic perspective, see Marjorie Grice-Hutchinson, *The School of Salamanca* (Oxford, 1952).

5.2.4. THE PRINCIPLE OF DOUBLE EFFECT

The central decision principle and analytic instrument of critical probabilism is the principle of double effect. This principle makes it possible to analyze and assess decision situations under conditions of uncertainty and expected (negative) side effects. It is a decision principle for poorly-constructed and ambiguous decisions. Most decisions of economic-ethical relevance do in fact have side effects and, therefore, are in fact poorly-structured decision problems under uncertainty. They cannot be converted into well-structured decision situations by calculi with unrealistic, scientistic premises, such as premises that the results of actions can be known certainly or that the probability distribution of the possible effects of actions and environmental events is known. The probabilistic principle of action with side effects, or double effect,[24] therefore, is especially applicable in economics ethics and decision theory, and is able to penetrate the poorly-structured economic-ethical decision situation and to reduce it to a clearer structure. The principle of double effect, in contrast to the principle of the categorical imperative, is concrete and makes it possible to perform comparisons of goods. It is, therefore, superior to the universalization principle, which is unable to judge the concrete individual case, only its universalization.

The principle reads: An action with negative side effects is sensible and permissible, if the following four conditions are met:

1) The goal of the action must be both good and sincere (i.e. the decision-maker may not intend a bad and impermissible effect). The side effects must be *praeter intentionem*.[25]

2) The type or form of the action must be intrinsically good.

3) The negative side effects must be true *side* effects. They must have the objective character of accidental effects arising in the pursuit of other goals, and may not serve as means to the good effect.

---

[24] On the problem of actions with double effects, see Peter Knauer, "The Hermeneutic Function of the Principle of Double Effect," *Natural Law Forum*, 12 (1967), pp. 132-62; Richard McCormick, "Das Prinzip der Doppelwirkung einer Handlung," *Concilium*, 12 (1976), pp. 662-70; R. A. Duff, "Absolute Principles and Double Effect," *Analysis*, 36 (1976), pp. 68-80; Joseph M. Boyle, Jr., Germain Grisez, and Olaf Tollefson, *Free Choice* (Notre Dame, Ind., 1976); Robert Spaemann, "Nebenwirkungen als moralisches Problem," in Spaemann, *Kritik der politischen Utopie* (Stuttgart, 1977), pp. 167-82; Boyle, "Toward Understanding the Principle of Double Effect," *Ethics*, 90 (1980), pp. 527-38; L. J. McNamara, *Direct and Indirect* (Ph.D. Thesis, University of Oxford, 1980); J. L. Mackie, *Ethics* (London, 1977), pp. 160-68; S. S. Levy, *The Doctrine of the Double Effect* (Ph.D. Thesis, University of Michigan, 1982); G. E. M. Anscombe, "Action, Intention, and 'Double Effect,'" *Proceedings of the American Catholic Philosophical Association*, 57 (1983), pp. 12-25. On judgment of consequences, see Rainer Specht, *Innovation und Folgelast* (Stuttgart, 1972).

[25] On *praeter intentionem*, see Boyle, "Aquinas on Praeter Intentionem," *Thomist*, 42 (1978), pp. 649-65; and M. Müller, *Ethik und Recht in der Lehre von der Verantwortlichkeit* (Regensburg, 1932).

4) There must be a proportionately grave reason to perform the action. The acting person may not be obligated by other duties to refrain from it completely.

This list of conditions summarizes the formulations of the principle by John of Saint Thomas,[26] from whom the first complete version of the principle is derived, and Jean Pierre Gury.[27] Conditions 1), 3), and 4) are the same for both authors. Condition 2) was expanded by Gury, in order to ensure that the principle is not applied in the sense of a universal comparison of goods. The principle of double effect is not identical to an uncritical, universal comparison of goods, with which the good and bad effects of *all* actions, including actions of an unambiguously unethical character, are taken into account and the lesser evil of several bad actions is chosen. Gury attempts with condition 2) to guarantee that intrinsically-immoral actions are excluded from the comparison of goods.

In more recent ethical discussion, the prevailing tendency is to drop the second criterion, of completely excluding intrinsically immoral actions, and to understand the morality of an action as a function of the comparative judgment of all of its foreseeable consequences, as a function of a universal comparison of goods. The statement above about the relationship between the dignity of the person and comparisons of goods[28] also holds true for this tendency: every comprehensive comparison of goods requires, as an absolute prerequisite of the comparison, that the dignity of the human person does not go into the process of comparison. At least *one* good must have an absolute character, so that it can be the condition and standard of the comparison of relative goods.

The question is discussed within general ethics whether the principle of double effect can be united with various normative, basic convictions, or whether it is a prerequisite of a normative ethical theory that judges particular actions as intrinsically bad and excluded from the comparison according to this principle.

Joseph M. Boyle, Jr. holds the view that the principle of double effect can be united with any normative theory that assumes the existence of types of actions that are good and types that are bad. Every ethical theory that makes such a distinction can make use of the principle of double effect.[29] This position shifts the debate, of course, from the question whether there are actions that are intrinsically good and bad and whether the answer to this question is a prerequisite for being able to apply the principle of double effect to the question of *which* actions are intrinsically good or bad.

---

[26] John of Saint Thomas, *Cursus Theologicus* (Madrid, 1645-56), tom. VI, disp. XI, a. 6, cap. 39 and 42.

[27] Jean Pierre Gury, *Compendium theologiae moralis*, 2 vols. (Lyon, 1850) ; 17th Ed. (1866). tr. I, cap. II, n. 9.

[28] Cf. above, p. 110.

[29] Boyle, "Toward Understanding the Principle of Double Effect," p. 537.

Elizabeth Anscombe believes that the principle does not say what one can or should do, but instead what one may not do, and thus that its applicability is restricted. The principle does not read that the predominance of good over bad makes an action permissible and recommends it, but instead requires that the side effects stand in a reasonable relation to the good. It permits only *good* actions with negative side effects, and only actions with which the negative side effects stand in an appropriate relationship to the (good) primary effect.[30]

The principle of double effect assumes that there are in fact actions that are intrinsically good or bad, that they establish the limits of individual comparisons of goods, and that they cannot be taken into account directly with secondarily good or bad side effects. But it does not say which actions are intrinsically good and which are intrinsically bad. Although economic ethics is not concerned primarily with general, foundational questions, but with comparisons of goods, it must also recognize intrinsically bad actions, such as lying and theft, which cannot be weighed against economic goods, such as profit.[31]

A principle that is effective with difficult cases and borderline decisions is able to be all the more helpful in less problematic areas of decision-making. If unstructured questions arise in economic ethics and decision theory about comparing the goodness of corporate objectives and the negative side effects of pursuing them, or between conflicts of the goals of economic policy and the negative side effects of the realization of one goal upon reaching the others, then questions of comparison, for which our principle is extremely useful, not fundamental questions, are under discussion.

For comparisons of goods within corporate and economic policy, the principle of double effect is an aid to decision-making, because it has the advantage of being more robust than mathematical decision rules. The data that go into it are not calculated categorially with precision. Furthermore, it is not the case, as with the calculi of decision theory, that the entire decision depends upon the correctness of the values of the data and the calculations. With the principle of double effect, judgment and analysis are instead performed simultaneously and holistically. The processes of structuring, assessing, and solving the decision situation happen simultaneously and independently. Decision-making and problem-structuring take place in the judgment of the decision-maker, not by external calculations, not by *probabilitas externa*.

The principle of double effect joins robustness with higher analytic power and compels personal penetration of a decision situation. This characteristic

---

[30] Anscombe, "Action, Intention, and 'Double Effect.'"

[31] On the practical application of the principle of double effect in business ethics, see below, Section 7.2, pp. 176-77.

makes it suitable for decisions in professional ethics, in medical ethics for example,[32] and for strategic decisions in corporate management.

The principle has been further explicated as follows: The necessity of tolerating negative side effects must be proportionally larger, when:

1) the primary goal is closer by nature to the negative effect,

2) it is certain that the bad effect will follow, and

3) there are fewer ways to avoid the bad effect than there would be if the goal or primary effect were to occur first.[33]

Additional aids to decision-making that can be derived from the principle of double effect in cases of actions with side effects, as well as in situations of conflicting goals, are:

1) How closely is the bad result or side effect dependent upon the action?

2) Is the damage that would result from omission of the intrinsically good action greater than the bad side effect that would result from performance of the action?[34]

The principle and its explications do not relieve the decision-maker of judgment and *probabilitas interna*, but they assist in penetrating the decision.

An example from economic policy may serve to the clarify the principle. In the case of a conflict of goals between combating unemployment and avoiding inflation, as depicted by the Phillips curve, the economic policy-maker must ask the following questions: Is the need to combat unemployment by this particular measure so great that the inflation, which is perhaps more directly and closely related to this measure (the expansion of the money supply, for instance) than to other measures (fiscal measures, for instance), must be accepted? With which measures of promoting employment is the probability of the occurrence of inflation the highest? With which measures is it most difficult to avoid inflation, if unemployment is already declining? Of all possible measures against unemployment, then, the one to choose, according to the principle of double effect, is the one that will have the smallest inflationary side effects.

The problem of side effects and the principle of double effect form a bridge between ethics and economics. This principle is a crucial instrument of the analysis and judgment of ethical economy and ethics related to economics. In the

---

[32] For an analysis of the problem of side effects of physicians' actions and the determination of the boundaries of physicians' conduct obligation with the help of the principle of double effect, see Koslowski, "Lebensverlängerung," in Koslowski, *et al.*, eds., *Die Verführung durch das Machbare* (Stuttgart, 1983), pp. 83-100.

[33] [Cursus] Collegii Salmanticensis, *Cursus Theologicus*, tom. 7, tract. XIII, disp. 10, dub. 6, n. 214-47 (*Comm. in S. Thomae s. th.* II-II, q. 64, a. 7), (= *Tractatus de bonitate et malitia actuum humanorum*), ed. Domingo de Santa Teresa. See also Mangan, "A Historical Analysis of the Principle of Double Effect."

[34] Nikolaus Seelhammer, "Doppelwirkung einer Handlung," *Lexikon für Theologie und Kirche* (Freiburg, 1959), Vol. III, p. 516-17.

coordination of the price system, the side effects between ethical and economic action orientations, between ethical pre-coordination and economic coordination in the market, refute the thesis that the economy is an ethically-neutral zone with no need of an ethical theory, because it already leads to the social optimum without one. The invisible hand of the market does indeed function, but not so strangely that it transforms the pursuit of immediate self-interest, by means of the externalities and side effects that economic egoists exert on one another in competition, into efficiency. This form of efficiency cannot be equated with the common good. Contrary to Mandeville's assumption, the common good does not originate as a "super externality" of the individual pursuit of self-interest.

In individual ethics and the decision theory of the individual economic decision, the phenomenon of side effects shows that ethics and economics have in common the function of achieving, in the conscious life and its decisions, a comprehensive weighing of goods, to which the perfection of action should aspire. Economics and ethics aim together at a weighing of goods that seeks to anticipate and to take into account all aspects of the good and all positive and negative effects and side effects. The law of intended positive side effects makes it possible to understand the managerial function as one of consciously bringing about, by creative imagination, positive externalities among the members of the firm. The principle of double effect, as it was developed within early-modern, Spanish natural law theory, proves to be particularly well suited for structuring decisions with side effects and under conditions of uncertainty, and for serving as a decision principle of ethical economy.

CHAPTER 6

ECONOMICS AND ONTOLOGY

Economic ethics and philosophy have three common spheres of research and intersect in three fields. Besides the fields of economic ethics or ethical economy, and cultural philosophy of the economy, which have been discussed above, there exists a third field, economic ontology, understood as the theory of the fundamental determinants of the sphere of being of the economy.[1] We turn now to the analysis of the ontology of the economy and its relationship to economic ethics.

The ontology of the economy investigates the basic determinants and "first causes" of its objects of study: the manager and the coordination of economic action. To the ontology of the economy belong the discussion of the categorial and ontological presuppositions of the science of the economy and its various schools of thought. The categories of an academic discipline form the basic concepts with which they conceptually comprehend reality. In the Kantian tradition, the categories of the mind constitute together the object of knowledge and form the mental concepts, such as cause, possibility, etc., that are valid for all academic disciplines. Human knowledge arises from the application of the categories of the mind to the material of sensory perception. The Kantian approach assumes that the categories are the same for all academic disciplines. In this discussion of economic ontology, however, the focus of attention will not be the general categories of thought and ontology, but the specific basic categories of the theory of the economy and their relevance to ethical economy.

The concept of ontology has a double meaning. It means an all-encompassing theory of complete reality, or metaphysics, and also the foundational theory of the sub-spheres of complete reality. In the latter meaning, ontology is the sphere of ontology and the fundamental theory of the particular spheres of being that stand in question in an academic discipline. The ontology of the natural sciences investigates their basic models, such as mechanism, teleology, organism, etc. In an analogous way, the ontology of the economy seeks to clarify the question whether the mechanistic and/or organistic ontology, or an ontology of self-consciousness and conscious action is suitable for the discipline of economics.

It is easy to see that the categorial and ontological foundations of an academic discipline are closely related. If the scholar adopts the position of realism in the philosophy of science, then the categories of his or her discipline are not on-

[1] These three fields are also distinguished by Werner Sombart, *Die drei Nationalökonomien*, 2nd Ed. (Berlin, 1967), p. 294.

ly the instruments of his or her research, but also the basic determinants and characteristics of reality. If, on the other hand, the researcher holds the position that cognition is a productive act of the mind or the conceptual construction of reality, then he or she follows the epistemological position of a Kantian criticism or of constructivism.

For the theory of the market and for the conceivability of economic ethics in the market context, the question of how to understand the relationship of the existence of economic reality in itself to its perception in the acting producer or consumer is of significance. For the fundamental theory of economics, the question is of significance whether market reality (e.g. its opportunities for profit) is reflected in the acting businessperson and whether he or she is determined by it to act in a certain, profit-maximizing way, or whether the ability to recognize and to take advantage of opportunities requires the will to take advantage, which does not arise on its own by the necessity of external reality. A broader, meaningful question of economic ontology is whether the basic category of economics, the economic principle, is an essential feature of reality and, therefore, also of nature, so that all movements in nature belong to the economic principle, or whether economics and ethical economy are activities of the intentional, human mind, and economic laws first become effective by human thought in action.

6.1. Intentional or Natural-Scientific Ontology of the Economy?

Both of the main approaches to market theory, the Austrian school and the neo-classical approach, see economics only as a theory of the choice of means, not as one including the consideration of ends.[2] Economics is directed toward the rational choice of means, not the assessment of ends. For both schools, ethical economy or economic ethics remains outside economics. The Austrian and neo-classical approaches are distinguished from one another, however, by the epistemological and ontological status that they assign to the economic principle and to economic theory. The neo-classical approach sees the economic principle as a law of nature,[3] based on the principle of least action in mechanics. In the neo-classical view, the economic principle and the rationality of the expression of the principle of least action lie in the social and cultural spheres. At the beginning of the development of modern mechanics, Maupertuis formulated the principle of least action as follows: "If there is a change in nature, the quantity

[2] On the Austrian school, see Ludwig von Mises, *Human Action* (New Haven, 1949), p. 15. On the neo-classical school, Lionel Robbins, *An Essay on the Nature and Significance of Economic Science*, 2nd Ed. (London, 1962), p. 24.

[3] Cf. Paul A. Samuelson, "Discussion – Problems of Methodology," *American Economic Review*, 53 (1963), p. 232.

of the action that is used in this change is always the least possible. The action is the product of the mass of the body (m) multiplied by its velocity (v) and the distance that it covers (s)." [4] The action is always the minimum of $m \cdot s \cdot v$. The principle of least action forms the basis of the variational principles of classical mechanics, as they were worked out by Euler, Lagrange, and Jacobi.

The discovery of variational principles was of greater significance for physics than for economics, since they made it possible to single out a definite path of movement or action, from all of the possible paths that a body might take from A to B, as the one determined by law of nature and discernable a priori. Variational principles permit the determination of the path of the maximum or minimum as the one that nature, according to physics, and the person who acts with economic rationally, according to economics, will choose from all possible paths. Variational principles make an unambiguous determination and prediction of the path of movement or action possible. Classical mechanics determines that, of all possible paths, the movement of the body always takes the maximum/minimum path, which is given by variational principles. Only because this astonishing simplicity of the way of nature holds true is it possible, according to mechanics, to give a simple solution to the problem of which way a moving body – for example, a ray of light in an inhomogeneous medium – will take.

The fundamental question of the ontology of economics and of the status of the economic principle is whether this principle should be understood as a law of nature in economics, analogous to the principle of least action, or as a rule of the mind, as a rule of the logic of choice. Neo-classical theory interprets the economic principle as a law of nature, which compels human persons. Utility maximization is seen as the force that moves the actions and "causes" their effects. In this view, the laws of microeconomic theory, such as the economic principle, the law of the equality of price and marginal cost with profit maximization, etc., unambiguously determine the solutions of utility maximization, which can be derived from the variational principles of Eulerian or Lagrangean mechanics and variational calculations. It must be stressed here that these unambiguous maximum/minimum solutions are applicable only if utility maximization is seen as the motivating force that drives economic man in the same way that inertia is the driving force that moves heavenly bodies in Newtonian mechanics. Without this assumption of the driving force of maximal utility, the "laws" of economics are no longer rules of a decision logic, or are mere approximations of actual behavior.

If, however, the assumption is made that utility maximization drives the acting person to act economically, in the sense of the economic principle, the question is raised: Why is economics distinguished at all from physics, and why is it

---

[4] P.-L., Moreau de Maupertuis, Letter XI: "Sur ce qui c'est passé à l'occasion du principe de la moindre quantité d'action," in *Oeuvres* (Lyon, 1768), Vol. II, p. 275 ff.

not, as the mechanics of human action, identical to the mechanics of the movements of nature? Although variational principles are identical in mechanics and economics, the ontological theories upon which they are both based are obviously not identical. The fundamental difference between the two fields of maximization consists in two points. First, in the fact that the maximum/minimum solution is always attained in mechanics, but not always in economics, because of error. While mechanical bodies are unable to err, human beings are quite capable of doing so. Error is possible, because human maximization is carried out by thinking beings, while mechanical minimization takes place according to laws of nature. Thought adds the dimension of the representation of reality in the thought to the reality itself, and introduces the element of negation into reality. Reality can be correctly thought, incorrectly thought, and consciously and deliberately refused and rejected. The representation of reality leads to a doubling of reality in thought. This doubling can, on one hand, be misdirected, as in the case of error, or reality can, on the other hand, be negated and criticized in the conceptual representation, as in the case of critique or unhappiness.

The movements of mechanics always attain the optimal solution, the least action. The "movements" of human action do not always attain the optimum, utility maximization. They sometimes fail to attain it because of error or because of critique (i.e. redefinition of the content of the utility function or the goals of the action).

The phenomena of error in the perception of reality and the conscious negation of goals lead to a second fundamental difference between mechanical and economic maximization. The maximandum or minimandum is not well defined in economics, while in mechanics it is clear. Utility is not an empirical concept, but a highly abstract, general concept with infinite and indefinite dimensions. It is impossible to determine externally which arguments are contained in a person's utility function. An external observer cannot determine whether another person has realized utility maximization by his or her behavior, because the dimensions of the individual utility function are not predefined and empirically verifiable. Since the maximandum "utility" is not objective in the way that the minimandum of mechanics is – Maupertuis's $m \cdot s \cdot v$, for instance – it can never be determined from without whether an acting person has actually attained a maximum solution according to the given dimensions of his or her utility function and under the given circumstances, or whether he or she has erred and missed the mark of utility maximization.

The premise of utility maximization becomes an irrefutable proposition, immune to criticism, if its content is given by the statement: "All individuals maximize utility in infinite dimensions." This proposition is the classic case of the logical fallacy of complete disjunction: "All things are either white or non-white," either white or some other color. Applied to the infinite dimensionality of utility maximization, this fallacy says: "Every person maximizes either this dimension or all other dimensions of utility." Utility maximization, without previously-defined dimensions of the concept of utility, means only the tautology that each person either maximizes this particular dimension of utility or all other dimensions of his utility. This proposition is always true, but without analytic value, since we do not know and cannot name the other dimensions.

Economic maximization, therefore, cannot be identical to mechanical maximization, since it runs the risk of error and is open to negation and redefinition of the goals of actions (i.e. to redefinition of the maximanda of the maximization calculus). The maximanda of economic maximization are not given by nature, but are instead chosen by human persons. The neo-classical understanding of utility maximization is unclear in its conception of the act of choice. It offers no genuine choice in utility maximization, since the goal of the action, utility, is always already predetermined and the assumption that maximal utility is the goal of action is always true. According to this theory, I have no choice other than to maximize my utility.

Maximization is a mathematical procedure and as such is indifferent to its application to natural and social phenomena. It is a truth-producing, analytic procedure, however, only in cases in which the maximanda are definable and defined (i.e. only in limited contexts and not as total maximization). Economics is fascinated by classical mechanics, because in the mechanical motion of bodies the minimandum is well-defined and, consequently, the path of motion can be determined unambiguously: nature chooses the shortest path, or the path of least action. In economics, on the contrary, as the discussion in Chapter 2 of the expansion of economic rationality to include ethical and religious rationality has shown, the definition of the maximandum is left open to the decision of the acting person. In human action, the maximization process is not deterministic and mechanical, but intellectual. Only in its realization in the external world is it causally mechanical. Because economic maximization is an intellectual process, it doubles the levels of causation. Action is, first of all, the perception of, imagination of, and choice between possible worlds and, only in a second step, the causal-mechanical realization of the one chosen possible world in the actual world.

Shackles' "paradox of choice"[5] is cited here once again. With its help, the situation can be formulated elegantly. If our actions have no influence on the course of our world after a decision, then we have no genuine choice. If we have a genuine choice and our decision changes the course of the world, we cannot know in detail which effects our actions will have, since the determined course of the world is interrupted by our action. Applied to the problem of maximization and the ontology of the economy, this means that if genuine opportu-

---

[5] G. L. S. Shackle, *Imagination and the Nature of Choice* (Edinburgh, 1979), p. 19. Cf. above, pp. 135-36.

nities for choice exist, the maximization calculus, understood as a precise calculation procedure, is not applicable, since the arguments of the equation are unknown. If, on the other hand, the maximization calculus is applicable in the calculating sense, it is of little use, because the equations of the constraints are known (i.e. the environment is parametric). The decision problem is then not a real decision problem at all, but instead a transformation of known relations between parameters and variables that are not really unknown.

The Austrian school of economics, and Mises especially, have clearly emphasized that economic laws and the economic principle are not laws of nature, but laws of the logic of decision-making, laws of the mind, and that the mechanistic analogy of classical and neo-classical economics is therefore misleading.[6] The a priori nature of Mises' economics follows from his insight that economic "laws" are rules of choice and action and not laws of *actio* and *reactio*. The economic principle is a rule that determines the logic of human preference action, the logic of the preference of one possible course of action to another. It is not a law of nature describing effects that external events exert on human conduct by making them react to stimuli. Economic laws are laws of a logic of choice. The solutions that the practical syllogism of the economic principle delivers do not assert themselves on their own in the acting person, but must instead be chosen by him or her. In other words, they must be intentionally affirmed and appropriated.

The Austrian school, in contrast to neo-classical economics, begins with the fact that action is effective intentionally, not merely reactively and physically. The acting person "reacts" to representations of reality, not to reality itself. Her perception of reality is intentional, voluntary, and active, not merely reactive and passive. Cognition and choice are intentional acts of the *intellectus agens*, not mere effects of an external world on an internal recipient.[7] Mises' approach represents a critical realism in economic epistemology that corresponds to the intentional character of perception and cognition. It is distinguished from the ultra-realism of the neo-classical approach (which is also shared by Marxist theory), according to which the perceptions and actions of economic actors are determined by economic reality. Neo-classical (as well as Marxist) theory assumes that economic reality can be recognized by an external observer as completely objective and can be understood simply to exist, independently of the intentions, perceptions, and expectations of persons acting in it.[8] The critical-

[6] Cf. Ludwig von Mises, "Soziologie und Geschichte," *Archiv für Sozialwissenschaften und Sozialpolitik*, 61 (1929), p. 505.

[7] See also Murray N. Rothbard, "Praxeology" and Ludwig M. Lachmann, "Austrian Economics in the Age of the Neo-Ricardian Counterrevolution," in Edwin G. Dolan, ed., *The Foundations of Modern Austrian Economics* (Kansas City, 1976), pp. 19-36 and 216-20.

[8] Frank Hahn, a leading advocate of equilibrium theory, does say, "I have laid great stress on the difference between the perceived environment and the environment, but very little seems to be

realist approach of the Austrian school is superior to the ultra-realism of the neo-classical approach, because it acknowledges that the acting person perceives reality intentionally, already chooses in her perception what she wants to perceive, and decides and acts as an acting person, *homo agens*, not as one acted upon, *homo actus*. Contrary to the assumption of neo-classical economics, the acting person is not affected passively by reality as *homo oeconomicus* and determined by it to act in one particular way.

The epistemological contrast between the theory of intentional cognition and the ultra-realist theory of the determination of cognition by external reality is of significance for the theory of economic coordination and economic ethics. Economic coordination does not automatically establish itself on its own, according to the critical-realist approach, in the sense that economic reality compels the acting person to act or react. Coordination must instead be brought about by economic – by their knowledge of reality and their acts of choice. The data of the market do not induce the persons acting in the market to behave in one way or another. The data must instead be intentionally perceived, indeed produced, by economic persons, by producers and consumers. Knowledge can be produced only by human striving and the human *intellectus agens*; it does not produce itself or force itself on the acting person. The world is neither "an accomplice of our knowledge" (Michel Foucault) nor completely inaccessible to it. Knowledge, understood as correspondence of the intellect to reality, is possible, but it must be intended and created. Knowledge of the market must be created by the persons acting within it, especially by business managers. Israel Kirzner has shown that the economic data of the market are not "there," but must instead be brought to consciousness intentionally by the businessperson.[9]

Economic knowledge is not compelled by the mechanics of the price system, but is instead created in the discourse of the market by economic persons. The epistemology of the Austrian school follows critical realism: One must imagine a part of reality, and then the being that imagines this part of reality, and then the reality and the being that imagines it, at the same time. There exists the market situation. There exist acting persons, with their perceptions of this market situation. And, finally, there exist the repercussions of the thoughts of the acting persons about the market situation on the market situation itself. The representation of reality in the heads of thinking persons causes repercussions on reality itself, as is shown by the role of expectations and the phenomenon of the self-

known of how the two are related" ("On the Notion of Equilibrium in Economics," in Hahn, *Equilibrium and Macroeconomics* (Oxford, 1984), p. 58). But little follows from the emphasis on the distinction between the perceived and recognized environment and the environment "in itself" for his theory, in which market equilibrium is nevertheless determined as a "final coherent state of balance" (p. 64).

[9] Israel M. Kirzner, *Competition and Entrepreneurship* (Chicago, 1973), pp. 226 ff.

fulfilling prophecy, for example, in the creation of price fluctuations of stock by speculation.

6.2. The Inconceivability of an Objective General Equilibrium and Universal Mechanism

The phenomenon of "doubling" reality by conceiving reality means that total reality cannot be conceived as a single, "general" equilibrium and as *one* universal, objective mechanism. Both the ontology of a general equilibrium of the world and the theory of total reality that understands it as a single, universal mechanism are impossible. First, considerations of the general ontology of mechanism and equilibrium will be discussed. Then, in a second step, they will be transferred to economic ontology and the economic theory of general equilibrium.

If the world forms a single, coherent mechanism, there can be no thinking beings in this total mechanism, because thought and representation of reality interrupt the homogeneity of a thoroughgoing mechanism. Human knowledge of the mechanism is not simply induced mechanically by the mechanism, because a thinking being can also think that the world is not a mechanism, and can think *at the same time* about the mechanism *and* about his or her thoughts about the mechanism.

The second objection to the general ontology of an objective, universal mechanism[10] and, therefore, to the concept of a general equilibrium of the world, is that the totality, or complete reality, cannot be conceived as a universal mechanism. The totality can arise from mechanisms only as a composition of parts that can form, in themselves, partial equilibria or disequilibria. Even if the totality consisted of parts in equilibrium, it would only be made up of partial-equilibrium systems, and would not for that reason be itself "in equilibrium." For its constituent sub-systems that are in equilibrium, the totality forms an environment that is itself incommensurable with the criterion of the equilibrium. The parts of the totality either are or are not in equilibrium; but they form a totality that is not in equilibrium. The totality is not an equilibrium of parts or partial equilibrium systems, but merely the mechanical composition of its parts or partial systems.

Complete reality cannot be seen as *one* equilibrium, because it cannot be conceived as a partial equilibrium system that finds itself again in a larger environment, which is incommensurable with the question whether it is as a whole

---

[10] On the critique of "objective mechanism," see also Robert Spaemann and Reinhard Löw. *Die Frage Wozu?* (Munich, 1981); and Löw, "Zur Kritik des objektiven Mechanismus," *Berichte zur Wissenschaftsgeschichte*, 6 (1983), pp. 29-39.

"in equilibrium." There is no "environment" for complete reality, and no area in it that is outside it. There exists, therefore, for the theory of complete reality, no reference point by means of which it could be judged whether complete reality is "in equilibrium." If the universe is conceived as a unity, it cannot be grasped as a universal mechanism, but only as an organism, because only an organism is self-sufficient and returns into itself. According to Friedrich Schelling, "an unrestricted mechanism would destroy itself," while in an organism "the succession of causes and effects is contained within definite limits and flows back into itself." Therefore, according to Schelling, with any comprehensive observation, "the opposition between organism and mechanism must disappear." It dissolves, when it is assumed that the organism is "earlier" than the mechanism.[11]

Mechanical systems of local equilibrium situations cannot be combined into a general equilibrium without external intervention. They do not assemble themselves into a general equilibrium mechanism by mechanical forces. Partial equilibria do not aggregate themselves mechanically to form a general equilibrium. In a complete reality conceived as mechanical, the condition of complete reality, which is formed from the combination of partial equilibria, is causally-mechanically determined. But one cannot say that this condition as a whole is in equilibrium. It is the result of a mechanical process. The entire universe has no equilibrium, since there nothing outside it by which we could judge whether one condition of complete reality is in greater mechanical equilibrium than another. In mechanical terms, one condition of the world is as good as any other condition. Only local mechanical equilibria are possible, because only they can be related to an external reference point or standard.

For these reasons, the mechanistic cosmology in physics was also superseded by a general theory of evolution or process cosmology. The theory of evolution overcame the static character of mechanics and its inapplicability to large contexts, for which there is no stable point of reference.

The limits of the mechanism as a model of the totality are visible in the minimum principle of classical mechanics. What does "least" action mean, if all motion in nature inevitably follows the minimum path? In comparison to what other actions is each action the least? If *everything* that happens in nature takes place at the smallest cost and with the least action, the expression "least" loses all meaning, since there is no *tertium comparationis*, according to which the least could be measured. If the economic principle had universal validity for all movements in the sense of the mechanical minimum principle, for movements in nature as well as those of human actions, one would have to ask: Why is there anything at all, why not instead nothing? Of what value is the economic principle, if everything that happens inevitable happens economically and there

---

[11] F. W. J. von Schelling, *Von der Weltseele*, in *Werke*, ed. Manfred Schröter, 3rd Ed. (Munich, 1979), Vol. I, pp. 416-18.

are no ends for which economic activity takes place? As Frank Knight has put it in a different context: "The notion of economy makes little sense where ends are not predefined."[12]

6.3. The Market Economy as Teleological Mechanism

The concept of a single general equilibrium and a thorough-going mechanism is not directly applicable to the economic context. The theory of general equilibrium as a state of general equilibrium of the economy is consistent and free of contradiction, only if the ontology of the economy is based upon a Leibnizian theory of the "teleological or metaphysical mechanism," which at the same time transcends the mechanistic ontology to attain the level of entelechial ontology. According to Leibniz, the components of the *mechanismus metaphysicus* are formed by entelechial, monadistic beings, whose entelechies or essences are ends in themselves, between which, however, mechanical cause-effect relationships exist.[13] In this Leibnizian sense, the coordination context of the market can also be seen as an entelechial mechanism, whose coordination takes place by an adjustment of external forces until an equilibrium point is reached, but whose moving forces are of a teleological nature. Human persons, who realize their entelechy or essence and consciously follow goals, are the teleological originators of the market forces that move one another to equilibrium.

In the economic model of a general equilibrium, the interiority of the moving forces of the equilibrium context, namely the will and the desires of the economic subjects, must be seen as goal oriented. Consequently, the concept of equilibrium can be applied to market theory only as a metaphor, because in the interior of the market forces, in contrast to the center of mass of a mechanical equilibrium, substantive and freely chosen goals are effective. An additional distinction within the final causes in the general equilibrium of the market must also be made between natural-teleological causes and conscious, intellectual-teleological goals. Natural-teleological causes are, with the human person, the physiological needs that represent not only subjective goals, but also goals natural to the acting person and predetermined by the organism. Conscious goals are those that human persons set and rationally seek to pursue as intellectual beings.

In the market economy and coordination by the price system, individual demand and welfare are at the same time cause and end – mechanical, effective cause, as well as the final cause of the economic process. The final cause of market equilibrium, individual decision and action, is itself determined by the

---

[12] Frank H. Knight, *On the History and Method of Economics* (Chicago, 1963), p. 295.

[13] Cf. Koslowski, "Economy Principle, Maximizing, and the Co-Ordination of Individuals in Economics and Philosophy," in Koslowski, ed., *Economics and Philosophy* (Tübingen, 1985).

natural teleology of the organism and by the conscious setting of goals by the intellectual self. The market forms a process that serves the optimal allocation of scarce resources for the goals of constantly growing demand, a demand that is, in turn, an expression of individual striving for *self-realization*. The market economy realizes no predefined, concrete goals other than those of individuals. The market is a coordination process, into which individuals enter, in order to adapt their preferences and strategies to those of other persons and to the conditions of the market. Individual preferences are aggregated to become market demand and to determine what the market is to produce. Individual self-realization is the reason and the purpose, the *causa efficiens* and the *causa finalis*, of the market process. The market economy, seen from outside, is a mechanical context that mediates market forces and supplies resources to their efficient application. This mediation takes place in a manner analogous to the adjustments of mechanical powers in nature. But, seen from the inner-perspective of the participants in the market process, the economy is a context of teleological and conscious interactions. The goal of the economic subjects is self-realization and the satisfaction of their subjective plans. Their adaptations to their interaction partners are not mechanistic, but anticipated.

Economic adaptation is more complex that mechanical adaptation. The phenomenon of anticipation transcends the law of mechanics that a being can be at only one position in space-time. The anticipating subject is at the same time with himself and others, when he attempts to understand the behavior of others. He is not moved by a force that is unambiguously identifiable in space and time. A constant exchange and mutual effect of expectations and adaptations oscillates between the ego and the others. This adaptation is not only a mechanical adaptation to other forces, but also an adaptation to other situations by empathy. Seen from within, the market is a social context of interaction among beings of a teleological-entelechial and conscious nature. Because of the organic *and* intellectual nature of these beings, who constitute the market forces in the market, the acting person, neither the mechanistic analogy of completely external market forces nor the organistic analogy of a complete integration of all societal members into an organism holds true for the particular character of the market process.[14]

Mechanistic analogies in economics and their expression in differential equations are useful and legitimate as abstract formulations of complex social processes, as long as one remains conscious of their analogical character. But the basic "ontological" difference between mental, "Lamarckian" adaptation or learning, on one hand, and mechanical "adaptation" and "Darwinian" selection,

---

[14] Cf. Knight, "Statics and Dynamics," in Knight, *The Ethics of Competition and other Essays*, (New Brunswick, N. J., 1997), pp. 153-77.

on the other hand, must be remembered. A "general equilibrium" in the mechanistic sense cannot be applied to economic theory in the literal sense.

6.4. General Equilibrium as Transcendental Ideal

Equilibrium is an ideal or a regulative idea that can help us to understand the market process, but not the description of the result of an empirical, *mechanistic*, variational process. General equilibrium, in the economic sense, is possible only because the economic entities are *not* mere forces existing at a position in space-time.

According to purely mechanistic concepts, it is impossible to unite partial equilibria into an all-encompassing total equilibrium, because there is no exogenous standard for the question: When is this total system "in equilibrium"? There can be, on the contrary, a Pareto-optimal adjustment and adaptation of strategies between anticipating and learning intellectual subjects, which can be called an "equilibrium," if the individual preferences and strategies are adjusted and adapted until a point is reached at which it is no longer possible to improve the situation of one person without worsening the situation of someone else.

This can be explained with the example of Walrasian *tâtonnement*. Léon Walras interprets the way that market participants or parties to contracts sound out their mutual readiness for exchange with and payment to one another, as *tâtonnement*, as a mutual sizing-up of preferences, expectations, the readiness to compromise, and the self-established, non-surpassable threshold values in the contractual or exchange transaction. The *tâtonnement*, understood as sounding-out, can be interpreted at first as a mechanical adjustment and self-balance of forces or intensities of preference. This is possible with preferences, expectations, and anticipations of anticipations, however, only in a remote, analogous sense. *Tâtonnement* actually implies adaptation to expected, mental situations and reactions, learning through communication, anticipation, and empathy. Intellectual adaptation and learning transcend the mechanical adjustment of external, unambiguously identifiable forces.

The problem of rational expectations also shows that economic adaptation is of a higher complexity than mechanistic causality and adaptation, since individuals rationally anticipate the reactions of others and adapt to anticipated behavior, as well as to mental situations. If the determining factors of the market were completely mechanical and additive, the market would be unnecessary as a system of interaction, since we would only have to apply the variation calculations of general mechanics as a calculation procedure in order to determine the maximum solution of the equations that describe economic forces. If, on the other hand, individuals formed an integrated organism, we could optimize the economy, with the help of a centralized decision process, according to the preferences of the central brain or head of the organism. That would mean, as Friedrich von Hayek put it, transforming the catallactic of the market process into a single, large household.[15] We would – in Max Weber's terminology – replace an "autocephalous order," an order of autonomous beings, with a "heterocephalous" or "monocephalous" order, a social order with only one head."[16]

A state of general equilibrium implies a static resolution of the self-altering forces of the market. Since, in human affairs and in the historical world, such a solution – even in theory – can be only provisional and approximate, and every equilibrium point of the market is only a transition to the next disturbance and re-adaptation, and since every point of equilibrium is historically unrepeatable and, therefore – in opposition to physical, partial equilibria – experimentally non-reproducible, it would be advisable to give up the concept of market equilibrium altogether, in favor of the concept of market process. The mechanistic connotations of the concept of general equilibrium have the tendency in economic theory to obscure the fact that the economy is not a mechanism, but instead a simultaneous context of mechanical causes in the production of material goods *and* of intellectual causes in economic interaction and the coordination of human individuals with self-consciousness and self-relationship. The economy belongs simultaneously to both worlds, the material world and the intellectual world.

The term "general equilibrium" blurs the ontological distinction between the various levels of reality, the physical and the social or mental. In interpreting "general equilibrium," economic theory oscillates between an interactionistic, "mental" interpretation and a mechanistic, physical interpretation of "equilibrium." In the Austrian tradition, equilibrium is understood as the interactionistic correspondence and balancing-out of the expectations of all concerned individuals. In the Ricardian and neo-classical tradition, in contrast, it is understood as the mechanistic adjustment of market forces toward reaching a state of equilibrium.[17] As Mises pointed out, this tradition treats equilibrium in the sense of an epistemological ultra-realism, as something existing: "The mathematical economists . . . deal with equilibrium as if it were a real entity and not a limiting no-

---

[15] Friedrich A. von Hayek, *Der Wettbewerb als Entdeckungsverfahren* (Kiel, 1968), p. 8.

[16] Max Weber, *Economy and Society*, ed. Guenther Roth and Claus Wittich (New York, 1968), Vol. I, pp. 49-50.

[17] Hahn, "On the Notion of Equilibrium in Economics," p. 65, summarizes the contribution of general equilibrium theory thus: It has made an important contribution to the knowledge of economies "by describing so precisely what would have to be the case if there were to be no Keynesian problems." But, since these Keynesian problems of the formation of expectations and uncertainty about the future are undeniable, a theory that assumes complete adaptation of all plans to the equilibrium is unrealistic.

tion, a mere mental tool. What they are doing is vain playing with mathematical symbols, a pastime not suited to convey any knowledge."[18]

The state of equilibrium of an economy as a whole can only be a transcendental ideal or a regulative idea in the Kantian sense, not a categorial concept of the analysis of reality. Kirzner, who represents a position between a radical subjective position, such as Shackle's, Lachmann's, or Wiseman's, and the neoclassical position, assumes that there is a potential state of equilibrium of the economy at every moment that is attained by the anticipations and actions of entrepreneurs. It is they who coordinate the plans of individuals and act as mediators between different expectations and plans, as they realize the differential profits that become possible because different opportunities for profit arise at various places and times. As arbitrageurs, they achieve coordination between the different plans and expectations that persons entertain at different places and times and that differ from one another according to individuals, places, and times. Profits are differential incentives and rewards for the arbitrageur-entrepreneur to achieve the coordination.[19] According to Kirzner's theory, the opportunities that entrepreneurs realize exist independently of whether the entrepreneurs perceive them. The entrepreneur uses opportunities that exist, even when they are not perceived or imagined.[20]

The following objection must be raised against this understanding of the market process as a means of bringing about general equilibrium through the arbitrage of entrepreneurs: Even if a potential equilibrium of the plans of all market participants existed independently of the acts of imagining this equilibrium, and if it was brought to reality by entrepreneurial activity alone, it would certainly be unrecognizable and no one would be able to say when it was actually realized. A general equilibrium is not recognizable in the categorial sense that one could state the conditions of its realization. It can only serve as an approximation ideal, as a regulative idea of the social process. The expansion of the category of equilibrium to the ontological idea of a "general equilibrium" is a category mistake, the logical fallacy of *metabasis eis allo genos*. Partial equilibrium is a categorial and verifiable concept; general equilibrium is a metaphysical and categorially-unspecifiable concept. The categorial concept of partial equilibrium, whose existence conditions can be given, is converted into the metaphysical concept of total equilibrium. The borders of this equilibrium, with other national markets and the global market, for instance, are also undefinable. A general equilibrium is general only if the entire global market is in the equilibrium, a

[18] Mises, *Human Action*, p. 251.

[19] Israel M. Kirzner, *Competition and Entrepreneurship*, pp. 81-87.

[20] Kirzner, *ibid.*, p. 81, clearly distances himself here from the other current of the Austrian school, from Joseph A. Schumpeter, who stressed the central importance of innovation in entrepreneurial activity.

situation of the world that is certainly unrecognizable. The problem of the demarcation of what must be "in equilibrium" reveals the difficulties involved in extending the concept of equilibrium to larger wholes. The borders of "general" equilibrium and the identity of what is in equilibrium can no longer be given.

The concept of "general equilibrium" achieves, in one respect, something quite important. It provides a concept of the economy's unity and completeness. It makes it possible to think of the economy as a coherent whole. This concept of the completeness of the economy that general equilibrium theory produces is problematic, however, because the transfer of the concept of complete equilibrium from mechanics into economics provides only an incomplete concept of social unity. The unity of social reality is conceived too analogously to the unity of a mechanical system.

An equilibrium, or a system in equilibrium, represents a whole only in the extrinsic sense, not in the intrinsic sense.[21] The fascination in economics with the concept of equilibrium is based on the ability of mechanical equilibrium theory to make a unity that is not a real unity conceivable. A system of equilibrium is a unity whose oneness is completely external to the parts of this unity. Just as the parts of an interdependent mechanical system (e.g. the planets of the solar system) constitute only an external unity, the economy, according to general equilibrium theory, forms a unity that does not really integrate the parts of the system, but nevertheless brings them together to form the whole of a system. The market participants, the members of an economy, form a unity that remains external to their existence as individuals and components. An equilibrium system represents a unity only in the extrinsic sense, because its parts are not integrated into a whole, but are only brought together. The concept that the general equilibrium of the unity of social reality develops is deficient, if the equilibrium context of the market is seen as the one unique, definitive form of unity. It is adequate, if the unity of the market is understood as the extrinsic unity of *economic* interaction.

Three forms of the unity of the social world are to be distinguished: forms of unity constructed in analogy to a complete equilibrium, to an organism, and to an intellectual whole. Individual persons are, first of all, *elements* of an economic equilibrium context. Second, they are defined by their *participation* in the whole of social reality and as participating *organs* of this whole. They are at the same time both instruments and purposes for one another and for the whole, and form a whole that is comparable to an organism. But the social whole, understood as a social organism, gives more room for the independence of the organs than does a natural organism. Finally, the individuals are *members* of a whole. Their unity is formed in the same way in which they, as parts, express or repre-

---

[21] Cf. Hans Driesch, *Über die grundsätzliche Unmöglichkeit einer Vereinigung von universeller Teleologie und Mechanismus* (Heidelberg, 1914), p. 12.

sent the whole. Their being as members of an intellectually meaningful unity is a representation of the unity and the wholeness in the individual. Their role of representing the whole expresses their *membership* in the whole.[22]

The social and economic order must be differentiated according to the degrees of being a unity. Various forms of social unity are valid in the social and economic order. The form of unity of market equilibrium is one that suffices for the union of self-interested actions in the market. This form of unity, however, cannot represent the entirety of social reality. But neither can being an organ and instrument for the whole of an organism be the totality of the unity, because the independence of the individual is not safeguarded within it. Only the relation of the parts to the whole as members and the intellectual representation of the whole in the individual do justice to social unity as *intellectual* union. The individual is neither only an atomistic, self-contained element nor only an instrument for an organic wholeness and outward-looking relationships with others. The individual is, on one hand, a relationship in himself as a self-referential intellectual being and as a being who has needs for himself and, on the other hand, at the same time a relation to the unity of social reality, in which he is both an element and an organ and member.

6.5. Poietic Imagination of New Possibilities in the Market Process

The arbitrage theory of the entrepreneur, as Israel Kirzner has developed it, underestimates the role of the imagination in the creation of new reality. Entrepreneurial imagination is not only the discovery of existing opportunities, but also the creation of new realities. An older distinction within the ability to imagine in the human faculty of the power of imagination can clarify the difference. Avicenna and Albertus Magnus distinguish between *imaginatio* and *phantasia*. *Imaginatio* is the ability that retains the images (*imagines*) that the impressions of the senses have caused after the sense-impressions themselves are no longer present. The *imaginatio* provides the person with a supply of mental images. For the intellectual ability of *imaginatio*, the images that it imagines are given in the external world. The imagination reproduces them only as ideas in the memory. It elevates potentially existing images to the level of intellectual reality. The images that already exist in the world and that the *imaginatio* brings before the mind thus constitute the material that the second imaginative faculty, *phantasia*, uses to create new and previously unknown ideas and images. Fantasy is the ability to recombine mental images by composition and division and to create new combinations of existing things or even completely new objects, for

[22] On the unity-forms of the social, see also Gustav Gundlach, "Sozialphilosophie," in *Staatslexikon*, 6th Ed. (Freiburg, 1962), Vol. VII, p. 338.

instance centaurs, to use Albert's example.[23] *Phantasia* is what the European romantics later called "poetic imagination" (Coleridge) or the "productive power of imagination" (Schelling), the power of imagination that creates new reality, both in poetry and in economic and political production or *poiesis*.[24]

The function of the entrepreneur is not only the *imaginatio* and the discovery of existing opportunities. His or her role also involves creating new reality by poietic and creative imagination and fantasy. There is no potential, pre-existing, general equilibrium that must merely be brought to reality. There is only the market process, in which new realities and new visions of goods and services are imagined and realized.[25]

The entrepreneur does not merely combine factors of production optimally and minimize production costs in order to sell his product at a given market price, as the neo-classical theory of the firm assumes.[26] Neither does he merely realize opportunities that already exist. He also creates new opportunities and situations by going beyond the role of the mere arbitrageur to that of the innovator, who imagines new products and ways of production (i.e. new *poiesis*) with "poietic imagination" and the "productive power of fantasy" and is, in that respect, similar to the artist.

---

[23] Albertus Magnus, *Summa de Homine*, in *Alberti Magni Opera Omnia* (Paris, 1896), Vol. 35, qu. 37, 1 ff. See also, Pico della Mirandola, *De Imaginatione*, 1501.

[24] Samuel Taylor Coleridge, *Biographia Literaria*, in *Collected Works*, ed. James Engell and W. Jackson Bate (London and Princeton, 1983), Vol. VII, pp. 304-6, distinguishes the ability of the imagination (thereby going beyond Albert in making distinctions) into primary imagination, secondary imagination, and "fancy" (fantasy). He identifies the primary imagination with the reproductive power and the secondary imagination with the poetic or productive power of imagination (thus with Albert's *phantasia*) and separates the mere "fancy" from both of these abilities. – *Phantasia* can be both a productive, creative imagination and an empty fantasy of illusory and deceptive worlds.

[25] Shackle's understanding of market processes in a kaleidoscopic, constantly-changing society is closer to the phenomenon of continual re-creation in the market than is Kirzner's theory of the market process. Kirzner still adheres too much to the mechanical ontology of equilibrium, while Shackle's ontology of the economy belongs to the process ontology of Alfred North Whitehead's tradition. For a comparison of the Austrian and Shackle's "kaleidoscopic" approaches, see Lachmann, "From Mises to Shackle," *Journal of Economic Literature*, 14 (1976), pp. 54-62.

[26] Hahn, "The Winter of our Discontent," in *Equilibrium and Macroeconomics*, p. 144, freely admits that the neo-classical portrayal of the task of the entrepreneur leaves much reality out of account: "[Janos Kornai's] insistence that prices constitute only a fraction of the information bundle economic agents must digest seems to me to be correct and to be one of the most important areas of further study."

6.6. The Market as Social Discourse and Process of Entelechial Coordination

The market economy is a *mechanismus metaphysicus*, insofar as it is, seen from within, entelechial and, seen from without, mechanistic. The interpretation of the market process as a discourse and *mechanismus metaphysicus* is in accordance with the dual nature of economic action. Economic coordination must achieve technological or mechanistic effectiveness in production and, at the same time, enable human beings to do what they want to do in production and consumption, and thus realize efficiency. The economy must not only produce with technological proficiency, but must also produce what human persons want to produce and what they want to consume. The latter meaning of economic efficiency can be called "entelechial efficiency." Entelechial efficiency means that the economy makes the maximal realization and expression of the human – entelechial – self possible. We realize ourselves in production more than in consumption. We consume in order to be creative producers more than we produce in order to consume. An economic order must begin with the postulate of freedom in production, and not primarily with consumer liberty or sovereignty.

The market forms something that is a contradiction at the level of basic ontological models, a "teleological mechanism," from mechanical, external adaptation and the internal pursuit of the goals of the elements out of which it is composed. The teleological mechanism and coordination process of the market is a formal process, insofar as the coordination system itself does not influence, or only secondarily influences, the substantive goals that it mediates. The coordination context as a whole, however, has a clear, purposeful orientation that cannot consist only in adjustment to external market forces until an equilibrium point is reached. The market serves the substantive purpose of making possible the individual pursuit of goals and their coordination, for the purpose of attaining the maximal realization of one's own self.

Completely formal coordination, in the sense of a mere adjustment of forces to reach an equilibrium point, cannot be the goal of the price system, because this coordination cannot normatively single out one form of coordination from other possible ways of coordination. A purely formal coordination process of a mechanical kind is not consciously organized, social cooperation and coordination, but merely a self-balancing of forces, whose output, a mechanical equilibrium point of an accidental constellation of forces, can make no claim to legitimacy. The market, competition, and the price system are a social discourse that serves the production of knowledge and social cohesion. They do not comprise a mechanical parallelogram of forces following from the physical adjustment of forces to reach an equilibrium point. Social and economic "forces" are not physical-mechanical forces, but conscious units of action seeking to realize their objectives in exchanges with one another. The market is the central discourse of society, because it makes possible the individual pursuit of goals and actions, the coordination of subjective judgments of costs and profits that arise from economic cooperation, and the simultaneous and continual control of the success of strategies to achieve low institutional costs.

As a social and formal discourse and "mechanism" of the coordination of the individual pursuit of goals, the market is at the same time socially organized and developed in the sense of an evolutionary process of selection. As a social discourse, the market has a goal that is substantive, not merely formal, because the organizers of the market, acting persons, have an internal dimension of establishing goals, not merely an external dimension of having been brought about, as with a physical mechanism. The market should achieve coordination, not as the merely external adjustment of forces, but as a process of mediation arriving at a situation that brings about the greatest possible realization of the subjectivity of the market participants. The efficiency of an economy in the broader sense means realizing in social coordination the maximum of entelechial self-realization and value-realization, not the maximum production of quantities of goods.

6.7. Not Value Subjectivism, but Subjective Value-Realization

The meaning of the market process as coordination, making possible the meeting of needs and the entelechial self-realization of the market participants, also does not follow from pure subjectivism in value theory. The position of value subjectivism can be described as follows: All value attitudes that go into the market process are subjective. Consequently, all members of society should be allowed as much as possible to make their own decisions concerning their own values and those of everyone else. Hartmut Kliemt recognizes here a naturalistic fallacy, which improperly draws from the premise of how the things of nature are the conclusion that that is how they should be. In the present case, from the "metatheoretical, descriptive premise that value judgments are ultimately incapable of being true," the conclusion is fallaciously drawn that "the members of society should make the fundamental value judgments of their lives with the least possible amount of social interference."[27]

In the case referred to by Kliemt, the naturalistic fallacy is not incorrect. Its presumed fallaciousness is asserted by many advocates of modern ethics and social science as a dogma, without it being made clear how one can come to any normative judgment without beginning with the nature of the subject matter and the decision situation and going back and forth between descriptive and normative propositions. If no member of the set of normative propositions ever fol-

---

[27] Hartmut Kliemt, "Ökonomik und Ethik," *Wirtschaftswissenschaftliches Studium*, 16 (1987), pp. 114-15.

lows from a member of the set of descriptive propositions, there are two completely unrelated classes of propositions and two separate realities and universes.[28] The uncritical assumption of the validity of the naturalistic fallacy also leads into the two-worlds theory of the separation of economics and ethics, of "is" and "ought" statements about the social world. In that case, the union of "is" and "ought," economics and ethics, their point of unity, would no longer be conceivable.

Two components of the theory of value subjectivism are false: First, the assumption that value subjectivism's premise – that no value judgment is ultimately capable of being true – is "meta-theoretically descriptive." Second, the conclusion that it follows from the assumption of value subjectivism that persons should be permitted the greatest possible latitude in making their own value judgments.

First, concerning the premise of value subjectivism: If one leaves aside the problem that it is unclear what a meta-theoretical theory is, the more serious objection remains that one cannot know that the proposition that all value judgments are ultimately not capable of being true is descriptive. As a proposition about a universal truth, this proposition is unprovable, and as a descriptive proposition, it presupposes a particular ontology (of separation) of the relationship between "is" and "ought." For, purely descriptively, there are many people in social reality who believe that the separation of "is" and "ought" is impossible. Descriptively, the proposition cannot be about the inability of *all* value judgments to be true. The proposition itself presents an ontology that does not understand itself to be an ontology, but instead to be a "metatheory." And the proposition dishonestly represents its establishment, not as ontological and metaphysical, but as empirical or descriptive. But since the adherents of the naturalistic fallacy reject the conclusion of "ought" from "is," they must also reject the ontological formulation of the naturalistic fallacy and replace it with the hypothetical principle that it is simply difficult to make a justified value judgment and to conclude "ought" from "is."

Second, concerning the conclusion of value subjectivism: The value-subjective position concludes from the premise that the descriptive world is separate from the normative world that the organization of the economy and the social order must be liberal. This conclusion, however, is not justified. If all value judgments are subjective, they are also arbitrary. If all value judgments are arbitrary, the social institutions corresponding to them are also arbitrary, because the institutions cannot be founded on definite, intersubjectively-universalizable value judgments. What follows from value subjectivism is not the constitutional state and market-economic order, but a power theory of social order: The subjective value judgments that become institutionally dominant are those that

---

[28] See also above, Section 3.3, pp. 89-91.

emerge as dominant. If all value judgments are subjective, the subjective value judgments that become objective and socially decisive are those that assert themselves as the most powerful, in the sense of external domination.

Drawing the conclusion of the subjectivism of all value judgments from the requirement that subjectivity and liberty should be safeguarded in the social order is a fallacy – not because of its naturalistic character, but because this conclusion misunderstands "subjectivity." Subjectivity, in the emphatic and substantial sense, should not be confused with subjectivity, in the sense of arbitrariness. Subjectivity does not mean the arbitrariness of a verdict and the mere idiosyncrasy or peculiarity of persons, but the inner dimension and liberty of the subject and self. Subjectivity is itself a value category, and denotes the inalienable inner- and self-relatedness of the human subject to himself and his liberty. If subjectivity is understood as the self-referential character of the person, in the conclusion cited above of the subjectivity of the human person to the requirement for social and political institutions that acknowledge and safeguard this subjectivity, this conclusion is not a fallacy. All value judgments are subjective, in the sense that they must be affirmed or rejected by a substantially free and ethical subject, because otherwise they would not be value judgments, but imposed judgments. From this concept of subjectivity, which is not identical to subjectivism, it follows that the institutions of the economy and the state must be organized in such a way that they permit subjectivity and liberty in the substantial sense.

If, on the other hand, the subjectivity of value judgments means that all value judgments are subjective, in the sense of arbitrariness and idiosyncrasy, it follows that nothing normative can be stated about the institutions corresponding to these value judgments. One can only venture the prognosis that these institutions will probably be similarly arbitrary and extremely idiosyncratic. The fallacy of concluding the subjective arbitrariness of value judgments from the observance of subjectivity in social institutions does not follow from any naturalism present here, but from the non-naturalism of this conclusion. It is not a case of concluding, from the descriptive statement that all value judgments are subjective and arbitrary, the corresponding naturalistic normative statement that the institutions following from these values must also be arbitrary, but simply a case of drawing, from the premise of the arbitrariness of value-subjectivism, a false conclusion that was not contained in the premise. From the premise of value subjectivism, the conclusion is drawn that it is necessary to realize a substantial concept of subjectivity and free self-referentiality of the person in society. This is a fallacy, but not a naturalistic fallacy. The position of value subjectivism is not identical to the viewpoint that subjectivity is a value.

From a substantial concept of subjectivity as a presupposition of value-realization also in the sphere of the economy, it follows, on the contrary, that the coordination of the market must make subjectivity in the substantial sense possible. Subjective value-realization and the realization of subjectivity or "self-hood" become the *telos* of the market process and the standard of market co-ordination. If this *telos* of the market process is not valid, and if the market is understood as a mechanism of merely natural forces that balance one another out until they reach a static resting point, this evening out of forces is not an equilibrium with normative significance, but only the result of a given combination of forces.

A balancing out of forces that reaches an equilibrium point cannot be the complete content of economic coordination, since this balance does not safeguard the subjectivity of everyone, but only provides a place for subjectivism to be itself. Market equilibrium cannot mean merely that the strongest arbitrary subjectivism has been achieved and balanced out, that the system has attained a static-mechanical point of rest. Market equilibrium involves, instead, the ideal of a social equilibrium, in which the subjectivity of each person, in the sense of self-realization, is safeguarded and is coordinated with that of each other person. The realization of the self and of subjectivity, not the mere subjectivism of arbitrariness, is the goal of human action. Making the pursuit of this goal possible represents the determination of the meaning of the arrangement of all social discourses that make up the market and price system.

The question whether subjectivity or subjectivism should prevail in the market is of crucial significance for its legitimation. From the premise that the purpose of the market is, besides meeting needs, to promote the subjective development of the human person in the economy, as much as it can coexist with the subjective development of everyone else, it follows that the legitimation of the market system as a social discourse must satisfy social and ethical criteria and requires a political structure. If, on the other hand, the purpose of the market is to mediate the subjectivisms of individual arbitrariness and to lead by mechanistic adjustment of the forces of the subjectivisms to their temporary balance, one must bring the naturalism peculiar to this theory to an end. From pure value subjectivism it follows that one should disturb the mechanical adjustment of forces as little as possible and must consider each result of the adjustment to be just as good as every other result with distinguishable combinations of forces. If, however, one were to draw, from the subjective premise of the arbitrariness of demand, substantial criteria for economic and political institutions, such as the assurance of liberty and the development of subjectivity, one would commit the fallacy of begging the question. One would presuppose unproven principles as proven and fail to state the reason for the conclusion. One would neglect to explain why *subjectivity* should be safeguarded. Without the assumption that teleology or entelechy is inherent to social reality, and therefore also to the market, to create the conditions of the development of human subjectivity, no theory of the legitimation of individualistic institutions of the economy that safeguard liberty can be developed, only a theory of the power of the social process, in which the strongest assert themselves.

The concept of the subjectivity and self-referential character of the intellectual human being forms the ontological basis that makes ethical decision and responsibility conceivable. Subjectivism, understood as the arbitrariness of every subjective demand, is, on the contrary, indeed able to include moral subjectivity as a demand besides others, but only morality as an arbitrary, idiosyncratic, subjective demand that is no better than any other. Subjectivism can represent ethical subjectivity in itself only in the improper sense, as a subjective, ethical demand. Ethical responsibility, the ability of ethical subjectivity, on the other hand, presupposes an ontology of the economy in which subjectivity can be conceived as something transcending mere subjectivism. An ontology of the economy that understands the market as a deterministic *mechanism* of equilibrium excludes ethics, in the sense of substantial subjectivity capable of universalization, in the sense of an "individual law," because it sees subjective demands as the unquestionable and predetermined stimuli of motion, which are only mechanically balanced in the price system. The mechanistic model of the economy must leave out of account the question of how ethical preferences or "subjective demands" capable of universalization can enter into the economy at all. Ethics cannot be understood within the ontology of mechanism, because intellectual self-reference and ethics, understood as the expression of self-consciousness, are not to be inserted into the "objective" mechanism. In the mechanism, everything is always as it is, because all components of the mechanism either are moved by another, external component or blindly continue their own movement. In the mechanism, there exists no ability of taking distance from oneself, of self-reference, and of the ability of consciousness to negate or to conceive that something can or should be different. In the mechanism, there is no difference between "is" and "ought" situations, only end states of partial equilibrium that are as they are and only represent transitions to other states, which are, like their predecessors, incommensurable with normative criteria.

6.8. Ethical Economy or Subjective Economics as General Theory of Human Action?

The theory presented here of the market as a *teleological* "mechanism," whose ontological foundation cannot consist in the model of mechanical equilibrium, raises the question of how teleology and mechanism, mental inner-connection and self-movement and external economic control can be merged into *one* ontological concept. This question is, at the same time, the ontological formulation of the problem of how ethical, freely-chosen maxims of action and economic determinants of action arising from the market situation can be understood to coexist. Since the time of Kant, the dualism of moral self-determination of the free will by mere observance of the law and external determination by the economic situation has been dominant in economics and ethics. The dualism of ethics and economics can be overcome, only if the perception of economic reality and its effect on businesspersons are already conceived as being determined by intentions. The intentional approach of economics, as represented by the Austrian school, already reduces the opposition of ethics and economics in economic theory to a greater degree than does the mechanical, ultra-realist approach of neo-classical economics. If the effect of economic reality on the acting person is already assumed to be subjected to the intentionality of being-perceived, intentional – ethical and economic – value perspectives already enter into the perception of economic reality and determine the perspectives from which the reality is intentionally recognized. The structure of the "mechanism" by which the external world of prices and market conditions makes an impression on the internal world of representations of reality and on the formation of ethical-economic preferences may not be analyzable in every detail.

Mises thus advocates the view that developing a theory of this mechanism, understood as a scientific theory, is impossible and that the relationship of the internal world of representations of the world to the external economic world represents for us a fact that cannot be further clarified and is, in this respect, comparable to the mind-body problem. In both cases – the mind-body problem and the theory of market coordination – the cause-and-effect relationship between the external world and internal perception is under discussion.[29] Mises' value subjectivism is, however, too radical here. Even if the "mechanics" of the repercussions between values and perceptions, between ethical convictions or preferences and economic action, cannot be explained in detail, and if ethical economy is, therefore, not possible as a causal-mechanical theory, the effectiveness of ethical convictions is still undeniable and universal ethical values can be distinguished, described, and "understood" as action-guiding preference perspectives.

Ethical convictions influence the external action of the human person, even if we no more understand *how* that happens than with other repercussions of cognitions of the external world on action in this external world. We do not know *how* the mind influences the body; but we do know *that* the mind and the will influence the body, and vice versa. The question of how a general equilibrium is conceivable in economics is a special case of the mind-body problem, which in market theory takes the form of a double question: How, on one hand, are teleological actions "moved" to an equilibrium by being led "mechanically" by market forces to adjust and adapt their efforts? And how, on the other hand, are the action intentions altered in this process of variation, which is to reach the

[29] Cf. Mises, "Soziologie und Geschichte," p. 507.

equilibrium by the perception of the market conditions and the other actions? At a high level abstraction and without explaining the cause-and-effect relationship between market conditions and perceptions of market conditions, the relationship between the intentions of economic persons and their reactions to market conditions can be described as a teleological mechanism.

Ethical economy, understood as the union of ethical and economic action orientations, can explain causally the relationship of values and preference perspectives or preferences to actions no more than pure economic theory can. For positive economic theory, the concrete value judgments of individuals can only be regarded as data. But ethical economy does not stop with this self-restriction of economics, because this relationship of the internal world of values to external action is precisely its object of study. Ethical economy is not in the position to *explain* the relationship of the world within us to the external world; but it is able to illuminate and to *understand* it. Its methodology is not that of causal-mechanical or nomological explanation, but that of the understanding, as it was portrayed above as circulation, which takes place in the expressions of experience, in the understanding and reexperience of the expression.

The basic model of ethical economy is the understanding and reexperience of the meaningfulness of action. Understanding and re-experiencing are operations of the mind, made possible by the self-experience of the subject and by the expansion of horizons resulting from understanding other persons. The human person's horizon of understanding is expanded and deepened in its effectiveness by understanding other persons and understanding their texts, by fusing one's own horizon with other persons' horizons of understanding.

The epistemology and ontology of the economy in the tradition of the Austrian school, which is "intentional" and provides more room for the understanding, is closer to the theory of ethical economy than is the "mechanistic" and ultrarealist ontology of neo-classical economics. The latter is not able in its ontological model to conceive the degrees of freedom of perception and decision necessary for the integration of ethics into economics. In the Austrian tradition, in contrast, the fact of the subjectivity and intentionality of the perception of reality and its significance for knowledge of economic reality is acknowledged.[30] While the ontology of the neo-classical economists is too objective for a theory of ethical economy, the ontology of the Austrian school is in danger of being too subjective for such a theory, because it sees ethical value preference perspectives as incapable of universalization and truth. In their opposition and affinity, neo-classical economics and radical value subjectivism represent the two sides of the scientistic understanding of human praxis. Scientism constantly

---

[30] See above all Mises' emphasis of the methodology of the understanding for economic and historical knowledge. Mises, *Human Action*, p. 50: "The discovery and the delimitation of understanding was one of the most important contributions of modern epistemology."

wavers back and forth between an excessive claim to objectivity in the economy and an arbitrary subjectivism in the question of ethics and aesthetics: "The scientific mind can rest only in one of two extreme positions, that there are absolute values, or that every individual desire is an absolute and one as 'good' as another. But neither of these is true; we must learn to think in terms of 'value-standards' which have validity of a more subtle kind."[31]

Ethical economy is the attempt to create, between the fiction of absolute values and the arbitrariness of value subjectivism, a theory of interpretive economics and an ethical-economic theory of the understanding and judgment of human actions that allows value questions to be dealt with scientifically, even if not scientistically. Ethics does not stand outside scientific reason in a state of mere arbitrariness. But neither is it a causal-mechanical theory of the explanation of action. It attempts, instead, to work out and establish value criteria whose validity is of a "more subtle" kind than the laws of nature and those of positive economics.

Ludwig von Mises undertook the ambitious attempt to establish economics as a general theory of human action. This attempt is convincing, in that it tries to understand action as a whole and to go beyond the reductionism of the economic action theory derived from the model of economic man. The attempt is dubious, however, in that it understands the inner world of the human person as merely subjective and inaccessible to the theory. In Mises' theory, ethics must remain outside the scientific theory of human action. According to him, the objectivity of his economic theory lies in this exclusion of subjective value questions.[32] Two objections can be made against this conception of economics as a general theory of action. First, Mises' theory excludes the most important questions of the understanding of human actions, those relating to understanding value orientations. Objectivity is attained by the renunciation of the completeness of the object of investigation. It is, therefore, no real objectivity, since value convictions and ethics also belong to the objectivity of action.

The incompleteness of the object of investigation in Mises' theory of human action leads to the second objection that must be raised against his praxeology from the perspective of a theory of ethical economy. Mises claims that his economic theory is a praxeological theory, a general theory of human action. On the other hand, he restricts his theory to an analysis of the means of action and excludes the analysis of ends and values.[33] Actions are, however, essentially determined by goals. A comprehensive theory of action must, therefore, include

---

[31] Knight, "Ethics and the Economic Interpretation," in *The Ethics of Competition and other Essays*, pp. 31-32.

[32] Mises, *Human Action*, p. 21: "It is in this subjectivism that the objectivity of our science lies. Because it is subjectivistic and takes the value judgments of acting man as ultimate data not open to any further critical examination, it is itself above all strife of parties and factions."

[33] *Ibid.*, p. 15.

the analysis of ends and values. If it restricts itself to the means-end relationship and excludes the analysis of means *and* ends, praxeology cannot be the desired comprehensive theory of action. Only ethical economy can be this comprehensive theory, because it unifies the economic theory of the relationships between means and ends and the ethical theory of the understanding and judgment of values and goals.

Mises is correct in maintaining that there is no difference between economic and non-economic motives,[34] because we *want* to pursue *all* of our goals economically, even if we do not always succeed in doing so. But it does not follow from this proposition that economics is the comprehensive theory of human action. All goals – ethical, aesthetic, economic, and political – can be realized either rationally or irrationally, economically or non-economically. But it is not the case that the content of all goals is absorbed into economics. A comprehensive theory of human action must be both a theory of the economics of pursuing objectives and a theory of the understanding and judgment of means and ends in their ethical, aesthetic, political, and cultural determination. Ethical economy, understood as a theory of ethics and the culture of the economy, attains the goal of a universal and integral theory of human action to a greater extent than does Mises' praxeology, which excludes the values of actions from its investigation. The agenda of a theory of ethical economy is, however, in accordance with Mises' project insofar as it acknowledges that ethics cannot do without pure economic theory, even if the latter is insufficient as a comprehensive theory of action. A general theory of human action must go beyond ethics and economics, to achieve a theory of ethical economy and ethics related to economics.

---

[34] *Ibid.*, p. 63.

CHAPTER 7

ECONOMIC ETHICS IN THE MARKET ECONOMY

The concept of mechanics and general equilibrium theory in economics is an analogy that has led, besides other misunderstandings, to the mistake that the coordination of the market and the equilibrium process of the price system do not need ethics, but instead lead to the economic optimum without it. The possibility and necessity of a theory of economic ethics in the market economy is rejected with the argument that decision room for the economic-ethical demands and maxims necessary for the acting person, whether manager or employee, exists only in a market that is monopolized or oligopolized, but not in a market with perfect competition. In a truly competitive market, the acting person has no room for ethical considerations, but also has no need of ethics, because the pressure of competition already compels him or her to economically-correct actions. Correct actions consist only in adapting to the decision variables of the acting person in the existing market conditions, in price taking with existing market price and the expansion of production until market price is equal to marginal cost.

Faith in the automatism of competition in the competitive market and the accompanying conviction that competition makes economic ethics superfluous, are expressed in two variants. One sees economic ethics as superfluous, but harmless. The other sees it as superfluous and also harmful or detrimental to economic efficiency. Both positions are to be distinguished from the objection that it can be extremely difficult for the individual to follow ethical rules in the competitive market when unethical practices have become habitual for all or most competitors.

7.1. Does the "Mechanism of Competition" Make Ethics Superfluous?

The theory of the superfluousness of economic ethics in the competitive market regards ethics as a dispensable luxury. The moral actions of an individual manager are seen as undesirable, even when possible, because they disturb the mechanism of competition and distort price signals.[1] Managers should be compelled by competition to produce efficiently and to earn profits. Their function is effectiveness, not morality. To cite the mechanism of competition as an argu-

[1] William J. Baumol, "Business Responsibility and Economic Behavior," in Edmund S. Phelps, ed., *Altruism, Morality, and Economic Theory* (New York, 1975), pp. 46-47.

ment against economic ethics is erroneous, however, because this argument is based on a nonestablishable faith in the mechanics of the price system and excessive optimism regarding the possibilities and speed of the movement of the factors of production (i.e. workers and investors) and the corresponding opportunities for the movement of customers, consumers, and suppliers. According to this "competitive optimism" and mechanistic understanding of market coordination, competition already compels firms sufficiently from outside to efficient *and* fair behavior in the firm's internal labor market and in the external customer market, without anyone having to consider the common good or ethics, because otherwise the workers would migrate to other employers and the customers to other suppliers.

This conception of the market economy is overly optimistic, however, because the mechanism of competition neither functions so well that it excludes market failure nor guarantees efficiency in such a way that all firms in the market already produce to the maximum of their capability without business ethics. As has been shown above,[2] if everyone pursues self-interest exclusively, market or economic failure can be avoided only by complete market transparency. Only if the transaction costs of enforcing contracts with repeated commercial relationships are exactly zero – if there are no natural monopolies resulting from uniqueness of resources and if there is no asymmetric knowledge among parties to contracts, in short, if there exist no producer's or consumer's surpluses in the competitive market – can market failure be avoided. According to the theory of perfect competition, all of these conditions would have to be met in order for economic ethics to be superfluous in the competitive market. There exist no situations in the real world that satisfies these ideal conditions. The ideal situation of perfect competition must be seen as a mere model assumption or ideal-typical situation. Asymmetric knowledge of suppliers and demanders about goods exchanged, quasi-monopolistic advantages and economic rents from location and time, or transaction costs with inflexibility of factors or the high cost of monitoring contracts destroy the ideal conditions of the superfluousness of economic ethics. At least one of the conditions restricting the automatism of competition will always be met in the market situation, which means that economic ethics is necessary in every real-world market as a corrective of partial market or economic failure resulting from the non-satisfaction of the ideal conditions.

The model of perfect competition and general equilibrium assumes, as conditions of the existence of a general equilibrium, that the price of the suppliers is predetermined in all markets, that profit is maximized by mere price taking in the market and, at the same time, is pressed down to zero as a tendency by competition, is "competed away," so that there are no producer's surpluses. These conditions are so highly specific and restrictive that they are the exception in

[2] Cf. above, Chap. 1, pp. 20-22.

real-world markets and cannot be used to argue for the superfluousness of a theory of economic ethics. Economic competition, as a market process, does not take place for the sake of normal profit, nor is it produced by competition for zero profit. It is undertaken for the sake of surplus profits or economic rents.

Only in the statistical, ideal model of perfect competition are there no economic rents, and also no longer any profits, because profit disappears under the pressure of competition that compels everyone to produce at the break-even point. Of such an ideal situation, however, Knight's statement is correct: "Under perfect competition there is no competition."[3] In the statistical situation of perfect competition and the unprofitableness of all producers, there are no longer any incentives to disturb the equilibrium situation by innovations, new products or production methods, or new rent seeking. As long as competition exists, it is competition for surplus rents and profits and, therefore, constantly breaks up the equilibrium situation of the "mechanism." Striving for profit and economic rents disturbs the equilibrium, a manifestation of liberty relative to the market mechanism and evidence of the possibility of ethical behavior in the competition. Each supplier attempts to gain producer's surpluses for herself by a quasi-monopoly or inimitable competitive advantages, such as location, innovation and novelty, goodwill, or patent advantages. Each buyer seeks to bring herself into the position of monopsony, in which she has special purchasing power, in order to gain consumer's surpluses for herself.

The fact that rent seeking exists is not of ethical importance. What is of ethical importance is the manner in which it takes place, whether it is pursued fairly or unfairly, in open or in dishonest competition. The phenomenon of rent seeking is ethically relevant, because it represents a phenomenon of freedom in opposition to an unambiguously determined market solution.[4] Because there are economic rents in the competitive market, it is not an ethically neutral zone.

Even with conditions approaching those of the ideal market, economic ethics is not superfluous as the ethics of the business enterprise, because it is able to increase the internal and life-world efficiency and culture of the firm. In all markets, not only those that have been oligopolized, a trade-off between convenience and profit-maximization, between an easy, pleasant life and greater production and higher profit is possible,[5] because firms do not constantly work at the limits of their capacity and at their break-even points, but instead exhibit latent potentials that can be activated by economic ethics. The hidden reserves of convenience and slack can, therefore, also be employed with competition and

---

[3] See also Israel M. Kirzner, *Competition and Entrepreneurship* (Chicago, 1973), p. 90.

[4] See also James M. Buchanan, "Towards the Simple Economics of Natural Liberty," *Kyklos*, 40 (1987), p. 16: "The maximization of individual liberties is equivalent to the maximization of the combined values of consumers' and producers' surplus."

[5] On the phenomenon of "slack," see Oliver E. Williamson, "Firms and Markets," in Sidney Weintraub, ed., *Modern Economic Thought* (Philadelphia, 1977), pp. 185-202.

can be "sacrificed" in favor of ethical conduct. A view that declares economic ethics to be superfluous, because it disturbs the laws of perfect competition, commits the fallacy that the market and competition form a mechanism permitting free decisions only within the logic of price taking. Such a mechanistic view of the firm underestimates the freedom of businesspersons and the openness of the market process. In the reality of conducting business within a social milieu, the range of alternative actions confronting the businessperson is wider and more complex than is represented by a mechanistic model of the market.

According to the mechanistic model, the manager can only minimize cost and maximize profit, or else receive the reward of his economic ruin. The practice of business management, however, takes place in a complete social context in which also taking ethical, psychological, and social-cultural aspects of economic action into account, thereby going beyond cost-efficiency and profit-maximization, promotes not only ethics, but also efficiency, because it improves the atmosphere of a firm and the readiness of its workers to produce, and also proves itself in the process to be profitable. "Price taking," profit maximization, and efficiency are the necessary conditions of meaningful economic action, but they are not sufficient. They must be satisfied, but they must not be the sole and ultimate orientations of action. In the complexity of human social life, they exist under constraints of an ethical nature, because, particularly within the firm, economic action is subject to the complexity of social life.

It can be seen that ethics is possible even in the market form in which action appears to be most strongly determined by market conditions: the market with perfect competition. In contrast to monopolistic competition, the environment and above all the price become parametric for the individual supplier under conditions of perfect competition. If ethics can be shown to be possible here, it is possible a fortiori in market forms with a less parametric environment, in which the acting person possesses greater power to shape the environment. The conclusion that the increasing degree of competition in the progression of market forms from oligopoly to perfect competition implies a decreasing degree of the importance of economic ethics is empirically untenable, as has already been shown, since the interior of the firm is a social group, not a mechanical machine, and ethics is therefore always present within it.

Drawing the conclusion of increasing competition from increasing expulsion of economic ethics is also untenable logically, because it represents a *metabasis eis allo genos*, a logical leap into a different way of thinking and a different category. The assumption that economic ethics becomes superfluous with increasing competition is based on an improper logical leap from the intentional to the mechanical-deterministic sphere of existence. The theory that ethics would be superfluous with perfect competition concedes that the monopolist and the oligopolist exhibit degrees of ethical freedom in their actions. It claims, however, that this freedom disappears as the price becomes parametric, because the businessperson is compelled to behave efficiently in the competitive market. Therefore, all considerations of economic ethics and, above all, of a just or fair price are assumed to become inappropriate with perfect competition, because the price becomes the parameter for the businessperson. It should be objected against this position that the price is neither the sole nor the decisive action variable within the firm. This means that economic action does not become mechanical in the competitive market, but instead remains intentional. Furthermore, the *individual* price is itself ethically relevant with parametric *market price* and perfect competition, because (as will be shown more fully below) individual price justice remains an ethical issue even in the competitive market.

The thesis that ethics becomes superfluous in the competitive market and that increasing competition drives out ethical considerations makes a logical category mistake, which follows in turn from an incorrect, mechanical ontology of the economy. The increase of competition as a social process of the creation of knowledge and the coordination of preferences and actions, the development from an oligopolistic or hierarchical economy to a market economy, cannot lead to a transformation of the economic process from an ethically-defined into a merely more economically-defined context of coordination and to a different ontological status of the economy. If the increase in competition also represents an increase of exchange, the growth of competition cannot logically transform a *social* process into a *deterministic-mechanical* process in which the actors become marionettes who no longer have room for ethical consideration. Intentionality and freedom of action survive the transition to perfect competition, even though the degree of freedom in setting prices decreases.

Seen economically, perfect competition does not represent a conversion into a different category of economic action whose character *eo ipso* excludes economic ethics. The competitive market is an especially efficient market form and, when ruinous competition is not present, is not only compatible with intentional and free action, but also challenges managerial intentionality and imagination and, therefore, ethics. Since perfect competition challenges the creative powers of the human person more than monopolistic competition – "The greatest of all monopoly profits is a quiet life" (John Hicks)[6] – ethical and aesthetic attentiveness, ability of perception, and power of imagination are required within it more than in other market forms and economic systems. The competitive market is not an ethically neutral zone, but instead an ethically challenging zone. Ethics is not "squeezed out" in the competitive market.

Faith in a mechanism of competition so "good" that it makes economic ethics superfluous is a scientistic illusion, the conclusion of a train of thought that starts out from the assumption of the mechanical analogy of "general equilibrium." In reality, businesspersons in the market are neither elements of a mobile

---

[6] Cited by Albert O. Hirschman, *Exit, Voice and Loyalty* (Cambridge, Mass., 1971), p. 55.

that finds its state of equilibrium according to an external stimulus, nor marionettes on the strings of market forces. They are, instead, rationally-acting, intellectual beings, whose pursuit of objectives is influenced not only by economic considerations, but also by economic-ethical imperatives and cultural values. An appropriate, fundamental theory or ontology of the economy must, therefore, go beyond the mechanistic ontology to one of intentional action.

The distinctive moral feature of the market and of free exchange cannot be that it has no need of ethics. This strange transformation of the cultural sphere of the economy into a mechanism and of economic action into the mere solution of a mathematical maximization problem, in which the values of the parameters are given and the equations for the solution of the unknowns are known, is just as fallacious a leap into a different category as is the inversion of ethics in the action sphere of the economy into mere economizing. What distinguishes the competitive market from other forms of coordination is, instead, that it permits and coordinates the individual pursuit of goals under economic and ethical value definitions, and does *not* restrict individual action to mere economizing for the predetermined goal of profit maximization.

It follows from the ontology of the market, understood as a discourse and an "entelechial mechanism," that economic ethics also increases the ability of the competitive market to function. Because the elemental particles of the entelechial mechanism "market" are not inanimate centers of mass, without interiority and self-reference, but consciously-acting individuals, ethical motives and action orientations, in addition to pure economic action objectives, form a component of its utility and production functions. Speaking in economic terms, ethics is, even with perfect competition, a necessary input of the coordination system market. By no means is ethics driven out of the coordination of the market by increasing competition.

7.2. Morality and Advantage: The Costs of Economic Ethics

If economic ethics is not superfluous even in the competitive market, it has nevertheless not yet been explained whether it is possible and feasible under conditions of competition. In discussions of the question of economic ethics, one often hears that ethics in the market is indeed desirable, but not possible, because, under conditions of competition, any individual manager who conducts business ethically will soon be ruined and driven from the market. A manager who adopted particular moral standards concerning, for instance, environmental conservation or handicapped and impoverished employees, would be outstripped by his less morally sensitive and morally active competitors, and would soon be driven into the red. Ethics is possible in the market, according to this view, only if *all* suppliers act ethically. Since not all suppliers act ethically, ethical action on the part of the individual is not a strategy with which one can survive, and leads to elimination by market selection.

This conception of the market economy and of competition is too optimistic regarding the effects of competition, and too pessimistic with regard to the costs of ethical action. Competition does not function so well that every ethical manager is quickly ruined. And the costs of ethical action are not so high that they exclude economic ethics from responsible business calculations. The "ethical" manager is driven out by the "merely efficient" manager as the direct consequence of ethical actions, only if all suppliers produce in the position of the marginal supplier and if there exist no economic rents (i.e. if all managers produce at the break-even point, in the economically least-expensive, cost-minimizing way, and none of them makes a profit). This case is, as has already been shown, improbable and not a true situation of competition, since competition is conducted precisely in order to attain economic rents and profits. The individual supplier does not strive to be a marginal supplier, but to be an intra-marginal supplier (i.e. to have a less expensive cost situation than his competitors, or at least a better cost situation than the marginal supplier). In every intra-marginal situation, the manager can afford ethical conduct, even if doing so produces costs. These costs can be met from producer's surpluses, from possible hidden reserves, such as slack, and from profit.

If the preceding argument shows that ethical "special performance" does not lead automatically to the ruin of the ethical manager, it has not yet been proven that motives to bring it about also exist and that the *costs* of ethical conduct – independently of the question of survival – do not make ethical conduct in the market improbable. The ethical entrepreneur or manager appears to "pre-deliver" and to create a public good whose profits are publicly appropriated, whose costs are paid by him or her individually, and to whose individual production, therefore, only extremely weak incentives exist.

The question of the private costs of the public good of ethics necessitates a case distinction according to the kinds of costs that ethics creates and the degree of the publicness of the good ethics. Therefore, it is also shown in the context of business ethics that ethics is neither a completely public nor a completely private good, but is instead a semi-public good, like other higher value-qualities. The ethical conduct of a manager can consist in:

1. An additional service that is appropriated somewhere else and creates tangible private costs;

2. Supplementary services that make a positive financial difference and cause either no costs or intangible costs outside the firm and within the firm itself ("cost-neutral ethics");

3. Refraining from permitting a competitive advantage and differential economic rent relative to ethical competitors as a consequence of taking advantage of a morally dubious opportunity, or by unethical conduct or violation of rules;

4. Accepting the competitive disadvantage and loss that the ethical manager experiences, if most other competitors attain differential economic rents by unethical practices, while the ethical manager renounces this opportunity and sustains the costs of this behavior, which may be uniquely rule-conforming.

Concerning 1: If the ethical action represents a purely public good or an act of charity, it is necessary to decide whether the costs to the firm of the action are justifiable and sensible. This case is not problematic, since it involves works of supererogation that are performed above and beyond the limits of obligation and are ethically optional. The responsibility of the manager here also includes asking whether the firm can pursue works of ethical supererogation, such as voluntary social services, before the duty of ensuring the long-term good of the firm.

Concerning 2: Ethical conduct consists here in what are called "virtues" in philosophical ethics. The conduct of businesspersons seeks to realize virtues, such as consumer friendliness, goodwill, leniency, patience, etc. These virtues create public and private goods, public goods within the firm and in its exchange with the surrounding area, and at the same time private goods, because the proceeds of these virtues benefit both the firm and individuals. Their costs do not consist in financial expenses, but instead, if at all, in personal expenditures, in the effort required to realize them. The virtues produce "goods" such as goodwill, corporate and sectoral culture, etc., whose utility is appropriated both publicly *and* privately. The ethical goods of the virtues are neither purely public nor purely private goods.

Concerning 3: In this case the firm incurs costs from its ethical conduct of foregoing a differential economic rent by refraining from unethical (i.e. duty- or rule-violating) conduct. Assume that the strategic plan of a competitor is leaked to the firm, and that it could be used to the firm's competitive advantage. If the firm abstains from taking this advantage and returns the strategic plan unread, it foregoes the differential economic rent that it could gain from the competitive advantage. Another, similar case would be the renunciation of bribery in order to receive an additional order ahead of a customer, where this is not usually possible in the industry, but is possible in a particular case.

In these cases, the ethical action does not create additional costs, but instead foregoes additional economic rent. Refusing to take advantage of an unethical opportunity does not jeopardize the firm, if it is not already producing at the break-even point. The renunciation of the unethical conduct is the foregoing of the unethical appropriation of differential economic rent, not the creation of additional costs by ethical conduct. The ethical conduct does not consist in the production of a public good, but in the renunciation of a public bad (bribery) at the cost of private enrichment. An additional incentive not to produce this public bad is the firm's interest in preventing a bad, for instance bribery, from becoming common practice and avoiding becoming itself the victim of the practice of bribery. Even in situations where the survival of the firm can be ensured only by unethical conduct, the acquisition of a large order by bribery, for instance, the production of the bad of bribery, in order to turn away an apparently even greater bad, namely the bankruptcy of the firm and the loss of jobs, cannot be justified.

According to the principle of double effect, as shown above,[7] an intrinsically bad action may not be performed in order to attain a good goal. It is only permissible to choose intrinsically ethical strategies of action, the pursuit of which may, under certain conditions, bring about unintended, negative side effects. To practice bribery, in order to preserve one's own firm as a side effect, is not ethically permissible. The reversal of the definition of the action, to preserve one's firm as the main intention and to practice bribery as a side effect of this goal, is objectively untrue, because the goal "preservation of one's firm" is not an action, but instead a general attitude, and therefore does not unintentionally and accidentally bring about bribery as side effect of its performance.

Economic considerations also confirm this ethical verdict. A firm that can be preserved only by bribery is no longer economically efficient. Its capital and employees would be employed more efficiently elsewhere. Even in economic terms, the goal of the preservation of the firm cannot justify the adoption of an unethical strategy.

Concerning 4: The most difficult case for the motivation to ethical conduct is the situation in which acting ethically leads to a genuine competitive disadvantage for the ethical businessperson. Such situations involve more than simply renouncing unethical conduct and the additional differential economic rent made possible by it. In a market in which duty- and rule-violating conduct, such as bribery or unfair competition, are general practices, the ethical action that renounces these practices produces a moral precommitment that serves the possible reconstruction of an economic ethos, the semi-public good of the universality of this economic ethos. The costs of this semi-public good are incurred only by the individuals who produce it; the profits accrue to everyone. The economic calculus would eliminate as unprofitable the option of privately producing this semi-public good of ethical conduct. There is no private-economic incentive to produce the good of rule-compliance in an environment that does not follow that rule. Against this line of reasoning, however, it must be objected ethically that the renunciation of a generally widespread rule violation does not represent the production of a genuine good, but the renunciation of the act of violating one's ethical duty. The conceptualization of the theory of public goods leads partially into error, if it represents the renunciation of violating ethical duty in an environment in which this violation is a common and general practice,

---

[7] Cf. above, Section 5.2.4., pp. 138-40.

already as the production of a good, whose production is a commendable work and resembles a work of supererogation.

The reason this case is difficult, in terms of economic ethics, is that, with a general erosion of the ethical rules, the manager experiences not only a loss of differential economic rent, as in Case 3, but a genuine competitive disadvantage that worsens the relative market position of the firm. It is, of course, not evident that this competitive disadvantage *must* economically eliminate the alternative obligatory action in the situation of pervasive unethical behavior. The negative spillovers and side effects of the unethical practice on the entire firm and the internal ethos of its members are to be compared to costs that individual obedience to the ethical rule would cause. If the ethics of the entire industry is worsened, this will also have repercussions on the workers' ethics, their motivation to work, and their productivity. The negative side effects that a low level of morality in the firm's operations brings about on the morality of the workers, by setting a bad example, the worsening of the internal corporate ethics and culture, and the negative repercussions of a lowering of the marginal morality of the firm's performance on the trust of the workers in the firm, must be included in the rational calculus and the economic consideration of whether taking full advantage of the rule is more advantageous than the costs of obeying it.

The individual observance of economic-ethical rules, the rule against bribery for example, in a milieu of general violation of the rules, not only creates costs in the form of a comparative disadvantage, but at the same time builds up hidden reserves of the good "ethics" within the firm, forming human capital, which must be included in the calculation of the costs of ethical action. Just as, according to the economic calculus, short-term advantages from unethical conduct or from the exploitation of rules normally acknowledged must be weighed against the long-term disadvantages of the erosion of the ethos, the short-term disadvantages that arise from rule conformity in comparison to the exploitation of an "opportunity" must be weighed against the long-term advantages of the formation of goodwill and trust.

7.3. Morality at the Margin

A situation of an increasing erosion of the universally valid ethical standards in an industry is a special case of the theory of ethical economy in the market economy and an important economic-ethical problem. Götz Briefs has identified the situation of the sinking of the socially obligatory ethos as "sinking marginal morality."[8] Marginal morality is the lowest level of ethical conduct that is still

[8] Götz Briefs, *Untergang des Abendlandes* (Freiburg, 1920), p. 5; and "Grenzmoral in der pluralistischen Gesellschaft," in Erwin von Beckerath, Willy Meyer, and Alfred Müller-Armack,

tolerated, the margin of ethically still-accepted and practiced behavior. If this marginal morality sinks with an increasing spread of unethical practices, pressure is exerted on the individual to conform his behavior to the sinking marginal morality, in order to avoid a worsening of his competitive situation. With sinking marginal morality and with a lowering of the ethical limit of business practices that are not permitted, the situation of the ethical manager, who previously was an intra-marginal supplier and produced below the break-even point at a profit, can move in the direction of the break-even point, because without his involvement in the unethical practices, his cost situation constantly appears to worsen relative to his unethical competitors.

Even here, however, it is not the case that a linear and necessary, inversely-proportional relation exists between ethical conduct and costs, so that a lowering of one producer's ethical level relative to his competitors *necessarily* leads to cost advantages for the unethical producer and cost disadvantages for the ethical producers. If such a relationship actually existed, as is suggested by the idea that one's own marginal costs could be sunk by a relative sinking of one's own marginal morality, the unethical manager would always exhibit the lowest relative costs in an industry. This relationship *cannot* exist, however, because unethical conduct also creates economic costs – costs that consist in the loss of reputation and informal sanctions by customers, suppliers, and competitors in the industry. Furthermore, informal sanctions, in the form of public opinion and opportunities to migrate to other suppliers, are greater in a competitive market than in centrally-controlled economies, in which, as Johannes Messner objected to Briefs, the phenomenon of profiting by sinking the marginal morality is just as virulent as in the market economy.[9]

The phenomenon of sinking marginal morality describes each social process in which the capital of ethics and of economic ethos is exhausted by the growth of the number of free riders on this ethos. The consumption of the public capital of economic ethics by a growing number of free riders is increased by the self-fulfilling prophecy of the ethical "un-assurance phenomenon" itself. In analogy to the assurance phenomenon of ethics, according to which an increasing readiness to comply with rules is created by increasing marginal morality, by the assurance of the generality of rule-compliance, with sinking marginal morality there appears unassurance concerning the meaningfulness of ethical action. If the incentives to produce the public good "ethics" sink, the assurance game of ethics is transformed into an unassurance game of sinking marginal morality.

---

eds., *Wirtschaftsfragen der freien Welt* (Frankfurt, 1957), pp. 97-108. See also Werner Schöllgen. "Grenzmoral," in *Staatslexikon*, 6th Ed. (Freiburg, 1959), Vol. III, pp. 1016-19. Geoffrey Brennan and James M. Buchanan, *The Reason of Rules* (Cambridge, 1987), p. 60, have described a similar phenomenon and in analogy to Gresham's Law, that bad money drives out good money, named it "Gresham's Law of Politics": bad conduct drives good conduct in the market.

[9] Johannes Messner, *Sozialökonomik und Sozialethik*, 2nd Ed. (Paderborn, 1929), p. 39.

The question is, therefore, how such a cumulative erosion process of the "unassurance" of economic ethics associated with sinking marginal morality can be slowed. The "assurance" of high marginal morality (as discussed in Chapter 2), the ethic of the categorical imperative, and religion prove to be inadequate during historical phases of sinking marginal morality. The phenomenon of sinking marginal morality is distinguished at two central points from the classical prisoner's dilemma situation, as it was determined above with the analysis of the assurance problem. In the prisoner's dilemma, the individual prisoner does not know how the other prisoners will act and wishes to follow the rules either not at all or only when *all* others do so as well. In the situation of sinking marginal morality, the individual suspects or senses, on the contrary, that the behavior of others tends more and more toward unethical options; but he himself *wants* to be ethical, if at least the majority or a large number of the competitors, though not necessarily all of them, act ethically.

Since in the case of sinking marginal morality, not the complete assurance of rule-compliance, but already the partial assurance of the "unassurance" phenomenon of the acting person, is eliminated or reduced, the behavior of the industry leaders and market-dominating firms plays a central role. These actors can, by setting an example of ethical conduct, slow and stop the erosion process of marginal morality. The leaders of the industry, its market and opinion leaders, must become "assurance-mediators" for the stability of economic ethics in the industry, or for an increase of marginal morality. The economic-ethical role of setting an example[10] consists in the assurance of high marginal morality, in the assurance that ethical conduct in the industry concerned is meaningful and does not endanger survival. The function of setting an example and of "reassurance" in a situation of sinking marginal morality cannot be demanded of the smallest and weakest forms in the industry, since they would be overtaxed under conditions of universally sinking marginal morality, because of their position as marginal suppliers. One does not require the beggar to set the standard and example for the observance of property rights. The largest firms also have the greatest self-interest in the validity of the rules of economic ethics, because they most of all are injured by the sinking marginal morality of others.

The market leaders must lead the way in the production of the semi-public good of economic ethics and, if possible, also produce moral precommitments for this semi-public good on the basis of their greater financial power. In the sphere of the semi-public good of economic ethos, an observation is repeated that is well known from the sphere of international public goods. Just as in the international sphere, particular institutions and regimes that are advantageous for all nations come into being only if a hegemonic power is first prepared to

[10] On the role of examples in ethics, see also Max Scheler, "Vorbilder und Führer," in *Schriften aus dem Nachlaß*, 3rd Ed. (Bonn, 1986), Vol. I, pp. 255-344.

produce financial and organizational precommitments for their coming into being,[11] a high economic marginal morality is developed in an industry, only if the market leaders are prepared to set an example and not to violate the ethical rules for the sake of every short-term advantage and to take an erosion of the economic ethos and ethical irregularities into account.

One can also see here the inevitable moral character of power. The market leaders in an industry, not the central authority of the state, must ensure the existence of the semi-public good of economic ethics – analogously to the function of the state to provide public goods within its sphere. Economic ethics and high economic marginal morality are neither purely private nor purely public goods, but semi-public goods that benefit both the public and the industry concerned. The private utility of economic ethics consists not only in economic, tangible utility, but also, as with general ethics as well, in the intrinsic rewards of ethical action, such as joy in the good itself and the certitude of contributing to the common good.

7.4. Proper Conduct and Appropriateness to the Nature of the Subject Matter in Question

The situation of sinking marginal morality in the economy is one in which violations of the nature of the subject matter of the economy meet increasingly general acceptance. There is a spreading of practices that provide a short-term advantage for some individuals, but which cannot be generalized without economic damage and are harmful in the long term, even for the recipients of the short-term advantage. Unfair competition, slush money, and corruption are practices that violate the rules and the nature of the subject matter of business. The rules that make the omission of these practices obligatory are ethical rules, because their content is not codified legally or cannot be sanctioned. They are ethical action demands, because their fulfillment is not economically rational in the sense that they represent the locally-maximizing strategy and follow from the immediate self-interest of the acting person. The omission of the unethical economic practices is distinguished as rationally imperative only in the rational calculus of a comprehensive, not merely locally-maximizing, ethically-oriented strategy.

The price system's appropriateness to the nature of the subject matter and full ability to function require ethical practices whose performance does not

[11] Cf. Richard N. Cooper, "Worldwide *versus* Regional Integration," in Fritz Machlup, ed., *Economic Integration* (London, 1976), pp. 41-60; Stephen D. Krasner, *International Regimes* (Ithaca, 1983); Robert O. Keohane, *After Hegemony* (Princeton, 1984); and Charles P. Kindleberger, "International Public Goods without International Government," *American Economic Review*, 76 (1986), p. 8.

follow from the pursuit of immediate self-interest. The intention of fulfilling the appropriateness to the nature of the subject matter of the economy is also required when short-term economic advantages could be obtained by unethical business practices. The appropriateness to the nature of the subject matter of the price system is impaired by, for example, the practice of slush money, because the resources and goods are not employed where the highest price is paid and the best alternative use for them exists. Bribery instead "buys" a missing link of resources in an inefficient manner by means of slush money, or pays an efficient allocation, which would take place anyway with competent management, with an additional price that is overly expensive by the amount of the slush money.

In terms of economic ethics, the problem of unethical practices can be formulated in two different ways. In the negative formulation, economic ethics requires the omission of these practices. Formulated positively, the imperative of economic ethics reads: "Act in accordance with the nature of the economy."[12] Making possible the objective goal of the economy – the meeting of needs and the self-development of the persons within a nation's economy – requires the realization of the efficient allocation of all resources. This efficient allocation, for its part, presupposes the omission of unethical practices. Efficient allocation does not come into existence "on its own" despite widespread unethical practices.

If the major premise of economic ethics, that proper conduct in the economy should be realized, is applied to the price system and the exchange transactions that make up the center of the market economy, it is concretized as the rule: "Follow the proper conduct of the price system" or "Obey the rules of the price system." The ethics of the price system is further concretized for exchange relationships and commutative justice as the rule: "Give each person in exchange that to which he or she is entitled according to the undistorted rules of the price system." The appropriateness to the nature of the subject matter of the price system, and therefore economic ethics as well, require that all persons receive in exchange that to which they are entitled according to the rules of market price control. The commutative justice of the price system, or price justice, requires giving to each person what is determined to belong to him or her according to the rules of the economy in a competitive market. Commutative justice proves to be a special case of the general principle of justice, to give to each person what is his *(suum cuique tribuere)*. Commutative justice is the application of the subjective-personal dimension of justice to the sphere of the market and exchange. In commutative justice, economic ethics and its imperative to follow universalizable maxims in one's own economic strategies become concrete in the demand to conduct oneself properly in exchange relationships. The formal

---

[12] See also Oswald von Nell-Breuning, "Wirtschaftsethik," in *Staatslexikon*, 6th Ed. (Freiburg, 1963), Vol. XIII, p. 775.

ethic of universalizable rules is realized in the duty and virtue of commutative justice, in the intention and state of character to give to each his own. Commutative justice is the state of character of justice applied to the sphere of commerce. The duty to comply with the rules of the economy, if it is not to remain merely formal and in the sphere of interiority and the good will, must be materialized as the intention to shape the maxim concretely and as the constant state of character and "virtue" to practice commutative justice.

CHAPTER 8

COMMUTATIVE JUSTICE

Justice is the realization of morality in human social relationships, the state of character and practice of giving to each person what is his or hers. This familiar concept of justice is what Aristotle calls special justice, and stands in contrast to Plato's general justice, which includes the entirety of virtue. Justice is the persistent state of character, supported by the will and controlled by the intellect, to give to each person what is his or hers, above all his or her due.[1] The principle of giving to all persons what is theirs is neither tautological, in the sense of Arthur Schopenhauer's objection – "How can you give someone what is already his?" – nor devoid of content, in the sense that the market automatically distributes to each person what is his or hers according to the rules of the market.[2] The principle "To each his or her own" is empty, only if all actual market coordination is regarded as the ultimate criterion of exchange, even when unethical practices dominate the market concerned, because the principle then requires only giving to each person what he or she receives anyway. The price system, however, is able to achieve coordination formally with the presence of completely different economic "marginal moralities," so that, with each different socially existing marginal morality, each person is given something different. Commutative justice, understood as the principle to give to each person that to which he or she is entitled, according to the rules of the price system, means to give him or her that to which he or she is entitled, if the price context complies with its own rules. The price system, however, can comply with its own rules only if these rules are also affirmed by the actors themselves and are followed ethically.

8.1. Commutative Justice as Appropriateness to the Nature of the Matter of Exchange: The Equivalence Principle

The principle of justice *suum cuique* becomes concrete as commutative justice in the principle of giving to each person that to which he is entitled in an undis-

[1] Thomas Aquinas, *Summa Theologiae*, II-II, q. 58, a. 1: *"Iustitia est habitus secundum quem aliquis constanti et perpetua voluntate ius suum unicuique tribuit."* This formulation follows Ulpian's well-known definition, as recorded in Justinian's *Digest*: *"iustitia est constans et perpetua voluntas ius suum cuique tribuendi"* (D 1,1,10).

[2] On the juristic context of the principle *"suum cuique,"* see also Wolfgang Waldstein, "Ist das 'Suum cuique' eine Leerformel?" in *Ius Humanitatis* (Berlin, 1980), pp. 285-320.

torted competitive market and with the performance of the economy's function. If each person receives that to which he is entitled in exchange transactions, each person receives the price-equivalent of his service or merchandise. He receives the monetary-equivalent of what is his, and vice versa. If each person receives what is his, the equality of equivalence in exchange is achieved. The exchange of equivalents brings about equality of service and service in return. The principle of justice "To each his own" is concretized in commutative justice with the principle "Exchange genuine equivalents." The equivalence of service and service in return expresses itself in the equality of the market value and the monetary price of the service. The equivalence makes the exchange just, because each receives what is his and neither party to the exchange gives too much to the other. According to Aristotle, all things must have a price, because exchange is then possible. But when equality or equivalence in exchange does not exist, no exchange and no community exists. And when no commensurability is ensured by money, there is no equality or equivalence.[3]

The principle of commutative justice "Exchange equivalents" is not an economic law, but an imperative of economic ethics. Not every exchange that actually takes place does so according to commutative justice. A just exchange requires that the equality of the equivalents is fulfilled and that the exchanging parties make the exchange rule the maxim of their concrete action of exchange and the state of character and virtue of their economic practice. Two fundamental problems are to be distinguished in the rule "Exchange equivalents" or "The value of the merchandise must be equivalent to the return in service or price."[4] This rule presupposes that one knows what the other person is entitled to and what is his, and that one has the will to give it to him. The rule "To each his own" contains two components. First, it assumes a prior rule, establishing how to determine what one is entitled to in exchange. Second, it requires an establishment of obligation that tells the basis of the obligation to give each person what is his. These two problems will now be addressed in turn.

8.2. How Do We Determine What Each Person is Entitled to in Exchange?

Commutative justice and that to which each person is entitled in exchange consist in price justice and appropriateness to the nature of the subject matter in exchange. The exchanging parties must preserve the price-justice and the appropriateness to the nature of the matter in exchange and should at the same time,

---

[3] Aristotle, *Nicomachean Ethics*, trans. Terence Irwin (Indianapolis, 1985), V, 8, 1133 b 15.

[4] Oswald von Nell-Breuning, "Das Äquivalenzprinzip," *Jahrbücher für Nationalökonomie und Statistik*, 133 (1930), p. 40, formulates the "exchange-equality of the commodity and the price" (*Tauschgleichheit von Ware und Preis*).

as an additional exercise of virtue not strictly required, strive for a just balance in the contract. The price-justice and appropriateness to the matter of exchange is defined by the following three criteria, to which the virtue of commutative justice is added as a fourth and less binding requirement. Commutative justice is defined by:

1) the requirement of joining the actual contract price to the prevailing price; in the market economy, to the market price;

2) the requirement that the item exchanged is appropriate and not a mere sham good;

3) the requirement that the exchange is mutually advantageous and neither party experiences a loss of net wealth; and

4) the requirement that a just balancing of interests takes place and that the virtue of commutative justice is exercised in the contract.

1) and 3) are the criteria of price justice. 2) is the criterion of appropriateness of the good-in-exchange. These four criteria will be discussed in order.

8.2.1. JOINING THE PREVAILING PRICE BY THE ACTUAL CONTRACT PRICE

Answering the question of price justice requires that the ethical and political-economic theory ethical economy distinguishes two levels of establishment: the constitutive level of the existing conditions of the market price or a different prevailing price, and the post-constitutive level of the conditions of justice, according to which the individual price joins the prevailing price. What someone is entitled to in exchange will first be determined by the prevailing price, the price that normally is paid and prevails for the object of exchange. The parties to the exchange are entitled to a price that does not oppose the prevailing price, but is instead joined to it. In a market economy, this prevailing price is the market price. The individual price, which should conform to commutative justice, must first join this price. The second level of questioning is about the justice of the constitutive conditions of the prevailing price and, therefore, about the constitutive conditions of commutative justice.

For the market economy, the question of the justice of the constitutive conditions of the market price is the question whether the prevailing market price is a genuine market price, in the sense of a price formed in a competitive market. The status of the market in which the prevailing market price is formed is determined by the market form, as well as by the legal and political structural conditions of the market and the historically-acquired rights of ownership and the distribution of wealth that existed in the market when it began. The economic theory of the market ideal-typically provides the values in exchange that come into being with given initial terms and factors in an unimpeded competitive market. Historical-legal theory provides a description of the source of the original endowment in existence when the market opened. Political theory reconstructs the constitutional and legal structure of the market existing at a definite point in time. Price formation in a market is determined by the market form, the legal and constitutional structural conditions of the economy, and the way in which the initial market conditions came into being.

Differences in the market form, legal conditions, and the historical initial distribution endowments lead to varying prices and, therefore, to differing distributions of what belongs to each person in the exchange. The values in exchange in a market are historically individuated. They are determined by the historical, initial distribution of the rights of ownership and the present price ratios in the market. Price formation according to the economic and legal norms prevailing at a specific point in time determines the prevailing price and, therefore, the most important standard for determining what belongs to each party in the exchange. The prevailing price is not identical to the actual, individual price, but is instead the price formed in accordance with the political and economic rules of the society and without distortion of the rules of ownership and exchange. It provides the equivalent of what is due each person for his or her good or service in the given economic order. The commutative justice of the individual is the price behavior that corresponds to and joins the prevailing price of the economic order to which he or she belongs.

It is obvious that there can be as many different prevailing prices in this sense as there are historical forms of ownership and price systems, and that prevailing prices deviate from the actual prices that always come into being under incomplete accordance with the economic-legal rules. The prevailing price that is to be taken as the starting point in commutative justice for the determination of that to which each of the exchange partners is entitled does not need to be a just price in the sense of natural law. It is the price that has come into being correctly in terms of the laws of the economy concerned. The prevailing price states the rule, according to which commutative justice must decide as a subordinate rule. The question of the justice of the prevailing price (i.e. the question whether the prevailing price is also the just price) goes beyond the level of commutative justice and requires rules of a higher order.

The question of what is the just price, whose validity goes above and beyond legal and economic rule-justice in a given system of rules, and which further determines what is due to each person, as the requirement to pay him the prevailing price, leads back to the question of which economic system and which of the legal systems prior to the economic relationships are just. The just price, in the sense of natural law, is then the price that comes into existence in the one price system, among all possible and realizable price systems, which is just. Just price theory must go beyond the question of the price justice of the individual exchange to settle the question of the justice and legitimacy of the exchange context and price system as a whole, in which the individual exchange takes place and whose generally prevailing price the individual price joins.

Commutative justice does *not* investigate *constitutive* price justice, which extends into the sphere of political justice and is at the same time the object of investigation, not only of ethical economy, but also of political economy and political philosophy. Commutative justice does not pose the question whether the constitutive conditions under which the prevailing prices have been formed meet the standard of justice, but the question whether the individual price and the actual exchange arrangements are in just accordance with the prevailing price. Commutative justice in the concrete economic action is neither entitled nor able to render verdicts and to make constitutive decisions concerning the prevailing price and the constitution of the prevailing prices. It does not decide the question whether the prevailing price should be a market price, a governmentally-administered appraised price, or a mixture of the two. The role of commutative justice is, instead, to make the decisions to be reached by individuals or groups (bargaining units, for instance) about the way in which the actual price individuates the prevailing price, and about the level of the actual price, and to question its commutative justice. The example of bargaining units already shows, of course, that the constitutive level of price formation and the justice of the prevailing prices cannot be completely separated from the post-constitutive level of commutative justice and individual price justice. Suppliers with great market power make *both* operative *and* constitutive decisions about the price level and price justice.

The Presumption that the Market Price Is the Just Price

The fulfillment of commutative justice, insofar as the price level is concerned, requires joining the individual price to the prevailing price in the individual contract. In a market economy, the prevailing price is in general the market price. The assumption can be made initially, until the contrary is proven, that the market price is just, because the conditions of the market price's formation, the market process and price formation by competition, are themselves constitutive criteria of the assessment of price justice, as will be shown in the next chapter. Within a competitive market, the market price can be presumed to be a just price.[5]

The market price is the just price, if both the scarcity relationships between the goods in the goods market and the factors in the market for the factors of production necessary to produce the good in question, and the readiness of all buyers to pay, their assessments of the value of the goods in question, and the

---

[5] Cf. Nell-Breuning, "Fortschritte in der Lehre von der Preisgerechtigkeit," in *Miscellanea Vermeersch* (Rome, 1935), Vol. I, p. 102; and Johannes Messner, *Sozialökonomik und Sozialethik*, 2nd Ed. (Paderborn, 1929).

readiness of all sellers to produce and sell are entered into in it under free price variation and under conditions of competition, and if an examination by the political action center of the society has taken place to determine whether the system of prices violates the minimum norms of the appropriateness of the subject matter of the economy.

The presumption that the market price is just is the presumption of the validity of the above prerequisites of genuine market price formation. The presupposition that the prevailing market price is the just price must usually be made anyway by each observer who does not have access to complete market information. In general, it is more probable that this prerequisite is satisfied than that the market is monopolized or distorted, because monopolies or oligopolies, as long as they are not governmentally supported and protected, are broken up by international competition and the substitution competition that comes from similar supplies of goods. The requirement to join the market price in price formation has the presumption of being in accordance with justice.

Joining the Individual Price to the Market Price: Individual Price Justice

The individual price is ethically relevant, even when a market price exists. Even with the validity of a just market price, the problem of individual price justice remains. The formation of the individual price in an exchange individuated by space-time is clearly distinguished from the formation of the market price, understood as the formation of the decisive and prevailing price. The individual price joins the general market price and reacts to it. It is, however, not identical to it, because it is individuated, as the actual contract price, by space, time, circumstances, and the parties to the contract. The relation of the individual price to the market price, its joining to or deviation from the general market price, is a problem of the price formation and commutative justice of the contract that is not already predetermined by the validity of a general market price. The parties to the contract have at their disposal, even in the competitive market, room for action in the formation of the individual price in relation to the general market price, room for action that is ethically relevant.

This individuated character of the actual contract price relative to the general market price is overlooked by economic price theory, if the individual price is understood as a mechanical result and, as it were, the equilibrium point of the total supply and demand forces. In the view of the microeconomic theory of market equilibrium, the price is, with perfect competition, an invariable piece of data for the individual businessperson. The supplier behaves as a passive price taker relative to the predetermined market price. The price cannot be ethically relevant in this view, because the action of the price taker relative to the price exhibits no degree of freedom at all. The price taker in the competitive market cannot influence the price.[6] This ideal situation of a market of mere price takers is accurate, however, only for perfectly competitive markets with homogenous goods, or goods that are not individuated as commodities by space and time, such as stocks and bonds.

The stock market represents a perfect market, with goods that are individuated neither by space nor by time. For this reason, the goods of the stock market are especially capable of and at risk from speculation and, consequently, raise other problems of justice.

In most markets, because of the uniqueness of the contract and the good at a particular point in space-time, suppliers have room for action in the formation of the price and contract, which is economic-ethically relevant and for which they must be ethically *responsible.* An ethic of price formation, for the discretion in price formation that exceeds the mere acceptance of the general market price, is necessary and is also a component of commutative justice in the competitive market.

For most goods, there exists no general, well-defined market price, only a normal market price with a bandwidth of variance above and below it that depends upon the place and time of the existence of the good, upon its position in space-time. The specific position in space-time at which an economic transaction takes place leads to an "individuation" of the good and its price according to the physical law of the irreversibility of each action, which follows the Second Principle of Thermodynamics, which has been mentioned above.[7]

Every material, tangible good and every good that is neither a trivial mass commodity nor a legal title for another absent good, such as a security, becomes by its place in the stream of reality, an individual in space and time, a distinctive good that is not completely interchangeable with any other. Supposedly identical goods are in fact distinguishable at another place and time, which means that the buyer or seller can say: "The same price as the market price is to count for this particular good, but not at this place and time." The uniqueness of positions in space and time means that the homogeneity of goods, which is the precondition of a unified market price in the strict sense, is constantly given only *cum grano salis*. Buyers and sellers can always point to the inhomogeneity of the good in question, which is caused by its unique occurrence at this point in space-time. The buyers can say: "We are prepared to pay the same price as others for a good from this good's class, but not for this particular, individual good from this class at this place and time."

---

[6] Thus, for instance, William J. Baumol, "Business Responsibility and Economic Behavior," in Edmund Phelps, ed., *Altruism, Morality, and Economic Theory* (New York, 1975), pp. 46-47.

[7] See also Israel M. Kirzner, *Competition and Entrepreneurship* (Chicago, 1973), p. 16, for the individuation of capital goods: "In a world in which no two assets are exactly the same, no opportunity offered by an asset owner can be exactly duplicated."

The individual price fluctuates above and below a normal price within a bandwidth that is relevant for economic ethics. Within it, price discrimination to the advantage or disadvantage of the buyer or seller can be pursued or be completely imperative. Within it, however, price discrimination can also be an ethical commandment of fairness. The economic-ethical discussion of the fair or just price is primarily a discussion of the formulation of the price in the individual exchange, not about the formation of the market price, which is valid as a guiding principle for the individual price and can be presumed to be just. The formation of the market price, free from governmental intervention, as the normal price, was already held as valid by early-modern, Spanish natural law theory as required and just in terms of ethics and natural law.[8] Not the formation of the market price, but the formulation of the individual price, which oscillates above and below the market or normal price, is the economic-ethical function of price formation among buyers and sellers. The individual price of a good, or the actual price of a good individuated in space and time, is not determined completely by the market price, but instead arises from ethically-relevant decisions.

An example that price formation is of economic-ethical significance and that price is not determined unambiguously by the market form, as a competitive price *or* monopolistic price, is provided by every case of price-setting and reduction of price competition in the market, which – in contrast to a monopoly – can be equally advantageous for buyers and sellers.

A reduction of price competition that is advantageous for both buyers and sellers takes place in markets in which the seller is a price setter and the buyer is a price taker. The question whether the reduction of competition by price-setting is fair or unfair, efficient or inefficient, cannot be decided in advance by the theory of market form. To be a price taker, as Tibor Scitovsky shows,[9] is not always disadvantageous or unfair treatment by the price setter. The situation of the price taker is not disadvantageous, if he refrains from some of the supplier's price competition and accepts the seller's price-setting, in order to receive in exchange greater non-price advantages made possible by the renunciation of perfect price competition. The reduction of price competition and the price increase for the consumer relative to perfect competition caused by the producer's price-setting can be compensated for the consumer by additional effort, increased friendliness, etc., on the part of the producer. The seller can offer these non-price advantages, which are greater than those of the competitive market, because with price-setting in response to the fluctuation of the price war and price pressure, he can focus to an increased extent on the other non-price variables of his supply-performance.

---

[8] Cf. Joseph Höffner, *Statik und Dynamik in der scholastischen Wirtschaftsethik* (Cologne, 1955).

[9] Tibor Scitovsky, "Pricemakers' Plenty," *Kyklos*, 38 (1985), pp. 517-36.

The price setter, to be sure, obtains an advantage comparable to the profit of a cartel member or oligopolist. But this may not be unethical, if the price setter offers services as compensation for higher prices. The price setter can offer greater availability, geographical proximity, faster transactions, etc., in exchange for prices higher than the equilibrium price with perfect competition, as is the case, for example, with retail business and its quasi-regional monopoly in most cities. In this case, the price setter's behavior is distinguished ideal-typically from the behavior of the oligopolist by the provision of non-price service in compensation for the relatively-excessive price. It must be decided in each individual case whether the exchange with price-setting is fair or unfair or, in other words, whether the contract and price are just or unjust.[10]

The price discretion of the price setter shows that the individual or actual price, as the spatiotemporally-determined individuation of the general market price, does not come into existence mechanically as an equilibrium point and is not extrinsic to or incommensurable with the requirements of economic ethics. The individual price belongs instead to the range of discretion in the formation of commercial transactions. It is one of the variables upon which the parties to the exchange must decide.

Commutative justice requires giving each party to the exchange what is his or hers in the exchange (i.e. exchanging equivalents). This rule has two components. First, it contains the requirement of *price justice*, that the individual price joins the market price, and that exchange equality of product and price is observed for singular goods, for which there exists no market price. Second, the rule of commutative justice involves the requirement of proper conduct as to the objective *nature of the item exchanged*. The proper conduct of the exchange requires the exchange of genuine goods, not sham goods. The two components of commutative justice – price justice and proper conduct or appropriateness to the nature of the matter – coincide and agree in the requirement that the exchange is advantageous to both parties. The requirement that the exchange is mutually advantageous summarizes and explicates the components of price justice *and* appropriateness to the nature of the matter in commutative justice. If sham goods are exchanged, or if one of the parties to the exchange suffers a loss of wealth, not everyone receives that to which he or she is entitled according to the price justice and proper conduct of the economy, according to commutative justice.

---

[10] *Ibid.*, p. 526: "Price makers do, indeed, earn monopoly or oligopoly profits, but they often provide services in exchange; and it remains to be decided in each particular case whether the exchange is fair or exploitative."

8.2.2. APPROPRIATENESS TO THE NATURE OF THE ITEM EXCHANGED: NO EXCHANGE OF SHAM GOODS

Sham goods contravene commutative justice and bring about unjustified incomes. If a transfer of income from a buyer to a seller takes place for a sham good, no added value is created by the seller. His or her income from this exchange is, therefore, unjust and violates the proper conduct of the economy.[11] The following causes of unjustified transfers of income resulting from the exchange of sham goods can be distinguished:

a) An unjustified transfer of income occurs when the stronger party, the seller, sells his commitment not to exploit *his own already existing power position* or *the buyer's already existing plight and predicament.* The good that is "produced" here consists only in the seller's renunciation of the use of power or in the non-exploitation of the plight of the buyer. It consists only in the renunciation of an unjust act by the seller. Income that originates merely from the non-exploitation of an already existing, given predicament is unjustified, because there is no economic production of added value. An example is the exploitation of a borrower's illiquidity, which has arisen through no fault of his own, by a lender. Not all high interest is unjust, however, because the creditworthiness of the borrower must be included in the calculation of the price of the credit. Distinguishing between the justified high price for a higher credit risk and the exploitation of a borrower's plight is, of course, often difficult.

b) A second form of income occurs if a *predicament* of the buyer or seller is *created* by the other party. In this case there is indeed "production" by the stronger party, namely the creation of a predicament, which distinguishes it from the mere exploitation of a pre-existing predicament. This creation of income, however, violates the commutative justice and proper conduct of the economy, since the creation of a predicament is the production of a sham good, not the economic production of added value. It is often not possible to distinguish income resulting from the creation of a predicament and income obtained by robbery. The exploitation of monopolies *without* the production of non-price quid pro quo, the creation and exploitation of predicaments by unjustified strikes or lockouts, etc., create unjust income.

c) The third type of sham good and of unjust income obtained from it is profiting excessively by aiding and abetting the self-delusion of the buyer and the exploitation of his inexperience. The income derived from an exchange-good, whose price has been driven up artificially by the seller's excessive encouragement of the buyer's self-delusion, vanity, search for prestige, etc., is unjust income, since the price does not correspond to the nature of the good.

[11] Cf. Julius Wolf, *Nationalökonomie als exakte Wissenschaft* (Leipzig, 1908), p. 143.

Here as well, of course, it is often difficult to distinguish between the satisfaction of existing vanity and the stimulation of new vanity.

d) The fourth type of unjust income arises from the misrepresentation of the facts of the matter (counterfeiting). This type of income is of economic-ethical importance above all when it is attained illegally.

The requirement that the price and the exchange transaction correspond to the nature of the good exchanged is neither trivial nor tautological, but a requirement of ethical and economic theories of goods and commutative justice. The exchange transaction must involve a genuine good, not a sham good about whose nature one of the parties has illusions, with the other party deriving profit from these illusions. Wheat, not counterfeit wheat with empty heads, should be exchanged. With an exchange, an income transfer for a genuine good, not an exchange of income for a sham good, must take place. In the case of a sham good, there exists an income transfer in favor of the seller, by which the subjective good of the buyer comes into being only by the manipulation of the seller, not by economic added value. The equality of price and commodity, the equivalence of commutative justice is, therefore, not fulfilled.

These four forms of unjust income are already partially anticipated and proscribed by law. Thus, one can ask what economic ethics can contribute here beyond commercial law. The law, as the order of coercion, functions with standardization, prohibition, and sanction. When the law becomes the order of obligation and intention – and no law can be only the order of coercion – it turns into ethics. Economic ethics forms, therefore, in questions of commutative justice the *order of obligation and intention of the economy*, which turns to the free will of the acting person for assistance in refraining from actions within the zone between what is still permitted and what is already forbidden by law.

This border cannot always be seen distinctly. For example, in case c), of unjust income from the self-delusion of the buyer, it is impossible to attain clear legal standardization. This increase or exploitation of the buyer's self-delusion by the seller can be neither proven nor made justiciable from without, because it concerns an internal relation of the buyer to himself or herself.

Economic ethics must acknowledge that the principle of *caveat emptor*, buyer beware, is also an important ethical principle, one that cannot be repealed simply by economic-ethical demands on the seller, since it contains the acknowledgement of the responsibility and liberty of the person. Economic ethics must find a path here between a ruthless *caveat emptor* principle of the strongest and an equally alienating principle of consumer care by legal and ethical restrictions. The seller cannot be his brother's, the buyer's, keeper. Nevertheless, the difference between deceiving and exchanging remains and is ethically relevant. The exchange transaction must correspond to the nature of the subject, not the appearance, so that equality of exchange between the good or service and the price is achieved.

8.2.3. MUTUALLY-ADVANTAGEOUS EXCHANGE: NEITHER PARTY SUFFERS A LOSS OF NET WEALTH

The fundamental principle of exchange is that it must be advantageous for both sides. The principle of mutually-advantageous exchange is, in contrast to many portrayals in positive economics, a normative principle, not an empirical one. It involves, following Heinrich Pesch, the requirement of requital according to the value of the good or service.[12] Neither of the parties to a contract may suffer a loss of wealth as a result of the exchange. The principle of the mutually-advantageous contract does not say that every contract proves that it is advantageous for both parties by the fact that it exists, because otherwise they would not have entered into it. The condition of mutually-advantageous exchange requires that *both* parties from the exchange transaction derive advantage. To derive advantage means that one at least does not suffer a loss of wealth by the contractual transaction. Thus, no party pays a price so excessive in relation to the value of the good that she is worse off economically as a result of the exchange than she would be if she had not conducted the exchange. The utility from the exchange transaction can be zero, but the change in the wealth from the transaction may not be negative.

The wealth of a party to a contract that he himself realized before the exchange may not be reduced by the exchange. This rule refers to real*ized* wealth. If the potential wealth is converted into considerably greater realized wealth by the exchange, but this increase in value is not completely settled in the exchange, there exists no unjust income for the person who acquires the good whose value has increased, because a relative wealth increase is brought about by the exchange. Assume that an art expert finds a valuable painting, which is considered by its owner to be worthless, in the attic of a house. If she buys it at a price far below what she knows to be its true value, the seller does not suffer a loss of wealth in the strict sense, since he did not know the value of the painting and thus had not realized its wealth, and since no immediate market price exists, to which it could be joined. Another question is whether economic ethics can say anything about when the difference between the estimated price and the agreed price in such a case is unethical. Rigorism is not required here, because the discovery of the painting is a wealth-increasing achievement.

The prohibition in economic ethics of a loss of wealth by a contractual transaction is only a different formulation of the theorem of the mutually-advantageous exchange and the demand of commutative justice that equivalents be exchanged. An exchange that leads to a loss of wealth for one party to a contract is not mutually advantageous and is not an exchange of equivalents. Transactions with sham goods are, therefore, also excluded, because they are not mutually

---

[12] Cf. Heinrich Pesch, *Ethik und Volkswirtschaftslehre* (Freiburg, 1918), pp. 50 ff.

advantageous and equivalent. They are not mutually advantageous, because they involve a loss of wealth on the side of the person who acquires the sham good. Seen economically, the exchange of money that a party to a contract *E (ego)* pays for the renunciation by the other *A (alter)* of exploiting a predicament of *E* is indeed a mutually-advantageous arrangement, because *E* suffers less loss by the transaction than he would have if the predicament were exploited. But this mutually-advantageous agreement is neither a mutually-advantageous *exchange* nor an economically correct achievement, in the sense of being just to the objective goal of the economy. *A*'s gain of wealth is brought about by *E*'s equal loss. There is no production of added value. The advantage to *E* from the exchange consists only in his not experiencing *even greater harm* and loss of wealth. The exchange of a small harm for a threatened greater harm is not an increase of wealth and not a mutually-advantageous exchange, if *both* the large *and* the small harm are caused by the same party. The theorem of mutually-advantageous exchange is not only a descriptive theorem about every actual exchange that takes place, but at the same time a normative principle: The exchange should be objectively advantageous, not merely apparently advantageous, for *both* parties, and should not merely bring about an apparent advantage, as in the case of exchanging a sham good.

Economic-ethical price theory cannot take refuge in the merely conventional price and regard every price to which parties have agreed as also an economic-ethically justified price. No party to a contract *wishes* to suffer a loss of wealth from an exchange, and thus to pay a price exceeding the value of the good. Therefore, if a wealth-diminishing exchange takes place "voluntarily," only to avoid an even greater harm that the other party could inflict, it is not an exchange at all, but coercion to a transfer of wealth from the weaker to the stronger, or from the one strong person to the many weak persons who have united against him.

The legal institution of bankruptcy is not an exception here. In bankruptcy, the creditor relinquishes some of his claims to the debtor, in order to gain a settlement of the bankruptcy proceedings. He does this to avoid an even greater loss. In this respect, bankruptcy is a wealth-diminishing contract for one of the parties, namely the creditor. As a contract transaction, however, bankruptcy, like other composition proceedings, is a consequential transaction of an original exchange that was advantageous for both sides. The bankruptcy contract is not an original contract, but a derivative contract. It is entered into in order to avoid or to limit the damage that has arisen outside the contract transaction of the bankruptcy. It is neither a contract concerning a sham good nor the exploitation of a predicament. The bankruptcy contract becomes the deliberate exploitation of the predicament of the creditor by the debtor, which consists in the debtor compelling the creditor to accept a smaller loss in order to avoid a greater loss of his claims in the bankruptcy, and therefore becomes a sham good for the creditor, only when a fraudulent bankruptcy of the debtor exists, where the debtor has thus intentionally brought about his own bankruptcy situation and the predicament of the creditor (i.e. the non-fulfillment of his claims). As a derivative phenomenon and as a contract subsequent to an original exchange transaction intended to be mutually advantageous, a bankruptcy proceeding is not a refutation of the requirement of commutative justice that each exchange transaction should be mutually advantageous and that sham goods should not be exchanged.

8.2.4. COMMUTATIVE JUSTICE AS VIRTUE

The criteria of commutative justice and the equivalence of goods exchanged, which have already been identified, are negative, up to the rule of joining the individual price to the market price: there must be no exchange of sham goods and no loss of net wealth by either party to the exchange. These negative determinants of commutative justice are unambiguous in their core. They forbid income from sham goods and from acts of exchange that lead to a diminution of wealth by either of the contracting parties. As negative determinants, they form the "irreducible core" of commutative justice.[13] But the negative formulation of this core allows room for the further positive ethical formulation of contracts.

These criteria of justice allow special room for bargaining in the formation of prices when a market price does not exist and, therefore, cannot be joined to a prevailing price, and when unique situations are to be developed. One situation in which no prevailing price *can* exist, one in which discretion in price formation is unavoidable, is that of the introduction of new goods and services. Additional situations of unique decision-making, which cannot be answered by general price rules, are those of distributing the producer's and consumer's surpluses arising from a particular exchange transaction with a given market price. In both forms of decision situation, the level of the price is under discussion. Neither decision situation can be attained from general rules of price justice. But neither are they economic-ethically neutral nor incommensurable with commutative justice. In both cases, justice remains an ethical obligation, not in the sense of the fulfillment of a rule, but in the sense of a state of character and exercise of virtue.

[13] The name *iustitia commutativa* originates with Josef Pieper, "Justice," trans. Lawrence E. Lynch, in *The Four Cardinal Virtues* (Notre Dame, Ind., 1966), pp. 76 ff., who calls *iustitia commutativa* in its *entirety* "the irreducible core of social relations." Pieper exaggerates, however, the unambiguousness of commutative justice. The arrangement of contracts is not completely determined by the principle of commutative justice.

Price Justice with Innovations

New products and services can be related to the market price of similar products only to an extremely limited degree, if at all. When new goods represent genuine innovations, they have no substitutes among already existing goods. There are no prices of similar goods, to which theirs can be compared. In such cases, commutative justice cannot be established by joining the existing price or prevailing price. It is up to the innovative firm to determine the price of an innovation or new good.

An additional argument for the economic-ethical liberty to set the prices of new goods and procedures is that pioneer profits and surplus economic rents from innovations are necessary as incentives for firms to strive to develop and introduce innovations. The innovative entrepreneur must utilize opportunities to make pioneer profits, so that she can begin mass production of the new good, finance the mass production with the help of the pioneer profits, and bring the new good to market as a common product. The innovator must see "what the market will bear" in certain situations, in order to meet the costs of the innovation. For her new product and innovation may already be withdrawn and eliminated from the market tomorrow.

The theory of commutative justice must take investment risk into account. Commutative justice, with the requirement of joining the market price, already relates primarily to goods that have a general price, even a static, constant price in the market, and therefore, primarily to average goods and services. New goods and procedures are not attained by the old, static price structure. The entrepreneurial risk of innovation is not compensated appropriately and justly by comparison with the constant price of similar goods. Average service is compensated by average prices, average interest, and average wages, not by profit or quasi-rent or at a loss.[14] Losses are the price of the opportunity to introduce innovations and to be able to make profit with innovations, the price for providing the entrepreneur the opportunity to pursue creative and long-term strategies and, therefore, to succeed or to fail. The individual must be allowed the opportunity to make profits or sustain losses, because no one can assess firms and, therefore, strategies for the future ex ante. The certain determination of which strategy, among the many possible long-term strategies, is the economically correct strategy is never possible ex ante, only ex post. Therefore, no unambiguous rules of commutative justice for innovations and the corresponding introduction prices or quasi-rents arising from them can be provided. The fact that the higher risk of innovation is balanced by higher prices does not violate commutative justice. The formation of equivalents in the form of the market price is only introduced by the innovative entrepreneur and the prevailing price is formed only by him.

---

[14] Cf. Ludwig von Mises, *Human Action* (New Haven, 1949), pp. 291 ff.

It is not possible to provide positive rules of exchange for price formation in cases of innovation that go beyond the negative rules prohibiting the exchange of sham goods and exchanges in which one of the parties sustains a loss of wealth. Nevertheless, these negative rules involve essential orientations for the evolutionary process of innovation. They formulate the ethical obligation to distinguish sham innovations from genuine innovations and the prohibition against introducing "innovations" that do not deserve the name, but are instead "false wheat." Innovation profits represent quasi-rents from the introduction of a good that is still unique, for which no substitute (yet) exists. Like all economic rents arising from the unique availability of resources, these economic rents are also not entirely neutral ethically in price formation, even though comparison to a market price is not possible. The question of how high the quasi-rent may be in individual cases must remain open, even if it does not stand outside all ethical considerations and criteria of justice.

The Distribution of Consumer's and Producer's Surpluses as a Problem of Ethical Equity

Like the question of the determination of the just price in the case of innovation and the level of the quasi-rents from the innovation, the dividing up of the producer's and consumer's surpluses between suppliers and demanders is also an open and, therefore, economic-ethically relevant question. The distribution of economic rents cannot be expressed by general rules, since questions about quasi-rents and consumer's and producer's surpluses are, by their very nature, about singular phenomenon. With such economic rents, the distribution of rents between the buyer and the seller is under discussion with every prevailing market price possible. The distribution of rents is not a problem of deontological ethics. It is, however, a problem of the economic-ethical exercise of virtue, a problem of the just state of character.

The virtue or state of character of justice requires, above and beyond the rules of commutative justice, doing the good in each individual case. Aristotle describes yet another ability, which is indeed a component of justice, but nevertheless surpasses it, by going beyond the rule of what is just: the *epikia*, the equitable or appropriate:

> What is equitable is better than one way of being just, but it is still just, and not better than what is just by being a different genus. Hence the same thing is just and equitable, and while both are excellent, what is equitable is superior. The puzzle arises because what is equitable is just, but is not what is legally just, but a rectification of it. The reason is that all law is universal, but in some areas no universal rule can be correct . . . . And this is the nature of what is equitable – rectification of law insofar as the universality of law makes it deficient . . . . It is also evident from this who the decent person is; for he is the one who decides for and does such actions, not an exact stickler for justice in the bad way, but taking

> less than he might even though he has the law on his side. This is the decent person, and his state is equity.[15]

The requirement of justice as equity is not a universal rule, but the orientation of action toward the virtue of justice. Equity requires the state of character of justice. For the law, the requirement of the state of equity is not relevant. The written and general law also cannot at all portray the virtue of equity in itself. Equity is for positive law "a silent goddess who cannot be heard, because nothing was stipulated about this in the contract, and a judge cannot pronounce in accordance with unstipulated conditions."[16] For ethics, equity is, on the contrary, not a silent goddess, but a requirement of the *ethical* decision-making of the individual.

When applied to the economic-ethical problem of quasi-rents and consumer's and producer's surpluses, this means that questions of justice and equity that are legally unobjectionable must also be included in contracts. The extent to which the quasi-rents resulting from an innovation are to be used, for instance, is a meaningful, economic-ethical question to the individual, even if little can be said about the level of the just price for an innovative good legally and from a general economic-ethical rule of price justice. The same is true of contracts with inexperienced persons who do not know the market value of their productivity. In terms of commercial law, the complete, unilateral appropriation of the economic rents from such contracts is of little significance. But in terms of economic ethics, it should be asked whether such an action is just. In assessing the justice of labor contracts, of course, it should also be considered that in situations where a unilateral appropriation of quasi-rents by the employer occurs, self-regulating mechanisms usually set in within the firm by which the employees recover a part of the economic rent in the form of slack or non-material advantages. A more difficult situation exists when the producer's surplus is appropriated unilaterally by the employees, because rigid labor law reduces the firm's ability to defend itself from the quasi-rent of the slack.

The economic theory of the market assumes that the parties to a contract have taken into account and have internalized all positive and negative side effects, all *economic rents*, that they themselves can acquire from the contract transaction, and that they express this internalization by agreeing to the contract. Any additional consideration of the externalities of the contract on the other party appears superfluous, even harmful, from this point of view, because the individual lacks adequate information about the "external" effects of the contract on the other party, and neither can nor should put himself in the position of the other person. Each party to the contractual transaction has his sphere, for

---

[15] Aristotle, *Nicomachean Ethics*, V, 14, 1137 b 10-35 (translation modified).

[16] Immanuel Kant, *The Metaphysics of Morals*, Part I: *The Metaphysical Elements of Justice*. trans. John Ladd (New York, 1985), p. 40.

which he should be concerned and which is no concern of the other party. For the time being, this argument will be accepted as satisfactory.

The difference between the ethical minimum of the law (i.e. non-interference in the sphere of the other person) and the ethical virtue of justice becomes visible here. Commerce can take place on the basis of individuals' consideration of their own interests, without anyone having to consider the side effects of actions on other persons. But the exchange transaction can also go beyond the consideration of self-interests, to a comparison of the interests of the other party. A fair contract is, from this perspective, a contract that goes beyond the price arising from a mere balancing of one's own interests and strives for a fair balance of the interests of the side effects and mutual consumer's and producer's surpluses.

The problem of the fair balancing of interests in the formation of contracts does not only arise when a price is possible only by convention. This may be the case when no market price, no assessment by society, and no shadow price or price by taxation exists. The ethical obligation of balancing interests also arises when a market price is present as the orienting price, although the problem presents itself in a less urgent form in the case of a given market price. Hobbes's proposition that every contract to which two parties agree is a just contract, is false. Not every conventional price and not every contract into which two parties enter is also a fair price and contract, as is shown by the problems of sham goods and of exchanges that bring about a reduction of net wealth for one party.

As has been shown above, the market price is not a completely fixed value, but is individuated by space and time within a certain, ethically-relevant bandwidth of variance above and below the market price. When the individual price oscillates around the market price within this bandwidth, price discrimination favoring the seller, as well as an equal price for everyone, can be practiced. Depending upon the situation and circumstances, price discrimination either in favor of a needy person or not in favor of a prosperous person can be demanded by ethics. Depending upon the situation, however, price indistinguishability can also be an ethical command of fairness to everyone.

It is of economic-ethical significance that the weighing of the individual price with regard to the market price cannot be dismissed as irrelevant for ethics. The acting person must decide concerning the individual price, whether it should be identical to or deviate from the market price. In general, one will accept the fixed market price, which is not ethically problematic, for goods that are highly homogenous, but also for inexpensive goods, because in these cases the costs of making decisions about the "individuation" of the price are higher than the profit to be gained by ethical reflection and the individual formation of a fair price. Kierkegaard's proposition that *the decision* is ridiculous in some life relationships, and necessary in others, is valid here.[17]

---

[17] Kierkegaard, *Either/Or*, Part II, pp. 170 ff.

Even when a market price exists, the distribution of the consumer's and producer's surpluses between the parties to a contract remains open. It is not highly ethical to seek strategically to obtain the entire possible rent from a contract for oneself and to exploit the ignorance, weakness, or inexperience of the other party. Economic ethics requires here the state of character of equity, the readiness to strive for a fair balance of interests between the producer's and consumer's surpluses. The problem of the distribution of economic rents is not a question of rules and prohibitions, but of the ethical virtue of justice and equity. Ruthless rent seeking is not highly ethical conduct, and probably is also not an advantageous, long-term strategy, because it will meet with equally harsh rent seeking from the other side. A generous, mutual concession of economic rents, with alternating preference to one party or the other according to different opportunities, will improve and humanize long-term, repeat business and is, therefore, sensible not only ethically, but also economically.

An economic exchange is optimal when the yields and economic rents of *both* the buyer *and* the seller are maximized. In this criterion, nothing is said about the distribution of consumer's and producer's surpluses between the two parties. A just balance with the appropriation of possible economic rents is neither economically inefficient nor Pareto-suboptimal. But in the view of ethics, it is an exercise of the virtue of justice. According to Aristotle, it is the nature of the virtues to maintain the mean in action between too much and to little. Thus, generosity must keep to a mean between extravagance and greed. The same is true analogously of the virtue of commutative justice. It is a mean between ruthless rent seeking and feeble compliance in the formation of contracts.

8.2.5. THE UNAVOIDABILITY OF THE QUESTION OF JUSTICE

Justice is, above all, a virtue of the powerful and knowledgeable person.[18] Such a person can draw quasi-rents for himself from his power and knowledge, and from the powerlessness and ignorance of the other person. The renunciation of the unjust exploitation of a position of power and knowledge can originate only from an ethical will and an ethical state of character, because nothing, neither the rule nor the sanction of public opinion and one's good reputation, can punish unjust rent seeking that remains within the legal rules and those of convention. In the sphere of *ethics*, which lies outside the merely conventional, power and knowledge can bind themselves only morally, but cannot be bound by external rules. Power and knowledge also prove themselves to be moral phenomena in the context of commutative justice.

A just action or solution is one that can raise claims to approval. In colloquial language, to say that a decision is just is to say that it claims approval and can

[18] Robert Spaemann, *Basic Moral Concepts*, trans. Armstrong (London, 1989), pp. 38-39.

raise a reasonable claim to the approval of those affected and disinterested observers. The statement "That is a just decision" means that claims and conflicts are negotiated in such a way that each impartial observer or judge, the "impartial audience in everyone's breast," can approve under the obligation to exchange roles and put oneself in the position of the other person. A just solution is one that *anticipates* an ideal discourse and its consent (i.e. the approval of everyone who has an undistorted perception of the situation). Justice does not mean the actual approval of all empirical subjects at every point in time, because the perspectives of persons concerned are always distorted and one sided. A just decision must be made under the conditions of impartiality, objectivity, and knowledgeability of the persons who have the will to these qualities and attempt to anticipate a consensus with their presence.

Justice is the characteristic of the prudent judge who weighs the claims of all sides and then decides impartially.[19] Justice requires the businessperson, accordingly, to weigh the claims flowing from the law and the performances of the parties concerned impartially, objectively, and favorably – in other words, justly. Justice assigns to the person who has decision power the requirement to test and decide impartially, and to seek the approval of the concerned parties. It assigns to the parties affected by the decision the requirement to approve and follow it, if they have acknowledged it as just. These two requirements form a constant and a dilemma of human society and economic order, one which cannot be removed – contrary to the hopes of the Marxist and anarchic-liberal utopians. The problem of justice cannot be avoided. It cannot be solved by implementing a perfect form of economic organization.

Justice, understood as an effort of the self to balance interests, is indispensable, because there will always be scarcity and conflicting claims to goods that must be brought into balance. The statement "In the sphere of production there is no justice" is not universally valid, because production is not only a technical and economic (i.e. poietic) matter, but at the same time also a social (i.e. practical) event. The work or product of the creative act may originate outside the conditions of justice, and the allocation of creative abilities may be incommensurable with concepts of justice. But the embedding of creative activity and production in the conditions of social life and, therefore, in practical norms of social cooperation and communication make it impossible to ban considerations of justice completely from the sphere of production.

Justice would be superfluous only if there were no longer any scarcity. Consequently, the utopias that believe it is possible to do without the concept of justice are those that also believe it is possible to overcome scarcity: anarchic liberalism and Marxism.

---

[19] This image is taken from a conversation with Robert Spaemann.

Anarchic liberalism pursues a pure ideal of efficiency and liberty in the economy. The norm of justice is completely replaced by the norm of efficiency or maximal output, or by the norm of freedom of action. The question of justice is considered to have been made superfluous by economic growth. According to the anarchic-liberal view, the growing quantity of goods to be distributed, the growing "pie," eliminates the problem of justice.

Marxism advocates a similar solution to the problem of justice. The production of superfluity, resulting from changes in the relationships of production in the perfect, communist society, would make conflicts and balances of interests, and therefore the requirements of justice, superfluous, because after the abolition of scarcity and in the superabundance there would be enough to meet all demands, without curtailment. Marx's motto "From each according to his abilities, to each according to his needs" is no longer a problem of justice under conditions of the end of scarcity, but the natural principle of the perfect society and the "justice-less" free self-realization made possible in it.

For the non-utopian present and for the firm that operates under conditions of scarcity of internal and external resources, however, the question of justice remains irrefutable. Neither the principle of liberty nor the principle of equality can completely replace the principle of justice. Justice must adopt perspectives of liberty and equality and take them into account in its weighing of claims; but it is identical with neither of them.

Just is a reasonable balance, capable of leading to a consensus, between conflicting, historically developed and historically conditioned claims to goods and services in the economy, a balance as it comes into being in anticipation of an ideal discourse that impartial advisors and judges would lead in the real conditions of the actual discourse of organizations, markets, and democracies that orient themselves toward the anticipation of an ideal discourse. There are conflicts that cannot be postponed in expectation of the future growth of the firm or the entire economy and a future greater quantity of goods to be distributed. There are also conflicts between historically developed individuals that cannot be resolved by the imposition to the individuals to give up the historicity of their own persons for the form of the ideal discourse partners and to transform their historical rights into "public" interests. In both conflict cases of the non-postponability of the oppositions of interests and of historical rights, only a just weighing of claims remains.

The preceding considerations of the determination of the just contract and fair price in the individual case show that not every price resulting from a contractual agreement is *eo ipso* automatically just, and that not every conventional price implies that the exchange is mutually advantageous. A consensus can be reached concerning even sham goods, as likewise a sham consensus concerning genuine goods can come about, because of inexperience and ignorance. Economic ethics studies those problems of the formation of contracts and price formation that, on one hand, are more than economic problems of the control and coordination of the economy by the price system and, on the other hand, do not yet lie in the domain of legal prohibitions and sanctions. The just contract's price is neither a price that market forces bring about automatically nor a legal institution that is justiciable or legally enforceable. Contractual justice is an exercise of virtue, which is, however, economically relevant. An economy directed toward the requirement of just prices and the principle of compensation according to the value of the product, a principle in which the market price represents the decisive criterion, but not the only criterion of price-justice in the particular case, will attain a greater degree of perfection than an economy of unrestricted rent seeking and the exhaustion of every opportunity for profit.

8.3. What Is the Basis of the Obligation to Give Each Person What Is His or Hers in Exchange?

The content of economic ethics can be summarized by the requirement to have the will and the state of character, guided by reason, to give to each person what is his or hers. This holds true for both exchange transactions and life within the firm, which represents in a wider sense an exchange event among the members of the firm in its internal market. The way to determine what each person is entitled to in exchange has just been explained. It remains to explain why one should give to each person what is his or hers and wherein the basis of the obligation to do this consists.

Economic ethics is concerned with situations in which the other person does not already have or does not receive what is his or hers, when it depends upon myself and my ethical judgment to see that he or she receives it. Contracts formulated in such a way that no deviation from the text of the contract is possible, or that monitoring them produces no transaction costs, are not relevant to economic ethics. Such situations are rare, of course, and the attempt to form situations in such a way that economic ethics is thereby superfluous in them, that complete external control is applied, presents an economic problem, because such control produces high costs. The attempt to eliminate economic ethics by external control presents a problem of general ethics, because it is ethically improper to attempt to exclude ethical decisions from the context of human action and, therefore, also from exchange transactions. An element of commutative justice and the virtue of equity remains, and must remain, in every non-trivial contract and exchange.

That which is due each person, what is his or hers, is determined by the rules and functional conditions of an economic order and the prevailing price. The determinants of the just price in a particular case (i.e. joining the market price, exchange of a genuine good, and no loss of net wealth by either party to the contract) describe the arrangement of exchange events that correspond to the nature of the economy and attain the objective goal of the economy: to ensure the meeting of needs and the self-realization of the businessperson in production. Those who participate in the exchange should make these rules their own. By participating in an exchange relationship and expecting the other party to follow the rules, they also implicitly agree at the same time to apply these rules to their own actions.

The question must be asked, therefore, whether in addition to the presentation of the rules of exchange in general, an ethical basis of obligation must still be provided to explain why the individual *should* make these rules his own. The ethical can be defined as the state of character to make the rules that follow from the nature of the situation, the appropriateness to the nature of the subject matter, also the motive of one's own action. The moral agent makes the general rules of an action-context and the nature of the situation also the motive of his own action. He pursues his own goals *and* the goals that are based on the universal rules of action in the concerned sphere of activity. In the action sphere of the economy, making the rules the motive of one's own action means that the acting person sees his individual economic pursuit of goals as a part of the realization of the objective goal of the economy as a whole and co-pursues the economic goal of the entire economy in his individual pursuit of goals.

Ethics consists in transforming one's own subjectivity and locally-maximizing strategies into subjectivity capable of universalization and globally-maximizing strategies. The person whose actions conform to economic ethics acknowledges that she cannot pursue her long-term goals in the economy separately from the rules of the realization of the objective goal of the economy as a whole. The transformation of short-term into long-term advantage considerations and from locally-maximizing into globally-maximizing strategies realizes the substance of the ethical, which, as shown above, does *not* follow from *immediate* self-interest. Making commutative justice the maxim of one's own actions and appropriating the state of character and virtue, to give to each person his or her own, does not mean maximizing one's short-term, local advantage, but acknowledging commutative justice as a condition of conduct and the perfection of one's own firm *and* the entire economy.

The difficulties that immediate self-interest has in making this universal interest also its own interest were discussed in Chapters 2 and 3. It appears advantageous to make the pursuit of the universal interest one's own self-interest, only if everyone else does the same. But because everyone else sees things the same way, the assurance that the individual pursuit of the universal interest is general practice comes about only with difficulty. If the religious perspective is based only upon long-term self-interest, it is certainly subject to limitations, since human beings are short-run minded. The religious-ethical perspective and the self-interested motive come together in ethical action, however; the ethical perspective takes an interest in the totality. The ethical perspective is supported by the nature of the subject matter of the economy, to achieve the maximum material well-being of all. The concept of appropriateness to the nature of the matter or goal of the economy supports the foundation of ethics from the structure of totality and from the interest that ethics and the global maximization of the ethically and religiously expanded self take in the state of totality. The natural-law ideal of appropriateness to the nature of the subject matter of the economy establishes an obligation to the good that is based not only on the pursuit of subjective self-interest and its coordination with other self-interests, but also on the nature of the goods, on the character of the will as an end in itself, and on the affirmative attitude towards the common good.

The basis of the obligation of commutative justice lies in the obligation to satisfy the rules of the economic order. The rules of the legitimate economic order must be fulfilled, because that is necessary for the attainment of the objective goal of the economy as a whole and the subjective goals of the persons within it. The goal of the complete economy is to meet the needs and to safeguard the conditions of the self-development of the individuals (i.e. to create the conditions of realizing the material and immaterial goods). The economic rules and duties follow from this objective goal.

To make these rules the rules of one's own actions is the ethical obligation of the individual for the economic sphere of his actions. If he affirms these rules as self-accepted duties of self-determined action, and not merely as heteronomous, imposed restrictions, he acts ethically – in Kantian terms, *from* duty and observance of the law, not merely *in accordance with* duty. The person who sees the objective rules of the economy, such as *pacta sunt servanda*, not as tiresome, external duties of conducting business, but instead makes them duties that he himself sets as maxims of his actions, conforms to the *deontological theory of economic ethics*.

The *theory of goods of economic ethics* encompasses material and immaterial goods, those of merely securing the means of subsistence and those of the "culture of securing subsistence" (Werner Sombart). The theory of goods of economic ethics represents in itself the ideas of human individuals and the things, whose realization in the structures of an order of the ideas is the realization of the idea of the good. The realization of the ideas of the goods and the order of these ideas according to *the* idea of the good, which places everything in order, is the realization of the maximum of compossible value fulfillment. The realization of the maximum of compossible value fulfillment is the material cause of the economy. To recognize this material objective goal of the complete economy as the background of one's own economic actions is to see oneself the idea of the economy in one's own actions as the model to make one's own, and one's own pursuit of goals and production of goods as a part of the complete realization of goods, as a part of the ethical *and* economic theory of goods. The business person follows the ethical theory of goods, if he or she produces and trades genuine goods. Commutative justice requires exchanging, not sham goods, but goods that correspond to the nature or idea of the subject matter.

Finally, the *ethical theory of virtues* encompasses the state of character and conviction, penetrating all of one's actions, to do justice to human persons and the nature of things. In economic ethics, virtue realizes itself as the virtue, state of character, and conviction to exercise justice and equity in the firm and in commercial transactions. This state of character has no further basis of obligation outside itself, but is instead its own motive and goal. The obligating and motivating basis of the virtue of justice is not another basis outside itself, but is itself. The virtue is itself the means and end; it is an end in itself. Its utility does not consist in something other than itself, but in its own realization and in the fact that the virtue of the acting person communicates the awareness of being on the way to doing justice to the nature of persons and things. "Happiness is not the reward of virtue, but virtue itself."[20] The utility of justice in the firm and in exchange transactions is not the wage or advantage from justice, but is instead justice itself – not in the sense of the pillow of the good conscience, but as the self-realization of human morality and the representation of the idea of the good in the economy. The person who makes justice in economic transactions the motive and the conviction of his or her economic actions for the sake of justice itself meets the standard of the virtue theory of economic ethics.

Duty, motive, and the good aspired to also belong together and mutually complete one another in economic action. The fact that they belong together shows that in economic ethics, as in general ethics, deontological theory, virtue theory, and the theory of goods form a unity and represent the aspects of the idea of the good in economic actions. The basis of the obligation to give every person what is his does not arise from an external basis, such as utility maximization or maximization of the economy's output, but from the relationship of the acting person to himself. The obligation to act ethically in the sphere of the economy expresses itself in the relationship of the human self to its will as duty, in the relationship of the self to its state of character and conviction as virtue, and in the relationship of the self to its goals as a question of the nature and form of the goods to which it aspires. The "self-relationships" of the human person to himself constitute his ethical obligations, as self-obligations. As self-obligations, the economic-ethical obligations do not follow from external goals and outer laws, but from the relationship of the self to its will and to the affirmation of the idea of the good as the order and appropriateness of totality.

The basis of the obligation to act ethically cannot originate only from enlightened self-interest or from obligations toward other persons. In the final analysis, only the self can obligate itself, though it cannot itself also be the com-

---

[20] Baruch Spinoza, *Ethica ordine geometrico demonstrata* (1677), Part V, Prop. 42.

plete content of the obligation. The content of the obligation is appropriateness to the nature of the subject matter, affirmed by the self; the good and the just, which penetrate everything. The self is the subject and the object of the obligation; the content of the obligation is appropriateness to the nature of the matter. The rules of justice – such as the rule to treat equals equally and unequals unequally in proportion to their relevant differences, and the rule of non-partiality, to give the burden of truth to the one who acts unequally, and not to the one who acts equally – are valid for all actions and cultural spheres of society, not only in the law, but also in economic exchange. They are established by the interests in the preservation of society and by the fact that moral justification implies impartiality and society's connectedness to rules. Establishing human social relationships without the formation of rules is unjust, because it does not treat equals equally and does not allocate the equal amount to the equal person, and thus does not give each person what is his or hers.[21] Moral reciprocity, that I see others as moral subjects like myself, and grant them the same subjectivity as myself, is the content of the categorical imperative. From the categorical imperative, the principle follows to give to each his own, because according to the categorical imperative, each person must be seen as a subject of rights and a being with moral freedom. Because I acknowledge myself as a moral creature and give to myself what is mine, I must also acknowledge all other persons as moral beings and give them what is theirs.

Commutative justice in the economy and market price formation follow the principle of equal liberty and equal legal status in their fundamental obligation to the acknowledgment of human subjectivity. The obligation to commutative justice in its concrete realization as appropriateness to the subject matter of the economy cannot, however, be derived completely from this transcendental, subjective-theoretical establishment of equal freedom, because this establishment is too formal. From the recognition of all human persons as equal legal subjects, the obligation to concrete commutative justice does not yet follow. The transcendental principle of the acknowledgment of liberty can be united with every formally rule-connected arrangement of legal institutions and forms of commerce. In the recognition of the liberty of the other person, something more than the acknowledgment of formal liberty must be present, namely, the affirmation at the same time of the objective goal and the nature of the subject matter of the economy. The objective goal of the economy is not only the realization of liberty, but also the realization of the idea of the good in the economy, the realization of the subsistence and wealth of persons. The acting person must adopt this goal in just the same way as the goal of liberty in his or her enduring state of character and conviction, determined by the will and guided by reason. The theory of liberty and the theories of the good, deontological theory, virtue theo-

---

[21] Cf. Waldstein, "Ist das 'Suum cuique' eine Leerformel?" p. 298.

ry, and goods theory must be united to form the obligation to the rules, to the state of character, and to striving toward the order of the goods in the realization of the idea of the good.

The obligations to rule compliance or action from duty, to perfection of action from virtue, and to the acknowledgment of the order of goods are united in the obligation to give each person what is his or hers. This obligation ensures that the objective goal of the economy is achieved and that the maximum of compossible value-realization is attained in the spheres of the economy. The objective goal of the economy is an essential component of the goal of totality, to realize the maximum of value-realization, the maximization of existence. The principle, to give each person what is his or hers also in economic exchange, follows ultimately from the fact that complete existence forms one single community of right, because the goal of the community of right of that which exists, the maximization of existence and value-realization, can be attained only if efficiency and justice are aspired to in the economy. The objective spheres of human culture and society, and among them above all the economy, must be in accordance with the community of right of that which exists and to the idea of justice that penetrates the totality.

CHAPTER 9

JUST PRICE THEORY

Commutative justice is dependent upon the guideline of the prevailing price. Without the prevailing price as the bench mark, one cannot determine which individual price and contract satisfies the demands of commutative justice. If the individual price is subject to (individual-)ethical norms of justice and fairness, the standard of the individual price, the prevailing price, must satisfy ethical norms. Since the prevailing price in a market economy is the market price, the market price, as the standard of individual actual prices, must also satisfy ethical and social-ethical norms.

The question of the justice of the prevailing price, and in the market economy, of the market price, is not a question of economic ethics in the narrow sense, but one extending beside ethical economy into the domain of political philosophy and political economy. The subjects of decisions about the prevailing price are not only individual economizing and the components of economic individual decisions in response to the price signals of the market, but also the political action center of the society, because the state also shapes market forces and, if necessary, must correct price relationships for political-economic ends.

The determination of the justice of the prevailing price, the question of the "just price," leads beyond commutative justice to the social-economic and social-ethical investigation of the constitutive conditions of the price system in question (i.e. into the analysis of market relationships, the conditions of ownership rights and social-state entitlement law, and the historically existing relationships of ownership). The categorial or even quantitative determination of the just price must achieve the analysis and evaluation of the totality of the factors of determination, determine the prices, and let them be economically correct in the sense of the objective goal of the economy. Such an analysis and evaluation must be the object of a categorial and causal "super theory," developed from price theory, political economy, jurisprudence, political science, political philosophy, and history. It is not possible to develop a theory of the just price in the categorial sense of a causal and complete analysis of the totality of the individual decisions that make a prevailing price just. That surpasses the capabilities of human knowledge. Nevertheless, regulative, "metaphysical" principles of the just price can be given.

Regulative principles are principles that do not achieve the concrete determination of something according to the categories of analytic understanding, but instead guide the application of the categories as ideas or rational concepts of a higher order. Regulative principles "regulate" the analysis of the understanding according to general ideas and make it possible to bring the categorial determinants together into constitutive unities. The regulative principles of price justice do not determine the concrete variables of supply and demand curves, but the rules according to which market price formation and its price formation processes take place and can be economic-ethically assessed and, if necessary, can be reoriented in their constitutive properties toward greater justice.[1] They guide the analysis of the constitutive presuppositions of just price formation and make up the idea according to which the process of price formation can be assessed. The regulative principles of price justice are, on one hand, the inclusion of the persons affected and the internalization of the side effects as formal process criteria of justice and, on the other hand, the attainment of the economy's objective goal and justice to the nature of the subject matter of the economy as the substantive, material principle and the criterion of justice.

9.1. Preliminary Historical Remark: The Significance of Early-Modern, Probabilistic Just Price Theory

Price formation is a part of the formation of a social will, and not only of an economic will, because the bilateral contract and the multilateral market price arising from the components of bilateral contracts are social forms of agreement, forms of the formation of a social consensus. The *implicit social contract of the price system* and the market price, which is permanently changing and renewing itself, contains, if the same formal freedom and market entrance laws are legally ensured, not only a self-balance of powers, but also peace-making and an equilibration of interests between the individuals.[2] This peace-making in the social contract of the price system requires minimum conditions of justice, because the economic form of social coordination of the society – like other forms of social coordination – cannot be successful without the expectation and imposition of striving toward justice. The peaceful and socially-embedded competition and the exchange within a society, which emerge from free contracts capable of being agreed upon, have a minimum measure of solidarity as a prerequisite. Exchange is itself an act of solidarity and social cohesion.

In its anthropological origins, exchange does not form any inner-societal act or interaction type. The exchange carried out from purely economic viewpoints and conditions of competition and without consideration of social reciprocity and justice is a form of interaction that ancient societies carried out only with

[1] On the distinction between categorial and idea knowledge (*Ideenerkenntnis*), see also Hermann Krings, "Vom Sinn der Metaphysik oder über den Unterschied von Ursache und Bedingung," *Philosophisches Jahrbuch*, 92 (1985), pp. 98-109.

[2] On the contract as self-contract, see also Josef Pieper, "Justice," trans. Lawrence E. Lynch. in *The Four Cardinal Virtues* (Notre Dame, Ind., 1966), pp. 77-78.

foreign persons, foreign tribes or even enemies. Ancient societies exchanged in the sense of modern market exchange only at their borders with foreign tribes. For ancient man, exchange has in common with war the foreign tribe and hostile person. The inner-societal exchange and the tradition of the just price attempt to attain an equilibrium between two extreme, economic forms of exchange, between the extra-societal, ethically and socially neutral exchange, on one hand, and the forms of exchange determined by pure reciprocity and love, the family and small groups, on the other hand. The fair exchange and just price seek to "domesticate" the hostility latent in the conflict of competition into a socially-tamed experience of coordination and to "care for" ethically the potentially socially eruptive competition of the pure price system.[3] The theory of just war and the international law of the early-modern period sought a limitation of international competition between states and even a limitation or "domestication" of war in similar ways at the inter-state level. They attempted to set normative limits to the power, escalation, and cruelty of war, to check the lack of norms in military clashes. In – admittedly extremely – analogous ways one must recognize in the theory of the just price an attempt to link the originally hostile conflict to the socially and ethically normative way of fair competition, to "care for" the conflict of competition.

In economic history prices were always also subject to social norms and, therefore, to ideas of justice. The complete autonomy of the market and price formation from the requirements of social justice and the assumption that prices are *only* the resultants of the power parallelogram of the market forces are necessary abstractions of price theory, but are the exception in the epochs of economic history and are correct only for the phases of Manchester liberalism, and even here only ideal-typically. Since the price system is a social institution, it underlies justice demands, not only in the commutative justice of individual price formation and price justice, but also demands of distributive justice in the distribution of participation rights. The ideas of commutative and distributive justice enter the process of price formation and influence the formation of market prices according to their criteria of justice.

A moralization of prices in just price theory is no more economic-ethically desirable than a total liberation of price formation from ethical norms. The early-modern discussion of just prices in the economic ethics of the Spanish natural law school gains again in significance with the question of the normative conditions of price formation, because the economy's process of differentiating out and becoming autonomous and, therefore, of price formation are completed

---

[3] According to Lujo Brentano, *Ethik und Volkswirtschaft in der Geschichte* (Munich, 1902), p. 18, the emancipation of the economy from social norms and the differentiating out of the economy began with the development of foreign trade. Starting out from the "natural law" of foreign trade, in which very few norms were institutionalized, the economy has both freed itself from certain norms and subjected the entire life of society to its own norms.

in the present era by a movement toward normative interpenetration and cultural formation of the societal subsystems, including the economy. The just price was, therefore, a problem for early-modern economic ethics, because it did not completely take the social interaction and formation of will existing in the price out of the system of ethical norms and make them autonomous. Early-modern economic ethics left price formation partially embedded in ethics and, therefore, considered a partial liberation of the economy and market price formation to be permissible and necessary. Karl Polanyi called the earlier economic form of the economy embedded in social norms the "embedded economy," in contrast to the modern "disembedded economy."[4] The gradual separation of price formation from the norms of social solidarity can be perceived in the development toward ethical probabilism and the prohibition of usury. Probabilism, the theory that one may follow the probable opinion *in dubiis* and need not hold to the certain opinion (*opinio tuta*, tutiorism), is applied to price determination and leads to a greater autonomy of decision about the price and to a stronger liberation of the economy from social ethics. Probabilism began with Johannes Nider (1380-1438)[5] and Thomas de Vio, Cardinal Cajetan (1469-1534).[6] Nider's ideas about probabilism were characteristically developed in his *Treatise on the Contracts of Merchants*.[7]

With the beginning of the modern period, which saw an increase in economic activity, the arrangement of a constant requirement and the duty of considering the situation of the contract party in price formation, which was valid until then, became problematic. Probabilism reduces the normative demands on price formation. According to Nider, in the event of doubt about whether the price is just and is becoming just to the situation of the contract party, a moderate probability that the price is "correct" and the price formation is just is sufficient: "Provided a value is fixed at a level within the extremes of a range of prices, it may be held to be done justly."[8] Cajetan affirms explicitly that a party to a contract may demand a price higher than necessary for his social class, and may use it to form capital in order to attain higher status and dignity. If someone has the ability to climb to a higher level and social status, he may acquire and collect

---

[4] Karl Polanyi, *Primitive, Archaic, and Modern Economies* (Boston, 1971), and *The Great Transformation* (Boston, 1944). See also Louis Dumont, *From Mandeville to Marx* (Chicago, 1977).

[5] The article "Probabilisme," in the *Dictionnaire de Théologie Catholique* (Paris, 1936), tome XIII 1, coll. 446, calls Nider one of the first advocates of probabilism.

[6] The works of Cajetan with significance for economic ethics are his *Commentary on the Summa theologica* (1508-28) of Thomas Aquinas, *De cambiis* (on trading companies?), and *Summula de peccatis* (1523). On Cajetan, see Joachim Giers, *Gerechtigkeit und Liebe* (Düsseldorf, 1941).

[7] Johannes Nider, *On the Contracts of Merchants*, trans. Charles H. Reeves (Norman, 1966).

[8] *Ibid.*, p. 23.

the goods necessary to it.[9] Consequently, the objection is sometimes raised against Cajetan that he abolished the borders of social rank and dissolved all conditions of social class. He is to have become the first patron of the coming capitalism.[10]

Probabilism in just price theory proves to be an intermediate position between the complete liberation of price formation and a rigid standardization of the price valid for the exchange. Tendencies to remove certain processes of price formation from the formation of market prices and to re-embed them in norms of social solidarity can be seen at the present time in the usury clauses of civil law, above all with interest on loans, and with the fixing of wage rates by collective agreement. These development show that price formation is not completely autonomous from social conditions, norms, and values, but must instead satisfy minimum conditions of justice.

The prevailing price for time and loans – the general discount rate – and the prevailing price for labor – the standard wage – are the most sensitive prices for price justice. They are, however, not the only prices relevant to price justice, as the historically significant debate of the price of grain and bread shows.

9.2. Natural Law and Forces of Nature in the Legitimation of the Price System

The price system of the market[11] is a method of the socio-economic formation of objectives and coordination and, at the same time, a system of social control of the correctness of economic strategies, whose success is seen in the profits they achieve and whose lack of success is seen in the losses they cause.[12] The coordination and control of social and political processes must, however, legitimate itself before those who are affected by the coordination and control method. This necessity of legitimation holds for all social or political coordination and control methods, for the market and for democracy. It is, therefore, just as necessary to pose the question of their legitimation and justice to the decisions

---

[9] Thomas de Vio Cajetan, *Comm. in II II s. th.*, q. 118, a. 1. On Scholastic and early-modern price theory, see Emil Kauder, "Genesis of the Marginal Utility Theory," *Economic Journal*, 63 (1953), pp. 638-50; John T. Noonan, *The Scholastic Analysis of Usury* (Cambridge, Mass., 1957); Kauder, *A History of Marginal Utility Theory* (Princeton, 1965); and Raymond de Roover, "The Scholastics, Usury, and Foreign Exchange," *Business History Review*, 41 (1967), pp. 257-71.

[10] Cf. Werner Sombart, *The Quintessence of Capitalism*, trans. Mortimer Epstein (New York, 1967), pp. 244-46.

[11] In the following, "price system" will always mean that of the market, since other systems of price determination are not systems of free price formation.

[12] The control aspect has been emphasized especially by Hans Albert. Cf. Albert, *Marktsoziologie und Entscheidungslogik* (Neuwied, 1967), pp. 66-67.

of the price system as to the decisions of the political system. It is social-ethically imperative that legitimation and justice questions are posed to the price system. It must find their answer in the analysis and evaluation of market events. The legitimation question of the price system answers itself neither on its own by referring to the naturalness of the market events that lead "by nature" to "natural prices," nor by reference to pure procedural correctness.

The assumption that every naturalistic, unhindered market leads to natural prices that are also just, because of these forces of nature, is a fallacy. It is not a naturalistic fallacy, arguing from "is" to "ought," from the fact of market price formation to the justice of market price formation, for instance. It is instead a fallacy, because a conclusion of an insufficiently definite "is" is drawn from an "ought" and is concluded from false premises. Market price formation has wide-reaching and non-self-evident legal and cultural presuppositions, such as rights of liberty and the legal protection of persons and property, etc., that do not establish themselves naturalistically, but must instead be established politically and economically and be affirmed by those who are active in the market. It has, in addition, economic-ethical presuppositions of the ethical conduct expectations of those who are active in the market, which likewise do not arise naturalistically, but must instead be acknowledged by these persons themselves as ethical demands. Finally, market price formation must serve the "natural" objective goal of the economy, namely safeguarding the means of sustenance and the self-development of businesspersons, which do not always come about on their own under market conditions and naturally in the price system, but in extreme situations of the economy require corrections of the "naturalistically" arising prices.

In the problem of the naturalness of the price system, the difference between the earlier, Aristotelian natural law tradition and the modern, Hobbesian natural law tradition becomes apparent. These two traditions have in common an orientation toward human nature and society and an emphasis on the order of individualistic property and exchange. They are distinguished, however, by their ways of defining "natural." For the Hobbesian tradition, the market is required by natural law, because it comes into being by natural egoism and the insight of natural reason that everyone's situation will be better if legal rules are valid and observed. For Hobbes, a price is just if it originates naturalistically from contracts in a market in which rights of ownership are in force and the sovereignty of the political ruler is acknowledged and enforced. For neo-Aristotelian natural law, the market is required, because it originates from the natural need to ensure life and the self-development of the entelechial individual and his or her interests in the exchange with other entelechial individuals. The state has the mission of safeguarding the legal order of the market and of intervening correctively in cases in which a clearly recognizable incorrect control of the market price exists. For the neo-Aristotelian natural law tradition, the market price is not the natural price and a price incommensurable with justice, but a price that may be presumed to be just, until the contrary is demonstrated. The refutation of this presumption is justified, only if an unambiguous and correctable false control can be demonstrated. The difference between the two types of natural law can be summarized as follows: For the natural law theory of the "neo-Aristotelian-liberal synthesis," the market price is the natural and just price, until decisive evidence of its injustice can be produced; for Hobbesian natural law, the market price is the naturalistic price, which cannot be derived from considerations of justice. Aristotelian natural law, which is based on the entelechy of the human person and things, points to naturalness; the natural law of the Hobbesian tradition, which belongs to a mechanistic worldview, is based on forces of nature.[13]

The question of the legitimation of the market price system cannot be answered by the argument of the naturalisticness of the market price, but only by a demonstration that the price system corresponds to human nature and the natural human need to exchange views with other persons, and at the same time attains the objective goal of the economy, achieving the maximum of value-realization. The natural law must hold on to this naturalness against the naturalisticness of a mechanistic interpretation of the market just as much as against the dissolution of the market and property order in the sociologism of discourse theory, which strives to disintegrate property law into participation laws without personal liability and legal control.[14] Discourse theory forms, in the question of justice, the opposite extreme to Hobbesian natural law. It disintegrates justice not into forces of nature, but into culturism, in which it disintegrates the boundaries of the individual and his opportunities for action, defined by his property, into an anarchic on-going discourse.

The question of the legitimation and justice of the market also cannot be answered formally by remarking that the participants of the market, the buyers and sellers, have by their very participation implicitly given their consent to the market. This implicit legitimation is inadequate, because there are people who, for accidental or systematic reasons, *cannot* participate as sellers in the market. Since those who are not able to work systematically as sellers in the market cannot participate, they cannot be included among those in the market segment who implicitly agree, although they certainly participate in other market segments as consumers, if they are supported by society. As persons incapable of discourse in the sense of the discourse market, these groups have no voice in the market. A market that does not take their interests into consideration is not just as a so-

---

[13] The natural law of Adam Smith fluctuates oddly in the middle between the Aristotelian and Hobbesian natural law theories. Smith describes a natural market price that arises naturalistically. Cf. Adam Smith, *The Wealth of Nations* (London, 1776), Book I, Chap. 7 "Of the Natural and Market Price of Commodities."

[14] For a comparison of market theory and discourse theory with the examples of the theories of James M. Buchanan and Jürgen Habermas, see Koslowski, *Gesellschaft und Staat* (Stuttgart. 1982), pp. 267 ff.

cial decision system. The interests of these groups that are not able to compete in the market must also be protected by representatives in the discourse market and the price system.

Finally, the question of the legitimation of the market also cannot be answered by purely economic arguments concerning the efficiency of the allocation of factors and goods and the maximization of material output. The economic efficiency and mutual advantageousness of market coordination are inadequate as legitimizing arguments of justice, since mutual advantageousness and efficiency can discriminate against certain aims or groups for long periods of time, even if the coordination is efficient, in the sense of an optimal allocation of resources. For example, entire groups can be excluded from market coordination by the law, without loss to the economic efficiency of the official economy, which is then defined only by the inner group of those not excluded.

If the question of the legitimation of the price system and of the justice of the market price is imperative, upon what is the presumption of the justice of the market price based?

9.3. What Distinguishes the Price System from Other Forms of Price Determination?

The presumption of the justice of the market price was based above on the fact that the procedural conditions of market price formation are at the same time criteria of the justice of all price formation, and are thus constitutional presuppositions of price justice as such. This presumption that the market price is the just price thus presupposes that the process of market price formation possesses a special quality ahead of all other processes of price formation. Is the price system of free exchange and the formation of the prevailing price by the competitive market ethically especially distinguished among the possible systems of price determination in the wider sense? Economic price formation is, besides the political process of formation of will, one of the central spheres of social formation of will. Economic formation of will, which leads to the prevailing price, takes place in the market by individual bilateral contracts and, after buyers and sellers have fit together and coordinated their plans with one another, by the composition of all bilateral contracts to an equilibrium price as the valid market price.

In contrast to central price-setting by a governmental authority, all individual offers and demands go into the market price according to their subjective evaluations, while central price-setting always determines prices authoritatively and *for other persons*. Price formation with the help of markets is not only a quantitatively more comprehensive way, but also a qualitatively, specifically different way of including the persons affected and internalizing side effects than administrative price-setting, because the subjectivity of those affected, the subjective assessments of utility alternatives of all buyers and sellers, and not only the quantitative relationships, go into the price formation. Therefore, only market prices that are formed in a competitive market are prices in the truest sense, that is, signals for opportunity costs of alternative uses of resources, which are formed from free evaluations of the use of factors and goods.[15] Market price formation is distinguished by this acknowledgement of human subjectivity in economic demand above other economic control systems and has, therefore, the presumption of being more just than the others, because it unites the individual evaluations of all buyers and sellers in a process of coordination, and not, as with the centrally-planned economy, in a procedure of subordination. The presumption for market price formation is a presumption in favor of coordination, rather than subordination.

9.4. Formal and Non-Formal or Substantive Conditions of Price Justice

A decision is just, if it corresponds to the nature of the subject matter and is made impartially and according to rules. A social system of decision-making and coordination can claim to be just if it satisfies the criteria of appropriateness to the nature of the subject matter of the economy, of impartiality, of inclusion, and of internalization. Justice completes the criteria of the inclusion of the persons affected and the internalization of side effects, the criteria of formal coordination, with the substantive criterion of appropriateness to the nature of the subject matter of the economy with respect to the goal of the economy and by the substantive-formal criterion of impartiality in the inclusion and internalization. The formal, substantive-formal, and substantive criteria comprise together the criteria of justice. The appropriateness to the nature of the subject matter of the economy poses, in addition to the question of the theory of social coordination according to the inclusion and internalization of the coordination process, the question whether all persons and groups are taken into consideration justly or unjustly, partially or impartially, in the coordination and receive a fair opportunity of entry to the market discourse. The formal coordination criteria do not deal completely with the substantive questions of appropriateness to the nature of the matter; the substantive questions of justice presuppose the formal criteria of free coordination.

The just price is, accordingly, one that comes into existence in a market process, that corresponds to the criteria of justice, and that thus achieves inclu-

[15] Cf. Friedrich A. von Hayek, ed., *Collectivist Economic Planning* (London, 1933); and Koslowski, "Economy Principle, Maximizing, and the Co-Ordination of Individuals in Economics and Philosophy," in Koslowski, ed., *Economics and Philosophy* (Tübingen, 1985), pp. 39-67.

sion and internalization and attains the objective goal of the economy. The just price can arise only within a market, because only a market satisfies the formal criteria and preserves the subjectivities of the economizing person. The just price is not identical to every market price that actually comes into existence, however, because actual market coordination often does not take place with complete observance of its own rules, and because market situations can arise in which the actual market does not attain the material, substantive goal of the economy – safeguarding the meeting of needs and the self-development of human persons – because of an inordinate inequality of opportunities for participation in the market.

Oswald von Nell-Breuning pointed out that just price theory must avoid determining prices exclusively by relationships of scarcity.[16] Relationships of scarcity are not the *sole* factors of price determination, since economic events are not oriented exclusively toward the formal control of scarce means for any ends whatsoever. They are also possible in market situations in which essential goals of the economy, for example, securing the basis of nourishment, are not attained, even though the price control follows scarcity signals. Beyond the coordination and efficient allocation of resources for any ends whatsoever, the economy is aimed at a predetermined and superordinate essential goal: securing the meeting of the needs and the self-development of its members. This realization of the objective goal of the economy makes market coordination according to scarcity relationships and the price system of free exchange necessary. The criterion of the objective goal of the economy requires just as much, however, the correction of price formation whenever this objective goal is not recognizably achieved by exclusive control according to scarcity and subjective demand. Incorrect prices can prevent the fulfillment of the economy's purpose and make corrections necessary. A market in which, for example, excessive amounts of disposable income are spent for health-damaging substances, and in which their prices are too low relative to those of other goods, may require governmental correction of these *prices* from above by means of taxation.

The just price criteria are criteria of the fulfillment of the economy's purpose and the coordination of businesspersons. They are neither predetermined, substantive ends nor exclusively formal criteria of coordination and efficient allocation. Just price theory is a synthesis of the principle of free coordination according to the subjectivity of the market participants and the principle of the objective goal of the economy. It joins the Aristotelian idea of the teleology of the economy to the idea of the free coordination of individual actions, as classical liberalism and Kantianism have developed it.

---

[16] Oswald von Nell-Breuning, "Das Äquivalenzprinzip," *Jahrbücher für Nationalökonomie und Statistik*, 133 (1930), p. 4.

The concept of the just price is not tied to a hierarchical society and its conception of a hierarchical demand, which prices must follow. The hierarchical justice ideal of socially structured rights went into the medieval theory of price justice and brought about a theory of the just price in which the hierarchical demand and the preservation of the hierarchical order in exchange and in the prices of goods and services became the criterion of price justice. Post-modern just price theory is not joined to hierarchical ideas of justice, but instead to the modern justice theory of equal basic rights and market entrance rights. The idea of justice that determines the just price is – so is to be gathered from the historical continuity of the problem of price justice and from the historical transformations of its institutional arrangement – subject to transformations, even if it has a common core in all epochs, which is given by human dignity and the *suum cuique*. Medieval, premodern just price theory, on one hand, and neo-Aristotelian, (post-)modern just price theory as the synthesis of liberalism and natural law, on the other hand, share the view that price formation is a piece of *social*, and not only of private formation of will and must, therefore, be subject to criteria of justice.

Ludwig von Mises saw a mistake in the distinction between economic and non-economic reasons of price determination. All reasons for price determination are economic reasons, because price determination follows exclusively from the subjective demand of individuals. The primary error of historical-realist political science consists, according to him, in the fact that it makes a distinction between economic and non-economic reasons for price determination.[17] In fact, at this point agreeing with Mises, political reasons for price determination cannot simply be advanced against economic reasons in the price system. On the other hand, it must be objected to Mises that ideas of justice as reasons for price determination always go and must go into price formation. Between the objective economic goal of meeting needs, on one hand, and the subjective purposes of the economic persons and their demands for the satisfaction of subjective demands, on the other hand, a tension can arise in certain historical situations that is so momentous that objective economic reasons for price determination, such as ensuring survival, must be asserted against the subjective reasons of price determination of market demand. Price justice does not forget that, beyond the subjectivisms of buyers, the price system must also still attain the objective goal of the economy.

Just price theory does not formulate positive norms, but negative norms of price formation, economic and social minimum requirements that the subjectivized price system must be able to satisfy. The formation of the market price at a specific point in time is determined, as far as the entire economy is concerned,

[17] Ludwig von Mises, "Soziologie und Geschichte," *Archiv für Sozialwissenschaften und Sozialpolitik*, 61 (1929), p. 483.

by existing scarcity relationships, by the existing subjective demand, and by market relationships or forms. These existing factors of market price formation can, in certain historical situations, lead to a price structure that is so far removed from the objective goal of the economy that corrective interventions by the governmental decision center are economically and economic-ethically imperative.

Ownership relationships and the market form are essentially influenced by the determining factors of the market price through the legal system and socio-economic structural conditions, which are likewise influenced ethically (i.e. according to criteria of social and political ethics) and are not neutral in terms of economic ethics. The formation of a universally valid market price is subject to ethical norms at the procedural level of price formation with given structural conditions and at the level of the constitutive presuppositions of the market process.

The historical conflict between the classical-liberal economic theory of positive price determination and the ethical and moral-theological theory of price justice[18] can be traced back to a unilateral emphasis on either the procedural or the constitutive aspects of price formation. The classical-liberal economic theory of price formation stressed the procedural aspect of the adaptation of all prices to relative scarcity and demand relationships and the determination of prices by market forms. Moral-philosophical and moral-theological theory, on the contrary, placed joining the individual price of a particular good to the socially valid price of the good, at the market price or the governmental estimated price, and the necessity of the validity of norms of justice for the individual and the prevailing price in the foreground.

As a consequence, the significance of understanding price theory for the theory of the economy and society and the importance of the observance of price laws for economic and social policy was often overlooked on the moral-theological side. On the side of the positive economic theory of price determination, with its mechanical analysis, the internal ethical presuppositions of the price system and its need for legitimation within a complete social order were forgotten.

The procedural dimension of price formation, as it is depicted by economic theory, is already subject to a constitutive structural condition that is not ethically neutral and does not come about on its own. It is subject to the condition that the subjectivity of every person in the market must be acknowledged. If this condition is not met, a mechanics of price is always still possible, but not a price system in the sense of a market discourse. A market price for slaves may develop according to scarcity relationships and norms of positive law. This market

[18] Nell-Breuning, "Fortschritte in der Lehre von der Preisgerechtigkeit," in *Miscellanea Vermeersch* (Rome, 1935), Vol. I, pp. 93-110.

price, however, cannot be called just, because the structural conditions of its formation exclude the essential group of suppliers affected by the price from making free offers of their "wares." It violates the criterion of inclusion. Therefore, the process is not one of free-market price formation in the strict sense (i.e. of free adjustment of supply and demand). The socio-economic value judgment for free procedural price formation, for the formation of a market price without the exertion of political influence, depends on the meta-economic and meta-procedural, substantial-ethical presupposition that the subjects of the process, the buyers and sellers, are acknowledged as free subjects, and that the subjective evaluations of *everyone* go into the market price. Otherwise, the arising price is not a market price at all, in the strict sense of an inclusion of all subjective supply and demand.

9.4.1. UNIFICATION OF PROCEDURAL AND STRUCTURAL JUSTICE

The significance of the theory of just price for price theory is that it makes it possible to remedy two deficiencies exhibited by the classical political economy of the market economy: the deficiency of the dichotomy of formal and substantive criteria of social coordination and the deficiency of a dichotomy of the procedural and structural theory of justice. Both dichotomies follow from the epistemic and ontological difficulty of conceiving contradictions together or unifying sub-contrary opposites. The opposition of formal and substantive, of rule-orientation and outcome-orientation, has accompanied the entire development of this book's argument and has proved itself to be central, above all, in the discussion of Kant's ethics. The opposition of process and end-state theories determines, in contrast, the discussion of the problem of justice in contemporary political economy.

Formalism and process thought belong together just as much as substantive theories of coordination and end-state theories. In both pairs of opposites, rule-oriented and pattern-oriented thought oppose one another. Formalism and process thought both require that the coordination of economic action and the origin of the distribution of wealth follow universal and formal rules that leave open the outcome-pattern of the regulated sphere. Substantive value thought and end-state theory require, on the other hand, that social coordination and distribution realize values with a specific content and structural conditions, structural patterns. From each of these two ontologies of social coordination, there arise difficulties that mirror those of the other.

The formalism-process ontology leads to two difficulties: either the process-context becomes so totalized within it that the immutable, that which remains the same, and structure can no longer be conceived, or the flow of the process-context becomes so far separated from the fixed structural conditions of the process that the mediation of the structural framework and the process is no longer achieved and the framework remains extrinsic to the process. How the framework and the process react toward one another and influence one another cannot be represented in the pure process ontology, because the total continuum of the all-encompassing process cannot be synthesized with the constancy and structure of the framework. A pure process theory of the economy and society is only capable of conceiving the continuum and the changes of the process, but not the becoming and passing away of individuals, or even the constancy of rules and structures in the process. For the total process theory, there are only the changes and variations of a single substrate, the process, which only takes on different configurations, in which, however, there is no becoming and passing away of individual things or persons. Therefore, in process theory, the arising of that which is new and has not yet been here, on one hand, and the becoming, the persisting, and the passing away of persons and institutions identical with themselves, on the other hand, cannot be conceived. Process ontology does not portray the individuality of outcomes in the process or even the identity of beings in time. What was stated as early as Anaxagoras is true of the pure process theory of social reality: Not the becoming and passing away of persons and things, but only their combining and separating can be conceived. The development of persons and institutional structures can no longer be judged by structures or criteria identical with themselves in a total process theory of society. The process can no longer be subject to criteria that transcend the process.

In contrast, it is true of end-state and structural theories that they are incapable of conceiving process and change, and always judge the changes of the social process only by fixed structures and patterns that are external to it. End-state theories remain external to their object, the changing social and economic process, and therefore have little effectiveness of control. For the purpose of conceiving a modern economy and society, therefore, process theories are, for the time being, more suitable than pure structure theories. A truly comprehensive theory of social reality must, however, understand process and structure together, in order to grasp change and constancy, a society's development and achievement of objectives, in a single theory.

The fact that process and structure belong together is crucial for the theory of justice, because the emphasis on formal rules and the substantive demands of appropriateness to the nature of the subject matter in question unify themselves in the concept of justice to form the idea of a just process. Justice is a principle that must be determined both formally and substantively, both by procedural and by structural conditions. Justice cannot, as with end-state theories of distribution, be brought only *ex post* to the completed process of the creation of economic value, with the process of the origins of goods itself seen as incommensurable with principles of justice. The theory of price justice takes into account the requirement that the process of coordination and price formation must itself be judged by demands of justice. In the social discourse of price formation, in the market itself, the demands of justice must be satisfied, must form prices that are just. The assertion that there is no justice in the sphere of production is false, because justice must also be fulfilled *in* the production of the national product. Justice must be realized simultaneously in the production *and* the distribution of the national product. If justice existed only in distribution, one would have to ask how a just pattern could get into a process that is, as a whole, incompatible with justice. According to a "substantial process ontology," both the process and its outcome must be just. The economy cannot be a justice-free zone, with justice first brought to it after the fact, from without, by distribution policy.

9.4.2. ALLOCATION AND DISTRIBUTION

The conditions of the production and of the distribution of a good, whether an individual product, a service, or the gross national product, cannot be separated. John Stuart Mill's belief that, if the national product exists (i.e. is produced), society can do with it whatever it wishes, is incorrect. Allocation and distribution, the conditions of the production and distribution of an individual good or the national product as a whole, can neither be completely separated nor be completely equated. The problem of justice is neither separable from the problem of allocation nor completely interchangeable with it. The process of the production of the national product in the coordination of the price system itself must satisfy the demands of justice.

With the formal and necessary conditions of justice, with inclusion and internalization, it is not decided with which evaluation and according to which substantive point of view the persons affected and the possible side effects of individual actions are to go into the coordination process. The question of weighting formal rights in a coordination process must be distinguished, as a substantive-formal criterion of the price system, from the substantive-substantive criteria. The substantive-formal criterion of coordination concerns the actual, substantive opportunities for the individual to collaborate in the market. The individual's opportunities for participation in the market are given by his or her productivity and buying power. The distribution of the ability to produce and the power to consume is unequal in the market. Therefore, the actually opportunities for participation are also distributed unequally.

An unequal distribution of buying power is not per se unjust. One must ask, in evaluating it, about the conditions of the creation of this inequality and distinguish between, on one hand, different opportunities for participation on the basis of historical rights of inheritance and, on the other hand, different participation rights on the basis of profits that have arisen by demand-satisfying market performance. In an ideal price system, the historically inherited rights represent, in turn, the result of economic output achieved by the testator in the preceding period. Only in the case of original conquest and the rights of ownership flowing from it and in the case of illegal acquisition in the preceding period do ethical problems arise with inheritance. In other cases, the will of the testator and owner to bequeath and the necessity of enterprises – and not only commercial enterprises – and family projects that extend over several generations to be able to plan and implement are the necessary and sufficient reasons for the right of inheritance. The concrete form of the right of inheritance, of course, has not yet been economic-ethically determined.

If, however, difficult and long-term disequilibria of the substantive opportunities for participation that endanger the formal rights arise through the market coordination, a correction of the opportunities for participation by the political action center of the society is possible and necessary according to the substantive-formal criterion of justice.[19] The remedies do not primarily concern the distribution of goods, but the allocation of opportunities for participation. These possible remedies are not based on substantive criteria of justice, on specific substantive goals, but on the substantive-formal presuppositions of the formal participation rights, on the preservation conditions of the formal rights. The substantive-formal safeguarding of opportunities for realization participation rights is achieved, above all, by opening up market entry and allocating basic opportunities to develop human capital by education. Opening up the entry to opportunities for education in the price system and governmental remedy in cases where the price system does not hold them open sufficiently are substantive-formal demands of justice.

The substantive-substantive demands of justice on the price system are given, instead, by the objective goal of the economy, to ensure that human needs are met. If market coordination according to subjective demand and scarcity relationships does not guarantee the attainment of the objective goal of the economy, the latter demands substantive corrections of the price system. Corrections of price relationships in favor of substantive goals may, however, only be carried out, first of all, if irrefutable reasons call for not attaining the objective goal of the economy by price control. The rules for these corrections must, secondly, be formulated as negative norms. Substantive justice does not require attaining specific quantitative objectives in the price system by governmental intervention, but preventing the non-attainment of vital goals of the economy. The two goals that demand such an intervention are the protection of vital interests, such as the basis of nutrition, and the preservation conditions of the culture of a given nation's economy. Both are corrections of the subjectivism of market coordination when allocation according to subjective demand does not guarantee the attainment of the objective goal of the economy. Violation of the safeguarding

---

[19] See also Allan Gibbard, "What's Morally Special about Free Exchange," in Ellen Frankel Paul, Jeffrey Paul, and Fred D. Miller, Jr., eds., *Ethics and Economics* (Oxford, 1985), pp. 27-28. – The materiality and formality of ethical principles, contrary to Kant's view, do not form disjoint classes, but a continuum.

of the basis of nutrition demands correctives of price control, because the end of life stands above the value of the uncoerced coordination of and non-intervention in the price system. The purpose maintaining the culture demands correctives of the price system, when a completely unimpeded subjectivism of market demand threatens to sap cultural solidarity and the public good or capital good of cultural solidarity is not produced in the necessary scope.

The just price is the market price in a market price system whose price and exchange relationships correspond to subjective demand and, at the same time, achieve the substantive goals formulated as side conditions (i.e. safeguard vital interests and the minimum of cultural solidarity). The substantive-formal criterion of safeguarding the opportunities for participation and the substantive-substantive criterion of protecting vital and cultural interests form the constraints of subjectivism, constraints which must not be formulated too narrowly. Governmental intervention, which, following distributive justice, takes corrective action in the market price relations on the basis of strict criteria, does not carry out a distribution, but an allocation of opportunities for elementary life goods.

9.5. International Price Justice

An extraordinarily difficult problem is posed by the question whether price justice also applies to price and exchange relationships that surpass the borders of a nation's economy, and whether internationally just prices can be determined. As has already been explained, exchange is in general free of normative obligations if the exchange goes beyond the borders of an entire national economy. The borders of the entire economy define the area within which the demands of justice can apply. With complete global economic interconnection, the borders to which the demands of price justice apply would be the borders of the world. But the world economy is not completely integrated; it exhibits different borderlines of national and transnational economic integration. Price justice, which places formal and substantive demands on price formation, therefore, cannot refer to "international price justice" in the same sense as with national price justice. The borders of economic and political integration do not coincide with international exchange relations. One cannot demand from the exchange relations of economic goods a degree of integration that does not correspond to political and cultural integration and is, therefore, also unable to create reciprocity of rights *and* obligations on the international scale.

The criterion of safeguarding vital interests, which is a criterion of the justice of the price structure for the integrative level of the nation or regional economic community, such as the European Union, cannot simply be carried over to the world economy as a whole and be invoked as the corrective for the terms of world trade. The duties that exist for small and highly-integrated communities are not transferable without modifications to larger communities. The subsidiarity between the global economy, continental economic communities, and national economies implies a degree of integration that decreases as it approaches the global economy and places decreasingly strong ethical demands on the price structure. An additional objection to the idea of equating global-economic and national-economic price justice is the lack of a political subject and center of action that could perform just corrections of the price structure of the global market in a non-self-interested manner. As long as such a political center of action (i.e. the world state) is lacking, price justice on the global scale is a utopia and concrete political correctives to the price structure amount to little more than taking advantage through cartelization.

Discretionary, local interventions in the global economy usually only increase the problem of corruption through their dirigisme and lead to losses of efficiency for the global-economic division of labor. It is also true of the international price structure that the questions of distribution and allocation cannot be considered independently of one another. The capital necessary to bring the Third and First Worlds into line is so considerable that its direct transfer from efficient use in the First World to use in the Third World, which in comparison to the former is still necessarily inefficient today, would lead to great losses of welfare for the entire global economy.

Finally, it must be objected, against a direct manipulation of the price relationships of the global market, that a central requirement of price justice is not only joining the (global) market price, but also the relationship between the current price and earlier prices. Prices are historically qualified and must start from earlier prices.[20] Even global market prices are historically qualified in this sense and the exchange relationships brought about by them are an expression of the historically-formed relationships of national economies' abilities to perform relative to one another. These performance relationships, which have found expression in price relationships, may not always have arisen in ultimately "pure" performance relationships and justly, but they have the presumption of corresponding to the actual relationships in which the historically-formed production potentials of nations stand relative to one another. The burden of proof of the contrary rests in each case with the person who calls the presumption for the market price into question. Therefore, the price relationships between finished products and raw materials are also shifted in favor of finished products, because a longer historical process of increasing social performance, of the formation of human capital in the form of education and the formation of material capital, has gone into the production of the latter. That the terms of trade in the comparison of finished goods and raw materials favor the finished products of the highly developed nations is also a consequence of a historical non-simulta-

[20] Cf. Nell-Breuning, "Das Äquivalenzprinzip," p. 38.

neity of social and technological development, which is incommensurable with considerations of international price justice and distributive justice.

The mission of developmental policy is not to transfer the substantive criteria of price justice that are valid for the national level to the international price context. This would be a fallacious transfer into a different category, if the differences between national and international integration are not taken into account. The mission of developmental policy is to carry through the formal demands of justice, the demands for market entry and the inclusion of all nations in an open, global market. As long as such barriers to market entry as tariffs, legal constraints, etc. are not removed, considerations of the substantive justice of the terms of trade and the price structure of the global market are the wrong starting point. The function of developmental policy is carrying through formal justice demands on the global scale and the requirement of all human and real capital formation in the nations of the Third World that allows these nations to improve the actual terms of trade, not by manipulations of the price structure, but by improved ratios of nations' abilities to perform for their own benefit.[21]

9.6. Justice as Satisfying a Criterion or as a Synopsis of Several Criteria?

The concept of distributive justice is inappropriate on the international and national scale, because there is no stock of goods independent of the preceding structure of ownership rights, only goods to which legal entitlements always already exist. The price system and claims to goods and rights are always historically mediated, because the concerned persons have always come into being historically. The conditions of the origin and development of claims and persons are to be considered in the search for the just price structure, not a quantity of goods that is always considered to be external to time and history, to distribute to equally abstract persons who are independent of time. The national product is not a pie to be distributed. It no more comes into existence suddenly out of nowhere than do the persons who raise their claims to it. Like them, it comes into existence in history. The persons who raise claims are always already "personalities," equipped with allocated and inherited rights. A just solution to the question of allocation and the price structure must take into account the legally inherited claims, the stability of expectations, the risks that grow out of the disappointment of stable expectations, and the conditions of the origin of the goods to be allocated. It must also take account of the consequences that redistributions might exert on retreat from business and reduction of performance.

---

[21] On the problem of the new global economic order, see also Eike von Hippel, *Grundfragen der Weltwirtschaftsordnung* (Munich, 1980); and Helmut Hesse, "Neue Weltwirtschaftsordnung," in *Handbuch der christlichen Ethik* (Freiburg and Gütersloh, 1982), Vol. III, pp. 337-48.

9.6.1. RAWLS' CRITERION OF A VEIL OF IGNORANCE

The discussion of the formal and substantive conditions of justice has shown that there is no universal "formula" or universal criterion of justice or just exchange. The distinction between special justice as calculation of the just exchange and just allocation with Aristotle and general justice as the order and harmony of the whole in the Platonic tradition already shows that a plurality of justice principles exists. The formulation of justice as "special justice" meets the need for a criterion of the just, for a formula of the just exchange and just allocation. Among contemporary philosophers, John Rawls above all has met this need for "criterial justice."

Rawls attempts to provide a criterion of allocation about which free and rational persons could reach an agreement in an original situation of equality. The original equality consists in their mutual ignorance of their later social positions and natural abilities. The persons decide how rights should be allocated to everyone behind a veil of ignorance about their own later individual characteristics and personalities. According to Rawls, rational individuals under conditions of uncertainty about the future would agree to the difference principle: "Social and economic inequalities are to be arranged so that they are both (a) to the greatest benefit of the least advantaged and (b) attached to offices and positions open to all under conditions of fair equality of opportunity."[22]

The difficulties of applying Rawls' theory can be seen in the fact that it has been interpreted both as extremely egalitarian[23] and as a conservative theory that maintains the status quo and severely restricts redistribution.[24] It in fact raises difficult objections. How is the least advantaged group to be determined and demarcated from above? What does "the greatest benefit of the least advantaged" mean? Moreover, why should one adopt a rule that takes as its starting point a highly abstract, barely comprehensible construction of total ignorance of oneself and one's later social status, and still wish to derive positive norms from this very construction? Rawls' model hides its ideal and ethical character behind the naturalistic assumption that a veil of ignorance is actually possible. But human persons actually are always historical persons and are characterized by their past and their life histories. If they were to remove this characterization in a state of ignorance about themselves, they would lose their character as "personalities," would no longer exist as particular individuals, and could make no decisions about or for themselves. The Rawlsian theory is a metaphysical, counterfactual, ideal theory that is forced to portray itself as naturalistic.

---

[22] John Rawls, *A Theory of Justice* (Cambridge, Mass., 1971), p. 83.

[23] Robert Nisbet, "The Pursuit of Equality," *The Public Interest*, 35 (1974), pp. 103-20.

[24] Buchanan, "A Hobbesian Interpretation of the Rawlsian Difference Principle," *Kyklos*, 29 (1976), pp. 20-23.

9.6.2. THE UTILITARIAN CRITERION OF TOTAL-UTILITY MAXIMIZATION

Not only in the case of Rawls does thinking about a criterion of the justice of allocation reveal the problem that satisfying a criterion always excludes the satisfaction of other possible criteria. Discovering and realizing a fundamental feature of justice conceals and excludes other features of justice. An especially vivid example of this relationship of discovering and concealing features of justice is offered by the different allocations that follow from the maximization of a society's total utility, the utilitarian criterion of justice. Slight differences in the formulation of the criterion of justice lead here to diametrically-opposed consequences for allocative justice and also would bring about – if the particular criterion were applied strictly – a completely different actual distribution.

Utilitarians refuse to see historical rights and the natural rights of talent and the ability to perform excellently as ethically neutral and preceding justice. Neither historically transmitted social status nor the accident of natural gifts can, according to utilitarianism, be valid as the starting point of a just allocation and transfer of goods. Consequently, no principle of permanently transferring property and the outcome of actions is possible. Goods and rights are assigned and transferred exclusively on the basis of the principle of total-utility maximization. Utilitarianism abolishes the concept of rights, because the attribution of resources is not based on and controlled by rights, but exclusively by the maximal total utility of society. Opportunities for utility and the allocation of goods are, according to utilitarianism, to be formed in such a way that they maximize the total utility of society. If they satisfy this criterion, they are also just.

The criterion of total-utility maximization leads, however, to an ambivalence and to entirely different "allocative justices." That is to say, the distribution of income that it requires depends completely upon which assumptions are made about persons' abilities to derive utility from given resources. Whether the criterion of the maximization of social total utility legitimates an equal or extremely unequal distribution of goods depends entirely upon the prior criterion of whether people's utility curves are equal or unequal. If people's utility curves (i.e. their ability to derive utility from resources) are equal, then, according to utilitarianism, equal distribution is demanded; if they are unequal, then the utilitarian criterion of total-utility maximization requires that the resources go in unequally large measure to those who have higher abilities to derive utility, that the resources are thus allocated unequally in accordance with the unequal capacities of different persons to derive utility.

For the case in which identical abilities to derive utility from resources (in this case from incomes) are assumed, the allocation rule can be depicted graphically as follows:

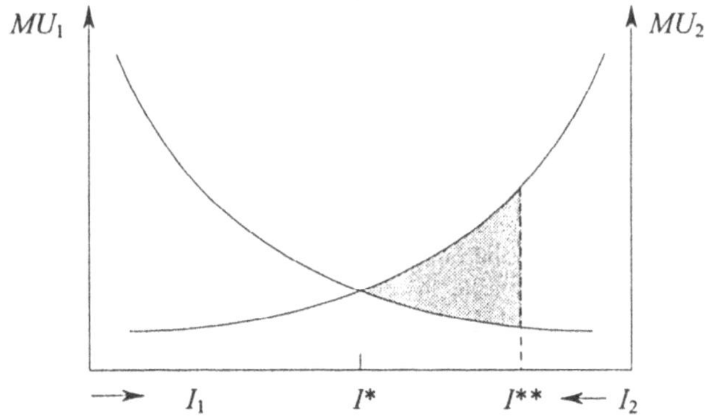

Figure 1

The ordinates MU_1 and MU_2 represent the ability to derive utility or the marginal utility (MU) of Income (I) of Persons 1 and 2. I_1 and I_2 represent their respective shares of the fixed, total disposable income. Total disposable income is depicted by the distance between the two axis-intersection points.

With an equal distribution of income, I*, the area under the marginal-utility curves, which measure the realizable total utility, is the largest. With the unequal distribution I^{**}, on the contrary, the shaded area outside the area depicting the total possible utility remains "unused."

If unequal abilities to derive utility from given incomes are assumed, a totally different picture arises. An extremely unequal distribution arises from the requirement that total utility be maximized:[25]

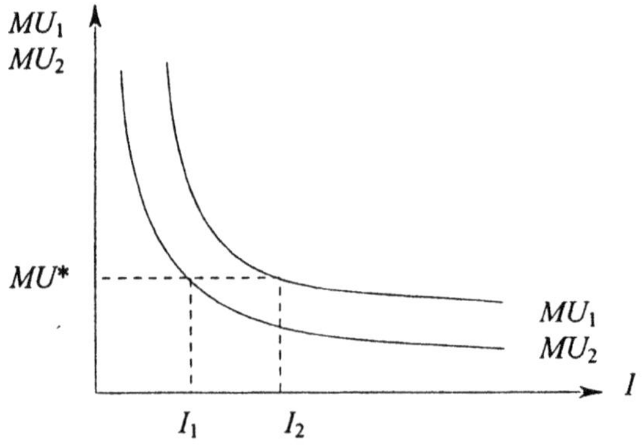

Figure 2

[25] The diagram follows Bernhard Külp, *Wohlfahrtsökonomik* (Tübingen, 1975), Vol. I: *Die Wohlfahrtskriterien*, p. 85.

Figure 2

Given the assumption of different abilities to derive utility, upon which these marginal-utility curves are based, Person 1 requires much more income than Person 2, in order to achieve the same marginal utility. The total utility of society, the sum of the integral under the two persons' marginal-utility curves, is therefore higher, the larger the share of the distributable income that Person 2 receives. In the case of different abilities to derive utility, the total utility is smaller with equality than with inequality. The distribution must be unequal, therefore, so that total utility is maximized.

For allocative justice, a two-fold rule follows from the criterion of the maximization of society's total utility:

1) Under the assumption that utility is interpersonally comparable and cardinally measurable, total-utility maximization requires as a criterion of justice that the distribution of income be egalitarian, if everyone's marginal-utility curves are identical (i.e. if everyone possess the same ability to derive utility from income). All persons should then have the income with which, on the average, the marginal utility of income is the greatest (Fig. 1).

2) The criterion of total-utility maximization requires an unequal distribution of income, if persons have differing marginal-utility curves. In this case, it requires that Person 2, who is able to derive more utility from a given income than Person 1, receives not only more utility, but also a larger share of income (Fig. 2). [26]

With differing abilities to derive utility, or with different marginal-utility levels, persons from wealthy families, who have better "taste," must be favored by distribution policies according to the criterion of total utility. Setting the goal of maximizing the total utility as the sum of the individual utilities leads to the rule of conserving the advantage of the classes with higher incomes and to maintaining an unequal distribution, if these classes exhibit a higher ability or competence to derive utility from income, because of their better taste.[27]

Johannes Hackmann has pointed out that the principle of total-utility maximization, in both its egalitarian and non-egalitarian forms, is totalitarian in its tendency, and that in the end it abolishes all responsibility. If the requirement of equal distribution is concluded from this principle and is then carried out, indi-

[26] J. J. C. Smart, "An Outline of a System of Utilitarian Ethics," in Smart and Bernard Williams, *Utilitarianism: For and Against* (Cambridge, 1973), p. 28, arrives at an intermediate solution in his utilitarian theory. The maximization of total utility (total happiness) is achieved, according to him, through the orientation toward *average* utility, not *marginal* utility: "For in most cases the most effective way to increase the total happiness is to increase the average happiness, and vice versa."

[27] Johannes Hackmann, *Zur wohlfahrtstheoretischen Behandlung von Verteilungsproblemen* (Berlin, 1972), p. 146.

viduals indeed possess a right to error and wrong economic decisions, whose consequences, however, they never have to accept, because they are always compensated for the loss of income from their incorrect decisions by additional income that they receive from others, so that the total utility maximization of everyone is ensured.

With total utility maximization, at the same time, the right to satisfy "apparent needs" or false needs must logically be taken from the individual, because it is not to be understood that one first should give him the right *not* to maximize utility, in order to maximize total utility and his utility afterwards by redistribution and, if necessary, against the will of the individual: "Scarce decision alternatives would be withheld primarily from those who use them for an especially intensive production of well-being."[28]

One must conclude, therefore, that the criterion of utility has become so popular only because it satisfies the desire for "criterial philosophy," and that it permits a *"scientific" derivation of the equal distribution of income*, if the assumption is made that the functions of marginal utility from income are sinking and identical for all individuals, and if the maximization of marginal utility is seen as the highest goal of the social order. The assumption of identical marginal-utility functions (= identical needs structures) and identical abilities to derive utility (= identical marginal utilities of income), however, are unrealistic, because there exist different educations, formations, social values, and reference groups, and contradict the concept of the person as a non-interchangeable individual who has come about historically.

In reality, the criterion of utilitarianism, the maximization of total utility, is unsuitable as the criterion of justice for a "scientific" derivation of equal distribution, because it has extremely anti-egalitarian consequences, if the assumption is made that the ability to use income increases with greater education and a higher level of income. Also, the income effect of better information and education leads to a redistribution in favor of the educated or informed classes, according to the principle of total utility maximization, because a larger total utility is achieved with greater inequality of income distribution. The criterion of total utility maximization, in this case, supports a stronger differentiation of distribution, but not bringing it into line. If "taste" is an ability that learns and a capital that must be acquired, and if the level of marginal utility of an individual increases more than proportionally with higher income, the total utility that can be derived from a given national product is greater with inequality than with equality.

John Stuart Mill has already pointed to the Social Darwinist meaning of the principle of utility maximization:

---

[28] *Ibid.*, p. 148.

> It is one of Nature's general rules, and part of her habitual injustice, that 'to him that hath shall be given, but from him that hath not, shall be taken even that which he hath'. The ordinary and predominant tendency of good is towards more good. Health, strength, wealth, knowledge, virtue, are not only good in themselves but facilitate and promote the acquisition of good, both of the same and of other kinds.[29]

The example of utilitarianism shows that basing justice on a single criterion runs the risk that the one dimension of the problem of justice that this criterion reveals hides other dimensions of justice. End-state theories and exclusively-substantive theories of justice are especially susceptible to this danger, because the concentration on the end state overlooks the conditions of its coming into existence and the justice of the self-changing process that leads to an – always only provisional – end state. Both utilitarian and non-utilitarian end-state criteria reduce the variety of the social process of producing and distributing wealth to a single dimension that describes only the particular end-state criterion.

9.6.3. JUSTICE AND GAMES: HAYEK

The form of distribution brought about by market success in a market economy, as it comes into being at the end of a period, cannot be predicted or anticipated, since it is not planned according to an end state. Its development is instead determined only by a framework of universal rules, and therefore also cannot be prescribed in detail by justice. Liberty, contingency, and necessity are interwoven in the manner of the appropriation of social wealth.

Friedrich von Hayek compares the events of the market with the model of a game, in which the rules are fixed, but the results of playing are subject to luck and the skill of the other players, who must follow the rules of the game, but in which the result cannot be determined from the outset by the rules alone: "It is competition according to rules, and is determined by superior skill and power, but also by luck. It is a game of skill and also one of luck."[30] Chance, therefore, receives a certain dignity in the market. Contingency becomes an acknowledged factor of the social order. The distribution of power and wealth also depend upon chance. The action orientation of the economic subjects is achieved by the rules of the game "economy" in such a way that the individual pursuit of goals, but not the achievement of a particular distribution of a good, a final distribution, are made possible. The rules of the game aim not at a particular distribution, but at an increase of the quantity of goods, disregarding its structure and distribution.

---

[29] John Stuart Mill, *Three Essays on Religion* (London, 1874), p. 35.

[30] Hayek, *Drei Vorlesungen über Demokratie, Gerechtigkeit und Sozialismus* (Tübingen, 1977), p. 27.

The first goal of the game is to play a non-zero-sum game of indifference to which distribution comes into existence, not a game with constant outcome distribution, because the conditions of constant distribution reduce the outcome of the game according to the quantity and would make it into a zero-sum game. The market process brings it about that "we play a non-zero-sum game whose rules aim at increasing the dividends (in the true sense of that which is shared), but which leaves the individual's share partly to chance."[31] Since chance must be a central generative factor in the emergence of the results of the market's production, the distribution that emerges remains in the end outside the market process, similarly accidental, or at least unwilled and not anyone's fault. The question of justice in the sense of distributive justice cannot be posed to it: "There can be no distributive justice, when no one distributes anything . . . . Since each individual's result is neither intended nor foreseen by others, the total outcome can be called neither just nor unjust."[32]

Even if Hayek exaggerates the contingent nature of the market outcome, important insights can be gained from his position. The distribution of goods in a market economy arises from the production of the individual for others. This production is the outcome of conscious plans and anticipations, the outcome of work, but also of contingent circumstances. The remuneration must, on one hand, correspond to the utility of the abilities and investments of the individuals, but, on the other hand, also reflect the objective successes for others and not only the subjective strivings of the individual. Both criteria, investment or subjective performance and success or objective achievement of the individual for others, must go into the payment of wages, in order to make possible an efficient individualistic order.

From the second condition, that neither subjectively-assumed desert of compensation nor effort, but the objective consequences of actions for the contingent needs of others, are decisive for the payment of wages, it follows that the question of the justice of the impersonal decisions of the market can be posed only limitedly, because the utility of our actions for the needs of others, which are constantly changing and unpredictable, is likewise unpredictable and contains a high degree of contingency.

The market forms a system of rules in which contingent changes can be discovered just as much as foreseeable and essential changes, and in which only the structure of the system and action types, but not individual courses of actions, are determined and stipulated. A planning system establishes, however, courses of action and goal variables as end-state variables and interprets both the entire process of the economy as goal-variable maximization and the action

---

[31] Hayek, *Der Wettbewerb als Entdeckungsverfahren* (Kiel, 1968), p. 12.

[32] Hayek, *Drei Vorlesungen über Demokratie, Gerechtigkeit und Sozialismus*, p. 24. See also Hayek, *Individualism and Economic Order* (Chicago, 1948), p. 22.

of the individual as instrumental functions for these goal variables. One weakness of the market system is that it cannot fix, but must leave open, the overall result of the process and its final distribution or end state. This openness of outcome of the market, however, forms at the same time the conditions for the individual establishment and pursuit of goals. There is no unambiguous solution to the distribution problem and no criterial justice in the sense of only a *single* criterion, because the distribution is the outcome of a game in which performance, luck, and chance work together. Within certain limits, the outcome of this game must simply be accepted.

James Buchanan[33] advocates the view that the distribution problem can be solved contractually by an agreement between the poor and the rich. The wealthy will obligate themselves to voluntary redistribution out of insight or fear of revolution. This makes possible, according to Buchanan, a redistribution according to the Pareto criterion. Wealth is redistributed in such a way that no one is worse off, but some are better positioned, because the rich derive utility from their reduced fear of revolution, but the poor derive direct utility from the redistribution.[34] With a voluntary scheme of redistribution, though, in comparison to governmental redistribution, a prisoner's dilemma[35] and an assurance problem arise. Many people are ready to give if everyone gives, but reduce their charitableness if they are the only benefactor. But the assurance of the universality of charitableness is possible only with governmental coercion, so that in this sense governmental coercion to "voluntary" Pareto-optimal charitableness could be rationally advisable, in order to overcome the prisoner's dilemma situation. Beyond the problem of ensuring the universality of the redistribution, the question is posed whether a Pareto-optimal, consensual redistribution will be sufficient.

9.6.4. NOZICK'S CRITERION OF THE JUSTIFIED CLAIM

Robert Nozick's theory of claim justice poses the question of which distribution is just and whether the state has the right to carry out such a distribution. First, Nozick also criticizes the notion that one could tackle the distribution problem in the way one could give children portions of a pie, and then "make last minute adjustments to rectify careless cutting."[36] This view assumes that there is a person or group entitled to control all resources and to decide how they should be

---

[33] Cf. Buchanan, "The Libertarian Legitimacy of the State," in Buchanan, *Freedom in Constitutional Contract* (College Station, 1977), passim; and "Die Verfassung der Freiheit," in Otto Molden, ed., *Zu den Grenzen der Freiheit* (Vienna, 1977), pp. 62-64.

[34] Cf. Buchanan, *Limits of Liberty* (Chicago, 1975), pp. 80-81.

[35] Alan T. Peacock, and Charles K. Rowley, "Pareto Optimality and the Political Economy of Liberalism," *Journal of Political Economy*, 80 (1972), pp. 481-84.

[36] Robert Nozick, *Anarchy, State, and Utopia* (New York, 1974), p. 149.

distributed. It is clear that in such a case, as already with the criterion of the maximization of a society's total utility, responsible actions would no longer be at all possible.

Nozick opposes making end-state ideas the standard of distribution measures. On the contrary, care must be taken that all steps leading to a distribution are just. Above all, historical principles must be satisfied: The origin of the distribution must take place in just steps. Nozick calls his own theory of claims of justice a theory of procedural justice oriented toward historical principles. According to this theory, one should not ask whether a distribution corresponds to one distribution scheme or another, but whether each person has a claim to that which he possess and whether the distribution has taken place justly.

Nozick provides three criteria of justice in holdings:

> 1. A person who acquires a holding in accordance with the principle of justice in acquisition is entitled to that holding.
>
> 2. A person who acquires a holding in accordance with the principle of justice in transfer, from someone else entitled to the holding, is entitled to the holding.
>
> 3. No one is entitled to a holding except by (repeated) applications of 1 and 2.[37]

A holding is just, if it originates by just original appropriation or by just transfer of rights of possession. Nozick's claim theory of justice repeats the rights of ownership requirements of civil law.[38] It calls just that which corresponds to the norms of civil law, with the exception that Nozick is prepared to carry out corrections to ownership relationships if they are based on earlier, unjust acquisitions and transfers of possession. But he adds the qualification that one cannot say how far one should go into the past.

9.6.5. UNIFICATION OF PROCEDURAL AND END-STATE CRITERIA

Since the element of contingency plays a significant role in the outcome of the market-economic process,[39] the distribution outcome of the market must be

---

[37] Nozick, p. 151.

[38] Amartya Sen, "The Moral Standing of the Market," p. 5, remarks with faint irony: "Its robustness raises questions of ethics."

[39] The significance of chance as a generative factor of the origin and distribution of income has been clearly presented by Armen A. Alchian. The income distribution of the market is so strongly determined by chance, because income from profit, which influences distribution most strongly, depends to a high degree on chance and luck. Alchian, *Economic Forces at Work* (Indianapolis, 1977), p. 20: "Positive profits accrue to those who are better than their actual competitors, even if the participants are ignorant, intelligent, skillful, etc. . . . the greater the uncertainties of the world, the greater is the possibility that profits would go to venturesome and lucky rather than to logical, careful, fact-gathering individuals." See also Frank H. Knight, *Risk, Uncertainty and Profit* (Boston, 1921), Chap. 12: "Social Aspects of Uncertainty and Profit."

seen as indifferent to the concept of justice. Since all property originates from three sources, investment, inheritance, and luck[40] – of which only the first can be called just with certainty, the second is only legal, and the third is incommensurable with justice and the law – the distribution resulting from these three sources cannot be called just, but for the time being only "not unjust." It can, however, also not be said of a general theory which final distribution in detail *would be* just, because no one has sufficient information for a complete analysis of the actually-occurring and at the same time historically-unique distribution. It is only possible to give negative and formal criteria of the justice of the total distribution and to determine minimum conditions of the justice of allocating opportunities for participation to individual persons by governmental action. Substantive end states of the distribution and patterns of the acquisition of social wealth, which would be predetermined by governmental actions and realized by governmental power, cannot be established theoretically.

From the impossibility of distinguishing and carrying out a definite pattern of the social distribution of wealth in the categorial sense as just, the insight follows that the formal criteria of the justice of the process are the necessary and decisive conditions of the justice of the price system, but also that the pattern for the justice of the process arising from the rules cannot be *completely* arbitrary. Or, in Hegel's words: "The maxim: 'Ignore the consequences of actions' and the other: 'Judge actions by their consequences and make these the criterion of right and good' are both alike maxims of the abstract Understanding."[41] A theory of the market that sees prices and the distribution of income resulting from them, which itself emerges according to the rules of the law and of the market with market closure, as justified a priori, is just as abstract as a theory that seeks to carry out a definitely structured, "just" end-state at each period.

The problem of the justice of the price system consists in the mediation between the "laissez-faire" of the pure process of rules and the carrying out of social end states or patterns.[42] The function of the state is both to ensure the market's freedom of action and to prevent situations of price relations from arising

---

[40] According to Michael Oakeshott, "The Political Economy of Freedom," in Oakeshott, *Rationalism in Politics and other Essays* (Indianapolis, 1991), p. 392, all forms of property "spring from [three] sources, investment, inheritance and luck." See also Knight, "Ethics and the Economic Interpretation," in Knight, *The Ethics of Competition and other Essays*, (New Brunswick, N. J.: 1997), p. 48: "The ownership of personal or material productive capacity is based upon a complex mixture of inheritance, luck, and effort, probably in that order of relative importance."

[41] Georg W. F. Hegel, *The Philosophy of Right*, trans. Dyde (Amherst, N. Y., 1996), § 118.

[42] Cf. G. A. Cohen, "Robert Nozick and Wilt Chamberlain: How Patterns Preserve Liberty," *Erkenntnis*, 11 (1977), pp. 5-23, who criticizes the abstractness and reduction of the concept of justice. It must be objected against the comparison of the distribution problem to a game, in which not the final distribution, but the observance of the rules of the game is decisive, that in games, if one party has lost, a second game under conditions of equal distribution can be begun. That distinguishes the game from human life, whose character is uniqueness.

that make formal rights of participation and the attainment of the substantive economic goal impossible. The state can understand justice neither only as process justice nor only as end-state justice.[43] Governmental actions do not aim at the distribution of a quantity of goods, nor at distributive justice, but must instead realize allocative justice in the sense of safeguarding minimum rights of participation and achieving the objective goal of the economy. That also means that the political can be determined neither in the manner of stark intervention rules nor exclusively by consensus, but that the problem of justice must instead be decided according to appropriateness and reasonableness. The political element consists in the anticipation of a possible consensus of rational persons concerning the solution of the problem of justice, and not in the carrying out of an actual consensus, because the latter will remain suboptimal regarding the problem of justice, if it is to be free of domination in the fullest sense, since it might undersupply distributive measures, due to the veto power of persons.

The limits of the reduction of political and economic actions to action according to rules become apparent in the problem of justice. Distribution cannot be oriented toward a single rule or a single parameter, because every sole rule leads necessarily to disregarding other essential perspectives of justice. The political problem of justice cannot be reduced to the satisfaction of a single distribution rule, but consists in bringing the claims to appropriateness and equitableness into line. From the low operationalizability of the problem of justice, its politically-risky character emerges.

The economic justice of the allocation of the opportunities for participation in the market does not start out from a definite picture of a just final distribution or of an optimal distribution that disregards the conditions of the origin of legitimate claims or original endowments. Justice must, instead, be conceived between pure process thought and end-state models in a theory that connects process ontology with the recognition of patterns in the process. End-state theories of justice are also unsuitable, therefore, because there exist no end states in the social process, only stages preliminary to new processes. On the other hand, as has already been shown, pure processes, not containing patterns or forms, are unrecognizable. A pure process theory understands only atomistic components and their configurations. It understands, in the strict sense, neither repetitions of patterns nor the new, the new creation of completely different patterns. The law and justice, however, already rely on the knowledge of stable patterns and the

---

[43] Cf. Knight, "Abstract Economics as Absolute Ethics," *Ethics*, 76 (1966), p. 177: "The freest economic order possible along with anything like modern civilization requires (a) extensive legislation to prevent intolerable divergences from free market conditions and (b) much more action to prevent intolerable consequences that would prevail if society were organized solely through exchange by individuals in the nearest possible approach to the perfectly competitive markets of 'pure' economic theory."

"stability" of the laws of reality for the knowledge of structures relevant to the law.

No *end* states, which could be called just or unjust, emerge within the market process and the price system, but instead patterns and price relations, whose agreement with the formal and substantive criteria of price justice can be questioned. The theory of price justice is not an end-state theory of justice, but a process theory of the justice of the price system, which at the same time provides basic presuppositions of the market process and criteria of its correction in clearly defined situations. It supplements the pure process thought of the price system with ideas about substantive-formal opportunities for participation in the market process and the obligation not to forget the substantive goal of the economy when considering the subjective goals of demand.

9.7. Justice in Interaction with Nature

The problem of interaction with nature is an aspect of the duty also to safeguard vital interests in the market system. It is an aspect of natural law that grows in significance with increasing endangerment of the natural environment. The interaction of humans with human and extra-human nature is also a problem of justice toward nature. It is not a social problem of justice and, therefore, it finds no observance in theories of justice that permit only humans and their social relationships to be the subjects and objects of justice. Justice in interaction with nature is also not a theme of special justice, but rather a problem of the general and ontological concept of justice. If, following Plato, the just is that which orders and penetrates reality, nature also belongs to the domain of things that should be appropriate and "just," and human beings must ensure justice in relation to it.

As in the social world, so also in relation to nature, the question of justice proves to be the function of mediating justified claims. In the case of justice toward nature, however, not the claims of legal subjects, but human claims to economic expansion and the conservation conditions of nature confront one another. Justice toward nature means taking nature into consideration, including nature with the help of advocates in the discourse of the price system, and observing the external effects of human economic activity on nature (internalization). Justice toward nature requires acknowledging that nature has certain rights, independently of its "utilization" by humans. Human persons may not see nature only as raw materials or only as an opportunity for utility, in the sense of the economic concept of the good, but must instead recognize in it the substantive value-qualities characteristic of it.

The requirement of commutative justice in interaction with nature presupposes, as an ethical demand, that not only human rights exist, but also rights of nature, which human persons must assert in representing voiceless nature against themselves and their urge to expand. Commutative justice in interaction with nature should protect the dignity, integrity, and "liberty" of nature. These liberty rights of nature are its right to its "natural" behavior. Nature's liberty rights are to be protected in a way analogous to economic liberty's protection of the right of human persons to rational conduct and goal-pursuing actions.[44] Justice toward nature requires acknowledging the "rights" of animals and plants to their natural behavior and of the earth to natural treatment as worth being protected, or at least as "rights" relevant for humans and weighing against the rights of humans to "use nature up" in the human decision discourse of power and democracy.

The weighing of goods between conserving the natural landscape or instituting nature-conservation parks, on one hand, and acquiring land available for agriculture, especially with growing population pressure, on the other hand, for instance, is a problem of the justice of our interaction with nature, in which the rights of nature are always in a weaker position. It is questionable whether the social decision systems of the market and democracy, which are restricted to human affairs, are in a position to protect the "rights" of nature. In the discourses of the market and democracy, only beings capable of speaking are the bearers of rights and are prepared for discourse. Since rights can be formed only by democratic discourse, the "right of nature" is without a voice, especially if a trans-discursive "natural right" of rights-creating discourse is not adopted.[45]

The difficulty of accomplishing a "discursive" establishment of justice toward nature points toward the strengths of the ontological concept of justice of the Solonian-Platonic tradition. The ontological concept of justice permits expanding the justice question in a holistic way from its social dimension to the interaction with nature and to equilibrating the claims of human beings and the claims of natural beings. There is not only social exchange, but also ecological exchange and, therefore, not only justice in the social world, but also commutative justice toward nature. Exchange is, according to Baudrillard's theory of the libidinal economy, a saving of time.[46] In exchange with others, we save life time, because we do not *have* to do everything ourselves. The thought of saving time by exchange leads beyond the commercial exchange to the ecological exchange of humans with nature. The theory of saving time by exchange transcends social exchange to the level of exchange with nature: In exchange with non-human nature and extra-human life, we gain the life that we are only able to

---

[44] Cf. Francesco Forte, "Tutor of Nature," in Koslowski, ed., *Individual Liberty and Democratic Decision-Making* (Tübingen, 1987), p. 97.

[45] Cf. Koslowski, "Market and Democracy as Discourses," in Koslowski, ed., *Individual Liberty and Democratic Decision-Making* (Tübingen, 1987), pp. 58-92.

[46] Jean Baudrillard, *Symbolic Exchange and Death*, trans. Ian Hamilton Grant (London, 1993).

receive at all only in exchange, because we are not *able* to do everything ourselves. In exchange with nature, life takes place as a process that combats entropy and consumes energy. The exchange of entropy for negentropy, of disorder for order, makes it possible to save the time that life must fight for against its disintegration and the constant destruction of its self by the increasing disorder and entropy of the world.[47] Only by exchange with the natural and social environment is the living organism able to receive at a level of greater order and reduced entropy.

The need for a theory of economic ethics, for an ethic of the relationship with nature, an "environmental ethic of economic activity," also appears in this exchange with nature, in the economy of ecological exchange. This environmental ethic of economic activity must take fairness arguments toward nature as the exchange partner into account. This necessitates, above all, including environmental consideration or environment damage as real returns or costs in the capital calculation of economic subjects and in total economic calculation, and no longer treating the character of the natural environment as an economically irrelevant quantity, as does classical economics. Classical political economy saw nature only as a free, and thus unprotected good, or as raw materials brought to the level of economic value by labor. The economic dimension of the ecology and of the law of entropy, the second principle of thermodynamics, has been brought to public attention again by Nicholas Georgescu-Roegen.[48]

Taking the fairness viewpoint toward nature into consideration does not impose itself by technical, economic argument. Taking nature into consideration is, instead, a problem of acknowledging that extra-human nature has relative rights of its own and a problem of the inclusion of the rights of nature and of the internalization of the costs to natural resources and evolved structures of nature in the social discourses of the market and democracy. Acknowledgment is always a voluntary and ethical phenomenon. Prudent management in relation to the natural environment is also an economic-ethical phenomenon of free acknowledgment. Acknowledging a right to ownership of nature means acknowledging that we must include and accept responsibility for the (side) effects of our actions on nature, whether intentional or unintentional, just as the side effects of our actions on other human persons – even if with a lower weighting.

---

[47] Cf. Erwin Schroedinger, *What Is Life?* (Cambridge, 1944).

[48] Nicholas Georgescu-Roegen, *Energy and Economic Myths* (New York, 1976), pp. 3-36.

CONCLUSION

Morality and Efficiency

The principles of ethical economy demonstrate that ultimately there exists no unbridgeable chasm between ethical and economic decisions, and that the ethical perspective is not one aspect among others, but instead a way to take the perspectives of the sciences and, in the case of economic ethics, above all economic theory into consideration, to order them, to evaluate them, and to enable them to become effective in practice. In this sense ethical economy aims, like general ethics, at the perfection of action, in which all aspects of the decision situation are taken into account. In an ethic of the totality of the aspects according to which action is structured toward purposes, intentions, effects, side effects, and circumstances, the instruments of analysis and understanding developed by ethics and economics join together to form a theory of ethical economy as a general theory of human action.

Ethical economy and economic ethics must orient themselves toward the nature of the subject matter of the economy. The content of economic ethics cannot consist exclusively in mere compliance with rules, formal agreement with a universal law, or in accordance with the outcome of the current consensus of some community of discourse, which is always contingent.

Since action has the character of a draft for the future, economic ethics, like all ethics, is future oriented and must, therefore, seek to recognize and decide the unique, the not-yet-tested, and the unrepeatable. There is only one ethic that aims at the perfection of human action and imparts itself to all cultural spheres – including the cultural sphere of the economy. Its basis of obligation and its support for decision-making arise from the nature of the subject matter in question: *obligatio oritur a natura rei.*[1]

The economy is not governed by economic laws alone, but is determined by human persons, in whose desires and choices a complete ensemble of economic expectations, social norms, cultural views, and ethical ideas about the good is always in effect. Consequently, this totality must also be taken into consideration, and reflection on the ethical character of economic action must be included in economic action and economic theory.

Economic ethics, therefore, does not consist in abstract opposition and the precociousness of the moralizing "ought" against objective economic argu-

[1] Luis de Molina, *De justitia et jure* (Moguntiae, 1602), tom. 1, disp. 4, n. 3.

ments. Economic ethics requires, instead, that in view of the totality of the action situation, the decision is made according to the nature of the subject matter, i.e. according to the function of the economy to safeguard the means of subsistence and to make creative action possible.

Ethical economy, economic ethics, and their economic-ethical imperative form the restriction of general ethics and the general formulation of the ethical imperative to the life and cultural sphere of the economy. Edmund Husserl has expressed the ethical imperative as follows: "Intend with insight the best among the achievable."[2] This is a further formulation of the unity of economics and ethics in ethical economy: the motives and intentions of actions must be directed with understanding and consideration of side effects and circumstances toward the perfection of actions under the conditions of what is economically possible and efficient, and must realize the best among the achievable. The goal of ethical economy is the optimization of actions under the ethical condition that human dignity is acknowledged and the economic condition of efficiency holds true. The following must be in effect as a maxim of the businessperson and as an economic-ethical imperative: Act in such a way that your economic actions correspond to the two-fold goal of the economy, to supply human persons with goods efficiently and to form a central sphere of human practice and self-realization.[3] It is important to remember, in contrast to mechanistic approaches to economic theory, that the businessperson is always an acting person, not someone acted upon by anonymous economic forces.

"Attentiveness as power or drive of imagination is the beginning of morality," writes Johann Fichte.[4] This is also true of the beginning of correct business management and of economic ethics. Taking the side effects of actions into consideration is ultimately a question of attentiveness. Decision theory has shown that attentiveness, not time, is the true scarce resource.[5] If morality is attentiveness, that means that the scarcity of the resource of ethics is greater than the scarcity of economic resources. Dennis Robertson's saying that economics makes understandable and teaches the "need of economizing on love,"[6] has more than merely an economic or aesthetic sense. It is not only the economic world view that requires morality not to strain the morality of the human person too greatly. It is, rather, the scarcity of the moral resource of attentiveness that

---

[2] Edmund Husserl, *Manuskript F I*, 21, 20, as cited by Alois Roth, *Edmund Husserls ethische Untersuchungen* (Den Haag, 1960).

[3] See also Oswald von Nell-Breuning, "Wirtschaftsethik," in *Staatslexikon*, 6th Ed. (Freiburg, 1963), Vol. XIII, p. 775.

[4] Johann Gottlieb Fichte, *Werken*, ed. I. H. Fichte (Berlin, 1971), Vol. I, p. 295.

[5] Herbert A. Simon, "Rationality as Process and as product of Thought," *American Economic Review*, 68 (1978), p. 13.

[6] Dennis H. Robertson, "What Does the Economist Economise?" in Robertson, *Economic Commentaries* (London, 1956), p. 154.

makes it necessary to economize on ethical demands and first to exhaust the possibility of economic thought. The unification of economics and ethics, the theory of ethical economy, shows the correct use of the capital of moral attentiveness or ethics in the economy. It acknowledges the power of economic thought and, at the same time, asserts the importance and meaning of the ethical in those situations and problems of the economy and of business in which ethics must not be ignored.

BIBLIOGRAPHY

Aeschylus, *Prometheus Bound*, trans. James Scully and C. John Herington, Oxford: Oxford University Press, 1975.

Albach, Horst, "Vertrauen in der ökonomischen Theorie," *Zeitschrift für die gesamte Staatswissenschaft*, 136 (1980), pp. 2-11.

Albee, Ernest, *A History of English Utilitarianism*, London: George Allen & Unwin; 1901; 3rd Ed., 1962.

Albert, Hans, *Marktsoziologie und Entscheidungslogik*, Neuwied: Luchterhand, 1967.

Albertus Magnus, *Summa de Homine: Secunda Pars Summae de Creaturis*, in *Opera Omnia*, Paris: Ludovicus Vivès, 1896, Vol. 35.

Alchian, Armen A., *Economic Forces at Work*, Indianapolis: Liberty Press, 1977.

Anscombe, G. E. M., "Action, Intention, and 'Double Effect,'" *Proceedings of the American Catholic Philosophical Association*, 57 (1983), pp. 12-25.

_____, *Intention*, Oxford: Basil Blackwell, 1957; 1963; 1979.

Anshen, Melvin, ed., *Managing the Socially Responsible Corporation*, New York: Macmillan, 1974.

Aristotle, *Nicomachean Ethics*, trans. Terence Irwin, Indianapolis: Hackett, 1985.

Arrow, Kenneth J., "Political and Economic Evaluation of Social Effects and Externalities," in Michael D. Intriligator, ed., *Frontiers of Quantitative Economics*, Amsterdam: North Holland, 1971; New York: Elsevier, 1975, pp. 3-25.

Augustine, *The City of God*, trans. Gerald G. Walsh and Grace Monahan, Washington: The Catholic University of America Press, 1952, Books VIII-XVI.

Axelrod, Robert, *The Evolution of Cooperation*, New York: Basic Books, 1984.

Backhaus, Jürgen, "Politische Ökonomie als Theorie der Begründung: Eine Auseinandersetzung mit Friedrich Kambartels Bemerkungen zum normativen Fundament der Ökonomie," *Zeitschrift für allgemeine Wissenschaftstheorie*, 8 (1977), pp. 91-117.

Banfield, Edward C., *The Democratic Muse: Visual Arts and the Public Interest*, New York: Basic Books, 1984.

Barrett, C. Richard and Prasanta K. Pattanaik, "On Vague Preferences," in Georges Enderle, ed., *Ethik und Wirtschaftswissenschaft*, Berlin: Duncker & Humblot, 1985, pp. 69-84.

Baudrillard, Jean, *Symbolic Exchange and Death*, trans. Ian Hamilton Grant, London: Sage Publications, 1993; *L'échange symbolique et la mort*, Paris: Gallimard, 1976; 1993.

Baumol, William J., "Business Responsibility and Economic Behavior," in Edmund S. Phelps, ed., *Altruism, Morality, and Economic Theory*, New York: Russell Sage Foundation, 1975, pp. 45-56.

Baumol, William J. and William G. Bowen, *Performing Arts: The Economic Dilemma*, New York: Twentieth Century Fund, 1966.

Becker, Gary S., *The Economic Approach to Human Behavior*, Chicago: University of Chicago Press, 1976.

Behrman, Jack N., *Discourse on Ethics and Business*, Cambridge: Oelschlaeger, Gunn & Hain, 1981.

Bell, Daniel, *The Cultural Contradictions of Capitalism*, New York: Basic Books, 1976.

Bennett, Jonathan, "Morality and Consequences," in Sterling McMurrin, ed., *The Tanner Lectures on Human Values*, Salt Lake City: University of Utah Press; Cambridge: Cambridge University Press, 1981, Vol. II, pp. 45-116.

Beuys, Joseph, Jannis Kounellis, Anselm Kiefer, and Enzo Cucchi, *Ein Gespräch: Una discussione*, ed., Jacqueline Burckhardt, Zürich: Parkett, 1986.

Blaug, Mark, ed., *The Economics of the Arts*, London: Martin Robertson, 1976.

Böhm-Bawerk, Eugen von, "Macht oder ökonomisches Gesetz?" *Zeitschrift für Volkswirtschaft, Sozialpolitik und Verwaltung*, 23 (1914), pp. 205-71.

Bollnow, Otto Friedrich, *Existenzphilosophie und Pädagogik: Versuch über unstetige Formen der Erziehung*, Stuttgart: Kohlhammer, 1959; 5th Ed., 1977.

Bossuet, Jacques-Bénigne, *Cinquième écrit ou mémoire de M. l'Évêque de Meaux à M. l'Archevêque de Cambrai* (on Fénelon, *Les Maximes des Saints*), in *Oeuvres Complètes*, Paris: Méquignon & Leroux, 1846, Vol. IX, pp. 346-68.

Boulding, Kenneth E., "Economics as a Moral Science," *American Economic Review*, 59 (1969), pp. 1-12.

_____, "Toward the Development of a Cultural Economics," *Social Science Quarterly*, 53 (1972), pp. 267-84.

Bowie, Norman E., *Business Ethics*, Englewood Cliffs, N. J.: Prentice Hall, 1982.

Boyle, Joseph M., Jr., "Aquinas on Praeter Intentionem," *The Thomist*, 42 (1978), pp. 649-65.

_____, "Toward Understanding the Principle of Double Effect," *Ethics*, 90 (1980), pp. 527-38.

Boyle, Joseph M., Jr., Germain Grisez, and Olaf Tollefsen, *Free Choice: A Self-Referential Argument*, Notre Dame, Ind.: University of Notre Dame Press, 1976.

Brennan, Geoffrey and James M. Buchanan, *The Reason of Rules: Constitutional Political Economy*, Cambridge: Cambridge University Press, 1985.

Brentano, Lujo, *Ethik und Volkswirtschaft in der Geschichte*, Munich: E. Reinhardt, 1902.

Briefs, Götz A., "Grenzmoral in der pluralistischen Gesellschaft," in Erwin von Beckerath, Fritz W. Meyer, and Alfred Müller-Armack, eds., *Wirtschaftsfragen der freien Welt* (Festschrift for Ludwig Erhard), Frankfurt: Fritz Knapp, 1957, pp. 97-108; in Briefs, *Ausgewählte Schriften*, Berlin: Duncker & Humblot, 1980, Vol. I, pp. 62-74.

_____, *Untergang des Abendlandes: Christentum und Sozialismus: Eine Auseinandersetzung mit Oswald Spengler*, Freiburg: Herder, 1920; 2nd Ed., 1921.

Brunner, Karl and William H. Meckling, "The Perception of Man and the Conception of Government,"*Journal of Money, Credit, and Banking*, 9 (1977), pp. 91-117.

Buchanan, Allen E., *Ethics, Efficiency, and the Market*, Oxford: Clarendon Press, 1985.

Buchanan, James M., *Cost and Choice: An Inquiry in Economic Theory*, Chicago: Markham, 1969; Chicago: University of Chicago Press, 1978.

_____, "Economics and Its Scientific Neighbors," in Sherman R. Krupp, ed., *The Structure of Economic Science: Essays on Methodology*, Englewood Cliffs, N. J.:

Prentice-Hall, 1966, pp. 166-83; in Buchanan, *What Should Economists Do?* Indianapolis: Liberty Press, 1979, pp. 115-42.

_____, "Ethical Rules, Expected Values, and Large Numbers," *Ethics*, 76 (1965), pp. 1-13; in Buchanan, *Freedom in Constitutional Contract: Perspectives of a Political Economist*, College Station: Texas A & M University Press, 1977, pp. 151-68.

_____, "A Hobbesian Interpretation of the Rawlsian Difference Principle," *Kyklos*, 29 (1976), pp. 5-25; in Buchanan, *Freedom in Constitutional Contract*, pp. 194-211; in Karl Brunner, ed., *Economics and Social Institutions*, Boston: Martinus Nijhoff, 1979, pp. 59-78; in Charles K. Rowley, ed., *Social Choice Theory*, London: Edward Elgar, 1993, Vol. III, pp. 127-46.

_____, "Individual Choice in Voting and the Market," *Journal of Political Economy*, 62 (1954), pp. 334-43; in Buchanan, *Fiscal Theory and Political Economy: Selected Essays*, Chapel Hill: University of North Carolina Press, 1960, pp. 90-104; in Buchanan, *Economics: Between Predictive Science and Moral Philosophy*, College Station: Texas A & M University Press, 1987, pp. 185-97; in Rowley, ed., *Social Choice Theory*, Vol. I, pp. 428-37.

_____, "The Libertarian Legitimacy of the State," in Buchanan, *Freedom in Constitutional Contract*, pp. 50-63.

_____, *The Limits of Liberty: Between Anarchy and Leviathan*, Chicago: University of Chicago Press, 1975.

_____, "Rent Seeking and Profit Seeking," in Buchanan, Robert D. Tollison, and Gordon Tullock, eds., *Toward a Theory of the Rent-Seeking Society*, College Station: Texas A & M University Press, 1980, pp. 3-15.

_____, "Social Choice, Democracy, and Free Markets," *Journal of Political Economy*, 62 (1954), pp. 114-23; in Buchanan, *Fiscal Theory and Political Economy*, pp. 75-89; in Helen Cameron and William Henderson, ed., *Public Finance: Selected Readings*, New York: Random House, 1966, pp. 158-74; in Buchanan, *Economics*, pp. 171-83; in Rowley, ed., *Social Choice Theory*, Vol. I, pp. 418-27.

_____, "Towards the Simple Economics of Natural Liberty: An Exploratory Analysis," *Kyklos*, 40 (1987), pp. 3-20.

_____, "Die Verfassung der Freiheit," in Otto Molden, ed., *Zu den Grenzen der Freiheit*, Vienna: Fritz Molden, 1977, pp. 57-67 (translation of "The Constitution of Freedom," plenary lecture presented at the Alpbach European Forum, September 1976).

_____, "What Should Economists Do?" *Southern Economic Journal*, 30 (1964), pp. 213-22; in Buchanan, *What Should Economists Do?* pp. 17-37; in Buchanan, *Economics: Between Predictive Science and Moral Philosophy*, pp. 21-33; in Rowley, ed., *Social Choice Theory*, Vol. I, pp. 438-47.

Buchanan, James M. and Gordon Tullock, "Economic Analogues to the Generalization Argument," *Ethics*, 74 (1964), pp. 300-01.

Cajetan, Thomas de Vio, *De Cambiis*, in *Scripta Philosophica: Opuscula Oeconomica-socialia*, ed. P. Zammit, Rome: ex Typographia missionaria dominicana, 1934.

_____, *In Summam Theologiae Divi Thomae Aquinatis*, Venice, 1508, 1514, 1518; Bologna, 1528.

Calabresi, Guido and Philip Bobbitt, *Tragic Choices*, New York: W. W. Norton, 1978.

Cohen, G. A., "Robert Nozick and Wilt Chamberlain: How Patterns Preserve Liberty," *Erkenntnis*, 11 (1977), pp. 5-23.

Coleridge, Samuel Taylor, *Collected Works*, ed. James Engell and W. Jackson Bate, London: Routledge & Kegan Paul; Princeton: Princeton University Press, 1983, Vol. VII: *Biographia Literaria: Biographical Sketches of My Literary Life and Opinions.*

Cooper, Richard N., "Worldwide *versus* Regional Integration: Is there an Optimum Size of the Integrated Area?" in Fritz Machlup, ed., *Economic Integration: Worldwide, Regional, Sectoral*, London: Macmillan, 1976, pp. 41-60.

Croce, Benedetto, "Über die sogenannten Wert-Urteile," *Logos*, 1 (1910/11), pp. 71-82.

[Cursus] Collegii Salmanticensis, *Cursus Theologicua*, 1647 ff.; Vols. VI and VII, Paris, 1877-78.

Dam, Cornelis van and Luud M. Stallaert, eds., *Trends in Business Ethics: Implications for Decision-Making*, Leiden: Nijhoff, 1978.

De George, Richard T., *Business Ethics*, New York: Macmillan, 1982; 5th Ed., Upper Saddle River, N. J.: Prentice Hall, 1999.

De George, Richard T. and Joseph A. Pichler , eds., *Ethics, Free Enterprise, & Public Policy: Original Essays on Moral Issues in Business*, New York: Oxford University Press, 1978.

Dilthey, Wilhelm, *Der Aufbau der geschichtlichen Welt in den Geisteswissenschaften*, 1910; Frankfurt: Suhrkamp, 1981.

Döllinger, Ignaz von and Friedrich Heinrich Reusch, *Geschichte der Moralstreitigkeiten in der römisch-katholischen Kirche*, Nördlingen: C. H. Beck, 1889.

Douglas, Mary, *Risk Acceptability according to the Social Sciences*, London: Routledge & Kegan Paul, 1987.

Driesch, Hans, *Über die grundsätzliche Unmöglichkeit einer Vereinigung von universeller Teleologie und Mechanismus*, Heidelberg: C. Winters, 1914.

Duff, Robert Antony, "Absolute Principles and Double Effect," *Analysis*, 36 (1976), pp. 68-80.

Dumont, Louis, *From Mandeville to Marx: The Genesis and Triumph of Economic Ideology*, Chicago: University of Chicago Press, 1977.

Dyke, Charles F., *Philosophy of Economics*, Englewood Cliffs, N. J.: Prentice-Hall, 1981.

Eide, Kjell, "Cultural/Economic Relationships," in Douglas V. Shaw, William S. Hendon, and C. R. Waits, eds., *Artists and Cultural Consumers: Proceedings of the Fourth International Conference on Cultural Economics, Avignon, May 12-14, 1986*, Akron: Association for Cultural Economics, 1987, Vol. III, pp. 202-6.

Elster, Jon, *Ulysses and the Sirens: Studies in Rationality and Irrationality*, Cambridge: Cambridge University Press, 1979; 2nd Ed., 1984.

Enderle, Georges, ed., *Ethik und Wirtschaftswissenschaft*, Berlin: Duncker & Humblot, 1985.

Falkinger, Josef, *Sättigung: Moralische und psychologische Grenzen des Wachstums*, Tübingen: J. C. B. Mohr (Paul Siebeck), 1986.

Farquhar, Peter H., "Advances in Multiattribute Utility Theory," *Theory and Decision*, 12 (1981), pp. 381-94.

Fénelon, François de Salignac de La Mothe, *Dissertatio de amore puro*, in *Oeuvres complètes de Fénelon*, Paris: Leroux, 1851; Geneva: Slatkine Reprints, 1971, Vol. III, pp. 420-571.

Fichte, Johann Gottlieb, *Grundlage der gesammten Wissenschaftslehre*, in *Fichtes Werke*, 11 vols., ed. Immanuel Hermann Fichte, Berlin: Walter de Gruyter, 1971, Vol. I, pp. 83-328.

Fischoff, Baruch and Christoph Hohenemser, "Handling Hazards," *Environment*, 20 (1978), pp. 16-20, 32-37.

Fishburn, Peter C., "Subjective Expected Utility: A Review of Normative Theories," *Theory and Decision*, 13 (1981), pp. 139-99.

Forschner, Maximilian, "Das Gute und die Güter: Zur Aktualität der stoischen Ethik," in Fondation Hardt, ed., *Aspects de la philosophie hellénistique*, Geneva: Fondation Hardt, 1986, pp. 325-59.

Forte, Francesco, "Tutor of Nature: Comment on Peter Koslowski," in Koslowski, ed., *Individual Liberty and Democratic Decision-Making: The Ethics, Economics, and Politics of Democracy*, Tübingen: J. C. B. Mohr (Paul Siebeck), 1987, pp. 93-97.

Franke, Günter, "Expected Utility with Ambiguous Probabilities and 'Irrational' Parameters," *Theory and Decision*, 9 (1978), pp. 267-83.

Gäfgen, Gérard, "Ökonomische Implikationen ethischer Prinzipien," in Dieter Duwendag and Horst Siebert, eds., *Politik und Markt: Wirtschaftspolitische Probleme der 80er Jahre* (Festschrift for Hans Karl Schneider), Stuttgart: Fischer, 1980, pp. 191-207.

Gapinski, James H., "The Production of Culture," *Review of Economics and Statistics*, 62 (1980), pp. 578-86.

Gauthier, David P., "Economic Rationality and Moral Constraints." *Midwest Studies in Philosophy*, 3 (1978), pp. 75-96.

Georgescu-Roegen, Nicholas, *Energy and Economic Myths*, New York: Pergamon Press, 1976.

Ghoos, Jozef, "L'acte à double effet," *Ephemerides Theologicae Lovanenses*, 27 (1951), pp. 30-52.

Gibbard, Allan, *Utilitarianism and Coordination*, Cambridge, Mass.: Harvard University Press, 1971; New York: Garland, 1990.

_____, "What's Morally Special about Free Exchange," in Ellen Frankel Paul, Jeffrey Paul, and Fred D. Miller, Jr., eds., *Ethics and Economics*, Oxford: Basil Blackwell, 1985, pp. 20-28.

Giers, Joachim, *Gerechtigkeit und Liebe: Die Grundpfeiler gesellschaftlicher Ordnung in der Sozialethik des Kardinals Cajetan*, Düsseldorf: Mosella, 1941.

Glastetter, Werner, "Zum Problem der 'abgeleiteten Verteilungskonzeption' – Einige kritische Bemerkungen zum vorliegenden Wachstumsprozeß aus der Sicht der Verteilungsgerechtigkeit," in Gottfried Bombach, Bruno S. Frey, and Bernhard Gahlen, eds., *Neue Aspekte der Verteilungstheorie*, Tübingen: J. C. B. Mohr (Paul Siebeck), 1974, pp. 269-304.

Goethe, Johann Wolfgang von, *The Maxims and Reflections of Goethe*, trans. Bailey Saunders, New York: Macmillan, 1893; *Maximen und Reflexionen*, Zürich: Artemis-Gedächtnisausgabe, 1962.

Greenwood, Peter H. and Charles A. Ingene, "Uncertain Externalities, Liability Rules, and Resource Allocation," *American Economic Review*, 68 (1978), pp. 300-10.

Grice-Hutchinson, Marjorie, *The School of Salamanca: Readings in Spanish Monetary Theory 1544-1605*, Oxford: Clarendon Press, 1952.

Grimm, J. and W., *Deutsches Worterbuch*, Munich: Deutscher Taschenbuch Verlag, 1984.

Gundlach, Gustav, "Sozialphilosophie," in *Staatslexikon*, 6th Ed., Freiburg: Herder, 1962, Vol. VII, pp. 337-46.

Gury, Jean Pierre, *Compendium theologiae moralis*, 2 vols., Lyon, 1850; 17th Ed, 1866.

Hackmann, Johannes, *Zur wohlfahrtstheoretischen Behandlung von Verteilungsproblemen*, Berlin: Duncker & Humblot, 1972.

Hahn, Frank, "On the Notion of Equilibrium in Economics" and "The Winter of our Discontent," in *Equilibrium and Macroeconomics*, Oxford: Basil Blackwell, 1984, pp. 43-71 and 134-44.

Harrod, Roy Forbes, "Utilitarianism Revised," *Mind*, 45 (1936), pp. 137-56.

Hayek, Friedrich A. von, ed., *Collectivist Economic Planning: Critical Studies on the Possibilities of Socialism*, London: George Routledge & Sons, 1935; repr. Clifton, N.J.: A. M. Kelly, 1975.

_____, *Individualism and Economic Order*, Chicago: University of Chicago Press, 1948; London: Routledge & Kegan Paul, 1949; Chicago: Henry Regnery, 1972.

_____, *Drei Vorlesungen über Demokratie, Gerechtigkeit und Sozialismus*, Tübingen: J. C. B. Mohr (Paul Siebeck), 1977.

_____, *Der Wettbewerb als Entdeckungsverfahren*, Kiel: Institut für Weltwirtschaft, 1968.

Hegel, Georg Wilhelm Friedrich, *The Philosophy of Right*, trans. S. W. Dyde, 1896; Amherst, N. Y.: Prometheus, 1996; *Grundlinien der Philosophie des Rechts*, 1821; 5th Ed., Frankfurt: Suhrkamp, 1996.

Hendon, William S., "An Observation on Arts and Economics," in Hendon, James L. Shanahan, and Alice J. MacDonald, eds., *Economic Policy for the Arts*, Cambridge, Mass.: Abt Books, 1980.

Hendon, William S. and James L. Shanahan, eds., *The Economics of Cultural Decisions*, Akron: Association for Cultural Economics; Cambridge, Mass.: Abt Books, 1983.

Hendon, William S., Nancy K. Grant, and Douglas V. Shaw, eds., *The Economics of Cultural Industries*, Akron: Association for Cultural Economics, 1984.

Henschel, Rudolf, "Ordnungsbedingungen und Einkommensverteilung – Enfluß der autonomen Gruppen auf die Ordnungsbedingungen," in Gottfried Bombach, Bruno S. Frey, and Bernhard Gahlen, eds., *Neue Aspekte der Verteilungstheorie*, Tübingen: J. C. B. Mohr (Paul Siebeck), 1974, pp. 319-42.

Heraclitus, Fragment 29, in Milton C. Nahm, ed., *Selections from Early Greek Philosophy*, 3rd Ed., New York: Appleton-Century-Crofts, 1947, p. 90.

Herder, Johann Gottfried, *Vernunft und Sprache: Eine Metakritik zur Kritik der reinen Vernunft*, in *Sämtliche Werke*, ed., Bernhard Suphan, Berlin, 1877-1913; Hildesheim: Georg Olms, 1967, Vol. XXI, pp. 191-339.

Hesse, Helmut, "Neue Weltwirtschaftsordnung: Ökonomische Kriterien zur Beurteilung konkurrierender Lösungsmodelle," in *Handbuch der christlichen Ethik*, Freiburg: Herder, Gütersloh: Mohn, 1982, Vol. III, pp. 337-48.

Hession, Charles H., *John Maynard Keynes: A Personal Biography of the Man who Revolutionized Capitalism and the Way We Live*, New York: Macmillan, 1984.

Hicks, John R., *Causality in Economics*, Oxford: Basil Blackwell, 1979.

Hippel, Eike von, *Grundfragen der Weltwirtschaftsordnung*, Munich: C. H. Beck, 1980.

Hirschman, Albert O., *Exit, Voice and Loyalty*, Cambridge, Mass.: Harvard University Press, 1971.

Höffner, Joseph, *Statik und Dynamik in der scholastischen Wirtschaftsethik*, Cologne: Westdeutscher Verlag, 1955.

Hume, David, *An Enquiry Concerning the Principles of Morals*, Sect. V: "Why Utility Pleases," in *The Philosophical Works*, ed. T. H. Greene and T. H. Grose, London, 1882, Vol. IV, pp. 202-17.

Institut für Gesellschaftswissenschaften Walberberg, ed., "Im Gespräch: Wirtschaftsethik – Ausweg aus der Ordnungskrise," *Die Neue Ordnung*, Special Edition, 1986.

Jaeger, Werner Wilhelm, *Paideia: The Ideals of Greek Culture*, 3 vols., trans. Gilbert Highet, New York: Oxford University Press, 1939; Vol I: *Archaic Greece and the Mind of Athens*; *Paideia: Die Formung des griechischen Menschen*, 3 vols., Berlin: Walter de Gruyter, 1933; 1935; 1989, Vol. I.

Jahoda, Marie, "Arbeitslose haben alles Recht der Welt, über ihre Lage unglücklich zu sein: Gespräch mit Marie Jahoda," in *Geschafft: Über Arbeit, keine Arbeit und Freizeit*, ed. Psychologie-heute-Redaktion, Weinheim: Beltz, 1985, pp. 16-23.

Jöhr, Walter A., *Der Kompromiß als Problem der Gesellschafts-, Wirtschafts- und Staatsethik*, Tübingen: J. C. B. Mohr (Paul Siebeck), 1958.

John of Saint Thomas, *Cursus Theologicus*, Madrid, 1645-56.

Jones, Donald G. and Helen Troy, eds., *A Bibliography of Business Ethics, 1976-1980*, Charlottesville: University Press of Virginia, 1982.

Justinian, *The Digest of Justinian*, trans. Alan Watson, Philadelphia: University of Pennsylvania Press, 1985.

Kant, Immanuel, *Critique of Practical Reason*, trans. Lewis White Beck, New York: Macmillan, 1985; *Kritik der praktischen Vernunft*, 1788.

_____, *Foundations of the Metaphysics of Morals*, trans. Lewis White Beck, New York: Macmillan, 1959; *Grundlegung zur Metaphysik der Sitten*, 1785.

_____, *The Metaphysics of Morals*, Part I: *The Metaphysical Elements of Justice*, trans. John Ladd, New York: Macmillan, 1985; *Metaphysik der Sitten*, 1797.

Katterle, Siegfried, *Sozialwissenschaft und Sozialethik: Logische und theoretische Probleme praktischer Sozialwissenschaften, besonders christlicher Soziallehren*, Göttingen: Otto Schwartz, 1972.

Kauder, Emil, "Genesis of the Marginal Utility Theory: From Aristotle to the End of the Eighteenth Century," *Economic Journal*, 63 (1953), pp. 638-50.

_____, *A History of Marginal Utility Theory*, Princeton: Princeton University Press, 1965.

Keohane, Robert O., *After Hegemony: Cooperation and Discord in the World-Political Economy*, Princeton: Princeton University Press, 1984.

Keynes, John Maynard, "Economic Possibilities for our Grandchildren," in Keynes, *Essays in Persuasion*, New York: W. W. Norton, 1963, pp. 358-73.

_____, *A Treatise on Probability*, London: Macmillan, 1921; 1973.

Kierkegaard, Søren, *Either/Or*, Part II, trans. Howard V. Hong and Edna H. Hong, Princeton: Princeton University Press, 1987; *Enten-Eller*, Copenhagen, 1843.

Kindleberger, Charles P., "International Public Goods without International Government," *American Economic Review*, 76 (1986), pp. 1-13.

Kirsch, Werner, Werner-Michael Esser, and Eduard Gabele, *Das Management des geplanten Wandels von Organisationen*, Stuttgart: C. E. Poeschel, 1979.

Kirzner, Israel M., *Competition and Entrepreneurship*, Chicago: University of Chicago Press, 1973.

Kliemt, Hartmut, "Ökonomik und Ethik," *Wirtschaftswissenschaftliches Studium*, 16 (1987), pp. 113-18.

Klomps, Heinrich, *Tradition und Fortschritt in der Moraltheologie: Die grundsätzliche Bedeutung der Kontroverse zwischen Jansenismus und Probabilismus*, Bonn: Bachem, 1963.

Knauer, Peter, "The Hermeneutic Function of the Principle of Double Effect," *Natural Law Forum*, 12 (1967), pp. 132-62.

Knight, Frank Hyneman, "Abstract Economics as Absolute Ethics," *Ethics*, 76 (1966), pp. 163-77.

_____, "Ethics and the Economic Interpretation," "The Limitations of Scientific Method in Economics," and "Statics and Dynamics: Some Queries Regarding the Mechanical Analogy in Economics," in Knight, *The Ethics of Competition and other Essays*, London: George Allen & Unwin, 1935; Chicago: University of Chicago Press, 1976; New Brunswick, N. J.: Transaction, 1997, pp. 11-33, 97-139, 153-77.

_____, *On the History and Method of Economics*, Chicago: University of Chicago Press, 1963.

_____, *Risk, Uncertainty and Profit*, Boston: Houghton Mifflin, 1921; Chicago: University of Chicago Press, 1971.

Koch, W., "Ethik und Ökonomik," *Zeitschrift für die gesamte Staatswissenschaft*, 117 (1961), pp. 577-609.

Kolm, Serge-Christophe, "Must One Be Buddhist to Grow? An Analysis of the Cultural Basis of Japanese Productivity," in Koslowski, ed., *Economics and Philosophy*, Tübingen, J. C. B. Mohr (Paul Siebeck), 1985, pp. 221-42.

Korff, Wilhelm, "Ethische Entscheidungskonflikte: Zum Problem der Güterabwägung," in *Handbuch der christlichen Ethik*, Freiburg: Herder; Gütersloh: Mohn, 1982, Vol. III, pp. 78-92.

Koslowski, Peter, "Economy Principle, Maximizing, and the Co-Ordination of Individuals in Economics and Philosophy," in Koslowski, ed., *Economics and Philosophy*, Tübingen: J. C. B. Mohr (Paul Siebeck), 1985, pp. 39-67.

_____, *Ethik des Kapitalismus*, with a comment by James M. Buchanan, Tübingen: J. C. B. Mohr (Paul Siebeck), 1982; 6th Ed., 1998.

_____, *Evolution und Gesellschaft: Eine Auseinandersetzung mit der Soziobiologie*, Tübingen: J. C. B. Mohr (Paul Siebeck), 1984.

_____, "Gerechtigkeit zwischen den Generationen: Die soziale Sicherung im Spannungsfeld von Eigenverantwortung und staatlicher Daseinsvorsorge," *Frankfurter Allgemeine Zeitung*, No. 248, 25 October 1986, p. 13.

_____, *Gesellschaft und Staat: Ein unvermeidlicher Dualismus*, with an introduction by Robert Spaemann, Stuttgart: Klett-Cotta, 1982.

_____, "Die Grenzen der ökonomischen Theorie: Plädoyer für eine gesamte Staatswissenschaft," *Merkur* 39 (1985), pp. 791-806.

_____, "Haus und Geld: Zur aristotelischen Unterscheidung von Politic, Ökonomik und Chrematistik," *Philosophisches Jahrbuch*, 86 (1979), pp. 60-83.

_____, "Lebensverlängerung: Nebenwirkungen und Grenzen der ärztlichen Behandlungspflicht aus philosophicscher und ökonomischer Sicht," in Koslowski, Philipp Kreuzer, and Reinhard Löw, eds., *Die Verführung durch das Machbare: Ethische Konflikte in der modernen Medizin und Biologie*, Stuttgart: S. Hirzel, 1983, pp. 83-100.

_____, "Market and Democracy as Discourses: Limits to Discursive Social Coordination," in Koslowski, ed., *Individual Liberty and Democratic Decision-Making: The Ethics, Economics, and Politics of Democracy*, Tübingen: J. C. B. Mohr (Paul Siebeck), 1987, pp. 58-92.

_____, "Markt- und Demokratieversagen? Brenzen individualistischer gesellschaftlicher Entscheidungssysteme am Beispiel der Umwelt- und Kernenergiefrage," *Politische Vierteljahresschrift*, 24 (1983), pp. 166-87.

_____, "Maximierung von Existenz: Leibniz' Theorie der besten aller möglichen Welten und die Wirtschaftstheorie," *Studia Leibnitiana*, 19 (1987), pp. 54-67.

_____, "Mechanistische und organistische Analogien in der Wirtschaftswissenschaft – eine verfehlte Alternative," *Kyklos*, 36 (1983), pp. 308-12.

_____, "Nebenwirkungen," in Joachim Ritter and Karlfried Gründer, eds., *Historisches Wörterbuch der Philosophie*, Basel: Schwabe, 1984, Vol. VI, pp. 659-62.

_____, "Philosopy and Economics: An Introduction," in Koslowski, ed., *Economics and Philosophy*, Tübingen, J. C. B. Mohr (Paul Siebeck), 1985, pp. 1-16.

_____, *Die postmoderne Kultur: Gesellschaftlich-kulturelle Konsequenzen der technischen Entwicklung*, Munich: C. H. Beck, 1987.

_____, "Religion, Ökonomie, Ethik: Eine sozialtheoretische und ontologische Analyse ihres Zusammenhanges," in Koslowski, ed., *Die religiöse Dimension der Gesellschaft: Religion und ihre Theorien*, Tübingen: J. C. B. Mohr (Paul Siebeck), 1984, pp. 76-96.

_____, "Sinnvolles Wirtschaften: Die Ökonomie entdeckt die Philosophie wieder," *Frankfurter Allgemeine Zeitung*, No. 179, 6 August 1986, p. 25.

_____, "Sozialstaat: Glück mit Illusionen," *Wirtschaftswoche*, No. 21, 16 May 1986, pp. 78-83.

_____, *Staat und Gesellschaft bei Kant*, Tübingen: J. C. B. Mohr (Paul Siebeck), 1985.

_____, "Über die Notwendingkeit von ethischen und zugleich ökonomischen Urteilen," *Orientierungen zur Wirtschafts- und Gesellschaftspolitik*, 33 (1987), pp. 7-13.

_____, Über Notwendigkeit und Möglichkeit einer Wirtschaftsethik," *Scheidewege: Jahresschrift für skeptisches Denken*, 15 (1985/86), pp. 294-305.

_____, *Zum Verhältnis von Polis und Oikos bei Aristoteles: Politik und Ökonomie bei Aristoteles*, Straubing: Donau-Verlag, 1976; 2nd Ed., 1979.

Koslowski, Peter, Robert Spaemann, and Reinhard Löw, eds., *Moderne oder Postmoderne? Zur Signatur des Gegenwärtigen Zeitalters*, Weinheim: VCH/Acta humaniora, 1986.

Krasner, Stephen D., *International Regimes*, Ithaca: Cornell University Press, 1983.

Krings, Hermann, "Vom Sinn der Metaphysik oder über den Unterschied von Ursache und Bedingung," *Philosophisches Jahrbuch*, 92 (1985), pp. 98-109.

Külp, Bernhard, *Wohlfahrtsökonomik*, Tübingen: J. C. B. Mohr, 1975, Vol. I: *Die Wohlfahrtskriterien.*

Lachmann, Ludwig M., "Austrian Economics in the Age of the Neo-Ricardian Counterrevolution," in Edwin G. Dolan, ed., *The Foundations of Modern Austrian Economics*, Kansas City: Sheed & Ward, 1976, pp. 216-20.

_____, "From Mises to Shackle: An Essay on Austrian Economics and the Kaleidic Society," *Journal of Economic Literature*, 14 (1976), pp. 54-62.

Laffont, Jean-Jacques, "Macroeconomic Constraints, Economic Efficiency and Ethics: An Introduction to Kantian Economics," *Economica*, 42 (1975), pp. 430-37.

Leibniz, Gottfried Wilhelm, *Theodicy: Essays on the Goodness of God, the Freedom of Man, and the Origin of Evil*, trans. E. M. Huggard, New Haven: Yale University Press, 1952.

Lenin, Vladimir Ilyich, "The State and Revolution," in *Collected Works*, Moscow: Progress Publishers, 1978, Vol. XXV, pp. 381-492.

Letwin, Shirley Robin, "Certainty Since the Seventeenth Century," in Philip P. Wiener, ed., *Dictionary of the History of Ideas: Studies of Selected Pivotal Ideas*, New York: Charles Scribner's Sons, 1968, Vol. I, pp. 312-25.

Levy, S. S., *The Doctrine of the Double Effect*, Ph.D. Thesis, Department of Philosophy, University of Michigan, 1982.

Lindenberg, Siegwart, "Utility and Morality," *Kyklos*, 36 (1983), pp. 450-68.

Lipsey, Richard G. and Kelvin Lancaster, "The general Theory of Second Best," *Review of Economic Studies*, 24 (1956), pp. 11-32.

Loccumer Protokolle, *Theologische Aspekte der Wirtschaftsethik*, Loccum: Evangelische Akademie Loccum, Vol. I, 1986; Vol. II, 1987.

Löw, Reinhard, "Zur Kritik des objektiven Mechanismus," *Berichte zur Wissenschaftsgeschichte*, 6 (1983), pp. 29-39.

Luce, R. Duncan and Howard Raiffa, *Games and Decisions*, New York: John Wiley & Sons, 1957.

Luckmann, Thomas, "Über die Funktion der Religion," in Koslowski, ed., *Die religiöse Dimension der Gesellschaft: Religion und ihre Theorien*, Tübingen: J. C. B. Mohr (Paul Siebeck), 1985, pp. 26-41.

Luhmann, Niklas, "Neue Politische Ökonomie," *Soziologische Revue*, 8 (1985), pp. 115-20.

Luijk, Henk van, *When the Market Fails: The Morality of Economic Man*, St. Gallen: Forschungsstelle für Wirtschaftsethik, 1986.

Mackie, John L., *Ethics: Inventing Right and Wrong*, London: Penguin Books, 1977.
Maier, Anneliese, *Die Mechanisierung des Weltbilds im 17. Jahrhundert*, Leipzig: F. Meiner, 1938; 2nd Ed., Rome: Edizioni di storia e letteratura, 1968.
Maiwald, Werner, *Ethik und Wirtschaft: Ein Beitrag zur Erkenntniskritik der Nationalökonomie unter Zugrundelegung des Problems der Gerechtigkeit*, Diss. rer. pol., University of Tübingen, 1922.
Mandeville, Bernard, *The Fable of the Bees: or, Private Vices, Publick Benefits*, London, 1714; ed. F. B. Kaye, 2 vols., Oxford: Clarendon Press, 1924.
Mangan, J. T., "A Historical Analysis of the Principle of Double Effect," *Theological Studies*, 10 (1949), pp. 41-61.
Marcus Aurelius Antoninus, *Meditations*, trans. George Long, London: Bell, 1862.
Marshall, Alfred, *Principles of Economics*, London: Macmillan, 1890; 9th Ed., 1961.
Matthews, R. C. O., "Morality, Competition, and Efficiency," *The Manchester School of Economic and Social Studies*, 49 (1981), pp. 289-309.
Maupertuis, Pierre-Louis Moreau de, *Oeuvres*, Lyon: J. M. Bruyset, 1756; 1768; Hildesheim: Georg Olms, 1974, Vol. II.
McCormick, Richard, "Das Prinzip der Doppelwirkung einer Handlung," *Concilium*, 12 (1976), pp. 662-70.
McKenzie, Richard B., "The Economic Dimension of Ethical Behavior," *Ethics*, 87 (1977), pp. 208-21.
McNamara, L. J., *Direct and Indirect: A Study in the Principle of Double Effect in Roman Catholic Moral Theology*, Ph.D. Thesis, Faculty of Theology, University of Oxford, 1980.
Menkes, Joshua, "Risk or Angst," *Risk Analysis*, 1 (1981), pp. 237-40.
Messner, Johannes, *Social Ethics: Natural Law in the Western World*, trans. J. J. Doherty, St. Louis: B. Herder, 1949; Rev. Ed., 1965; *Das Naturrecht: Handbuch der Gesellschaftsethik, Staatsethik und Wirtschaftsethik*, 2nd Ed., Innsbruck: Tyrolia, 1950; 7th Ed., Berlin: Duncker & Humblot, 1984.
_____, *Sozialökonomik und Sozialethik: Studie zur Grundlegung einer systematischen Wirtschaftsethik*, Paderborn: Ferdinand Schöningh, 1928; 1929.
Mill, John Stuart, *Three Essays on Religion*, London: Henry Holt, 1874.
Mises, Ludwig von, *Human Action: A Treatise on Economics*, New Haven: Yale University Press, 1949; Chicago: Henry Regnery, 1966; San Francisco: Fox & Wilkes, Irvington-on-Hudson, N. Y: Foundation for Economic Education, 1996; *Nationalökonomie: Theorie des Handelns und Wirtschaftens*, Geneva: Editions Union, 1940.
_____, "Soziologie und Geschichte: Epilog zum Methodenstreit in der Nationalökonomie," *Archiv für Sozialwissenschaften und Sozialpolitik*, 61 (1929), pp. 465-512.
Mishan, E. J., "The Postwar Literature on Externalities: An Interpretative Essay," *Journal of Economic Literature*, 9 (1971), pp. 1-29.
Molina, Luis de, *De justitia et jure*, Moguntiae, 1602.
Moore, George Edward, *Principia Ethica*, Cambridge: Cambridge University Press, 1903.
Morgenstern, Oskar, "Thirteen Critical Points in Contemporary Economic Theory: An Interpretation," *The Journal of Economic Literature*, 10 (1972), pp. 1163-93; in Morgenstern, *Selected Economic Writings*, ed. Andrew Schotter, New York: New York University Press, 1976, pp. 267-93.

Müller, M., *Ethik und Recht in der Lehre von der Verantwortlichkeit*, Regensburg: Habbel, 1932.

Musgrave, Richard A. and Peggy B. Musgrave, *Public Finance in Theory and Practice*, 2nd Ed., New York: McGraw Hill, 1976.

Nell-Breuning, Oswald von, "Das Äquivalenzprinzip," *Jahrbücher für Nationalökonomie und Statistik*, 133 (1930), pp. 33-47.

_____, "Fortschritte in der Lehre von der Preisgerechtigkeit," in *Miscellanea Vermeersch* (= *Analecta Gregoriana*, Vol. IX), Rome: Pontificia Università Gregoriana, 1935, Vol. I, pp. 93-110.

_____, *Kapitalismus – kritisch betrachtet: Zur Auseinandersetzung um das bessere "System,"* Freiburg: Herder, 1974; 1986.

_____, "Wirtschaftsethik," in *Staatslexikon*, 6th Ed., Freiburg: Herder, 1963, Vol. XIII, pp. 773-80.

Nelson, Benjamin N., "Sources of 'Probabilism' and 'Anti-Probabilism' in 16th and 17th Century Science," in Nelson, *On the Roads to Modernity: Conscience, Science, and Civilizations*, ed. Toby E. Huff, Totowa, N. J.: Rowman and Littlefield, 1981, pp. 115-20.

Netzer, Dick, *The Subsidized Muse: Public Support for the Arts in the United States*, Cambridge: Cambridge University Press, 1978.

von Neumann, John and Oskar Morgenstern, *Theory of Games and Economic Behavior*, Princeton: Princeton University Press, 1944; 3rd Ed., 1953.

Newman, John Henry, *An Essay in Aid of a Grammar of Assent*, London: Burns, Oates, 1870; ed. Ian Ker, Oxford: Clarendon Press, 1985.

Nider, Johannes, *On the Contracts of Merchants*, trans. Charles H. Reeves, ed. Ronald B. Shuman, Norman: University of Oklahoma Press, 1966; *Tractatus de Contractibus Mercatorum*, Cologne: Ulrich Zell, c. 1468.

Nisbet, Robert, "The Pursuit of Equality," *The Public Interest*, 35 (1974), pp. 103-20.

Noonan, John T., Jr., *The Scholastic Analysis of Usury*, Cambridge, Mass.: Harvard University Press, 1957.

Nozick, Robert, *Anarchy, State, and Utopia*, New York: Basic Books, 1974.

Oakeshott, Michael, "The Political Economy of Freedom," in Oakeshott, *Rationalism in Politics and other Essays*, London: Methuen, 1962, pp. 37-58; Indianapolis: Liberty Press, 1991, pp. 384-406.

Oelmüller, Willi, ed., *Materialien zur Normendiskussion*, 3 vols., Paderborn: Schöningh, 1978-79.

Olson, Mancur, *The Logic of Collective Action: Public Goods and the Theory of Groups*, Cambridge, Mass.: Harvard University Press, 1965.

Parfit, Derek, "Prudence, Morality, and the Prisoner's Dilemma," *Proceedings of the British Academy*, Oxford: Oxford University Press, 1981.

Pascal, Blaise, "The Provincial Letters," trans. Thomas M'Crie, in *Great Books of the Western World*, ed. Mortimer J. Adler, 2nd Ed., Chicago: Encyclopædia Britannica, 1990, Vol. XXX: *Blaise Pascal: The Provincial Letters, Pensées, Scientific Treatises*, pp. 1-169.

Peacock, Alan T. and Charles K. Rowley, "Pareto Optimality and the Political Economy of Liberalism," *Journal of Political Economy*, 80 (1972), pp. 481-84.

Pesch, Heinrich, *Ethik und Volkswirtschaftslehre*, Freiburg: Herder, 1918.

Peter Lombard, *Libri Quattuor Sententiarum*, 1158.

Pico della Mirandola, *De Imaginatione*, 1501.

Pieper, Josef, "Justice," trans. Lawrence E. Lynch, in Pieper, *The Four Cardinal Virtues*, Notre Dame, Ind.: University of Notre Dame Press, 1966, pp. 41-113; *Über die Gerechtigkeit*, Munich, Kösel, 1953; 4th Ed., 1965.

Pius XI, Encyclical *Quadragesimo Anno – On Reconstruction of the Social Order*, Rome, 15 May 1931.

Plato, *Cratylus*, trans. Benjamin Jowett, and *Republic*, trans. Paul Shorey, in *The Collected Dialogues*, ed. Edith Hamilton and Huntington Cairns, New York: Pantheon Books, 1961, pp. 421-74 and 575-844.

Polanyi, Karl, *The Great Transformation*, Boston: Beacon Press, 1944; 1957.

_____, *Primitive, Archaic, and Modern Economies*, Boston: Beacon Press, 1971.

Pondy, Louis R. and David M. Boje, "Bringing Mind Back In," in *Paradigm Development as a Frontier Problem in Organization Theory*, unpublished manuscript of the Department of Business Administration, University of Illinois, Urbana, 1976.

Popper, Karl, "La rationalité et le statut du principe de rationalité," in Jacques Rueff and Emil M. Claassen, eds., *Les fondements philosophiques des systèmes économiques*, Paris: Payot, 1967, pp. 142-50.

Pseudo-Dionysius Areopagita, *De divinis nominibus*, after 485 A.D.

Radbruch, Gustav, *Der Handlungsbegriff in seiner Bedeutung für das Strafrechtssystem: Zugleich ein Beitrag zur Lehre von der rechtswissenschaftlichen Systematik*, Berlin, 1904; Darmstadt: Wissenschaftliche Buchgesellschaft, 1967.

_____, *Die Lehre von der adäquaten Verursachung*, Berlin: Reimer, 1902.

Rawls, John, *A Theory of Justice*, Cambridge, Mass.: Harvard University Press, 1971.

Recktenwald, Horst C., *Das Selbstinteresse – Zentrales Axiom der ökonomischen Wissenschaft*, Wiesbaden: F. Steiner, 1986.

Reder, Melvin W., "The Place of Ethics in the Theory of Production," in Michael J. Boskin, ed., *Economics and Human Welfare: Essays in Honor of Tibor Scitovsky*, New York: Academic Press, 1979, pp. 133-46.

Regan, Tom, ed., *Just Business: New Introductory Essays in Business Ethics*, Philadelphia: Temple University Press, 1983.

Rescher, Nicholas, "Economics vs. Moral Philosophy," *Theory and Decision*, 10 (1979), pp. 169-79.

Rich, Arthur, *Wirtschaftsethik*, Vol. I: *Grundlagen in theologischer Perspektive*, Gütersloh: Mohn, 1984.

Rickert, Heinrich, *Science and History: A Critique of Positivist Epistemology*, trans. George Reisman, ed. Arthur Goddard, Princeton: D. Van Nostrand, 1962; *Kulturwissenschaft und Naturwissenschaft*, Tübingen: J. C. B. Mohr (Paul Siebeck), 1899; 1910; 1915.

_____, *The Limits of Concept Formation in Natural Science: A Logical Introduction to the Historical Sciences*, Abr. Ed., trans. and ed. Guy Oakes, Cambridge: Cambridge University Press, 1986; *Die Grenzen der naturwissenschaftlichen Begriffsbildung:*

Eine logische Einleitung in die historischen Wissenschaften, Tübingen: J. C. B. Mohr (Paul Siebeck), 1902; 5th Ed., Tübingen 1929.

Riesenhuber, Klaus, "Gut," in Joachim Ritter and Karlfried Gründer, eds., *Historisches Wörterbuch der Philosophie*, Basel: Schwabe, 1974, Vol. III, pp. 951-60.

Riesman, David, *Abundance for What? and other Essays*, New York: Doubleday, 1964.

Riklin, Alois, *Wissenschaft und Ethik*, St. Gallen, 1982 (= Hochschule St. Gallen, *Aulavorträge* 17).

Rinderspacher, Jürgen P., "Der Feierabend, der keiner ist," in *Geschafft: Über Arbeit, keine Arbeit und Freizeit*, ed. Psychologie-heute-Redaktion, Weinheim/Basel: Beltz, 1985, pp. 38-41.

Robbins, Lionel, *An Essay on the Nature and Significance of Economic Science*, London: Macmillan 1932; 2nd Ed., 1962.

Robertson, Dennis H., "What Does the Economist Economise?" in Robertson, *Economic Commentaries*, London: Staples, 1956, pp. 147-54.

Röpke, Wilhelm, "Spekulation," *Handwörterbuch der Staatswissenschaften*, 4th Ed., Jena: G. Gischer, 1926, Vol. VII, pp. 706-10.

Röpke, Wilhelm, Josef Hünermann, and Eberhard Müller, *Wirtschaftsethik Heute: Drei Reden an jeden, der produziert, kauft und verkauft*, Hamburg: Furche, 1956.

Romberg, R., "Ethik," in Joachim Ritter and Karlfried Gründer, eds., *Historisches Wörterbuch der Philosophie*, Basel: Schwabe, 1972, Vol. II, pp. 759-805.

de Roover, Raymond A., "The Scholastics, Usury, and Foreign Exchange," *Business History Review*, 41 (1967), pp. 257-71.

Roth, Alois, *Edmund Husserls ethische Untersuchungen*, Den Haag: Nijhoff, 1960.

Rothbard, Murray N., "Praxeology: The Methodology of Austrian Economics," in E. G. Dolan, ed., *The Foundations of Modern Austrian Economics*, Kansas City: Sheed & Ward, 1976, pp. 19-36.

Rowley, Charles K. and Alan T. Peacock, *Welfare Economics: A Liberal Restatement*, London: Martin Robertson, 1975.

Sainte-Foi, Charles, "Du Probabilisme," *Le Correspondant*, 2 (Paris, 1843), pp. 145-59.

Samuelson, Paul A., "Consumption Theory in Terms of Revealed Preference," in *The Collected Scientific Papers*, ed. Joseph E. Stiglitz, Cambridge, Mass.: MIT Press, 1966, Vol. I, pp. 64-74.

_____, "Discussion – Problems of Methodology," *American Economic Review*, 53 (1963), pp. 231-36.

Sartre, Jean-Paul, *Existentialism and Humanism*, trans. Philip Mairet, London: Eyre Methuen, 1948; *L'Existentialisme est un humanisme*, Paris: Editions Nagel, 1946.

Scheler, Max, *Formalism in Ethics and Non-Formal Ethics of Values: A New Attempt toward the Foundation of an Ethical Personalism*, 5th Ed., trans. Manfred S. Frings and Roger L. Funk, Evanston: Northwestern University Press, 1973; *Der Formalismus in der Ethik und die materiale Wertethik: Neuer Versuch der Grundlegung eines ethischen Personalismus*, 1913-16; 6th Ed., Bern: Francke, 1980.

_____, "Vorbilder und Führer," in *Schriften aus dem Nachlaß*, 2nd Ed., Bern: Francke, 1957; 3rd Ed., Bonn: Bouvier, 1986, Vol. I: *Zur Ethik und Erkenntnislehre*, pp. 255-344.

Schelling, Friedrich Wilhelm Joseph von, *Von der Weltseele, eine Hypothese der höheren Physik zur Erklärung des allgemeinen Organismus*, in *Werke*, ed. Manfred Schröter, Munich: C. H. Beck, 1798; 1965; 1979, Vol. I, pp. 413-651.

Schelling, Thomas C., *Choice and Consequence: Perspectives of an Errant Economist*, Cambridge, Mass.: Harvard University Press, 1984.

Schleiermacher, Friedrich Ernst Daniel, *Grundlinien einer Kritik der bisherigen Sittenlehre*, Berlin: Realschulbuchhandlung, 1803; 2nd Ed., Leipzig, F. Meiner, 1928.

Schmoller, Gustav, "Die Gerechtigkeit in der Volkswirtschaft," *Jahrbuch für Gesetzgebung, Verwaltung und Volkswirtschaft im Deutschen Reich*, 5 (1881), pp. 19-54.

Schöllgen, Werner, "Grenzmoral," in *Staatslexikon*, 6th Ed., Freiburg: Herder, 1959, Vol. III, pp. 1016-19.

Schönke, Adolf and Horst Schröder, *Strafgesetzbuch: Kommentar*, 22nd Ed., Munich: C. H. Beck, 1982.

Schroedinger, Erwin, *What Is Life?* Cambridge: Cambridge University Press, 1944.

Schütz, Alfred, *The Phenomenology of the Social World*, trans. George Walsh and Frederick Lehnert, Evanston: Northwestern University Press, 1967; *Der sinnhafte Aufbau der sozialen Welt: Eine Einleitung in die verstehende Soziologie*, Vienna: Julius Springer, 1932; 1960; Frankfurt, Suhrkamp, 1981.

Schwemmer, Oswald, *Philosophie der Praxis*, Frankfurt: Suhrkamp, 1971.

Scitovsky, Tibor, "Pricemakers' Plenty: A Neglected Benefit of Capitalism," *Kyklos*, 38 (1985), pp. 517-36.

Seel, Gerhard, "Struktur und Geltung des wirtschaftlichen Handelns," in Karl Bärthlein and Gerd Wolandt, eds., *Lehrstücke der praktischen Philosophie und Ästhetik*, Basel: Schwabe, 1977, pp. 113-89.

Seelhammer, Nikolaus, "Doppelwirkung einer Handlung," *Lexikon für Theologie und Kirche*, Freiburg: Herder, 1959, Vol. III, pp. 516-17.

Sen, Amartya K., "Isolation, Assurance, and the Social Rate of Discount," *Quarterly Journal of Economics*, 81 (1967), pp. 112-24.

_____, "The Moral Standing of the Market," in Ellen Frankel Paul, Jeffrey Paul, and Fred D. Miller, Jr., eds., *Ethics and Economics*, Oxford: Basil Blackwell, 1985, pp. 1-19.

_____, *On Economic Inequality*, Oxford: Clarendon Press, 1973; 1997.

_____, *On Ethics and Economics*, Oxford: Basil Blackwell, 1987.

_____, "Plural Utility," *Proceedings of the Aristotelian Society*, 81 (1980/81), pp. 193-215.

_____, "Rational Fools: A Critique of the Behavioral Foundations of Economic Theory," *Philosophy and Public Affairs*, 6 (1976), 317-44.

Sen, Amartya and Bernard Williams, *Utilitarianism and Beyond*, 3rd Ed., Cambridge: Cambridge University Press, 1984.

Service, Elman R., *Origins of the State and Civilization: The Process of Cultural Evolution*, New York: W. W. Norton, 1975.

Shackle, George L. S., *Decision, Order, and Time in Human Affairs*, Cambridge: Cambridge University Press, 1961; 2nd Ed., 1969.

_____, *Epistemics and Economics: A Critique of Economic Doctrines*, Cambridge: Cambridge University Press, 1972.

_____, *Imagination and the Nature of Choice*, Edinburgh: Edinburgh University Press, 1979.

_____, "Time and Choice: Keynes Lecture in Economics 1976," *Proceedings of the British Academy*, 62 (1976), pp. 309-29.

Sidgwick, Henry, *The Scope and Method of Economic Science*, London: Macmillan, 1885.

Sihler, Helmut, "Ethik und Unternehmensführung," in Wissenschaftlichen Gesellschaft für Marketing und Unternehmensführung, ed., *Unternehmensführung in sozialer Verantwortung: Dokumentation einer Veranstaltung am 11. Mai 1987 in Münster*, pp. 25-31.

Simon, Herbert A., "Rationality as Process and as product of Thought," *American Economic Review*, 68 (1978), pp. 1-15.

Smart, J. J. C., "An Outline of a System of Utilitarian Ethics," in Smart and Bernard Williams, *Utilitarianism: For and Against*, Cambridge: Cambridge University Press, 1973, pp. 3-74.

Smith, Adam, *An Inquiry into the Nature and Causes of the Wealth of Nations*, London: W. Strahan and T. Cadell, 1776; Oxford: Clarendon Press, 1976.

_____, *The Theory of Moral Sentiments*, London: A. Millar, 1759; ed. E. G. West, Indianapolis: Liberty Classics, 1976.

Sombart, Werner, *The Quintessence of Capitalism: A Study of the History and Psychology of the Modern Business Man*, trans. Mortimer Epstein, London: T. F. Unwin, 1915; New York: Howard Fertig, 1967; *Der Bourgeois: Zur Geistesgeschichte des modernen Wirtschaftsmenschen*, Leipzig: Duncker & Humblot, 1913.

_____, *Die drei Nationalökonomien: Geschichte und System der Lehre von der Wirtschaft*, Leipzig: Duncker & Humblot, 1930; 2nd Ed., 1967.

_____, *Der moderne Kapitalismus: Historisch-systematische Darstellung des gesamteuropäischen Wirtschaftslebens von seinen Anfängen bis zur Gegenwart*, Leipzig: Duncker & Humblot, 1902; 1916; Munich: Deutscher Taschenbuch Verlag, 1987, Vol. II: *Das europäische Wirtschaftsleben im Zeitalter des Frühkapitalismus, vornehmlich im 16., 17. und 18. Jahrhundert.*

Spaemann, Robert, *Basic Moral Concepts*, trans. T. J. Armstrong, London: Routledge, 1989; *Moralische Grundbegriffe*, Munich: C. H. Beck, 1982.

_____, "Die Herausforderung," in *Mut zur Erziehung*, Stuttgart: Klett, 1978.

_____, "Nebenwirkungen als moralisches Problem," in Spaemann, *Kritik der politischen Utopie*, Stuttgart: Klett, 1977, pp. 167-82.

_____, *Reflexion und Spontaneität: Studien über Fénelon*, Stuttgart: Kohlhammer, 1963; 2nd Ed., Stuttgart: Klett-Cotta, 1990.

_____, "Über die Unmöglichkeit einer universalteleologischen Ethik," *Philosophisches Jahrbuch*, 88 (1981), pp. 70-89.

Spaemann, Robert and Reinhard Löw, *Die Frage Wozu? Geschichte und Wiederentdeckung des teleologischen Denkens*, Munich: Piper, 1981; 1985; 1991.

Specht, Rainer, *Innovation und Folgelast: Beispiele aus der neueren Philosophie- und Wissenschaftsgeschichte*, Stuttgart: Frommann, 1972.

Spinoza, Baruch, *Ethica ordine geometrico demonstrata*, 1677.

Spranger, Eduard, *Das Gesetz der ungewollten Nebenwirkungen in der Erziehung*, 6th Ed., Heidelberg: Quelle & Meyer, 1960.

_____, "Vom Wesen des Geistigen," in Spranger, *Gesammelte Schriften*, ed. Hans Walter Bähr, Tübingen: Max Niemeyer, 1980, Vol. VI: *Grundlagen der Geisteswissenschaften*, pp. 305-12.

_____, "Wilhelm Dilthey: Gedächtnisrede," in Spranger, *Vom pädagogischen Genius: Lebensbilder und Grundgedanken großer Erzieher*, Heidelberg: Quelle & Meyer, 1965.

_____, "Die Wirtschaft unter kulturphilosophischem Aspekt," in Spranger, *Kulturphilosophie und Kulturkritik*, ed. Hans Wenke, Tübingen: Niemeyer, 1969.

Stegmüller, Friedrich, "Zur Literaturgeschichte der Salmanticenser Theologen," *Theologische Revue*, 29 (1930), pp. 55-59.

_____, "Die spanischen Handschriften der Salmanticenser Theologen," *Theologische Revue*, 30 (1931), pp. 361-65.

Stegmüller, Wolfgang, *Probleme und Resultate der Wissenschaftstheorie und Analytischen Philosophie*, Berlin: Springer, 1973, Vol. IV: *Personelle und statistische Wahrscheinlichkeit*, Part I: *Personelle Wahrscheinlichkeit und rationale Entscheidung.*

Steiner, Rudolf, *Nationalökonomischer Kurs*, Dornach: Rudolf Steiner-Verlag, 1979.

Stigler, George J., "Economics or Ethics?" in *The Tanner Lectures on Human Values*, Salt Lake City: University of Utah Press; Cambridge: Cambridge University Press, 1981, Vol. II, pp. 143-92.

Sufrin, Sidney C., *Management of Business Ethics*, Port Washington, N. Y.: Kennikat Press, 1979.

Suppes, Patrick, "Decision Theory," in *Encyclopedia of Philosophy*, ed. Paul Edwards, New York: Macmillan, 1967, Vol. II, pp. 310-14.

_____, *Probabilistic Metaphysics*, Uppsala: University of Uppsala, 1974.

Surányi-Unger, Theo, "Scope and Problems of Economic Philosophy," *Zeitschrift für die gesamte Staatswissenschaft*, 116 (1960), pp. 385-401.

_____, *Wirtschaftsphilosophie des 20. Jahrhunderts*, Stuttgart: G. Fischer, 1967.

Tautscher, Anton, *Wirtschaftsethik*, Munich: M. Hüber, 1957.

Thielicke, Helmut, *Theological Ethics*, 2 vols., ed. William H. Lazareth, Philadelphia: Fortress Press, 1966; *Theologische Ethik*, Tübingen: J. C. B. Mohr (Paul Siebeck), 1965.

Thomas Aquinas, *Summa contra Gentiles*, trans. Vernon J. Bourke, Notre Dame, Ind.: University of Notre Dame Press, 1975.

_____, *Summa Theologiae*, trans. Fathers of the English Dominican Province, New York: Benzinger Brothers, 1948.

Thun-Hohenstein, Matteo, *Ein neues Affektverhältnis zwischen Mensch und Objekt*, unpublished manuscript, Vienna School of Applied Arts, October, 1984.

Troeltsch, Ernst, *The Social Teaching of the Christian Churches*, trans. Olive Wyon, Chicago: University of Chicago Press, 1981, Vol. I; *Die Soziallehren der christlichen Kirchen und Gruppen*, in *Gesammelte Schriften*, Tübingen: J. C. B. Mohr (Paul Siebeck), 1912, Vol. I.

Trux, Walter and Werner Kirsch, "Strategisches Management oder die Möglichkeit einer 'wissenschaftlichen' Unternehmensführung," *Die Betriebswirtschaft*, 39 (1979), pp. 215-35.

Tullock, Gordon, "An Application of Economics in Biology," in *Toward Liberty: Essays in Honor of Ludwig von Mises on the Occasion of his 90th Birthday*, Menlo Park: Institute for Humane Studies, 1971, Vol. II, pp. 375-91.

Ulrich, Peter, *Transformation der ökonomischen Vernunft: Fortschrittsperspektiven der modernen Industriegesellschaft*, Bern: P. Haupt, 1986.

Utz, Arthur Fridolin, ed., *Kann der Christ Marxist sein? Muß er Kapitalist sein?* Bonn: WBV und Scientia Humana-Institut, 1982.

Van Leeuwen, Henry G., "Certainty in Seventeenth-Century Thought," in Philip P. Wiener, ed., *Dictionary of the History of Ideas: Studies of Selected Pivotal Ideas*, New York: Charles Scribner's Sons, 1968, Vol. I, pp. 304-11.

Ver Eecke, Wilfried, "Ethics in Economics," *Philosophy and Social Criticism*, 9 (1982), pp. 145-68.

Waibl, Elmar, *Ökonomie und Ethik: Die Kapitalismusdebatte in der Philosophie der Neuzeit*, Stuttgart-Bad Cannstatt: Frommann-Holzboog, 1984.

Waldstein, Wolfgang, "Ist das 'Suum cuique' eine Leerformel?" in *Ius Humanitatis* (Festschrift for Alfred Verdross), Berlin: Duncker & Humblot, 1980, pp. 285-320.

Weber, Max, *Economy and Society: An Outline of Interpretive Sociology*, trans. Ephraim Fischoff, *et al.*, ed. Guenther Roth and Claus Wittich, New York: Bedminster Press, 1968; Berkeley: University of California Press, 1978; *Wirtschaft und Gesellschaft: Grundriß der allgemeinen Wirtschaftsphilosophie*, Tübingen: J. C. B. Mohr (Paul Siebeck), 1921; 5th Ed., 1976.

_____, "The Social Psychology of the World Religions," in *From Max Weber: Essays in Sociology*, trans. and ed. H. H. Gerth and C. Wright Mills, New York: Oxford University Press, 1946, pp. 267-301.

Weber, Wilhelm, *Wirtschaftsethik am Vorabend des Liberalismus: Höhepunkt und Abschluß der scholastischen Wirtschaftsbetrachtung durch Ludwig Molina*, Münster: Aschendorff, 1959.

Weinberger, Ota, *Grundriß der allgemeinen Wirtschaftsphilosophie*, Berlin: Duncker & Humblot, 1958.

Weizsäcker, Carl Friedrich von, "Die Einheit von Wahrnehmen und Bewegen," in Weizsäcker, *Der Garten des Menschlichen: Beiträge zur geschichtlichen Anthropologie*, Frankfurt: S. Fischer, 1980, pp. 153-66.

Wiese, Leopold von, *Ethik in der Schauweise der Wissenschaften von der Gesellschaft*, Bern: Francke, 1947.

Williamson, Oliver E., "Firms and Markets," in Sidney Weintraub, ed., *Modern Economic Thought*, Philadelphia: University of Pennsylvania Press, 1977, pp. 185-202.

_____, "The Modern Corporation: Origins, Evolution, Attributes," *Journal of Economic Literature*, 19 (1981), pp. 1537-68; in Williamson, *The Economic Institutions of Capitalism: Firms, Markets, Relational Contracting*, New York: Free Press, 1985, pp. 273-97.

Wittgenstein, Ludwig, *Tractatus logico-philosophicus*, trans. David F. Pears and Brian F. McGuinness, London: Routledge & Kegan Paul, 1961; in *Werkausgabe*, Frankfurt: Suhrkamp, 1984, Vol. I, pp. 7-85.

Wolf, Julius, *Nationalökonomie als exakte Wissenschaft*, Leipzig: Deichert, 1908.
Wünsch, Georg, *Evangelische Wirtschaftsethik*, Tübingen: J. C. B. Mohr (Paul Siebeck), 1927.
Wundt, Wilhelm M., *System der Philosophie*, 2 vols., Leipzig: Engelmann, 1889; 3rd Ed., 1907.

INDEX OF PERSONS

Italicized numbers refer to occurrences of names in footnotes or the bibliography.

Aeschylus *136*, *247*
Agnelli, Giovanni 117
Albach, Horst *24*, *247*
Albee, Ernest *247*
Albert, Hans *82*, *215*, *247*
Albertus Magnus 157f., *247*
Alchian, Armen A. 130f., *238*, *247*
Alembert, Jean Le Rond d' 135
Anaxagoras 224
Anscombe, G. E. M. *137*, 139, *247*
Anshen, Melvin *247*
Aristotle *5*, 81, 96, 102, 108, 119, 184f., 199f., 202, 230, *247*
Arrow, Kenneth J. *25*, *247*
Augustine 49-51, *95*, *247*
Avicenna 157
Axelrod, Robert 24f., *45*, *247*

Backhaus, Jürgen *247*
Banfield, Edward C. *114*, *247*
Barrett, C. Richard *247*
Bartholomew Medina 136
Baudrillard, Jean 242, *247*
Baumol, William J. *114*, *169*, *190*, *247*
Bayes, Thomas 133-35
Becker, Gary S. 74f., *248*
Behrman, Jack N. *248*
Bell, Daniel 11, *248*
Bennett, Jonathan *248*
Beuys, Joseph *114*, *248*
Blaug, Mark *114*, *248*
Bobbitt, Philip *249*
Böhm-Bawerk, Eugen von *248*
Boje, David M. *8*, *259*
Bollnow, Otto Friedrich *90*, *248*
Bossuet, Jacques-Bénigne 52f., *248*
Boulding, Kenneth E. *114*, *248*
Bowen, William G. *114*, *247*
Bowie, Norman E. *248*
Boyle, Joseph M., Jr. *137*, 138, *248*
Brennan, Geoffrey *179*, *248*
Brentano, Lujo *213*, *248*
Briefs, Götz A. 178f., *248*
Brunner, Karl *248*
Buchanan, Allen E. *248*
Buchanan, James M. *9*, *18*, 27f., 45, *46*, 68, 108f., *171*, *179*, *217*, *230*, 237, *248f.*, *255*

Cajetan, Thomas de Vio 214f., *249*
Calabresi, Guido *249*
Carlyle, Thomas 15
Cicero, Marcus Tullius *86*
Cohen, G. A. *239*, *250*
Coleridge, Samuel Taylor 158, *250*
Cooper, Richard N. *181*, *250*
Croce, Benedetto *250*
Cucchi, Enzo *248*

Dam, Cornelis van *250*
Descartes, René 118
De George, Richard T. *6*, *250*
Dilthey, Wilhelm 87, *250*
Döllinger, Ignaz von *133*, *250*
Domingo de Santa Teresa 136, *140*
Douglas, Mary *250*
Driesch, Hans *156*, *250*
Duff, Robert Antony *137*, *250*
Dumont, Louis *214*, *250*
Dyke, Charles F. *250*

Eide, Kjell *115*, *117*, *250*
Elster, Jon 41, 47f., 69, *250*
Enderle, Georges *250*
Esser, Werner-Michael *254*
Euler, Leonhard 144

Falkinger, Josef *117*, *250*
Farquhar, Peter H. *251*
Fénelon, François 52f., *251*
Fichte, Johann Gottlieb 42, 245, *251*
Fischoff, Baruch *251*
Fishburn, Peter C. *251*
Forschner, Maximilian *251*
Forte, Francesco *242*, *251*
Foucault, Michel 148
Franke, Günter *251*
Freud, Sigmund 119

Gabele, Eduard *254*
Gäfgen, Gérard *251*
Gapinski, James H. *251*
Gauthier, David P. *251*
Georgescu-Roegen 7, 243, *251*
Ghoos, Jozef *136*, *251*
Gibbard, Allan *3*, *226*, *251*
Giers, Joachim *214*, *251*
Glastetter, Werner *251*
Goethe, Johann Wolfgang von *8*, 19, *252*
Grant, Nancy K. *252*
Greenwood, Peter H. *252*
Gresham, Thomas *179*
Grice-Hutchinson, Marjorie *136*, *252*
Grimm, J. *103*, *252*
Grimm, W. *103*, *252*
Grisez, Germain *137*, *248*
Gundlach, Gustav *157*, *252*
Gury, Jean Pierre 138, *252*

Habermas, Jürgen *217*
Hackmann, Johannes 233, *252*
Hahn, Frank *147f.*, *154*, *158*, *252*
Harrod, Roy Forbes *252*
Hayek, Friedrich A. von 154, *219*, 235f., *252*
Hegel, Georg Wilhelm Friedrich 19, 30, 33, *50*, 99, 118, 239, *252*
Hendon, William S. *114*, *252*
Henschel, Rudolf *252*
Heraclitus *103*, *252*
Herder, Johann Gottfried 30, *253*
Hesse, Helmut *229*, *253*
Hession, Charles H. *253*
Hicks, John R. 173, *253*
Hippel, Eike von *229*, *253*
Hirschman, Albert O. *173*, *253*
Hobbes, Thomas 13, 201, 216f., *249*
Höffner, Joseph *191*, *253*
Hohenemser, Christoph *251*
Hume, David *253*
Hünermann, Josef *260*
Husserl, Edmund 245

Ingene, Charles A. *252*
Innocent XII *53*

Jacobi, Carl Gustav Jacob 144
Jaeger, Werner Wilhelm *103*, *253*
Jahoda, Marie *119*, *253*
James, William 52
John of Saint Thomas 136, 138, *253*
Jöhr, Walter A. *253*
Jones, Donald G. *6*, *253*
Jung, Carl Gustav 48
Justinian *184*, *253*

Kant, Immanuel 4, 8, 13f., 30-36, 42, 45f., 59-67, *68*, 79, 100f., 104-7, 110f., 165, *200*, *226*, *253*
Katterle, Siegfried *253*
Kauder, Emil *215*, *254*
Keohane, Robert O. *181*, *254*
Keynes, John Maynard v, 11, 20, 135, *154*, *254*
Kiefer, Anselm *248*
Kierkegaard, Søren 46, 201, *254*
Kindleberger, Charles P. *181*, *254*
Kirsch, Werner *35*, *254*, *263*
Kirzner, Israel M. 148, 155, 157, *158*, *171*, *190*, *254*
Kliemt, Hartmut 160, *254*
Klomps, Heinrich *133*, *254*
Knauer, Peter *137*, *254*
Knight, Frank H. 151, *152*, *167*, 171, *238*, *239*, *240*, *254*
Koch, W. *254*
Kolm, Serge-Christophe *99*, *254*
Korff, Wilhelm *87*, *254*

Kornai, Janos *158*
Koslowski, Peter *4, 6, 11, 18, 19, 26, 48, 49, 50, 78, 107, 110, 113, 126, 131, 140, 151, 217, 242, 254-6*
Kounellis, Jannis *248*
Krasner, Stephen D. *181, 256*
Krings, Hermann *212, 256*
Külp, Bernhard *232, 256*

Lachmann, Ludwig M. *147*, 155, *158, 256*
Laffont, Jean-Jacques *256*
Lagrange, Joseph-Louis de 144
Lancaster, Kelvin *131, 256*
Leibniz, Gottfried Wilhelm 42, *48*, 99, *111*, 151, *256*
Lenin, Vladimir Ilyich 14, *256*
Letwin, Shirley Robin *136, 256*
Lévi-Strauss, Claude 118
Levy, S. S. *137, 256*
Lindenberg, Siegwart *256*
Lipsey, Richard G. *131, 256*
Locke, John 118
Löw, Reinhard *149, 256, 262*
Luce, R. Duncan *134, 256*
Luckmann, Thomas *33, 256*
Luhmann, Niklas *256*
Luijk, Henk van *256*

Mackie, John L. *137, 257*
Maier, Anneliese *13, 257*
Maiwald, Werner *257*
Mandeville, Bernard 13, 19-21, 141, *257*
Mangan, J. T. *136, 140, 257*
Marcus Aurelius 98, *257*
Marshall, Alfred 1, 24, *257*
Marx, Karl 13f., 118, 203f.
Matthews, R. C. O. *22, 61*, 64, *257*
Maupertuis, Pierre-Louis Moreau de 143ff., *257*
McCormick, Richard *137, 257*
McKenzie, Richard B. *44*, 66f., *257*
McNamara, L. J. *137, 257*
Meckling, William H. *248*
Menkes, Joshua *257*
Messner, Johannes *72*, 179, *188, 257*
Mill, John Stuart 225, 234f., *257*
Mises, Ludwig von *4, 13, 54*, 55f., 77, *143*, 147, 154f., 165-68, *198*, 221, *257*
Mishan, E. J. *6, 257*
Molina, Luis de *244, 257*
Moore, G. E. 20, 109, *257*
Morgenstern, Oskar *21, 257, 258*
Müller, Eberhard *260*
Müller, M. *137, 258*
Musgrave, Peggy B. *92, 258*
Musgrave, Richard A. *92, 258*

Nell-Breuning, Oswald von *9, 182, 185, 188*, 220, *222, 228, 245, 258*
Nelson, Benjamin N. *258*
Netzer, Dick *114, 258*
von Neumann, John *21, 258*
Newman, John Henry *134, 258*
Nider, Johannes 214, *258*
Nisbet, Robert *230, 258*
Noonan, John T., Jr. *215, 258*
Nozick, Robert 237f., *258*

Oakeshott, Michael *239, 258*
Oelmüller, Willi *258*
Olson, Mancur *32, 258*

Parfit, Derek *258*
Pascal, Blaise 7, 135, *258*
Pattanaik, Prasanta K. *247*
Peacock, Alan T. *131, 237, 259, 260*
Pesch, Heinrich *34*, 195, *259*
Peter Lombard *111, 259*
Pichler, Joseph A. *250*
Pico della Mirandola *158, 259*
Pieper, Josef *102, 197, 212, 259*
Pius XI *44, 259*
Plato 31f., 74, 83f., 102-7, 126, 184, 230, 241f., *259*
Polanyi, Karl 214, *259*
Pondy, Louis R. *8, 259*
Popper, Karl 56f., *259*
Pseudo-Dionysius Areopagita 110f., *259*

Radbruch, Gustav *125, 259*
Raiffa, Howard *134, 256*
Rawls, John 230f., *259*
Recktenwald, Horst C. *259*
Reder, Melvin W. *259*
Regan, Tom *6, 259*
Rescher, Nicholas *259*
Reusch, Friedrich Heinrich *133, 250*
Ricardo, David 14
Rich, Arthur *2, 259*
Rickert, Heinrich *14*, 63, *87, 259*
Riesenhuber, Klaus *260*
Riesman, David *120, 260*
Riklin, Alois *19, 260*
Rinderspacher, Jürgen P. *120, 260*
Robbins, Lionel *143, 260*
Robertson, Dennis H. 245, *260*
Röpke, Wilhelm *260*
Romberg, R. *260*
de Roover, Raymond A. *215, 260*
Roth, Alois *245, 260*
Rothbard, Murray N. *147, 260*
Rowley, Charles K. *131, 237, 259, 260*

Sainte-Foi, Charles *133, 260*
Samuelson, Paul A. *143, 260*
Sartre, Jean-Paul 129, *260*
Scheler, Max 84-87, 106f., 118, 130, *180, 260*
Schelling, Friedrich W. J. von 150, 158, *261*
Schelling, Thomas C. *261*
Schleiermacher, Friedrich E. D. 100f., 104-7, *261*
Schmoller, Gustav *261*
Schöllgen, Werner *179, 261*
Schönke, Adolf *125, 261*
Schopenhauer, Arthur 184
Schröder, Horst *125, 261*
Schroedinger, Erwin *243, 261*
Schumpeter, Joseph Alois *155*
Schütz, Alfred 77f., *261*
Schwemmer, Oswald 43f., *261*
Scitovsky, Tibor 191, *261*
Seel, Gerhard *261*
Seelhammer, Nikolaus *140, 261*
Sen, Amartya K. *28, 238, 261*
Service, Elman R. *261*
Shackle, George L. S. *91, 127, 130, 135*, 146, 155, *158, 261f.*
Shanahan, James L. *114, 252*
Shaw, Douglas V. *252*
Sidgwick, Henry 14f., *262*
Sihler, Helmut *15, 262*
Simon, Herbert A. 76, *245, 262*
Smart, J. J. C. *233, 262*
Smith, Adam 2, 4, 9, 13, 19f., 39, 44, *217, 262*
Socrates 103
Solon of Athens 103, 242
Sombart, Werner 14, *34*, 118, *142*, 207, *215, 262*
Spaemann, Robert *6, 53, 76, 125, 137, 149, 202, 203, 256, 262*
Specht, Rainer *137, 262*
Spinoza, Baruch *208, 262*
Spranger, Eduard *11*, 87f., *90, 114*, 125, *262f.*
Stallaert, Luud M. *250*
Stegmüller, Friedrich *136, 263*
Stegmüller, Wolfgang *132, 263*
Steiner, Rudolf *263*
Stigler, George J. *263*
Strigl, Richard 82
Sufrin, Sidney C. *263*
Suppes, Patrick *132, 134, 263*
Surányi-Unger, Theo *263*

Tautscher, Anton *263*
Thielicke, Helmut *136, 263*
Thomas Aquinas 19, *44, 86, 111, 184, 214, 263*
Thun-Hohenstein, Matteo 116, *263*
Tönnies, Ferdinand 10
Tollefsen, Olaf *248*
Troeltsch, Ernst 49, 51, *263*
Troy, Helen *6, 253*
Trux, Walter *35, 263*
Tullock, Gordon *46, 126, 249, 264*

Uexküll, Jakob von 7
Ulpian (Domitius Ulpianus) *184*

Ulrich, Peter *264*
Utz, Arthur Fridolin *264*

Van Leeuwen, Henry G. *136*, *264*
Ver Eecke, Wilfried *264*

Waibl, Elmar *264*
Waldstein, Wolfgang *184*, *209*, *264*
Weber, Max 14, *34*, 54-6, 58, 90, 154, *264*
Weber, Wilhelm *264*
Weinberger, Ota *264*
Weizsäcker, Carl Friedrich von *7*, *264*
Whitehead, Alfred North *158*
Wiese, Leopold von *264*
Williams, Bernard *261*
Williamson, Oliver E. *23*, *36*, *171*, *264*
Wiseman, Jack 155
Wittgenstein, Ludwig 48, 57, *264*
Wolf, Julius *193*, *265*
Wünsch, Georg *265*
Wundt, Wilhelm *90*, *265*

INDEX OF SUBJECTS

acedia 119
action
    cultural shaping of action decisions 112f.
    effects of as causal effects 130f.
    effects of one's own 75ff., 123ff.
    ethical conduct of managers 174ff.
    ethically good 96, 108ff., 137ff., 208ff., 239
    individuality of 63f.
    intrinsically bad 135, 139
    necessary conditions of meaningful economic action 172
    pre-coordination of 68ff.
    strategic 39ff.
    summation problem of individual actions 71
    theory of human action 164ff., 244
    unity of moral action 104ff.
    and virtue 96f.
    see also decision, rationality
advantage 174ff.
    from quasi-monopolistic position 23, 170
    greater advantage from rule compliance 41ff.
    mutual 18, 25, 32, 122, 195ff., 218
    short-term 22f., 42, 178, 181, 206
aesthetics 82, 87ff., 109ff.
allocation 152, 181ff., 218, 220, 225ff.
    versus distribution 225ff.
    in global price structure 228
    suboptimal allocation of resources 23
    in utilitarianism 231ff.
altruism 24f., 74f.
anonymity 9
    facilitating rule-breaking 27f.
anticipation 25, 43, 68, 70f., 130f., 152f.
a priori 14, 30, 54, 56ff., 73f., 85, 147
appropriateness to the nature of the matter (*Sachgerechtigkeit*) 13, 101ff., 106, 181ff., 184ff., 192ff., 206f., 209, 219, 224
art 87, 93, 95, 121f., 124
assurance game 29, 41ff., 47, 51, 66, 69, 124, 179
attentiveness 7, 173, 245f.
autonomy
    of the economy 10, 213f.
    of scientific and technological research 8
    of will and action 14, 60f.

bankruptcy 177, 196f.
Bayesian decision rule 133ff.
bribery 176ff., 182.

capital formation 44f., 229
capitalism 11, 110, 215
categorical imperative 14, 30f., 43, 46, 61f., 65f., 74, 79, 81, 102, 106, 137, 180, 209
    see also universalization
category 142, 155, 211
caveat emptor 194
claims, justice of 229
    criterion of the justified claim 237f.
cognition 143, 147f.
common good 18, 21, 32ff., 50, 141, 170, 181, 207
communist society 204
community 10, 118, 185
commutative justice 102, 182f., 184ff., 192ff., 197ff., 211, 213, 241f.
competition
    competitive market 37, 38, 169ff., 174ff., 179, 182, 185f., 219

mechanism of 169ff.
perfect 18, 21, 40, 67f., 169ff., 189ff.
composition, problem of 70f.
conflicts 203f.
constraints 131
consumption
coordination of subjective consumer needs 59
culture of 10f., 115ff.
of culture 94
ethics of 101
contingency 235f., 238
contract 18, 21ff., 32, 36f., 38ff., 68f., 101, 170, 186, 200ff., 204ff., 211ff.
commutative justice of 189f., 195ff.
implicit social contract of the price system 212
control 17, 37, 38, 64, 66, 72f., 95, 114, 123ff., 205, 215ff.
impossibility of 21ff.
cooperation, social 24f., 72, 159, 203
coordination
coordination system 17f., 215ff.
corrective for lack of 72ff.
criteria of social coordination 67, 219
economic coordination by the market 2f., 38, 60ff., 67ff., 93
ethics as form of social coordination 59ff.
purpose of 80
social 1, 69f.
uncontrolled 25
see also competition, pre-coordination through ethics, price system,
corporate ethics 34f.
corporate culture 4, 111, 114
corporate identity 113f., 121
costs 58f., 97, 179
of economic ethics 174ff.
of environmental pollution 243
critical realism 142f., 147f.
culture 9ff., 87
consumption of 94
of consumption 10f., 115ff.
corporate 4, 111, 114
cultivation/refinement of the economy 120
cultural economics 4, 112ff.
cultural marketing 116f.
cultural philosophy 87, of the economy 4, 11f., 112, 142
cultural society 120
the economy as cultural sphere 77, 111, 112ff.
post-industrial 116
of production 10f., 114f.

deception 194
decision 6ff., 17ff., 42f., 47f., 56ff., 68, 81, 100f., 106, 146f., 160, 169, 188, 200ff., 211, 219, 234, 244f.
analysis 48, 132
anticipation of decisions of others 40, 70ff.
decision problem 128ff.
duty of making responsible decisions 21, 197
models 43
political 76
professional-ethical decisions 140
systems 17f., 59, 70, 72, 125, 218, 242
theory 123ff.
degrees of publicness 86, 91ff., 108, 175
democracy 18, 59, 70, 204, 215, 242f.
development, ethical-cultural 96f.
development policy 117ff., 229
difference principle 230
diriger l'intention 135
dirigisme 228
discourse
ethical and religious 34
ideal 203f.
of market and democracy 241ff.
social 159ff.
theory 217
distribution 225ff., 235ff.

distributive justice 102, 213, 227, 229, 236, 240
double effect, principle of 125, 137ff., 177
duty
ethical 1, 55, 81, 96ff., 104ff., 176f., 183, 199, 201, 207f.
of making responsible decisions 21, 197

ecology 6f., 78, 241ff.
economic ethics 140f., 244ff.
defined 1ff., 36
and competition 169ff.
costs of 174ff.
as decision theory 129
function of 34f.
imperative of 182, 185, 245
economic/market failure 20ff., 26ff., 32f., 37f., 40, 64, 70, 92, 96, 169ff.
economic man, see *homo oeconomicus*
economic order 12, 38ff., 110, 157ff., 187, 203ff.
economic principle, see rationality, principle of
economic surpluses/rents
consumer's and producer's surpluses 170f., 175, 199ff.
quasi-rents 3, 99, 198ff.
rent seeking 171, 202, 205
see also profit
economics 13ff., 112ff., 142ff., 244ff.
defined 8, 98f.
Austrian school 67f., 143., 147., 154f., 166ff.
bio-economics 39, 78, 113
cultural 4, 112ff.
economic law-governed regularity 14, 124, 147
economic theory 1ff., 12f., 39f., 72, 78f., 92, 111, 153f., 166ff., 186, 222, 244f.
environmental 7f.
interpretive 77f., 167
macroeconomics 13, 77f., 112f., 167, 222
microeconomics 1, 15, 40, 127, 144, 189
neo-classical 13f., 21, 127, 143f., 154f., 158, 165f.
New Institutional 3
positive 61, 167, 195
universal 108, 123
economies of scale 23, 117, 121, 135
economy
as context of meaning 77f.
cultural philosophy of the 4, 11f., 112, 142
global 227ff.
not an ethically-neutral zone 37, 141, 171, 173
objective goal of 182, 206f., 209ff., 217, 220ff., 226
ontology of 142
planned 21, 179, 219
education 88, 120, 226, 228
law of unintended side effects in education 125
income effect of better information and education 234f.
efficiency 18f., 67f., 159f., 169ff., 218, 244f.
entelechial 159f.
no optimal efficiency with pursuit of mere self-interest 22, 46
as a social good 18f.
egalitarianism 230, 233f.
egoism 19f., 24f., 51, 75, 141, 176, 216
embedded economy 214
end-state justice 235, 240f.
enduring 7f., 32, 62, 75ff., 90
energy 7f., 113, 243
libidinal 100
entrepreneur, see manager
entropy 243
environment 40ff., 89, 93f., 117ff., 241
defined 7
environmental economics 7f.
environmental ethics 78
equality 18, 185, 204, 209, 230, 233ff.

equivalence principle 184f.
equilibrium, general 21, 67f., 149ff., 153ff., 169f.
  equilibrium system 156
  inconceivability of objective, general equilibrium 149ff., 170
equity, ethical 199ff.
erosion of ethical standards 178ff., 184
error 145f.
esprit de finesse/esprit de géometry 7, 124
ethical economy 11ff., 78ff., 108f., 112, 123, 140f., 142f., 223, 244ff.
  defined 1ff., 164ff.
  as economic theory of the ethical or ethics related to economics 3
  as substantive theory of goods and cultural economics 4f.
  as theory of the ethical presuppositions of the economy 3f.
ethical failure 31ff., 38f., 52
ethics
  as ability to endure 75ff.
  consequentialist 129ff.
  corporate 34f.
  as corrective for economic/market failure 26
  deontological 13ff., 36, 80, 81, 92, 96ff., 104, 106, 124, 199, 207ff.
  dualism of ethics and economics 14ff., 109, 123ff., 165ff.
  environmental 241ff.
  ethical principles 226
  as form of social coordination 59ff.
  formal 38ff., 60, 63f., 67ff., 73f., 79f., 81f., 91, 106
  function of 10, 34f., 78f. 81f., 129
  individual and social 110
  Kantian 64ff.
    see also categorical imperative
  natural law 13, 62f., 66, 106, 141, 187, 191, 215ff., 241
  necessity of 20ff., 25ff., 40
  as obligation to self 69f., 72, 208
  philosophical 1, 5, 14ff., 33
  substantive/material ethics of values 80, 81ff., 85f., 92, 96, 106ff.
  unity of 1ff., 36f., 102, 104ff., 208
  utilitarian 2, 76, 130f., 231, 234f.
  virtue ethics 96ff.
  see also *pacta sunt servanda*
eudaemonism 51f., 83f.
evolution, theory of 150
exception/excuse, problem of 26, 28, 41, 45ff., 64ff.
exchange 21f., 32, 39, 95, 102f., 182f., 152f., 159, 173f., 182f., 184ff., 212f., 215ff., 227f., 230, 242f.
  mutually-advantageous 122, 195ff.
expectations 229
  rational 153f.
experiences 89ff.
externalities see side effects

fairness 23, 191, 201, 211
  toward nature 243
fallacy, naturalistic 160ff., 216
form of the good 31, 83f., 105ff., 207ff.
formalism 73, 223
  objections to 80
formality 78ff.
free rider problem 27, 64, 179
freedom, see liberty

game theory
  assurance game 29, 41ff., 47, 51, 66, 69, 124, 179
  game-theoretical instability of economic behavior 27ff.
  and justice 235ff.
  of rational action 39ff.
  super-assurance game 41ff., 47, 51, 78
  unassurance game of sinking marginal morality 179
gnosis, Christian 53
good
  highest 83ff, 105ff.

idea/form of the good 31, 83f., 105ff., 207ff.
goods 121, 231
defined 82
allocation and distribution of 225
individual 189f.
merit 92
public 86, 91ff., 124, 175ff., 227
sham 186, 192ff., 199, 204
theories of 4, 14, 36, 80, 82ff., 88f., 92, 105f., 108, 194, 207f.
weighing of 110, 135ff.
government
governmental action 59, 239f.
governmental failure 25, 70
market correction by the state 220ff., 226
price-setting by the state 218f.
world government as political action center in global market 228

happiness 49ff., 75, 208
convergence of morality and 31
pursuit of 49ff., 53, 83
hedonism 10f.
hidden reserves of the good "ethics" 178
homo actus 148
homo agens 148
homo faber 121
homo oeconomicus 5, 25, 39f., 43f., 47, 121, 144, 148, 167
homo strategus 39
homogeneity of goods 190
human persons 11, 20, 151, 173f., 217f., 245f.
best and strongest motives of 1, 15f.
conditions of human finitude 30
and God 52ff.
human action 52, 56, 110, 145f., 150, 163f., 167f., 205, 244
human nature 110, 216f.
and nature 241ff.
rediscovery of 6, 8f.
relationship of the human person to him/herself 101, 208ff.
religious-ethical person as global maximizer 41ff.
and work 118ff.
human rights and rights of nature 241f.

idea of the good 31, 83f., 105ff., 207ff.
idealism, German 15, 95
idealistic self-over-evaluation 30
imagination
creative 127, 141, 158
po(i)etic/poietic 121f., 157f.
impartiality 203f., 219
imperative, categorical, see categorical imperative
imperative of economic ethics 182, 185, 245
inclination 44, 81, 97f., 100
inclusion of persons affected 17ff., 43f., 47f., 67, 73ff., 125, 212, 219f.
income
unjustified 193ff.
marginal utility of 231ff
individual persons 156f.
individual price 173, 186ff., 201, 211, 222
individualism 49f.
economic 60
religious 51
information
as substitute for energy 8
see also education
inheritance 118, 225f., 229, 239
innovation 171, 198f.
institutions 1f., 16, 90, 113, 161ff.
integration, political and economic, with international exchange relationships 227ff.
intentionality 41, 47, 143, 147f., 165f., 172ff.
interaction patterns 21, 70ff., 152
interdependence of utility functions 75f.

interests 135, 201ff.
just balancing of interests 186, 201f.
see also *diriger l'intention*
internalization of side effects 17ff., 43f., 48, 54, 67f., 74, 125, 212, 219f., 243
impossibility of complete internalization 21
international price justice 227
interpretative sociology 77f., 112, 167
intuition 56, 124
investment 239
in ethical conduct 97
invisible hand 18ff., 141
irreversibility 190
"is" and "ought" 89ff., 161, 164
isolation paradox 28ff., 34
iustitia commutativa 102, 182f., 184ff., 192ff., 197ff., 211ff., 241f.
iustitia distributiva 102, 213, 227, 229, 236, 240
iustitia legalis 102

just price 12f., 185ff., 198ff., 205, 211ff., 227, 229
early-modern just price theory 191, 212ff.
according to natural law 187, 191, 213ff., 215ff.
post-modern just price theory 221ff.
presumption that the market price is just 188f., 191, 216ff., 228
see also, price justice, international price justice
justice
of claims 229, 237f.
commutative 102, 182f., 184ff., 192ff., 197ff., 211, 213, 241f.
criteria of 197ff., 212f., 218ff.,
distributive 102, 213, 227, 229, 236, 240
divine 42
end-state 235, 240f.
minimal norms 215
problem of 80, 225
procedural 223ff., 238f., 240
as satisfaction of a criterion 229ff.
structural 223ff.
see also price justice

knowledge 202
asymmetric 21f., 64, 170

labor see work
law 199ff.
economic 14, 124, 143, 147, 185, 244
of ethical universalization and market coordination 60ff.
of intended side effects in the firm 125ff.
international 213
just 102ff.
legal systems 40, 102, 187, 222
of nature 7, 104, 167, 143ff.
obedience of 46
problem of enforcement 22
least action, principle of 57, 143ff., 150
legitimation
of institutions 163f.
of the market system 163
of the price system 215ff.
of rules 207
leisure time 115ff.
liberalism, classical 220
liberty/freedom 2, 14f., 34f., 61, 73f., 162ff., 194
of creative work 118
economic 10, 159
and equality 18, 204, 209
in relation to the market mechanism 171ff.
rights of nature 241ff.
logic 56f.
love 42, 48ff., 86, 213, 245
luck 235ff.
see also contingency
lying 63, 139

manager/entrepreneur 113, 127f., 157ff.
entrepreneur as arbitrageur 155f.
"ethical" manager 175ff., 179
innovative entrepreneur 198
managerial action 124ff., 139ff.
as maximizer of positive side effects in the firm 125ff.
market
as automatic mechanism 21
as coordination mechanism 20f., 38, 58f.
free market 18, 223
global market 155, 227ff.
labor market 23
market data 148
market form 172f., 186f., 191, 222
market process 68, 151ff.
market theory 18, 61, 79, 143f., 151, 165
opportunities for individual participation 225ff.
perfect market 190
as social discourse 159ff., 217
see also economic failure, price, price formation, society
market economy 11, 19, 38, 69, 73, 79, 159, 169ff., 186ff., 211, 223, 235f.
as teleological mechanism 151ff.
marketing 89, 113, 115ff., 121
materialism 15
materiality 78ff.
maximization 91, 129f.
of existence 12, 107f., 210
global and local 39ff., 46ff., 51f., 54, 65, 73ff., 124, 181, 206f.
of positive side effects 124, 128
of profit 18, 35, 170ff.
of utility 25f., 43, 85, 130f., 144ff., 231ff.
maxims 14f., 25, 28ff., 44ff., 51, 60ff., 73f., 79f., 82, 100, 107, 130f., 164, 169, 182f., 185, 206f., 239, 245
maxims as object of universalization 63
the universal as maxim of the acting person 25, 28
maximum
compossible value-realization 78, 107f., 124, 207, 210
expansion of limits of realizable maximum 95
impossibility of direct intention on a global maximum 48
meaning 9f., 14f., 48
of action 42, 47, 114, 119, 172, 179, 166
context of 77ff.
cultural understanding of 86ff., 112f.
of ethics 31ff., 42, 246
of work 117ff.
mechanics 12, 143ff., 150, 152f., 156
mechanism
of competition 169ff.
market not a deterministic mechanism of equilibrium 164f.
teleological 151ff., 159, 164ff.
universal 149ff.
metaethics 5, 17
metaphysics 12, 33ff., 40, 142
see also religion
modernity 13ff., 120f.
money 44, 185, 196
monetary calculation 55
monopoly
of the resources of one's own actions 22ff.
natural 170
breaking up 189
moral aggression 9
moralism 9, 30, 36, 213
morality 14f.
and advantage 174ff.
and efficiency 244ff.
marginal 178ff., 184
meaning of 31ff., 42, 246
transcendental 30
see also ethics
motivation to act ethically 65, 96, 175ff., 205

national product 60, 225ff., 229, 234
naturalistic fallacy 160ff., 216
nature 6f., 39, 63, 110, 146, 152
  forces of (*Naturwüchsigkeit*) 215ff.
  justice in exchange with 241ff.
  laws of 7, 104, 167, 143ff.
  natural economics 78, 98
nepotism 23
non-zero-sum game 236
norms 5, 10, 36, 69, 112, 189, 204, 211, 213ff., 221f.

ontology 39, 46f., 52f., 62, 78, 103, 109, 241f.
  economic 12f., 142ff., 173f.
  entelechial 151f.
  ontological trust 33f.
  process ontology 223ff., 240
operations research 128f.
optimality 68
  unattainability of absolute 130f.
order
  economic 12, 38ff., 110, 157ff., 187, 203ff.
  social 1, 15, 38ff., 80, 154, 157, 161f., 222, 234f.
organism 104, 142, 150ff., 243
  social 156f.
ownership 3, 11, 59, 186f., 211, 216, 222, 225, 229, 237ff., 243

pacta sunt servanda 3, 36f., 39f., 65, 207
paradox of choice 135f., 146
Pareto principle 153, 202, 237
penetration
  of the economy, normative 9f., 214
  of the social sphere 11, 121f.
perfection
  of action 36, 110, 141, 244f.
  degree of the perfection of the economy 205f.
  the good as 108ff.
Phillips curve 140
philosophy 120, 142
  cultural 4, 11f., 87, 112, 142
  political 2, 188, 211
  practical 4ff., 108
physics 12, 144f., 150
planned economy 21, 179, 219
po(i)etic imagination 121f., 157f.
political economy 11f., 108, 188, 211, 223, 243
  defined 1ff.
politics
  expansion policy 11
  foreign cultural policy 116f.
  political co-determination 18
  political philosophy and political economy 211
  political structural conditions 1, 186ff.
post-modern just price theory 221ff.
postulates, theory of 31f., 42, 66, 159
power 6f., 161f., 164, 180f., 202f.
  exploitation of 193
pragmatism, morally irrelevant 14
precision 128f.
pre-coordination through ethics 68ff.
predicament, exploitation of 193f., 196f.
preferences
  question of the arbitrariness of 79f.
  formation of 82
price
  actual 187f., 191, 211
  constant 198
  fair 173, 201, 204
  global market 227ff.
  individual 173, 186ff., 201, 211, 222
  joining the prevailing price 101, 186ff., 197f., 205, 211
  market 9, 21, 55, 169, 182, 186ff., 195, 197ff., 205, 211ff.
  signals 59, 169, 211
  wage and interest rates 215
  see also just price
price formation 187, 212ff.
  determining factors of prices 221ff.
  market price formation 9, 55, 189, 191, 209, 212ff.

price-setting 191f., 218f.
price justice 173, 182, 185ff., 197ff., 212ff., 218ff., 241
price discrimination 191, 201
see also just price, international price justice
price system 181ff., 215ff., 218f., 225f., 239f.
coordination of 67ff., 78f., 81, 141, 169f., 184, 225
price taking 21, 27, 169ff., 189ff.
prisoner's dilemma 26ff., 46, 64ff., 124, 180, 237
probabilism
objections to probabilistic decision calculus 134ff.
probabilistic decision calculus 131ff.
probabilistic just price theory 212ff.
probabilitas externa 133f., 136, 139
probabilitas interna 134, 136, 140
procedural justice 223ff., 238f., 240
production 10ff., 203, 225,
culture of 10f., 114f.
factors of 127, 158
innovations 171, 198f.
producers 11, 89, 113, 159, 170f., 179, 191
products 109, 115f.
see also economies of scale
profit 130, 155, 169ff., 215, 225
pioneer 198
maximization 18, 35, 170ff.
progress, technological 117ff.
proper conduct, or appropriateness to the nature of the matter (*Sachgerechtigkeit*) 13, 101ff., 106, 181ff., 184ff., 192ff., 206f., 209, 219, 224
property, question of 11
publicness of goods
degrees of 86, 91ff., 108, 175
semi-public goods 94ff., 124, 175ff., 180f.
rationality
expanded 39, 78
of formal ethics 81, 91f.
instrumental/formal (*Zweckrationalität*) and substantive/material (*Wertrationalität*) 54ff., 58ff.
"super-rationality" 38f., 42
theory of rational action 1f., 39ff.
rationality, principle of (or economic principle) 1f., 46, 73f., 76, 143f., 147, 150
defined 54
a priori character of 54ff., 74
rationalization 39f., 117f.
reality 20f., 29f., 34f., 40ff., 142f., 147ff., 154ff., 165f.
reason 2, 205, 209
practical reason 13f., 31, 42, 65, 79
primacy of practical reason 8
redistribution 237
religion 17, 37, 38ff., 46ff., 65f., 68f., 72f., 79, 86, 93, 95, 120, 180, 206f.
as corrective for ethical failure 31ff., 51f.
religious failure 33
responsibility 2, 7, 10, 21f., 118, 128, 134, 164, 175f., 190, 194, 233f., 238, 243
and conscientiousness 22
rules 17, 58f., 71f., 81f., 235ff., 239f.
of a code of corporate ethics 34f.
of commutative justice 192, 198f., 205ff.
ethical 181ff.
exceptions 46ff.
Golden Rule 62
regulative principles 211f.
trust in rule-compliance 22, 96

sanction 24f., 27, 41, 68f., 194, 205
sanction of public opinion 179, 202
saving 44
and capital formation as proto-ethical phenomena 45
and investment as ethos of inner-worldly asceticism 11

scarcity 17, 56, 93, 110, 115, 152, 188, 203f., 226, 245
  not sole factor of price determination 220ff.
scientism 129, 137, 166f., 173
self-delusion 193f.
self-fulfilling prophecy 32, 148f., 179
self-interest 1, 15, 17ff., 22, 32f., 34ff., 44ff., 64f., 74, 93, 97f., 141, 180ff.
  transcendence of immediate 38ff., 48ff., 72, 206ff.
self-legislation 89
  of the market 14, 21
self-realization 49, 111, 118, 152, 160ff., 204, 206, 208, 245
sham goods 186, 192ff., 199, 204
side effects 128ff., 241ff.
  defined 6ff., 125
  between experiences and value convictions 89ff.
  controlling 12, 123ff.
  intended/positive 7, 18ff., 36f., 75, 95, 98ff., 123ff., 125ff., 141
  internalization of 17ff., 21, 43f., 48, 54, 67f., 74, 125, 212, 219f., 243
slack 171, 175, 200
Social Darwinism 234f.
social order 1, 15, 38ff., 80, 154, 157, 161f., 222, 234f.
society 9ff., 67, 94ff., 117ff., 204, 209f.
  ancient 212f.
  market 10, 18, 27, 58f., 67
  service 8, 113ff.
  theory of 224f.
  with neither market nor ethical failure 38
  work in 117ff.
sociobiology 78, 126
sociology, interpretative 77f., 112, 167
spillovers, social 124
standard wage 215
stock market 190
strike 193
structural justice 223ff.
subjective value-realization 160ff.
subjectivism 226f.
  value subjectivism 160ff.
  subjective economics 164ff.
subjectivity
  preservation of 220
  realization of 160, 163
  transcendence of 43ff.
sublimation 123
  economics of 98ff.
super-assurance game 41ff., 47, 51, 78
suum cuique 184ff., 205ff.
symbiosis 7, 126ff.

tâtonnement 153
technology 6, 11f., 112ff., 120f.
  technological progress 117ff.
teleology 81, 88, 142, 151ff., 159, 163ff., 220
terms of trade 228f.
thought 56f., 145, 149
time
  and attentiveness 245
  saving 242f.
  temporal transcendence of present utility 45
  time horizon of maximization 42, 44f.
tit-for-tat strategy 24f.
transaction costs 20, 23ff., 36f., 38ff., 64f., 71, 170, 205
transcendence
  of economics and ethics 32ff.
  strategic, moral, and religious transcendence of subjectivity 47
  transcendental ideal 153ff.
trust 3, 21ff., 69, 178
  in the meaning of ethics 31ff.
  ontological 33f.
truth 20
  no ultimate assurance of the truth of religion 33
uncertainty 24, 36, 131ff., 230
  about the consequences of actions 20f., 128ff.

about the rule-compliance of other persons 27ff.
reduction of 69ff.
understanding, theory of 87ff.
unethical practices 181f.
universalization, ethical 27ff., 41, 45ff., 59ff., 124
the universal 25ff., 37, 50, 54, 63f.
universalization ideal 80, 106
universalization problem 64f., 237
see also categorical imperative
unity of ethics 1ff., 36f., 102, 104ff., 208
usury 214f.
utilitarianism 2, 76, 130f., 231, 234f.
utility 14, 18, 42ff., 74ff., 82f., 88, 92ff., 99, 123, 133ff., 145, 181, 208, 219
maximization 25f., 43, 85, 130f., 144ff., 231ff.
utopias 118, 203f., 228

value
in exchange 85, 116, 186f.
loss of values and norms 10
rank-ordering of values 87ff., 104f.
subjective value-realization 160ff.
in use 85, 116
value convictions/judgments 10, 61, 89ff., 123, 160ff., 166, 223
value experience 87ff.
value of life and dignity of the person 110
value-qualities 4, 79f., 82ff., 91ff., 104ff., 111, 113, 124, 175, 241
value subjectivism 160ff.
variational principles 144f.
veil of ignorance 230
virtue 1, 4, 11, 36, 86, 110, 176, 183, 184ff., 208ff.
commutative justice as 197ff.
as means and end 208
virtue ethics 96ff.
virtue-duty 100f.
virtue of justice 93f., 102ff., 200ff.
see also unity of ethics

wage 126f.
just 236
standard 215
war 213
wealth 119, 186
inheritance of 225f.
loss of 192, 195f.
potential and realized 195
welfare 24f., 37, 95, 117, 228
will 205, 207f.
wisdom 99
work/labor 8, 119ff., 127
character of in the post-industrial economy 113f.
ethics of 5, 10f., 21ff.
labor contract 21, 23, 200
labor market 23
redistribution of 120
in society 117ff.
unemployment 19, 117ff., 140
work relationship 23
worker motivation 34ff.
worker, question of the 11
see also wage

Issues in Business Ethics

1. G. Enderle, B. Almond and A. Argandoña (eds.): *People in Corporations.* Ethical Responsibilities and Corporate Effectiveness. 1990 ISBN 0-7923-0829-8
2. B. Harvey, H. van Luijk and G. Corbetta (eds.): *Market Morality and Company Size.* 1991 ISBN 0-7923-1342-9
3. J. Mahoney and E. Vallance (eds.): *Business Ethics in a New Europe.* 1992 ISBN 0-7923-1931-1
4. P.M. Minus (ed.): *The Ethics of Business in a Global Economy.* 1993 ISBN 0-7923-9334-1
5. T.W. Dunfee and Y. Nagayasu (eds.): *Business Ethics: Japan and the Global Economy.* 1993 ISBN 0-7923-2427-7
6. S. Prakash Sethi: *Multinational Corporations and the Impact of Public Advocacy on Corporate Strategy.* Nestle and the Infant Formula Controversy. 1993 ISBN 0-7923-9378-3
7. H. von Weltzien Hoivik and A. Føllesdal (eds.): *Ethics and Consultancy: European Perspectives.* 1995 ISBN Hb 0-7923-3377-2; Pb 0-7923-3378-0
8. P. Ulrich and C. Sarasin (eds.): *Facing Public Interest.* The Ethical Challenge to Business Policy and Corporate Communications. 1995 ISBN 0-7923-3633-X; Pb 0-7923-3634-8
9. H. Lange, A. Löhr and H. Steinmann (eds.): *Working Across Cultures.* Ethical Perspectives for Intercultural Management. 1998 ISBN 0-7923-4700-5
10. M. Kaptein: *Ethics Management.* Auditing and Developing the Ethical Content of Organizations. 1998 ISBN 0-7923-5095-2; Pb 0-7923-5096-0
11. R.F. Duska (ed.): *Education, Leadership and Business Ethics.* Essays on the Work of Clarence Walton. 1998 ISBN 0-7923-5279-3
12. R. Mohon: *Stewardship Ethics in Debt Management.* 1999 ISBN 0-7923-5747-7
13. P.H. Werhane and A.E. Singer: *Business Ethics in Theory and Practice.* Contributions from Asia and New Zealand. 1999 ISBN 0-7923-5849-X
14. R.J. Burke and M.C. Mattis (eds.): *Women on Corporate Boards of Directors.* International Challenges and Opportunities. 2000 ISBN 0-7923-6162-8
15. J.M. Lozano: *Ethics and Organizations.* Understanding Business Ethics as a Learning Process. 2000 ISBN 0-7923-6463-5
16. B. Goodwin: *Ethics at Work.* 2000 ISBN 0-7923-6649-2
17. P. Koslowski: *Principles of Ethical Economy.* 2001 ISBN 0-7923-6713-8

KLUWER ACADEMIC PUBLISHERS – DORDRECHT / BOSTON / LONDON

GPSR Compliance

The European Union's (EU) General Product Safety Regulation (GPSR) is a set of rules that requires consumer products to be safe and our obligations to ensure this.

If you have any concerns about our products, you can contact us on ProductSafety@springernature.com

In case Publisher is established outside the EU, the EU authorized representative is:

Springer Nature Customer Service Center GmbH
Europaplatz 3
69115 Heidelberg, Germany

Batch number: 10823959

Printed by Printforce, the Netherlands